Children's Understanding of Biology and Health

This book uses new research and theory to present the first state-of-the-art account of children's understanding of biology and health. The international team of distinguished contributors views children's understanding in these areas to be to some extent adaptive to their well-being and survival and uses evidence collected through a variety of different techniques to consider whether young children are capable of basic theorizing and understanding of health and illness. Topics ranging from babies to elderly people including birth, death, contamination and contagion, food, and pain are examined and close links between research and practice are made with obvious attendant benefits in terms of education and communication.

MICHAEL SIEGAL is Professor of Psychology at the University of Sheffield. He has researched and taught internationally and has published extensively in the area of developmental psychology; a second edition of his book *Knowing children: Experiments in conversation and cognition* was published in 1997.

CANDIDA C. PETERSON is Professor of Psychology at the University of Queensland and a Fellow of the Academy of Social Sciences in Australia. She has published a wide range of popular and academic texts in the field of child development, including *A child grows up* (1974) and *Looking forward through the lifespan*, 3rd edn. (1996).

Cambridge Studies in Cognitive Perceptual Development

Series Editors
George Butterwroth (General Editor), University of Sussex, UK
Giyoo Hatano, Keio University, Tokyo, Japan
Kurt W. Fischer, Harvard University, USA

Advisory Board
Patricia M. Greenfield, University of California, Los Angeles, USA
Paul Harris, University of Oxford, UK
Daniel Stern, University of Geneva, Switzerland
Esther Thelen, Indiana University, USA

The aim of this series is to provide a scholarly forum for current theoretical and empirical issues in cognitive and perceptual development. As the twentieth century draws to a close, the field is no longer dominated by monolithic theories. Contemporary explanations build on the combined influences of biological, cultural, contextual and ecological factors in well-defined research domains. In the field of cognitive development, cultural and situational factors are widely recognized as influencing the emergence and forms of reasoning in children. In perceptual development, the field has moved beyond the opposition of "innate" and "acquired" to suggest a continuous role for perception in the acquisition of knowledge. These approaches and issues will all be reflected in the series, which will also address such important research themes as the indissociable link between perception and action in the developing motor system, the relationship between preceptual and cognitive development to modern ideas on the development of the brain, the significance of developmental processes themselves, dynamic systems theory and contemporary work in the psychodynamic tradition, especially as it relates to the foundations of self-knowledge.

Forthcoming titles include

Paul Light and Karen Littleton
Social Processes in Children's Learning

Nobuo Masataka
The Onset of Language

Children's Understanding of Biology and Health

Edited by

Michael Siegal
University of Sheffield

and

Candida C. Peterson
University of Queensland

CAMBRIDGE
UNIVERSITY PRESS

PUBLISHED BY THE PRESS SYNDICATE OF THE UNIVERSITY OF CAMBRIDGE
the Pitt Building, Trumpington Street, Cambridge, United Kingdom

CAMBRIDGE UNIVERSITY PRESS
The Edinburgh Building, Cambridge CB2 2RU, UK http://www.cup.cam.ac.uk
40 West 20th Street, New York NY 10011–4211, USA http://www.cup.org
10 Stamford Road, Oakleigh, Melbourne 3166, Australia

First published 1999

Printed in the United Kingdom at the University Press, Cambridge

Typeset in Plantin 10/12 pt [VN]

A catalogue record for this book is available from the British Library

Library of Congress cataloging in publication data

Children's understanding of biology and health / edited by Michael
Siegal and Candida C. Peterson. – 1st ed.
    p.   cm. – (Cambridge studies in cognitive perceptual
development)
ISBN 0 521 62098 8 (hardcover)
1. Cognition in children.   2. Biology.   3. Health.
I. Siegel,
Michael.   II. Peterson, Candida C. (Candida Clifford) III. Series.
BF723.C5C514   1999
370.15'2 – dc21   99–10567 CIP

ISBN 0 521 62098 8 hardback

Contents

Contributors

TERRY KIT-FONG AU
Department of Psychology
University of California, Los Angeles
405 Hilgard Avenue,
Los Angeles, CA 90024–1563
USA

LEANN BIRCH
Department of Human Development and Family Studies
Penn State University
110 Henderson Building South
University Park, PA 16802
USA

SUSAN CAREY
Department of Psychology
New York University
6 Washington Place
7th Floor
New York, NY 10003,
USA

CAROLYN J. CAVANAUGH
Department of Psychology
Arizona State University
Box 871104
Tempe, AZ 85287–1104
USA

JENNIFER E. DEWITT
Department of Psychology
University of California, Los Angeles

405 Hilgard Avenue,
Los Angeles, CA 90024–1563
USA

JENNIFER FISHER
Department of Human Development and Family Studies
Penn State University
110 Henderson Building South
University Park, PA 16802
USA

BELINDA GOODENOUGH
Pain Research Unit
Sydney Children's Hospital
Randwick, NSW 2031
Australia

KAREN GRIMM-THOMAS
Department of Human Development and Family Studies
Penn State University
110 Henderson Building South
University Park, PA 16802
USA

ROBIN L. HANSEN
Department of Pediatrics
University of California Davis Sacramento Medical Center
2516 Stockton Boulevard
Sacramento, CA 95817
USA

GIYOO HATANO
Human Relations
Keio University
2–15–45 Mita
Minato-ku
Tokyo 108–8345
Japan

MELODY R. HERBST
Department of Psychiatry,
University of California–Davis Medical College

2315 Stockton Boulevard
Sacramento, CA 95817
USA
current mailing address:
1724 Irving Curve
Bloomington, MN 55431
USA

KAYOKO INAGAKI
Faculty of Education
Chiba University
1–33 Yayoi-cho
Inage-ku, Chiba-shi
Chiba 263–8522
Japan

RAQUEL JAAKKOLA
Department of Biology
MS-34, Redfield 1–32
Woods Hole Oceanographic Institute
Woods Hole, MA 02543
USA

CHARLES W. KALISH
Department of Educational Psychology
University of Wisconsin-Madison
1025 Johnson St.,
Madison, WI 53706
USA

JOHN E. B. MYERS
McGeorge School of Law–UOP
3200 5th Avenue
Sacramento, CA 95817 USA
USA

CAROL J. NEMEROFF
Department of Psychology
Arizona State University
Box 871104
Tempe, AZ 85287–1104
USA

CANDIDA C. PETERSON
School of Psychology
University of Queensland
Brisbane
Queensland 4072
Australia

LAURA F. ROMO
Department of Psychology
University of California–Los Angeles
405 Hilgard Avenue,
Los Angeles, CA 90024–1563
USA

MICHAEL SIEGAL
Department of Psychology
University of Sheffield
Western Bank
Sheffield S10 2TP
UK

VIRGINIA SLAUGHTER
School of Psychology
University of Queensland
Brisbane
Queensland 4072
Australia

KEN SPRINGER
Department of Psychology
Southern Methodist University
Dallas, TX 75275–0442
USA

MARGARET S. STEWARD
Department of Psychiatry
University of California-Davis Medical College
2315 Stockton Boulevard
Sacramento, CA 95817
USA
current mailing address:
687 The Alameda

Berkeley, CA 94707
USA

JOHN E. TAPLIN
School of Psychology
University of New South Wales
Kensington, NSW 2033
Australia

LAURA VOGL
Sydney Anxiety Disorders Clinic
3/26–32 Ewos Parade
Cronulla, NSW 2230
Australia

JOAN R. WEBB
Youth Health
NSW Department of Health
Gosford, NSW 2250
Australia

Preface

Anyone who deals with children knows the importance of answering their questions about birth and death, of promoting their health through proper diet, exercise, and hygiene, and of caring for them when they fall ill or suffer pain. However, probably no area of children's understanding is in greater need of fresh insights.

This collection of essays is intended to provide the first state-of the-art examination of what children can and do know about biology and health. It represents a reappraisal of traditional stage-like conceptions in which it has been proposed, for example, that young children cannot understand contamination and contagion as causes of illness.

Based on research gathered by a variety of techniques, each of the contributors addresses the question of whether young children may be capable of demonstrating at least a skeletal knowledge of the causes of human health and illness (ranging from the origins of babies to the causes of aging). Referring to experimental studies, case histories, and historical changes in views of biology and health, the authors review and evaluate children's understanding of birth, life, and death, their knowledge of contamination and contagion as well as processes related to food, digestion, and pain. The chapters focus tightly on the connection between research and practice in examining the positive implications for communication with children about a wide variety of illnesses and diseases – implications that extend to children's ability to make informed decisions about medical and therapeutic treatment.

Our hope is that the balance of theory and practice contained in the chapters will appeal to students and professionals in psychology and disciplines such as education, law, medicine, nursing, physiotherapy, counselling, social work, and child welfare. But above all, we hope that the contents will engage the interest and curiosity of readers who are simply concerned to know more about how children think and learn about issues that are central to their wellbeing and survival.

MS, CCP
June, 1999

1   Becoming mindful of biology and health: an introduction

Michael Siegal and Candida C. Peterson

Despite the large amount of investigation devoted to cognitive development, it has been only recently that attention has come to be directed to children's understanding of biology and health. The aim of this book is to provide a comprehensive view of the research that has been accomplished to date on development of children's biological understanding, its relevance to health issues, and applications in educational and legal settings, and to offer prospects for the future.

In this introduction, we examine alternative theoretical and methodological approaches to what children know in this vital area. First, we give a historical background in terms of the knowledge and beliefs about biology and health that were held by lay adults and health professionals in the nineteenth century. Such consideration leads to the conclusion that magic and religion as well as science retain prominent roles in the explanation of illness. In this respect, three contemporary research orientations – Piagetian, naive theory and conceptual change, and adaptive-evolutionary – are discussed in terms of predictions for what children can and do know about the mind–body distinction, processes of birth and death, illness transmission, food selection, pain, and the nature of disease prevention and cure. We then turn to considering the extent to which the predictions generated by these orientations differ from adults' expectations of what children can and do know, and how different types of methodologies may reveal the extent of children's knowledge. Although young children may not be credited with a full understanding, new evidence suggests that they are constrained towards learning about biology and health and possess an implicit "skeletal" causal knowledge that is highly dependent on the nature of the problem and the way in which it is encountered. This knowledge may be used as a basis for preventive health education.

Views on biology and health in the nineteenth century

Knowledge of biology and the implications for health cannot be considered independently of concepts of disease that are influenced by culture.

1

Reznek (1987, p. 211) has addressed two key questions: "Do we invent diseases or do we discover them? Do disease judgments express value-judgments or are they purely descriptive judgments?" According to Reznek, some putative diseases are not diseases because they do the individual no harm. However, the notion of "harm" can be broadly constructed so as to extend rather than limit conferral of disease status on a person's physical or mental condition. Shweder *et al.* (1997), for example, maintain that there are three moral codes and that each have implications for health: (1) an ethics of autonomy that aims to protect individual freedom and promote individual choices; (2) an ethics of community that aims to protect the duties and hierarchies in communities; (3) an ethics of divinity that aims to protect the soul and spirit of humans against pollution and degradation. Harm may thus occur not only through restricting individual liberty but also through violating family and community obligations or engaging in behavior that jeopardizes the divinity and purity of the self such as through the ingestion of disgusting substances.

On this basis, a broad concept of disease emerges in that diseases are invented by those who make and share judgments of harm in relation to one or more moral codes. But at the same time, as Reznek (1987) points out, the conferral of disease status is restricted by the need to determine that the objects of such judgments have distinct identities that are grounded in biology. For prediction, treatment, and cure, we need to be able to determine whether the causal agents of disease share the same explanatory or unique natures. In this respect, contagious diseases such as hepatitis and tuberculosis certainly qualify as these have a biological basis and there is a consensus that such diseases cause harm in relation to one or more moral codes. Alcoholism and smoking – or even masturbation and homosexuality to use Reznek's provocative examples – can be classified as diseases if these are judged to be harmful in keeping with the ethics of divinity and if the identity of these "diseases" can be established in terms of a physiological addiction rather than one that is learned. Nevertheless, it is important to recognize that a judgment that harm has occurred is incompatible with a position of relativism in that those who judge are set against those who disagree.

During the nineteenth century, both physicians and lay people granted disease status to conditions that were viewed to reflect moral vices rather than unique biologically determined identities, and beliefs about the nature of illness that are tied to visible events have endured in the twentieth century throughout innumerable societies (Murdock, 1980). As Thomas (1997, p. 18) has observed, the commonest reaction to severe sickness throughout modern British history has been to ask, "What have I done to deserve this?" To the extent that morality accommodates the biological determination of disease, moral codes endure such as aspects of Christianity and Judaism that focus on the importance of cleanliness and hygiene that have a clear biological utility (Thomas, 1997, p. 29).

In nineteenth-century North America, the most frequent interpretation of ailments labelled as disease was that these were due to leading an immoral lifestyle. This was the case for cholera epidemics that affected New York in 1832 and 1849. Rosenberg (1962) documents the common belief that those who succumbed to cholera were morally depraved in that they lived in filth and squalor, were intemperate, were not gainfully employed, and did not attend church. When people of substance did perish, it was suspected that they had engaged in secret moral vices. Many doctors held an "atmospheric" theory of the transmission of cholera in that those who breathed filthy air were likely to become ill. They often rejected the proposal that cholera has a contagious basis as the acceptance of such a theory would mean that persons from all walks of life could succumb to the epidemic and thus jeopardize the moral structure of society. Even by the time of the third epidemic of the century in 1866, only one in seven North American doctors believed in some kind of germ theory of the transmission of cholera (Rosenberg, 1962, p. 199). Instead, many subscribed to the view that the "intemperate" would be predisposed to drink filthy water. Only slowly did the medical profession and lay people come to accept that cholera could be prevented through destroying micro-organisms and education about hygiene rather than through fasting and prayers.

Even more vehement was the resistance against accepting the role of micro-organisms in the transmission of venereal disease. Most authorities in nineteenth-century America believed that the epidemic of syphilis and gonorrhoea in the United States was due to punishment for leading an immoral lifestyle involving sexual promiscuity and consorting with prostitutes (Brandt, 1987). The treatment prescribed by doctors was justly seen as painful and thus appropriately punitive. Doctors often attempted to conceal the cause of suffering if possible from reputable patients and their spouses. At all costs, it was to be kept out of the newspapers. Though there were those who advocated sex education as a means of preventing the spread of disease, frank discussion of venereal disease was often condemned as an exaggerated risk that could jeopardize marriage. It is often held that talking about sexually transmitted disease would encourage undue interest in sex and lead to wickedness and sin. Similar beliefs are present today among many adults in both industrial and non-industrial societies. They exist as formidable obstacles against efforts to prevent the spread of AIDS, as well as sexually transmitted diseases such as syphilis, gonorrhoea, and herpes that remain in massive numbers, affecting millions each year throughout world.

The heterogeneity of explanations for specific diseases that were held by adults in nineteenth-century America and Britain persist now. These draw on magic and religion, as well as science, and reflect an imperfect relationship between increasing age and cognitive development in the domain of biology. Rather than confining their explanations of disease to conceptions that are limited to biology and heredity, contemporary adults commonly view illness in terms of divine punishment or a "price to be paid" for genius and exceptional achievement or a "modern way of life" that involves the debilitating effects of diet and work (Herzlich and Pierret, 1986). Thus it is hardly surprising that there are numerous accounts of what children can and do know about the biological identity of specific diseases as distinct from judgments based on considerations of harm.

Approaches to conceptualizing what children can and do know about biology

Piagetian accounts

A good deal of the work on children's understanding of biology has been influenced by the seminal work of Piaget. According to Piaget ([1932]1977), young children have a belief in immanent justice. They believe that transgressors against adult authority will inevitably meet with a mishap and that adults are so powerful that they can enlist inanimate objects to punish the naughty.

Piaget's method was to present stories to children aged 6 to 12 and to probe for responses. For example,

There was a little boy who disobeyed his mother. He took the scissors one day when he had been told not to. But he put them back in their place before his mother came home, and she never noticed anything. The next day he went for a walk and crossed a stream on a little bridge. But the plank was rotten. It gave way and he falls in with a splash. Why did he fall into the water? (And if he had not disobeyed would he have fallen in just the same?)

According to the results reported by Piaget ([1932]1977, p. 243), 86 percent of 6 year olds believe in immanent justice as an explanation for the mishap declining to 34 percent by age 11–12.

Kister and Patterson (1980) gave similar stories to children aged 4 to 9 years to examine the development of conceptions of illness. Again there was a strong relationship between age and belief in immanent justice. Compared to older children, 4–5 year olds were more likely to say that illness such as colds result from disobedience of parents. Nevertheless, from the Piagetian viewpoint on immanent justice, there is no such thing as "clear-cut" stages (Piaget, [1932]1977, p. 257) – a qualification that has been echoed by researchers over and over again in the decades since Piaget first wrote on the topic.

Following Piaget, Bibace and Walsh (1979, 1981) proposed a stage analysis of children's knowledge of the causes of illness. Children between 2 and 6 years of age account for illness by immediate temporal or physical cues. People are said to catch colds from magic, or from the sun, trees, or God. Disease is defined in terms of a single perceptual event that is relevant to their own experience. Later children say that colds are caught when someone else goes near them and when touched by sick persons. Thus physical contact may be seen as important in the transmission of some illnesses, and that these may involve the ingestion of germs. Finally, at approximately 11 years of age, they give "formal-logical" explanations. There is a differentiation between external and internal causal agents. While a cold may be transmitted by an external agent, the illness is located within the body and develops in multiple external systems through the malfunctioning of internal structures. Children may describe colds as transmitted by viruses and consisting of blockages in the sinuses and lungs.

In fact, according to Bibace and Walsh, young children may regard all illness as contagious and believe that toothaches, as well as colds, can be caught by proximity to a sick person. Because children do not reason about causality, they may view illness as punishment. Bibace and Walsh speculate that the clinical usefulness of a Piagetian theory for the prevention and treatment of illness in children is to alert health professionals to children's immature understanding in order to promote empathy with their irrational fears. For example, health workers should be told that children may find closeness to a sick person unnerving. Because children have only a limited appreciation of the nature of contagion, they may want to be moved lest they catch the illness themselves. This situation may involve the need for health workers to prepare children for possible distress or to take measures to prevent this distress from occurring in the first place.

Though Bibace and Walsh (1979, p. 285) observe that "children's beliefs and assumptions about health, illness, and medical procedures differ dramatically and in unexpected ways from those of adults," they are careful to note that even adults may not have a well-formed scientific view of illnesses such as heart disease. They go to some lengths to recount incidents such as one in which a 30–year-old woman explained to her family doctor that the pain in her side resulted from having touched her sister who was under a "curse." Both children and adults may be prone to immanent justice explanations in an environment where alternatives are not available or are unappealing (Siegal, 1988; Nemeroff and Rozin, 1994). In their respective chapters (2, 5, and 6), Inagaki and Hatano, Kalish, and Taplin, Goodenough, Webb, and Vogl consider the extent to which a Piagetian analysis of children's biological knowledge can apply to voluntary and involuntary bodily processes, the understanding of contamination and contagion, and knowledge of the determinants of pain. Moral overtones are also seen to be pervasive in the incisive chapter 8 by Nemeroff and Cavanagh on the development of perceptions of body image.

Theory change account

Carey (1985, 1995) has proposed that that the heterogeneity in which children respond on measures of their cognitive development reflects reasoning on tasks that is specific to the domains of knowledge in which these are situated. Thus there is no need to appeal to general Piagetian stages as an *explanation* of development.

According to Carey (1995), young children's ideas about biology go through two phases of development. In the first phase, from the preschool years to approximately age 6, children learn facts about the biological world. For instance, preschool children know that animals are alive, that babies come from inside their mothers and look like their parents, that people can get sick from dirty food or from playing with a sick friend, and that medicine makes people better. As Carey points out, knowing these facts is an impressive achievement, and children certainly benefit from having this sort of encyclopedic knowledge as a basis for making decisions and learning new facts. Having access to a mass of biological facts, however, is quite different from having a "framework theory" of biology. A framework theory (Carey, 1995; Wellman and Gelman, 1992; Keil, 1994) involves the connecting of facts to create a coherent, unified conceptual structure. Carey and her colleagues have claimed that it is not until the age of 7 years or so that children begin to construct a coherent framework theory of biology, through a process of "conceptual change."

One of the most important conceptual changes that occurs within children's biological knowledge is the construction of the category "living thing" from two initially separate categories of plants and animals. As an example, young children tend to deny that plants and animals share any biological properties. They commonly say that plants aren't alive, can't die, don't eat or move. After the age of 6 years, children's knowledge undergoes a conceptual change and restructuring, and the concepts of plants and animals become joined to create a new biological concept "living thing." Carey and her colleagues have proposed that other conceptual changes occur alongside the development of a concept of living thing. For instance, the concept of "not alive" becomes more precise, so that children differentiate biological death (the cessation of bodily function) from the concepts "inanimate" (as in a telephone is not alive) and "unreal" (as in Bugs Bunny is not alive). Another concomitant conceptual change is a new concept of babies. Young children see the origin of babies in terms of the intentional behavior of parents who purchase them from stores or who manufacture them and place them in the mother's tummy; by contrast, older children and adults recognize that babies originate from intercourse that is intentional and that babies then grow by themselves through cell reproduction that occurs through nourishment and protection within the womb (Carey, 1985, p. 58).

Of particular concern is whether or not children have an understanding of properties that are transmitted through biological inheritance and those that are transmitted by cultural influences such as through non-biological, adoptive parentage. According to Solomon *et al.* (1996, p. 152), "to be credited with a biological concept of inheritance, children need not understand anything like a genetic mechanism, but they must have some sense that the processes resulting in Resemblance to Parents differ from learning or other environmental mechanisms." Based on this criterion, they claim that previous research in which it is concluded that young children have an explanatory biological framework is flawed as it does not provide a clear comparison of how children regard the respective contributions of biological and adoptive parentage (Gelman and Wellman, 1991; Springer, 1992; Springer and Keil, 1989).

To support the position that young children do not have an explanatory framework in the domain of biology, Solomon *et al.* carried out a series of four studies. In study 1, children aged 4 to 7 years were asked to indicate whether a child born to a biological parent but adopted by another would be more like one than the other in his or her physical traits and beliefs. The children were told a story about a little boy, who, depending on the counterbalanced version of the story, was born to a shepherd but grew up in the home of a king or vice versa. Before proceeding with the testing, the children were asked two control questions to ensure their comprehension in the sequence, "Where was the little boy born? Where did he grow up?" They were then asked questions concerning, for example, pairs of physical traits and beliefs such as, "When the boy grows up, will he have green eyes like the king or brown eyes like the shepherd?" and "When the boy grows up, will he think that skunks can see in the dark like the shepherd or that skunks cannot see in the dark like the king?" Many of the 4–year-olds answered that both physical traits and beliefs are determined environmentally. Not until 7 years of age did children often report that physical

traits are associated with the biological parent and beliefs with the adoptive parent. The results of study 2 indicated that preschoolers recognize
that physical traits cannot change whereas beliefs can change. However,
their judgments of whether beliefs can change were dependent upon
whether this change was desirable or not. Study 3 replicated the results of
study 1 using female story characters as did study 4, in which an attempt
was made to lessen the environmental focus of the stories by showing the
children only schematic pictures of the adoptive mothers rather than
pictures of their homes.

The important findings of Solomon *et al.*'s research suggest that only
after age 6 do children start to differentiate biological from cultural
influences within a framework theory of biology (see also Solomon and
Cassimatis, 1999). Resistance to training about the nature of biology
simply means that the child's whole theory must undergo a restructuring.
Whether children can and do understand these issues is taken up
by Springer and by Slaughter, Jaakkola, and Carey in their chapters (3
and 4).

Adaptive-evolutionary accounts

Naive framework theories such as those proposed by Carey have often
been viewed to operate on the basis of domain-specific constraints that
reflect the problem solving that is evolutionarily adaptive (Cosmides and
Tooby, 1994). Vosniadou (1994; Vosniadou and Brewer, 1992, 1994)
claims that such constraints can be seen as "entrenched presuppositions"
that are resistant to change as these are constantly confirmed by everyday
experience. In the domain of physics, for example, children's early
models of the earth appear to be constrained by two beliefs: (1) the earth
is a flat plane (the "flatness" constraint) and (2) unsupported objects fall
"down" on an up–down gradient (the "support" constraint). Thus they
initially have the misconceptions that people live on a world that contains
a flat surface, that the sky is above the earth rather than around, that the
earth moves around the sun, and one could reach and fall off the "edge"
of the earth. Theory revision can be very difficult to achieve when the
information to be acquired is inconsistent with these presuppositions. In
fact, in some cultures, indigenous cosmologies may come to rival those of
western science in that children may readily construe the information
presented by the culture as consistent with the flatness and support
constraints. For example, children in India often ascribe to the Hindu
religious mythology that the earth floats on an ocean that provides separation from "nether worlds" populated by other beings (Samarapungavan
et al. 1996).

Yet it is by no means certain that presuppositions such as the flatness and support constraints must be entrenched and that misconceptions inevitably flow from these. The significance of evolution goes beyond the notion that exerts constraints on early cognitive development in the form of entrenched presuppositions that are confirmed by everyday experience. Rather evolution can be seen to have a more powerful role in development in relation to a process of cultural evolution. For example, Australian Aborigines have exceptional visuo-spatial memories that are highly adaptive in tracking and pathfinding in deserts (Kearins, 1981). Australian children generally are advanced in their geographical and astronomical concepts; even preschoolers often express the beliefs that the world is shaped as a sphere, that one cannot fall of the edge, and that the earth goes around the sun (Butterworth *et al.*, 1999). These beliefs seem ones that are cultivated through Australia's distinctive remoteness and position in the southern hemisphere and close cultural ties with people in the northern hemisphere – a unique set of conditions to which even very young children are exposed in the course of conversation with others. Furthermore, it is now well established that immediate experience is not all that contributes to the growth of children's scientific understanding as even infants have mental representations that go beyond immediate experience and guide their expectations of behavior (Leslie and Keeble, 1987; Mandler, 1992; Spelke, 1994).

Similarly, in the domain of biology, presuppositions from everyday experience that animals are unlike plants in that they eat, move, and are alive or that children resemble their parents irrespective of biological inheritance do not exhaust the range of constraints on early biological knowledge. As Rozin (1990, 1996) has proposed, an adaptive intelligence must to some extent be present to avoid the catastrophic consequences of illness on health and survival. In particular, solutions to the problem of procuring a safe diet require an adaptive, specialized intelligence that involves an awareness of health-endangering contaminants that involves a preparedness for knowing what to identify as safe to eat. In the same way, Hatano and Inagaki (1994) have perceptively observed that children's grasp of human biology is adaptive in that it performs three functions. First, it enables children to form predictions about the behavior of familiar natural kinds such as mammals regarding food procurement, sheltering, and reproduction. Second, it enables children to make sense of biological phenomena such as animals and plants that become unhealthy when they are fed too little or too much or with inappropriate food. Third, it helps children to learn rules for taking care of animals and plants, as well as themselves. Their knowledge of internal bodily functions constrains their choices of the variety and quality of food. Therefore children should be capable of an early understanding in the domain of biology to the extent that they may in some respects be credited with an incipient framework theory that accurately accounts for the facts of biology.

Several studies support this view. Inagaki and Hatano (1993) examined children's understanding that some bodily characteristics such as eye colour are not modifiable in contrast to the modifiability of bodily characteristics such as the speed of running and mental characteristics such as memory. Most 4 and 5–year-olds were able to distinguish accurately among the modifiability of these three categories, and almost all were able to say that they could not stop their heartbeat or stop their breathing for a couple of days. In a series of studies carried out by Hickling and Gelman (1994), children aged as young as $4\frac{1}{2}$ years were generally able to identify that same-species plants are the sole originator of seeds for new plants of that species. Similarly, according to a series of experiments reported by Springer (1995), 4 and 5–year-olds who understand that human babies grow inside their mothers (77 percent of the total number of 56 children in his first experiment) possess a "naive theory of kinship" in that they could use this knowledge to predict the properties of offspring. They can say that a baby which is physically dissimilar to the mother will likely share her stable internal properties (e.g., "gray bones inside her fingers") and lack transitory properties (e.g., "scrapes on her legs though running through some bushes"). Finally, Hirschfeld (1995, experiment 5) gave children aged 3 to 5 years two simple situations. In one, they were asked to indicate whether the baby of a black couple who grew up with a white couple would be black or white. The other situation involved the inverse in which the child of the white couple grew up with the black couple. Both the 4 and 5–year-olds clearly favored nurture over nature and were able to give justifications to this effect.

Hirschfeld (1995, p. 239) contends that these results differ from those of Solomon *et al.* because children in the Solomon *et al.* studies were asked to infer biological and cultural traits from the same event. According to Hirschfeld, by asking children to make many more judgments about traits that are environmentally as opposed to biologically transmitted, they may have been prompted to respond that even biological traits such as eye colour are the result of adoptive parentage. Nevertheless, Hirschfeld's method does not provide a stringent test of what children know about family resemblance as his subjects were not asked to differentiate between biologically and culturally transmitted traits. In chapter 3, Springer picks up on this theme in examining the relation between specific knowledge such as adoption and children's understanding of biological traits and resemblance to families and discusses it in relation to theory change accounts. In chapter 7, Birch *et al.* examine how children come to learn about diet.

The coexistence of magic, religion, and science in culture and cognitive development: methodological and interpretative issues

Might it be that adults themselves are so willing to accept that children are capable of interpreting illness only in terms of magic and religion since they themselves retain components of these in their own theorizing? One of us vividly recalls a visit to a city in the Yucatán Peninsula of Mexico in the 1970s in which a cleaner carefully boiled, filtered, and cooled drinking water for guests, and then added ice cubes that were made from straight tap water! Given the lack of understanding of hygiene in many parts of the world, are we expecting too much of children to have this sort of knowledge? Yet work generated from an adaptive-evolutionary perspective indicates that even many young children should be able to build on an understanding of the microscopic basis of contamination as this understanding is close to survival, and perhaps other conditions that are associated with chronic illness (Eiser, 1990).

The authors of the chapters in this book attribute different sorts of competence to children and adolescents. This competence can be partly seen in terms of children's implicit and explicit knowledge. As Karmiloff-Smith (1986) points out, we can usefully examine knowledge in terms of that which is consciously accessible and that which can be implicitly represented in behavior. Although each of these terms have connotations with different levels of awareness, knowledge that is consciously accessible has at times been called "explicit" or "declarative knowledge" and implicit knowledge has at times been referred to as "procedural knowledge." For example, in communication tasks, young children can implicitly identify linguistic forms such as sentences by responding correctly when they are asked to repeat the last sentence that they heard in a story. However, if asked directly and explicitly to say whether linguistic forms such as the articles "a" and "the" are words, they may not be able to reply explicitly. Similarly, children may demonstrate a procedural or implicit knowledge if the experimenter examines their understanding as a means to obtain a clear-cut goal such as the detection of pretence in familiar situations or the procurement of food and the avoidance of illness. Even many 2–year-olds, for example, may implicitly demonstrate health knowledge by labelling as inedible food that appears safe but is contaminated in reality. Certainly, we would feel more secure in these circumstances if they could display a convincing explicit knowledge by spontaneously telling us that "Even if a drink looks OK it may have had a bug in it. So the drink may be contaminated." But to recognize that their knowledge in a domain may be mainly of the implicit sort is very different from embracing the conclusion that they have little or no understanding at all. The need for food drives children to an awareness of reality and deception. Kass (1994, p. 98) remarks that the possession of a incipient concept of cuisine as shown by "what and how a person eats reveals who you are, humanly speaking."

The issue of drawing out children's implicit knowledge can be examined with respect to children's understanding of the purpose and relevance of questions. As Trabasso (1997, p. 430) notes, how children understand questions is a powerful determinant of "what and how much is reported ... one major influence on the child's 'memory' is what is asked and what the child 'remembers' is not solely the child's creation."

Philosophers of language such as Grice (1975) have shown that adult conversation is characterized by rules or maxims which enjoin speakers to: "Say no more or no less than is required. Try to say the truth and avoid falsehood. Be relevant and informative. Avoid ambiguity and obscurity." In communication between adults, it is usually mutually understood that the rules may be broken to make "conversational implicatures." For example, adults know that speakers may be uninformative and state the obvious for purposes of irony or that they may be redundant and speak more than is required to probe an initial answer out of politeness or curiosity to ensure that this is the respondent's choice. However, children who are inexperienced in conversation may not share the scientific purpose underlying departures from conversational rules in adults' questioning. There may be a communication barrier which can prevent children from identifying the purpose and implications of adults' questions. As a consequence, children frequently do not disclose the depth of their understanding when questioned in cognitive developmental experiments.

In children's responses to instances of microscopic contamination, experimenters may present children with an apparently fresh substance that in reality is not good to consume in order to determine whether children understand the microscopic basis of contamination. In response to such direct questioning, preschoolers often say that they would like to drink juice that has been in prior contact with contaminants. Once a contaminant such as one described as a ground-up grasshopper has been dissolved or removed and the drink no longer appears contaminated, they may indicate that it can be safely consumed (e.g., Rozin *et al.*, 1985). Such responses are consistent with Piaget's theory in that these focus on states rather than transformations and are in keeping with Piaget's notion of a preoperational childhood realism in which the appearance and reality of an object are undifferentiated.

However, although children may know that a drink that has been in contact with a foreign substance is harmful, they may not truly recognize that a well-meaning experimenter would contravene the quality rule to be sincere by offering them a polluted drink in order to probe for their understanding of the causes of illness. The implied question (e.g., "Would you like to have this drink that may be contaminated?") is almost certainly one that they would have never encountered before. Instead they may defer to a unskeptical belief that the purpose inherent in the experimenter's question is to make a sincere offer of a drink; indeed, the very act of offering implies that the drink would not be polluted. By contrast, children may be given a naturalistic situation such as one in which a cockroach is made to fall accidentally into a drink and is then removed with a spoon so that the drink looks fresh but is in reality contaminated. In this type of situation that aligns children's interpretation of the purpose and relevance of the questioning with that of an experimenter, preschoolers in industrialized countries such as Australia and the United States can often say that an apparently fresh drink that had previously been in contact with a contaminant is not good to consume (Siegal and Share, 1990; see also Kalish, 1996; Springer and Belk, 1994). In many cases, providing children with explicit representations of expected and changed states permits them to identify readily that the changed situation *is* something other than what it appears (Saltmarsh *et al.*, 1996). In solving problems that are relevant to the food domain and are germane to survival, children are therefore more likely to share the purpose for an experimenter's question. With respect to this domain of knowledge which is highly relevant to their own concerns (in line with the Gricean conversational rule, "Be relevant"), they are apt to recognize that the purpose is to determine their ability to detect edible substances and reject those that are inedible. Therefore, even 3–year-olds should often be able to distinguish reality from appearance in recognizing that a food that looks edible may be in reality contaminated.

All the same, young children cannot be expected to justify their responses and their behavior by giving an elaborate account of the microscopic basis of contamination. They are very unlikely to say that a drink that has been in contact with a foreign object may be infected with germs that grow and multiply or, for that matter, to say that the AIDS virus can be transmitted only through the transmission of bodily fluids in intimate contact that almost always involves sexual contact (see chapter 9 by Au, Romo, and DeWitt). To state that illness can occur only in a specific manner that focuses on biological causation involves a great deal of sophistication that in many cases eludes adults. Nevertheless, researchers from any of the three perspectives that we have outlined may credit children with competence in their operations only if they explicitly use logical necessity to justify their solution to a problem. As Smith (1993, p. 2) has described the position of Piaget, "Necessary properties lay down both why something is, and has to be, what it is, and why it is not, and cannot be, anything else." Both the explicit and implicit is important.

However, this requirement goes beyond the normal facility that children whose conversational awareness is not well developed (or, for that matter, adults, particularly in cases involving intercultural communication or communication between superiors and subordinates) can often exhibit (Siegal, 1996, 1997). Not only does it assume that children recognize the purpose and relevance of questions, but also it assumes that children can boldly portray the strength of their beliefs in providing an explanation that they know the adult already knows – one that involves spontaneously evaluating the often inscrutable actions of the experimenter. At the same time, it does not accord recognition to the rather obvious fact that, regardless of characteristics such as age, a person may have a grasp of logical necessity but not be able to justify his or her understanding in a dialogue with the investigator.

While acknowledging that justifications are needed to determine the operational competence underlying children's judgments, followers and defenders of the orthodox Piagetian approach refer to children's performance on tasks that "appeal strongly to the child's nonverbal performance" (e.g., Piaget, 1952; Piaget *et al.*, 1960) as the other major source of evidence to support the contention that children's persistent difficulties on such tasks are not owing to difficulties in conversation (Lourenço and Machado, 1996, p. 154) . Yet as these tasks still require a modicum of language, ambiguity may persist. The minimization of conversationally obscure instructions in cognitive developmental tasks does not detract from the need to ensure that the remaining information is clear, relevant, and explicit and embedded within a purposeful dialogue with the experimenter.

Does this analysis mean therefore that we should be confined only to measuring children's appreciation of logical necessity and abandon the search for scientific knowledge that is anything less than fully explicit? Ironically, perhaps the best starting point comes from the considerable research on infancy in which children cannot misrepresent questions because none have been asked. In such cases, infants often stare longer at impossible than at possible events, indicating their surprise that some necessary physical principle of object identity and constancy has been violated (Baillargeon and Graber, 1988; Spelke, 1994; Wynn, 1992). Of course infants' responses may reflect a disposition to regard such events as unexpected or unfamiliar rather than as impossible and a violation of necessity. In the absence of language, it is difficult to distinguish between these alternatives. However, research with preschoolers who do have language points to a very good knowledge of necessity – one that can be violated only through "magic" as a term that is applied to events that are judged as impossible. As Subbotsky (1994) has proposed, for both children and adults, there appear to be certain cultural conventions that permit the *practice* of magic even though magical *events* such as magical causality and magic in time and space are defined in terms of the violation of logical necessity. In the case of children, magic can take place in the form of a belief in the activities of fairy tale characters; in the case of adults, it can take the form of a belief in protection from disease through an association with loved ones irrespective of their state of health (Nemeroff and Rozin, 1994; Rozin *et al.*, 1986; Rozin and Nemeroff, 1990). Johnson and Harris (1994) have shown that children often distinguish between the causality of physical events that are possible or necessary and those that are impossible with the exclusion of some form of special magic. As they point out, the "credulity" of young children in wishing to investigate "magical" outcomes can be deemed rational in the absence of evidence that invalidates the existence of supernatural creatures. Guided by cultural conventions that permit them to engage in the practice of magical fantasies, children often strive to reveal charming violations of logical necessity, that fit in with Piagetian viewpoints on development.

Shultz *et al.* (1979, p. 100) have noted that "one might well question whether human cognition could ever be entirely logical to the total exclusion of empirical content and, conversely, whether it could be ever be entirely empirical to the total exclusion of logical structure." According to Shultz *et al.*, children do not ordinarily feel that judgments of equivalence between two quantities do not need to be checked empirically. Thus the logical aspect of the children's knowledge such as that shown in their performance on conservation of quantity tasks is developmentally stable. However, when children are actually asked to do perform this empirical check after a quantity undergoes a perceptual transformation (e.g., when two formerly "equivalent" stimuli such as two rows of seven counters each that were once in one-to-one correspondence are now put out of alignment), their verbally expressed confidence in conservation can waver. Thus the empirical basis of conservation judgments is influenced by its dependence on relevant experience; whether children actually do make conservation judgments depends upon their familiarity with the purpose and relevance of the task. In this connection, the "magic" inherent in the perceptual transformation induced by an experimenter may prompt children to dispense with logical necessity and to look instead for an empirical basis for their initial responses. Even if children are quite certain of the answer, they may not share the conversational implications of questions as experimenters have intended and respond incorrectly.

Therefore interviewing techniques that have resulted in well-meaning investigators' assessment of a low level of early competence often involve the assumption of an early conversational wizardry. Even tasks that are assumed to appeal to children's nonverbal performance can jeopardize determining what they know. Explicit understanding in Piaget's sense may be the ultimate aim and certainly would give us confidence in predicting and accepting what children know about medical procedures. It would better enable us to prepare children with the capability to make intelligent, health-related decisions as evidenced in chapters 10 and 11 by Herbst, Steward, Myers, and Hansen, and Peterson and Siegal. Even so, for both children and adults, there may be considerable implicit knowledge of biology present that is infused with beliefs in magic and religion. It is this competence that may be used as foundation to draw out a deeper, explicit discussion and knowledge of the biological determinants of specific diseases in conjunction with normative judgments of harm.

As Kleinman (1986, p. 226) has pointed out, primary medical care has frequently overlooked psychology and related disciplines despite the "epidemiological reality" that over 50 percent of clinical practice deals with the psychological and social aspects of illness. Investigations of what children can or do know about biology such as those reported in this book should enable adults to have a more accurate appreciation of this knowledge and to promote communication with children on health matters.

Acknowledgments: preparation of this chapter was supported by the Australian Research Council. Some of the work discussed here has been adapted from Siegal (1999).

REFERENCES

Baillargeon, R., and Graber, M. (1988). Evidence of location memory in 8–month-old infants in a nonsearch AB task. *Developmental Psychology* , *24*, 502–511.

Bibace, R., and Walsh, M. E. (1979). Developmental stages in children's conceptions of illness. In G. C. Stone, F. Cohen, and N. E. Adler (eds.), *Health psychology: A handbook* (pp. 285–301). San Francisco: Jossey-Bass.

(1981). Children's conceptions of illness. In R. Bibace and M. Walsh (eds.), *New directions for child development: Children's conceptions of health, illness, and bodily functions, no. 14.* San Francisco: Jossey-Bass.

Brandt, A. M. (1987). *No magic bullet.* New York: Oxford University Press.

Butterworth, G., Siegal, M., Newcombe, P. A., and Dorfmann, M. (1999). Children's knowledge of the shape of the earth in Australia and England. Unpublished paper, School of Cognitive and Computing Sciences, University of Sussex.

Carey, S. (1985). *Conceptual change in childhood.* Cambridge, MA: MIT Press.

(1995). On the origin of causal understanding. In D. Sperber, D. Premack, and A. J. Premack (eds.), *Causal cognition* (pp. 268–301). Oxford: Oxford University Press.

Cosmides, L., and Tooby, J. (1994). Origins of domain specificity: The evolution of functional organization. In L. A. Hirschfeld and S. A. Gelman (eds.), *Mapping the mind: Domain-specificity in culture and cognition* (pp. 85–116). New York: Cambridge University Press.

Eiser, C. (1990). *Chronic childhood disease.* Cambridge: Cambridge University Press.

Gelman, S. A., and Wellman, H. M. (1991). Insides and essences: Early understandings of the nonobvious. *Cognition,* 38, 213–244.

Grice, H. P. (1975). Logic and conversation. In P. Cole and J. L. Morgan (eds.), *Syntax and semantics,* vol. III, *Speech acts* (pp. 41–58). New York: Academic Press.

Hatano, G., and Inagaki, K. (1994). Young children's naive theory of biology. *Cognition,* 50, 171–188.

Herzlich, C., and Pierret, J. (1986). Illness: From causes to meaning. In C. Currer and M. Stacey (eds.), *Concepts of health, illness, and disease* (pp. 73–96). Leamington Spa, UK: Berg.

Hickling, A. K., and Gelman, S. A. (1994). How does your garden grow? Early conceptualization of seeds and their place in the plant growth cycle. *Child Development,* 66, 856–876.

Hirschfeld, L. A. (1995). Do children have a theory of race? *Cognition,* 54, 209–252.

Inagaki, K., and Hatano, G. (1993). Young children's understanding of the mind–body distinction. *Child Development,* 64, 1534–1549.

Johnson, C. N., and Harris, P. L. (1994). Magic: Special but not excluded. *British Journal of Developmental Psychology,* 12, 35–51.

Kalish, C. (1996). Preschoolers' understanding of germs as invisible mechanisms. *Cognitive Development,* 11, 83–106.

Karmiloff-Smith, A. (1986). From meta-processes to conscious access: Evidence from children's metalinguistic and repair data. *Cognition,* 23, 95–147.

Kass, L. R. (1994). *The hungry soul.* New York: Free Press.

Kearins, J. M. (1981). Visual spatial memory in Australian Aboriginal children of desert regions. *Cognitive Psychology,* 13, 434–460.

Keil, F. (1994). The birth and nurturance of concepts by domains: The origins of concepts of living things. In L. A. Hirschfeld and S. A. Gelman (eds.), *Mapping the mind: Domain-specificity in culture and cognition* (pp. 234–254). New York: Cambridge University Press.

Kister, M. C., and Patterson, C. J. (1980). Children's conceptions of the causes of illness: Understanding of contagion and use of immanent justice. *Child*

Development, 51, 839–846.

Kleinman, A. (1986). Some uses and misuses of the social sciences in medicine. In D. W. Fiske and R. A. Shweder (eds.), *Metatheory in social science* (pp. 222–245). Chicago: University of Chicago Press.

Leslie, A. M., and Keeble, S. (1987). Do six-month-old infants perceive causality? *Cognition*, 25, 265–288.

Lourenço, O., and Machado, A. (1996). In defense of Piaget's theory: A reply to 10 common criticisms. *Psychological Review*, 103, 143–164.

Mandler, J. M. (1992). How to build a baby: II. Conceptual primitives. *Psychological Review*, 99, 587–604.

Murdock, G. P. (1980). *Theories of illness: A world survey*. Pittsburgh, PA: University of Pittsburgh Press.

Nemeroff, C., and Rozin, P. (1994). The contagion concept in adult thinking in the United States: Transmission of germs and of interpersonal influence. *Ethos*, 22, 158–186.

Piaget, J. ([1932]1977). *The moral judgement of the child*. Harmondsworth, UK: Penguin.

   (1952). *The child's conception of number*. London: Routledge and Kegan Paul.

Piaget, J., Inhelder, B., and Szeminska, A. (1960). *The child's conception of geometry*. London: Routledge and Kegan Paul.

Reznek, L. (1987). *The concept of disease*. London: Routledge and Kegan Paul.

Rosenberg, C. E. (1962). *The cholera years: The United States in 1832 and 1866*. Chicago: University of Chicago Press.

Rozin, P. (1990). Development in the food domain. *Developmental Psychology*, 26, 555–562.

   (1996). Towards a psychology of food and eating: From motivation to module to model to marker, morality, meaning, and metaphor. *Psychological Science*, 5, 18–24.

Rozin, P., Fallon, A., and Augustoni-Ziskind, M. (1985). The child's conception of food: The development of contamination sensitivity to 'disgusting' substances. *Developmental Psychology*, 21, 1,075–1,079.

Rozin, P., and Nemeroff, C. (1990). The laws of sympathetic magic: A psychological analysis of similarity and contagion. In J. Stigler, G. Herdt, and R. Shweder (eds.), *Cultural psychology: Essays on comparative human development* (pp. 205–232). New York: Cambridge University Press.

Rozin, P., Millman, L., and Nemeroff, C. (1986). Operation of the laws of sympathetic magic in disgust and other domains. *Journal of Personality and Social Psychology*, 50, 703–712.

Saltmarsh, R., Mitchell, P., and Robinson, E. J. (1996). Realism and children's early grasp of mental representation: Belief-based judgments in the state change task. *Cognition*, 57, 297–325.

Samarapungavan, A., Vosniadou, S., and Brewer, W. F. (1996). Mental models of the earth, sun and moon: Indian children's cosmologies. *Cognitive Development*, 11, 491–521.

Shultz, T. R., Dover, A., and Amsel, E. (1979). The logical and empirical bases of conservation judgments. *Cognition*, 7, 99–123.

Shweder, R. A., Much, N. C., Mahapatra, M., and Park, L. (1997). The "big three" of morality (autonomy, community, divinity) and the "big three" explanations of suffering. In A. M. Brandt and P. Rozin (eds.), *Morality and health* (pp. 119–169). New York: Routledge.

Siegal, M. (1988). Children's knowledge of contagion and contamination as causes of illness. *Child Development*, 59, 1,353–1,359.

(1996). Conversation and cognition. In R. Gelman and T. Au (eds.), *Handbook of perception and cognition*, vol. XIII: *Perceptual and cognitive development* (pp. 243–282). San Diego, CA: Academic Press.

(1997). *Knowing children: Experiments in conversation and cognition*, 2nd edn. Hove, UK: Psychology Press.

(1999). Language and thought: The fundamental significance of conversational awareness for cognitive development. *Developmental Science*, 2, 1–34.

Siegal, M., and Share, D. L. (1990). Contamination sensitivity in young children. *Developmental Psychology*, 26, 455–458.

Smith, L. (1993). *Necessary knowledge*. Hove, UK: Erlbaum.

Solomon, G. E. A., and Cassimatis, N. L. (1999). On facts and conceptual systems: Young children's integration of their understanding of germs and contagion. *Developmental Psychology*, 35, 113–126.

Solomon, G. E. A., Johnson, S. C., Zaitchik, D., and Carey, S. (1996). Like father, like son: Young children's understanding of how and why offspring resemble their parents. *Child Development*, 67, 151–171.

Spelke, E. (1994). Initial knowledge: Six suggestions. *Cognition*, 50, 431–445.

Springer, K. (1992). Children's beliefs about the biological implications of kinship. *Child Development*, 63, 950–959.

(1995). Acquiring a naive theory of kinship through inference. *Child Development*, 66, 547–558.

Springer, K., and Belk, A. (1994). The role of physical contact and association in early contamination sensitivity. *Developmental Psychology*, 30, 864–868.

Springer, K., and Keil, F. C. (1989). On the development of biologically specific beliefs: The case of inheritance. *Child Development*, 60, 637–648.

Subbotsky, E. (1994). Early rationality and magical thinking in preschoolers: Space and time. *British Journal of Developmental Psychology*, 12, 97–108.

Thomas, K. (1997). Health and morality in early modern England. In A. M. Brandt and P. Rozin (eds.), *Morality and health* (pp. 15–34). New York: Routledge.

Trabasso, T. (1997). Whose memory is it? The social context of remembering. In N. L. Stein, P. A. Ornstein, B. Tversky, and C. Brainerd (eds.), *Memory for everyday and emotional events* (pp. 429–443). Mahwah, NJ: Erlbaum.

Vosniadou, S. (1994). Capturing and modeling the process of conceptual change. *Learning and Instruction*, 4, 45–69.

Vosniadou, S., and Brewer, W. F. (1992). Mental models of the earth: A study of conceptual change in childhood. *Cognitive Psychology*, 24, 535–585.

(1994). Mental models of the day/night cycle. *Cognitive Science*, 18, 123–183.

Wellman, H. M., and Gelman, S. A. (1992). Cognitive development: Foundational theories of core domains. *Annual Review of Psychology*, 43, 337–375.

Wynn, K. (1992). Addition and subtraction by human infants. *Nature*, 358, 749–750.

Part I

Development of biological understanding

2   Children's understanding of mind–body relationships

Kayoko Inagaki and Giyoo Hatano

Until the mid-1980s, it had been believed that young children do not understand the mind–body distinction; they tend to interpret and explain bodily phenomena or processes within a working framework of the mind, i.e., in terms of intentional causality (Carey, 1985). For example, when asked why children grow bigger, preschool children often say, "Because they want to grow bigger." Even when children know that an input (e.g., eating a lot) is related to an output (e.g., becoming fatter), they know nothing about what mediates the process at a physiological level. They either give no explanation or offer an intentional explanation.

However, an increasing number of studies conducted since the late 1980s have revealed that young children have reasonable, if not accurate, understanding of bodily phenomena. That is, they can distinguish somatic phenomena or processes from mental ones, though the characterization of their understanding is still a subject of debate. Needless to say, such understanding does not mean that children regard the mind and the body as two totally separate entities. We believe that children and lay adults do distinguish between the mind and body but recognize their interdependence, as exemplified by their acknowledgement of psychosomatic diseases. The issue of the mind–body distinction, especially in relation to illness causality, is more complex than is assumed by western modern science, in which the workings of the mind are explained by psychology, and bodily processes are explicated in terms of physiological mechanisms.

In this chapter we discuss naive views of the relationship between the mind and body and provide some evidence for the claim that young children consider the mind and body as distinguishable but interdependent to some degree. The chapter consists of four sections. First, we claim that young children before schooling have the mind–body distinction, and try to explain bodily phenomena in terms of vitalistic causality. Even lay adults may use vitalistic causality as a fallback mode of explanation for bodily phenomena. Second, we specify the nature of this vitalistic causality, with an emphasis on how vital power is thought to operate, and how it is acquired, sustained, or lost. Vitalistic causality assumes more or less unspecified mechanisms, and thus often allows for contributions of multiple factors to bodily phenomena. Third, we consider young children's understanding of bodily susceptibility (or resistance) to illness as a sub-domain of this vitalistic biology. We show that the assumption that people completely distinguish between the body and mind may be false; rather, young children, and even some adults, recognize that the body and mind are interdependent in some cases. Finally, we discuss some implications for health practice and education of the idea that people view the mind and body as distinguishable but interdependent.

Young children's understanding of the mind–body distinction

Distinction between the mind and body

Since the late 1980s the issue of the mind–body distinction has become of interest to researchers who are concerned with whether young children have acquired an autonomous domain of biology. This is because the mind–body distinction, as well as the living–non-living distinction, is one of the essential components of naive biology.

In her influential book, Carey (1985) claimed that children before approximately age 10 have no form of biology differentiated from a domain of psychology, and thus they neither differentiate biological phenomena from psychological ones, nor recognize that biological processes (e.g., those producing growth or death) are autonomous; they are ignorant of physiological mechanisms involved. Most of the studies that she cited used an open-ended interview. For example, Gellert (1962) reported that, when asked to describe the function of internal bodily organs, most children under 11 or 12 years old could not refer to the physiological mechanisms involved in the workings of those organs, such as blood circulation for the heart, or the transformation of food in the stomach. Contento (1981), also using an open-ended interview, reported that, though young children have some knowledge about input–output relationships, they do not understand the mediating processes. It should be noted that these studies revealed that children lack explicit understanding of bodily processes, but not necessarily that they possess no biological knowledge of the processes. It is possible that young children have a significant implicit understanding of what the biological world is like before they reveal an explicit understanding of it (Gelman, 1979).

In fact, studies using more sophisticated methods than the open-ended interview have confirmed that possibility; these studies indicate that children can distinguish biological phenomena from psychological ones at ages much younger than those claimed by Carey. Let us give some examples. Siegal (1988) asked 4–8-year-old children to judge whether a protagonist's remarks stating causes of illness were true or false, and found that these children recognized that colds were caused, not by moral, but by medical factors (i.e., contact with contaminants). Springer and Ruckel (1992) confirmed Siegal's findings in a study in which they asked preschoolers to predict whether a protagonist who was exposed to contaminants or one who misbehaved would get sick. Coley (1995) used an attribution task. He presented pictures of predatory (e.g., tiger) and domestic (e.g., guinea pig) animals to 6- and 8-year-old children (and adults) and asked them whether each animal displayed various biological (e.g., has blood) or psychological (e.g., is smart, can feel angry, can feel scared) properties. He found that 6 year olds, as well as 8 year olds and adults, showed clearly different attribution patterns for biological versus psychological properties.

More direct evidence for the mind–body distinction in children was provided by Inagaki and Hatano (1993). In experiment 1 of their study, 4 and 5 year olds were given two tasks: a modifiability task and a controllability task. In the modifiability task the children were asked whether each of three types of characteristics (hereditary, physical, and mental) was modifiable and, if so, by what means. For example, for a hereditary characteristic children were told: "A boy, Taro, has black eyes. He wants to make his eyes blue like a foreigner's [a Caucasian's]. Can he do that?" "How can he do so?" A great majority of the children correctly denied the modifiability of the hereditary characteristics (e.g., eye color). In contrast, many of them answered that they could modify the physical characteristics (e.g., running faster), and about half of them acknowledged the modifiability of the mental ones (e.g., forgetfulness). A majority of the children who recognized the modifiability of the changeable physical characteristics asserted that modifications could be brought about by physical practice, such as more exercise, diet, and so on, whereas nobody accepted such practice as a means of modifying the mental characteristics. To modify the mental characteristics, about half of the 5 year olds replied that one needed effort or determination, and some referred to mental practice (i.e., concrete strategic means), as shown in one girl's answer, "[we can become less forgetful] if we rehearse *this and that* in our mind." These results suggest that the children thought that mere effort or determination might play a role in modifying mental characteristics, but not in modifying physical characteristics.

In the controllability task the children were asked whether organic activities inside the body (e.g., heartbeats) could be controlled by children's intention or desire. A majority of the children of both age groups recognized that the activities of internal organs are beyond their own control.

In another study, Inagaki (1997b) gave the controllability task with some modification to 3 year olds as well as 4 and 5 year olds. She also examined whether these children were aware of their bodily processes. She found that the awareness of bodily processes developed markedly from age 3 to 4. In addition, the more the children were aware of their bodily processes, the more often they recognized that bodily processes are independent of their intention; this tendency was especially clear for the heartbeat item. The 3 year olds clearly differentiated between heartbeats or respiration as involuntary acts and gratifying thirst or hunger (e.g., by drinking water) as voluntary acts, although they tended to overestimate the mind's ability to control heartbeats.

Kalish (1997a) examined whether preschool children would distinguish between the effects of contamination on the mind and the body. In this study, children heard stories about a character who did or did not eat some contaminated food, and who did or did not know if the food was contaminated. They were asked to predict whether or not the character in the story would get sick (i.e., biological responses), and whether the character would think the food was yummy or yucky (i.e., emotional responses). Results indicated that the children distinguished between physical and mental reactions to contamination in that knowledge determines mental reactions to contamination, but physical contact determines bodily reactions.

Vitalistic causal explanations for biological phenomena

Although the above findings are informative regarding the mind–body distinction, they do not necessarily indicate that young children understand the mechanisms or mediating processes involved in bodily functions or that they can offer causal explanations for the workings of bodily organs in terms other than those of a person's intention. However, it should be noted that young children's inability to give articulated mechanistic explanations for biological phenomena does not mean that they always give intentional explanations for them. Inagaki and Hatano (1993) propose that young children who are reluctant to rely on intentional causality for biological phenomena but cannot yet use mechanistic causality often rely on an intermediate form of causality which can be called "vitalistic causality."

Intentional causality means that a person's intention causes the target phenomenon, whereas mechanistic causality means that physiological mechanisms cause the target phenomenon, more specifically, a specific bodily system enables a person, irrespective of his or her intention, to exchange substances with the environment or to carry them to and from bodily parts. Inagaki and Hatano assert, in contrast, that vitalistic causality indicates that the target phenomenon is caused by the activity of an internal organ, which has "agency" or an activity-initiating and sustaining character. This activity is often described as a transmission or exchange of "vital power," which can be conceptualized as some unspecified substance, energy, or information. Vitalistic causality is clearly different from person-intentional causality in the sense that the organ's activities inducing the phenomena are independent of the intention of the person who has the organ.

Two types of evidence for young children's vitalism were provided by studies using specific questions. The first type of evidence was obtained from children's justifications for their predictions about bodily processes. In Inagaki and Hatano's (1990) study, several children, ranging in age from 5 to 8, gave explanations referring to something like vital force as a mediator when given novel questions about bodily processes. For example, when asked what effect the halt of blood circulation to the hands would have, one child said, "If blood does not come to the hands, they will die, because the blood does not carry energies to them," and another said, "We cannot move our hands, because energies fade away if blood does not come there."

Inagaki (1995) reported in another study that kindergarten children aged 6 years seem to think that energy taken in through eating helps people live a long life, prevents them from becoming ill, and can even heal them quickly of an injury. For example, 6 year olds were asked the following question: "What will happen to you if you eat nothing for several days?" Half of these children referred to death due to the lack of nutriment or energy; for example, "If we eat nothing, we shall die, because we lose power (or energy, or nutriment)." Most of the children who used the word "nutriment" paraphrased it in response to further inquiry, saying, "It's what makes us vigorous," "It gets our body active," or "It gives us power." One of the children justified his response by saying, "[We shall] die, because the stomach will suffer from the decrease in nutriment." When given a question such as, "Can Taro's grandpa, who is now 80 years old, live until 100 or 200 years of age, if he eats a lot and regularly?" a majority of 6 year olds gave affirmative responses, and one-third of them justified them by saying, "Because eating food produces energy," "Eating a lot makes him vigorous," and so on. When asked, "Can Natuko, who injured her leg, heal more quickly if she eats a lot?" one of the children answered, "She can turn an injury off more quickly [if she eats a lot], because nutriment in her stomach can be sent to the injured leg."

The second type of evidence was obtained through children's responses to forced-choice questions. Inagaki and Hatano (1993, experiment 2) asked 6-year-olds, 8-year-olds, and college students to choose one from three possible explanations for each of six bodily phenomena, such as blood circulation and respiration. The three explanations represented intentional, vitalistic, and mechanistic causality, respectively. For example, a question on blood circulation with three alternative explanations was as follows: Why does the blood flow to different parts of our bodies? (1) Because we move our body hoping the blood will flow in it (intentional); (2) Because our heart works hard to send our life and energy with blood (vitalistic); (3) Because the heart sends the blood by working as a pump (mechanistic). Results indicated that the 6-year-olds chose vitalistic explanations as most plausible most often; they chose them 54 percent of the time. They applied non-intentional (vitalistic plus mechanistic) causalities 75 percent of the time, though they were more apt to adopt intentional causality than the 8-year-olds or adults. With increasing age the subjects came to choose mechanistic explanations most often.

In addition, Inagaki and Hatano (1993, experiments 3 and 3a) revealed that 6-year-olds, as well as 8-year-olds and adults, relied on vitalistic causality only for biological phenomena and not for social-psychological phenomena. In other words, these subjects differentially applied vitalistic and intentional causalities to biological phenomena and social-psychological ones.

Miller and Bartsch (1997) examined whether Inagaki and Hatano's finding that 6-year-olds were vitalists would be confirmed among US subjects, and found that US children also preferred vitalistic causal explanations to intentional ones for biological phenomena. At the same time, they found that, contrary to Inagaki and Hatano (1993), college students were also vitalists; that is, these students chose vitalistic explanations for biological phenomena as often as the 6 and the 8-year-olds did.

However, this difference may be only apparent. As Hatano and Inagaki (1996, 1997) described elsewhere, vitalistic causality is never completely replaced by mechanistic causality with increasing age; in other words, it may continue to work as a basis of understanding and to be used in situations where people do not think they are required to provide answers based on so-called scientific biology. The college students in Miller and Bartsch's (1997) study may have been interviewed in such a situation. Even in Inagaki and Hatano's (1993) study, a few college students seemed to use vitalistic causality as an informal or fallback mode of explanation. When a student who consistently chose vitalistic explanations was interviewed after the experiment, she said, "We usually choose something like 'oxygen' or 'the heart works like a pump' because we have learned in school to do so. However, I chose other explanations because they were most convincing and comprehensible to me."

In sum, recent studies, using sophisticated assessments, have revealed that young children possess an informal biology which is based probably on vitalistic causality, and that they recognize that the functions of the mind and body are distinguishable from each other. Children almost never interpret or explain bodily phenomena or processes only in terms of intentional causality.

Nature of vitalistic causality

Let us discuss in more detail the nature of the vitalistic causality that young children possess and that even adults may use as a fallback strategy. We shall focus on the functions and dynamics of vital power, the causal device in vitalistic explanations, with an attempt to connect the notion of vital power to illness and ill health, the topic of the present volume. This discussion is inevitably speculative, because there have been few systematic studies that examine the notion of vital power entertained by young children and lay adults. However, whenever available, we refer to empirical findings, many of which are mentioned in the preceding and following sections.

Differences from mechanistic causality

How is vitalistic causality different from the mechanistic causality that refers to physiological mechanisms? Whereas mechanistic causality is applied to both living and non-living entities without distinction, vitalistic causality is applied only to organisms. As many other investigators (e.g., Atran, 1998; Gelman and Hirschfeld, 1999; Keil, 1995) have asserted, we assume that because human minds interpret behaviors of living entities differently from those of non-living things, it is appealing to rely on different modes of explanation between living and non-living things (including artifacts). When applied to bodily phenomena, mechanistic causality means that specific bodily systems exchange specific substances between each other or with their environment. In contrast, in vitalistic causality a bodily phenomenon is attributed to the workings of vital power, which refers to some unspecified substance, energy, or information that is essential for maintaining and enhancing life.

In somewhat elaborate vitalistic explanations, internal organs or bodily parts are given "agency," or an activity-initiating and sustaining character. To put it differently, organs are supposed to work hard to take in vital power from the external physical world including food, air, and so on, and exchange it with one another, so that all parts of the body can function well. Thus, vitalistic causality can be regarded as a product of personification – an attempt to understand the workings of internal organs by assigning them agency or regarding them as human-like agents.

Such a mode of elaborate explanation can be found in the Japanese endogenous science before the Meiji restoration (and the beginning of Japan's rapid modernization), which had evolved with medicine and agriculture as its core (Hatano and Inagaki, 1987). This endogenous science was not mechanistic and atomistic, but vitalistic and holistic. Bodily functions were interpreted in terms of vitalism, often as exchanges of unspecified "vital power" (*ki* in Japanese). For example, "The internal organ X works hard to produce such and such effects, sending vital power."

How vital power operates

How do young children assume vital power operates for living kinds? Our studies have shown that their understanding includes at least two very important functions of vital power for an organism's survival. First, young children assume that all other living things, like humans, take in vital power from food and/or water to maintain their vigor. Humans, children believe, can live for 100 years or even longer if they take in a sufficient amount of vital power (Inagaki, 1995). In contrast, if they are not provided with vital power for an extended period of time, children believe they will die. This is applied not only to organisms as a whole (Inagaki and Hatano, 1996, experiments 2 and 3) but also to their parts (e.g., hands no longer supplied with blood in Inagaki and Hatano's [1990] study). Second, young children assume that living things can grow in size using surplus of vital power. Therefore, if animals are fed little or plants are watered little, they will not become bigger (Inagaki and Hatano, 1996, experiments 2 and 3). Although we have not systematically examined it yet, some preliminary data suggest that young children believe that a lot of vital power is also needed for producing many offspring.

We claim that young children's biology is vitalistic, because naive biology is about living things, and that children's concept of living things is defined by a triangular structural relationship consisting of food and/or water, active and lively states ("becomes active by taking in vital power from food"), and growth ("surplus of vital power induces growth"), based on the notion of vital power (Hatano and Inagaki, 1996). This triangular structural relationship seems to be applied readily to animals, and may also be applied to plants, partly because children lack understanding of photosynthesis. This relationship seems to constitute the core of young children's understanding of the bodily phenomena of humans and other living things.

Vital power also seems to function in children's understanding of illness causality. Young children assume that (as will be discussed in the next section) vital power prevents living things from being taken ill; in other words, a body full of vital power is unlikely to fall ill, even when its owner comes in contact with a person suffering from the illness. Moreover, a person who has a great deal of vital power can recover rapidly even when he or she becomes ill or injured. Many Japanese people, both adults and children, believe in folk preventive medicine that advocates the importance of one's susceptibility or resistance to illness and that offers various specific recommendations for improving resistance. At a conceptual level, it refers, at least implicitly, to ingesting and sustaining vital power.

How vital power is ingested

Vital power has to be taken in from the outside. The obvious sources for ingesting vital power are food and water. In more elaborated forms of vitalism, some additional sources like air (taken through breathing) and other people's vital power (taken through sympathy) are also included, but in young children's biology, food and water are far more salient than other sources, as the study by Inagaki (1995) has revealed.

Do some kinds of food involve more vital power than others? Because the notion of vital power corresponds in part with that of nutrition, those foods that are considered to be better for one's health (e.g., vegetables) are believed to contain more vital power than those that are not particularly healthy (cakes or candies) or are too luxurious (marbled beef). This point will be discussed later in relation to susceptibility to illness. Young children are often asked by their parents to eat certain healthy foods (e.g., carrots or spinach) for both biological and moral reasons. These parental attempts may potentially be based on the notion of vital power; although parents cannot always explain which components in the food that they recommend are good for health, they believe that their recommendation is correct because the food seems to possess a lot of vital power.

Because food is the most salient source for vital power, young children's vitalistic biology is established around eating or nutrition. Although preserving the species or one's own genes is probably the supreme goal of animate entities, and even young children have an intuition that offspring resemble their parents (Solomon *et al.*, 1996; Springer, 1992), whether they readily understand the biological nature of inheritance is debatable (Springer, 1992; Springer and Keil, 1989; Hirschfeld, 1994; Solomon *et al.*, 1996).

How vital power is sustained or lost

An organism has to spend more vital power to be active and lively than just to survive. Thus it has to take in food or water more or less regularly. However, whether vital power is conserved or lost quickly depends on internal bodily conditions. For example, many lay adults in Japan assume that people who are old and/or physically weak tend to promptly lose vital power taken from food and other sources.

As we shall see in the next section, adults as well as young children believe that vital power can be lost quickly if a person experiences stress, either physical or psychological. The former (i.e., physical stress) includes extremely cold or hot weather, unseasonable weather, continuous engagement in hard exercise, and lack of sleep. The latter (i.e., psychological stress) includes difficulties in human relations, financial problems, and anticipated or actual failure in work or study. This implies that some psychological variables influence people's susceptibility to illnesses, even when the illnesses are caused by specific entities like germs and viruses. In other words, not only psychosomatic but also contagious illnesses are partly psychological in nature. Vitalistic biology insists that the mind and body are always interdependent to some degree in illness causality.

Understanding of the mind–body interdependence

In this section, we shall examine young children's understanding of illness causality as a sub-domain of their vitalistic biology. As alluded to in the preceding section, the notion of vital power as some unspecified substance, energy or information that greatly influences whether a person becomes ill, relates the mind and the body, because both psychological and physical stresses quickly reduce the vital power taken from food and other sources.

Alternative view of illness causality

Studies on children's conception of illness causality have often dealt with their understanding of germs as invisible causal agents. Although there have been studies reporting that preschool children invoke germs as causes of illness (e.g., Kalish, 1996, chapter 5 in this volume; Springer and Ruckel, 1992), it is debatable whether they understand germs as uniquely biological entities. Solomon and Cassimatis (1995) assert that these results simply indicate that children understand the pragmatics of utterances involving germs (e.g., "Don't eat that cheese, it has germs on it"), that is, germs are something that makes a person sick. In other words, these children do not understand germs as part of a uniquely biological process through which people become ill. Au and Romo (1999) also demonstrated, using kindergarteners through sixth graders as subjects, that these children generally did not possess an inherent biological understanding of germs. They found that only 6 percent of their subjects said that the "incubation of germs" phenomenon explains why it takes time for germs to multiply or reproduce inside the human body, and concluded that it is difficult for children (and probably lay adults too) to acquire and use knowledge about uniquely biological causal mechanisms, without being taught scientific biology.

Considering that germs were discovered to cause illness as recently as the nineteenth century, it is unlikely that young children easily understand germs as uniquely biological causal agents, and thus Au and Romo's (1999) conclusion seems reasonable. However, it is also unlikely that children have no biological knowledge about causes of illness, because the understanding of illness causality (or prevention of illness) is important from an evolutionary perspective. As we have seen in the previous sections, young children do have a biological (or vitalistic) understanding about bodily functions, and thus it is plausible that they have a substantial understanding of illness phenomena from perspectives other than a germ theory. Keil *et al.* (1999) claim, based on reviews of the history of knowledge about disease and on observations of traditional cultures, that ancient people represented by Hippocrates in Greece and people from traditional cultures possessed folk theories of medicine that are biological in nature. One of these, the imbalance theory, indicates that disease or poor health is a result of difficulty in maintaining balance in a person's humors.

Vitalistic explanations of disease described in the previous section seem to be a variant of this imbalance theory, and continue to exist as an explanation for susceptibility (or resistance) to illness. Whether or not a person who is exposed to germs gets sick often depends on his or her susceptibility to illness. Since the imbalance theory does not seem to have developed very much in western cultures, researchers who are strongly influenced by a germ theory tend to ignore the role of physical or psychological factors contributing to susceptibility to illness in determining whether a person gets sick. For example, Kalish (1997b) considers whether any given infected individual will fall ill is just probabilistic-uncertain.

Young children's understanding of susceptibility to illness

Human physical conditions are often affected by daily activities. For example, the more imbalanced a person's diet, or the more irregular someone's daily routines, the more susceptible they are to illness. Inagaki and Hatano (see Inagaki, 1997b) examined whether young children recognize that physical and social/psychological aspects of daily activities contribute to susceptibility to illness and if so, to what degree.

In experiment 1 of their study, kindergarten children aged 4–6 years were presented with pairs of drawings of two characters, and asked which of the two was more likely to catch cold with the question, "When these two boys, X and Y, play with a child who has a cold and is coughing a lot, which is more likely to catch cold, or are both equally likely?" The two characters were allegedly different in terms of the physical or social/psychological factors in their daily activities. The physical factors included imbalanced diet, insufficient food intake, insufficient intake of fresh air, and irregular daily routines. The social/psychological factors involved telling a lie and misbehaving.

A majority of the children in each age group, with the exception of the 4 year olds' responses to a fresh air item, chose the character who engaged in biologically bad activities as being more likely to catch cold. More specifically, the character who ate only a little every day, who ate few vegetables, who stayed up late watching TV, or who did not air out the room by opening windows was more likely to catch cold than the character who ate a lot, who ate a lot of vegetables, who went to bed early, or who aired out the room.

Although the 4 and 5-year-olds could give few reasons for their choices, about half of the 6-year-olds justified their responses for the items involving eating a little and eating few vegetables. For example, one 6-year-old child said, "[A boy who has] little nutriment does not have energy, so germs easily enter his body." Another 6-year-old child similarly justified, "When this boy X eats a lot, his throat is full of nutriment. This boy Y eats little, so his throat is not full of nutriment, and so the coughing can pass through his throat." Very few children could give reasonable explanations why the boy who didn't air out the room was more likely to catch cold. However, one of the 6-year-olds justified his choice, saying, "Old air makes this boy weaker, and when he plays with a child who has a cold, he will be even weaker and catch cold," and another said, "We cannot take in nutriment without airing out the room." Since the choice patterns of the 4 and 5-year-olds were very similar to those of the 6-year-olds, it is strongly suggested that the 4 and 5-year-olds, like the 6-year-olds, considered that the lack of energy or vital power due to, for example, eating too little, would make the protagonist susceptible to illness.

These children believed that social/psychological factors would also influence susceptibility to illness. A majority of children not only aged 4 and 5 but also of age 6 answered that the boy who often hit/pinched a friend or who told a lie was more likely to catch cold than the boy who was a good friend or who never lied. None of the 4 and 5-year-olds gave any reasons for their choices. Only 30 percent of the 6-year-olds justified their responses by referring to something like immanent justice. There were very few who chose both alternatives or rejected both alternatives, i.e., responses indicating that telling a lie, or misbehaving, was irrelevant to catching cold. In other words, most children recognized that physical aspects of daily activities would affect one's susceptibility to illness, but at the same time they believed that social/psychological factors also contributed.

In experiment 2, children aged 4 and 6 from another kindergarten were asked which of the two characters who had caught cold was more likely to become more ill, instead of asking which one was more likely to catch cold. The items used were similar to those used in experiment 1. The response tendencies found in experiment 1 were confirmed in experiment 2. The children predicted that not only physical factors but also social/psychological factors would contribute to making the cold worse.

The response that social/psychological factors would increase one's susceptibility to illness was not due to the experimental artifact of children's failure to make "equally likely" responses. When the children were asked to choose between two neutral alternatives, e.g., between a character whose name was Taro and a character whose name was Jiro, in terms of whose cold was more likely to become worse, they showed random responses for the three alternatives including the "equally likely" choice. Thus, these children seemed to believe that misbehaviors would increase the susceptibility to illness.

Do children believe that the contributions of psychological factors are the same as those of biological factors to becoming ill? The answer is "No." In experiment 3 we found that children aged 4 and 5 years evaluated biological factors as being more important than psychological ones for determining susceptibility to illness. Here we examined, devising a conflict task, whether children would differentially apply biological factors (e.g., nutrimental) to illness and moral factors to social phenomena (i.e., being invited to a party). The conflict task, consisting of six items each for biological items and social items, was constructed by combining three physical factors and three social/psychological ones so that these combinations were in conflict.

Children were presented with a pair of drawings and asked to choose one (or both) between a child X who engaged in biologically good activities (e.g., eats a lot of vegetables) but behaved badly (e.g., often hits and misbehaves) and a child Y who engaged in biologically bad activities (e.g., eats few vegetables) but behaved well (e.g., is a good friend) in terms of which was more likely to catch cold. For example, "When playing with a child who has a cold and is coughing a lot, who is more likely to catch cold (or are both equally likely), a boy who often hits or pinches his friend on the back but eats a lot of vegetables every day, or a boy who is a good friend but eats few vegetables?" After finishing the six biological items, they were also asked, as social items, which of the two would be more likely to be invited to a birthday party by a classmate.

We classified children's responses into three categories each for the biological (i.e., cold) items and for the social (i.e., party) items: (1) biological-cue dominant response, making a choice relying on the biological condition more than the moral one; (2) social-cue dominant response, making a choice relying less on the biological condition than the moral one; (3) equivalent response, choosing both or neither alternatives.

The 5-year-olds made biological-cue dominant responses more often than social-cue dominant responses for the cold questions, and social-cue dominant responses more often than biological-cue dominant responses for the party questions. They justified their choices by referring to biological aspects for the cold questions, while they referred to moral aspects for the party questions. In contrast, the 4-year-olds showed as many social-cue dominant responses as biological-cue dominant responses for the cold question, although they made social-cue dominant responses more often for the party questions. Statistical analyses showed significant differences in the numbers of biological-cue dominant responses between the cold questions and the party questions among both the 4-year-olds and the 5-year-olds. These findings indicate, on the one hand, that not only the 5-year-olds but also the 4-year-olds clearly differentiated biological phenomena from social/psychological phenomena in their reasoning. Moreover, the 5-year-olds considered biological (e.g., nutrimental) factors to be more important for illness susceptibility and moral factors as critical for popularity. On the other hand, the above findings indicate that the 4-year-olds weighed psychological factors in determining susceptibility to illness more heavily than the 5-year-olds, and failed to differentiate them from biological factors in the evaluation of their influence on illness susceptibility.

In sum, we can conclude from the above studies that, by age 5, children recognize that physical aspects of daily activities affect susceptibility to illness, but at the same time they believe that morally bad behaviors make some additional contribution to illness susceptibility, though they recognize biological factors as more important for illness.

In addition, we asked twenty college students the questions used in experiment 1 described above. Although a majority of them answered that telling a lie or misbehaving was irrelevant to catching cold, some of them chose the same alternative that young children did. That is, three students responded that the boy who often told a lie was more likely to catch cold than the boy who did not and another four, though they first made "equally likely" responses, added notes that it was probable that the character telling a lie was more likely to catch cold than the character who did not lie; for the misbehavior item such students were two and two, respectively. These students provided explanations, such as, "Psychologically anxious states, such as telling a lie, may influence health," or "The child who is not fine in both mind and body may be more likely to catch cold." These adult data seem to suggest that there exists a public belief that the mind and the body are not totally independent but interdependent to some degree. If so, the children's responses admitting some contribution of social/psychological factors to illness may reflect in part such a public belief.

Adults' understanding of an interdependence between the mind and body

In order to explore further lay adults' belief about mind–body interdependence, we examined how college students weighed infections, physical factors, and psychological factors as contributors to getting diseases. We used three kinds of diseases, i.e., dysentery, a common cold, and a duodenal ulcer, which were chosen to represent strongly infectious, moderately infectious, and non-infectious diseases, respectively, and which would differ in the degree that psychological factors contribute to becoming ill. We assumed that psychological factors would make a small contribution to the dysentery and the cold, while they would make a large contribution to the duodenal ulcer. We also assumed that physical factors contribute to susceptibility for all these diseases.

About fifty students were first asked in written form what factor they thought was the most important as a cause for getting dysentery, a cold, or a duodenal ulcer. For dysentery, one-fifth of the students pointed out that dysentery germs enter inside the body, and one-fourth of them just referred to bad sanitary conditions including a toilet without referring to any germ. One-third of them either did not know what dysentery was or could not suggest any risk factor as being important.

For the cold, one-fourth of the students referred to viruses entering inside the body and half of these students pointed out interactions between viruses and bodily susceptibility to illness, such as, "Viruses enter inside the body when the resistance to illness is weakened," "We are beaten by the viruses that enter inside our body when its resistance to illness is reduced, because we are weak at that time," or "Disturbance in bodily conditions due to insufficient sleep or fatigue makes us susceptible to the virus." About 70 percent of the students offered physical factors as contributing to illness susceptibility, that is, irregular daily routines or the lack of self-control of health, fatigue, deterioration of physical strength, a sudden change of temperature, or staying too long in a cold temperature. For example, "Bodily resistance to illness is lost due to shortage of sleep and/or fatigue," "Insufficient sleep or staying in the cold weather increases bodily susceptibility to illness," or "The body cannot adjust to sudden change of temperature." Only one student referred to the psychological factor, such as "When we are depressed." However, it should be pointed out that students' expressions of "irregular daily routines" or "the lack of self-control of health" often connote somewhat morally unfavorable meanings, because they imply that individuals are responsible for their own shortage of sleep, imbalanced diet, and so on.

For the duodenal ulcer, about 60 percent of the students suggested psychological factors, such as stress or trouble as a cause. About 15 percent of the students referred to the lack of self-control (e.g., irregular diet).

After having responded to the above open-ended questions, the students were presented with twelve items describing possible risk behaviors for each disease, and asked to assess each behavior in terms of the probability of getting the disease by choosing from the options "unlikely" (0), "slightly likely" (1), "moderately likely" (2), and "highly likely" (3). The twelve items were divided into four clusters consisting of three possible risk behaviors each: (a) exposure to a patient (e.g., Mr. H drank a can of juice in turn with his friend who got [the disease]); (b) physical factors involving imbalanced diet or insufficient sleep (e.g., Mr. D, who had strong likes and dislikes about food, ate few vegetables because he disliked them); (c) psychological factors involving depression or frustration (e.g., Mr. C has been depressed since he failed in his business); (d) irrelevant factors involving non-causal or positive events (e.g., Mr. L talked on the phone with a friend who got [the disease]).

We computed individual total scores for each of the four clusters by giving a score of 0 through 3 for each item, and averaged them. We excluded from the analyses subjects who answered that they were not familiar with the disease. Almost all the students judged "unlikely" the irrelevant cluster items for any disease (means were 0.1–0.3). For dysentery, the students rated exposure to the patient as the most likely risk factor (mean 5.8) and the physical factors as the second most likely (mean 3.3), whereas for the cold, they assessed exposure to the patient and the physical factors as highly likely risk factors (means 6.6 and 6.2, respectively). Means of the psychological cluster items were 1.5 for dysentery and 2.0 for the cold; these were significantly higher than the means of the irrelevant cluster items, suggesting that the students did not believe that contributions of psychological factors to the dysentery or to the cold were null. For the duodenal ulcer, the students rated the psychological factors as the most likely risk factor (7.3), the physical factors as the second most likely factor (5.5), and exposure to the patient as unlikely (0.3), indicating that they recognized the duodenal ulcer as a non-infectious, psychosomatic disease.

To examine further the students' beliefs about contributions of psychological factors to diseases, we counted the numbers of subjects who gave the score 1 ("slightly likely") or more to each of the three items (i.e., a total score of 3 or more) in the psychological and the irrelevant clusters. These patterns of responses were observed among 31.8 percent of the students for the psychological cluster versus 0 percent for the irrelevant cluster for dysentery; 43.6 percent versus 1.8 percent for the cold; 98.0 percent versus 2.0 percent for the duodenal ulcer. It should be noted that substantial proportions of the students (30–45 percent) believed that psychological factors would make some contribution even to infectious diseases. This suggests that they recognized that the mind and body are not independent but interdependent to some degree.

We would like to emphasize that the adults' beliefs of illness causality described above are not necessarily peculiar to Japanese people. Indeed, these beliefs may be salient and easily recognized in Japanese culture, where vitalistic explanations for illnesses are often observed in everyday life and due attention is paid to the role of physical or psychological factors contributing to susceptibility to illness in getting sick. However, as Miller and Bartsch's (1997) study indicated, US adults also prefer to rely on vitalism when in a non-scientific mode. It has also been reported that US adults who are supporters of a germ theory believe that colds are caused by cold weather or air. For example, when asked open-ended questions, about 20 percent of US college students gave cold weather and another 20 percent gave fatigue as potential risk factors for getting a cold (Sigelman et al., 1993). In addition, when allowed to choose unlimited number of risk factors, many more students were willing to choose cold weather or air as (folk) agents for a cold (Sigelman and Alfred-Liro, 1995). Western developmental researchers have not discussed lay adults' notion of susceptibility to illness explicitly, because the researchers regard the cold weather theory as wrong or unreasonable (e.g., Sigelman and Alfred-Liro, 1995).

Implications for health practices and education

We have shown that young children can distinguish bodily functions from mental ones; in other words, they never distort all biological observations so that they can be incorporated into the framework of intuitive psychology, nor are they ignorant of mediating processes between input and output. They can understand bodily phenomena or processes including illness in terms of vitalistic causality, although they do not know the specific physiological mechanisms involved. However (as also shown), young children, and lay adults too, believe that the mind and the body are not totally independent but interdependent to some degree, especially in their understanding of illness causality. They recognize that susceptibility to illness is important in determining whether a person becomes ill, and that not only physical aspects but also social or psychological aspects of daily activities contribute to it, although the former aspects are more important than the latter.

What implications can we derive from these findings for health practice and health education? We propose three of them. The first implication is that we should regard children who are taken ill as capable of understanding their illness and needed treatments. This notion is derived from the fact that even young children have the mind–body distinction, and understand that the body is relatively independent from the mind. Because children who are suffering from illnesses can understand their bodily phenomena and processes "biologically," parents or health practitioners can expect children's full cooperation based on informed consent. Needless to say, practitioners should give explanations translated into vitalistic terms, rather than purely technical or scientific terms. Thoughtful explanations for the significance and necessity of medical treatments would be expected to remove unnecessary fear, frustration, and confusion from child patients, and create favorable conditions for the treatments. This recommendation can be applied to even preschool-aged children.

The second implication is that even young children can understand preventive medicine or health practices. They know not only that they may be taken ill through exposure to patients or contagion, but also that whether they become ill depends on their susceptibility to illness. Moreover, they know that susceptibility to illness is determined by their daily activities. From the perspective of health practice and education, personal responsibility for health should be emphasized (e.g., eating a balanced diet, engaging in regular daily routines, avoiding stress in everyday life, and so on) by appealing to or triggering their notion of vital power and understanding of the mind–body interdependence. Such responsibility may include the avoidance of unnecessary and close contacts with patients, which is problematic, as will be discussed in the next paragraph. However, many other recommended activities are desirable ones, as far as children themselves try to engage in them with some biological understanding.

It should be pointed out that this emphasis on personal responsibility for maintaining health or preventing disease should be offered by health educators with great care. This is the third implication. Emphasizing that we can reduce the risk of becoming ill through self-control is double-edged in that it may develop a prejudice against patients and/or restrict opportunities for natural interactions with them. As we have seen in the previous sections, children are at least prepared to accept that whether they become ill depends on their susceptibility to illness, which is determined by their daily activities. A corollary of this belief is that sick people may be responsible for their illness to some extent. Although this is not true, the emphasis on self-control for good health may increase sick people's guilt feeling, and/or may result in blaming other sick persons for their failure in self-control (Wilkinson, 1988). A germ theory interpretation of diseases is guilt-free, because the causes of illness are attributed to exogenous factors. However, this interpretation may make children overly cautious about the risk of contagion (Kalish, 1997b; Springer and Ruckel, 1992), which tends to violate the basic human rights of patients.

Considering the last two implications simultaneously, we must develop a balanced and sensitive program for health education. On the one hand, children need to be instructed about causal mechanisms of germ transmission, but in a way that clearly eliminates undue anxiety over having contact with a patient. The program must also indicate that preventing contagion is not always possible, and thus patients should not be blamed. Fortunately, Au and Romo (1996) report that at least middle elementary schoolchildren can understand the causal mechanisms of AIDS transmission following appropriate biological instruction. On the other hand, we must emphasize the notion of self-care and personal responsibility for health, as the above second implication indicates. For effective health practices and education, we need not only to integrate the vitalistic causality of Oriental medicine and the germ theory of western medicine, but also to keep a balance between emphasizing children's initiatives for their own health and the protection of patients' human rights.

Acknowledgments: preparation of this chapter and some of the research reported in it were supported by Grant-in-Aid for Scientific Research from the Japanese Ministry of Education to Kayoko Inagaki (no. 07610114) and by Grant-in-Aid for Scientific Research on Priority Areas from the Japanese Ministry of Education to Giyoo Hatano (no. 09207105).

REFERENCES

Atran, S. (1998). Folkbiology and the anthropology of science: Cognitive universals and cultural particulars. *Behavioral and Brain Sciences*, 21, 547–609.
Au, T. K., and Romo, L. (1996). Building a coherent conception of HIV transmission: A new approach to AIDS education. In D. Medin (ed.), *The psychology of learning and motivation*, vol. XXXV (pp. 193–241). New York: Academic Press.
    (1999). Mechanical causality in children's "folkbiology." In D. Medin and S. Atran (eds.), *Folkbiology*. Cambridge, MA: MIT Press.
Carey, S. (1985). *Conceptual change in childhood*. Cambridge, MA: MIT Press.
Coley, J. D. (1995). Emerging differentiation of folkbiology and folkpsychology: Attributions of biological and psychological properties to living things. *Child Development*, 66, 1,856–1,874.
Contento, I. (1981). Children's thinking about food and eating: A Piagetian-based study. *Journal of Nutrition Education*, 13, 86–90.
Gellert, E. (1962). Children's conceptions of the content and functions of the human body. *Genetic Psychology Monographs*, 65, 291–411.
Gelman, R. (1979) Preschool thought. *American Psychologist*, 34, 900–905.
Gelman, S. A., and Hirschfeld, L. A. (1999). How biological is essentialism? In D. Medin and S. Atran (eds.), *Folkbiology*. Cambridge, MA: MIT Press.
Hatano, G., and Inagaki, K. (1987). Everyday biology and school biology: How do they interact? *Quarterly Newsletter of the Laboratory of Comparative Human Cognition*, 9, 120–128.
    (1996). Cognitive and cultural factors in the acquisition of intuitive biology. In D. R. Olson, and N. Torrance (eds.), *Handbook of education and human development: New models of learning, teaching and schooling* (pp. 683–708). Cambridge, MA: Blackwell.
    (1997). Qualitative changes in intuitive biology. *European Journal of Psychology of Education*, 12, 111–130.
Hirschfeld, L. (1994). Is the acquisition of social categories based on domain-specific competence or on knowledge transfer? In L. Hirschfeld and S. Gelman (eds.), *Mapping the mind: Domain-specificity in cognition and culture* (pp. 201–233). Cambridge, UK: Cambridge University Press.
Inagaki, K. (1995). Young children's spontaneous vitalistic explanations for bodily phenomena. Paper presented at the fifty-ninth meeting of the Japanese Psychology Association, Okinawa [in Japanese].
    (1997a). Endogenous variables mediating disease transmission. Paper presented at the meeting of the Society for Research in Child Development, Washington, DC.

(1997b). Emerging distinction between naive biology and naive psychology. In H. M. Wellman and K. Inagaki (eds.), *The emergence of core domains of thought: Children's reasoning about physical, psychological, and biological phenomena* (pp. 27–44). San Francisco: Jossey-Bass.

Inagaki, K., and Hatano, G. (1990). Development of explanations for bodily functions. Paper presented at the annual meeting of the Japanese Educational Psychology Association, Osaka [in Japanese].

(1993). Young children's understanding of the mind–body distinction. *Child Development*, 64, 1,534–1,549.

(1996). Young children's recognition of commonalities between animals and plants. *Child Development*, 67, 2,823–2,840.

Kalish, C. W. (1996). Preschoolers' understanding of germs as invisible mechanisms. *Cognitive Development*, 11, 83–106.

(1997a). Preschoolers' understanding of mental and bodily reactions to contamination: What you don't know can hurt you, but cannot sadden you. *Developmental Psychology*, 33, 79–91.

(1997b). Recognizing probabilistic causation: Children's predictions of illness. Paper presented at the meeting of the Society for Research in Child Development, Washington, DC.

Keil, F. C. (1995). The growth of causal understandings of natural kinds. In D. Sperber, D. Premack, and A. J. Premack (eds.), *Causal cognition* (pp. 234–262). Oxford: Clarendon.

Keil, F. C., Levin, D. T., Richman, B. A., and Gutheil, G. (1999). Mechanism and explanation in the development of biological thought: The case of disease. In D. Medin and S. Atran (eds.), *Folkbiology*. Cambridge, MA: MIT Press.

Miller, J. L., and Bartsch, K. (1997). The development of biological explanation: Are children vitalists? *Developmental Psychology*, 33, 156–164.

Siegal, M. (1988). Children's knowledge of contagion and contamination as causes of illness. *Child Development*, 59, 1,353–1,359.

Sigelman, C., and Alfred-Liro, C. (1995). Wear your coat: Age and ethnic differences in cold weather and germ theory of infectious disease. Paper presented at the biennial meeting of the Society for Research in Child Development, Indianapolis.

Sigelman, C., Maddock, A., Epstein, J., and Carpenter, W. (1993). Age differences in understandings of disease causality: AIDS, colds, and cancer. *Child Development*, 64, 272–284.

Solomon, G. E. A., and Cassimatis, N. L. (1995). On young children's understanding of germs as biological causes of illness. Paper presented at the biennial meeting of the Society for Research in Child Development, Indianapolis.

Solomon, G. E. A., Johnson, S., Zaitchik, D., and Carey, S. (1996). Like father, like son: Young children's understanding of how and why offspring resemble their parents. *Child Development*, 67, 151–171.

Springer, K. (1992) Children's awareness of the biological implications of kinship. *Child Development*, 63, 950–959.

Springer, K., and Keil, F. C. (1989). On the development of biologically specific

beliefs: The case of inheritance. *Child Development,* 60, 637–648.
Springer, K., and Ruckel, J. (1992). Early beliefs about the causes of illness: Evidence against immanent justice. *Cognitive Development,* 7, 429–443.
Wilkinson, S. R. (1988). *The child's world of illness: The development of health and illness behavior.* Cambridge, UK: Cambridge University Press.

3   How a naive theory of biology is acquired

Ken Springer

Two of the most important questions we can ask about theory change are what happens, and what makes it happen. The descriptive question is comparatively easy, and has given rise to numerous studies comparing children with varying degrees of biological knowledge – as can be seen in this volume, and in reviews by Carey (1985), Wellman and Gelman (1992, 1997), and others. Perhaps because the explanatory question is more difficult, there have been relatively few detailed suggestions as to what drives changes in an early theory of biology, and about how such a theory emerges in the first place.[1]

Existing proposals about the acquisition of a framework theory of biology can be divided into two types. Type 1 proposals link the emergence of a theory of biology to innate predispositions. In particular, it has been suggested that naive essentialism, and a teleological stance, contribute to the acquisition of a naive biology, by constraining the type of input that children notice and the way they put the input to use (e.g., Gelman and Hirschfeld, 1990; Keil, 1992; Kelemen, 1998). In each case there is some debate over the extent to which the predisposition is domain-specific, but most Type 1 proposals reflect the assumption that a theory of biology is an early, autonomous competency rather than an offshoot of some other theory.

Type 2 proposals are based on the assumption that a naive theory of biology is originally not fully distinct from other framework theories, in particular a naive psychology (e.g., Carey, 1985), or, according to one recent proposal, a naive mechanics (Au and Romo, 1999). According to such proposals, a naive biology emerges through a variety of processes, including the acquisition and reorganization of biological knowledge (Carey, 1985), and the use of personification and vitalistic causality to account for somatosensory experience and other observations of biological phenomena (Hatano and Inagaki, 1994; Inagaki, 1997). Type 2 proposals differ from the first type in that a naive biology is not considered autonomous initially, somewhat less specificity is granted to the role of innate constraints, and somewhat more emphasis is given to the role of everyday experience. (Type 1 theorists do not deny the importance of experience, any more than Type 2 theorists deny genetic constraints on theory acquisition. Differences on these points are merely a matter of emphasis and specificity.) These two types of proposals pertain to theory acquisition, and thus do not reflect views according to which the child's first systematic biological knowledge is atheoretical (e.g., Atran, 1994).

In this chapter I introduce a third type of proposal, one which shares features with each of the other two types. Like Type 1 theorists, I argue that a naive theory of biology is autonomous, at least by age 4 or 5, and does not emerge from other framework theories, even though it may be informed by them. However, in the spirit (if not the specifics) of Type 2 proposals, I claim that the critical factor driving the acquisition of a naive biology may be the acquisition of factual knowledge, combined with certain key inferences generated from this knowledge. Although nobody would deny that learning and inference are important components of theory building, I place special emphasis on certain kinds of knowledge and inference as sufficient for the initial construction of a theory. I shall say little about the role of innate competencies, despite the fact that there must be constraints, perhaps innate ones, on the inductions I attribute to children. I shall argue that by age 4 or 5 many children acquire a naive theory of biology, one which results in a conceptualization of certain biological phenomena which is incommensurable with children's prior understanding. In developing these arguments, my focus will be on children's theoretical beliefs about kinship. I shall not attempt a broader statement about theory acquisition within the biological domain, because it seems obvious that some theoretical changes will be driven more by new data and/or inference than others.

The family is a familiar social category for most of the world's children. Most children grow up in a family, interact with other families in their community, and hear talk about families from stories and other media. Owing in part to this experience, kin terms are among children's earliest vocabulary, and shortly thereafter preschoolers begin to conceptualize families as interpersonal units (e.g., Hirschfeld, 1989). In this chapter I shall be describing, and attempting to account for, the emergence of US children's theoretical understanding of family relations.[2]

Although researchers disagree on how to characterize the lay adult's conceptualization of the family, this does not prevent our describing early changes in children's understanding. I believe that such descriptions can be made on the basis of a useful distinction between two possible, though somewhat idealized, conceptions of the nuclear family. One conception is based on observable features that are readily available to young North American children: families are composed of some number of adults and children who may share common surnames, physical resemblance, and personal property. These individuals tend to live together and engage in common activities, both spontaneous and ritualized, and exhibit nurturing behaviors and other signs of emotional interconnectedness. An individual who identifies families on the basis of some or all of these features might be said to have a "social" conception of the family. (I have chosen this phrase for convenience; it should be noted that some of the features in question, such as physical resemblance, are not really social.)

An alternative, "biological" conception of the family is based on awareness of genetics. Kinship can be defined in terms of genetic relatedness and concepts such as genes, chromosomes, and DNA, which are neither observable nor typically explained to small children.

Biological and social conceptions of the family differ in the types of features that mark a group of people as a family (social/perceptual and readily observable vs. biological and not readily observable). Among adults, both types of features seem to play a greater or lesser role in our theories of family relations, depending on both the culture and the individual. However, despite the difficulty that researchers might face in characterizing this end state toward which children develop, it is at least clear that in the United States a mature, adult-like understanding of kinship is based on a distinction between biological and social relations. For example, even if we happen to believe that an adoptive parent is the "real" parent of an adoptive child in every possible sense – legal, economic, social, emotional, etc. – we nonetheless recognize a physical distinction between biological and adoptive parentage, and this distinction plays a fundamental role in our naive theory of kinship.

The main question I want to address in this chapter is what takes children beyond the surface features of families, such as nurturance and proximity, toward the notion that family relations can be defined in terms of unobservable, biological ties. In short, how do children first begin to move from a social construal toward a genetic one? I shall argue that the critical development leading to children's first theoretical reasoning about kinship occurs when they learn that babies grow inside their mothers. Knowledge of gestation allows children to link certain kin relations to birth, and to make theoretically based (though sometimes incorrect) predictions about the phenotype. This knowledge also allows children to develop some incorrect, though internally consistent, notions about inheritance. In short, learning about an unseen process changes children's understanding of observable features. I shall argue that children's first theory of kinship is a biological one, but not genetic, and that its acquisition is strongly data-driven. I shall suggest that this theory does not develop from a theory of psychology, that it is constrained only in a general way by a naive mechanics, and that it is implicit rather than explicit. I shall describe the effects of adoption on the coherence and sophistication of children's reasoning. Finally, I shall argue that children's earliest theory of kinship is incommensurable with their prior understanding of families, and that the emergence of this theory thus reflects fundamental cognitive change at the level of concepts such as *mother*.

Two claims about the acquisition of a theory of biology

As I describe children's earliest theory of kinship, I shall be making two claims which are somewhat distinctive in the literature on early biological thought. The first claim is that an implicit theory of biology is possessed by at least some 4 and 5-year-olds. Although it is widely acknowledged that young children have naive theories of physics and psychology, there is some debate as to whether they also have a naive theory of biology. My claim that some 4 and 5-year-olds have such a theory contrasts with other claims that it does not emerge until around age 6, if not later (Carey, 1985, 1995; Hatano and Inagaki, 1994; Johnson and Solomon, 1997; Solomon et al., 1996). My strategy will be to show that at least some younger children have an understanding of kinship that meets widely accepted criteria for possession of a biological theory (i.e., domain-specificity, ontological commitment, and explanatory mechanisms: Carey, 1985; Keil, 1989; Wellman, 1985), and that a framework theory of biology is reflected in children's beliefs about the specific topic of kinship. However, my emphasis will not be on age but rather experience. I believe that some 4 and 5-year-olds have a theory of biology because they have the right factual knowledge, not simply because they are 4 or 5. In the same vein, I shall present data that children who know they are adopted develop distinctive conceptions of kinship owing to their unique experience.

The second claim I shall develop here is that children's earliest theory of kinship is acquired through inductive inference from a set of simple facts about prenatal growth. My emphasis will be on the fact that babies both originate and gestate inside their mothers prior to birth. I shall argue that this fact is conceptually special, in two senses: first, children use the fact that babies grow inside their mothers as a basis for inductive inferences about phenotypic qualities and mechanisms of inheritance. For example, because the baby is physically close to the mother prior to birth, children who are aware of this fact expect babies to physically resemble their mothers more than their fathers (Springer and Hirschfeld, 1995).

Second, children who know where babies grow treat location of prenatal growth as a criterion for kinship. That is, they think that a baby belongs to a certain mother if and only if it originated in her body, regardless of who takes care of or lives with the baby (Springer, 1996).

My second claim thus focuses on how a particular piece of knowledge functions in children's conceptual thinking. In the case of adopted children, I shall show that other kinds of knowledge also play an important role. Although I shall be fairly concrete about how a theory of kinship is acquired, I shall be able only to speculate as to what motivates children to treat factual knowledge about prenatal growth as special, and what constrains the inductions they subsequently make. A second limitation is a dearth of attention to children above the age of 7, despite the fact that by age 7 most children still clearly lack even the rudiments of an adult-like genetic theory (e.g., Springer and Keil, 1989, 1991; Johnson and Solomon, 1997), and that older children exhibit beliefs about kinship and inheritance which do not fit a simple developmental trajectory between the beliefs of younger children and adults (Springer and Hirschfeld, 1995). Another limitation is an almost exclusive focus on the parent–offspring connection, and lack of attention to what adults would call degrees of genetic relatedness. The two basic claims in this chapter – that 4 and 5-year-olds have a theory of kinship, and that this theory is acquired through inductive inference – will be developed simultaneously rather than separately.

Methodological note

Most of the data described in this chapter come from studies in which children who know where babies grow prior to birth are contrasted with children who do not. I have found that about two-thirds of American 4 and 5-year-olds, and about three-quarters of 6 and 7-year-olds, understand that babies grow inside their mothers prior to birth (Springer, 1995, 1996). I shall refer to children who know this fact as "informed" children, while those who do not know where babies come from will be called "uninformed." The difference between informed and uninformed children is limited to knowledge about where babies grow. In other words, the label "informed" should not be taken to imply that such children know anything else about kinship and inheritance, such as where exactly babies grow, what the father contributes to the process, and so on. There is no evidence that 4 and 5 year olds know much of anything about such things. However, I shall argue that if these children are informed, in my limited sense of the term, they may develop a naive theory that allows them to make sense of other aspects of kinship and inheritance.[3]

This chapter is organized around three conceptual functions that a naive theory of kinship would serve. Anyone, child or adult, who possesses this particular theory would derive these conceptual benefits, despite the fact that the child's theory might be based on the conditions of birth, in contrast to the adult's genetic theory.

A theory of kinship provides explanations of and predictions about family resemblance

Family resemblances are perceptually given. But as Solomon *et al.* (1996) and others have pointed out, someone who merely recognizes that offspring physically resemble their parents does not necessarily have a theory. With a theory one can understand why offspring physically resemble their parents, and why the resemblance is restricted to certain kinds of parents (biological, not adoptive). One can also generate predictions about specific patterns of physical resemblance.

Although in the history of biology a variety of explanations for family resemblance have been proposed (Mayr, 1982), one characteristic that most theories share is the attribution of parent–offspring resemblance to some sort of physical substrate and/or mechanism. Currently, the lay adult who has some familiarity with genetics, however limited, can account for phenotypic similarities in terms of the extent to which two individuals share genes. The lay adult expects babies to resemble their biological parents more than, say, their grandparents (at least most of the time), and to resemble their grandparents more than unrelated individuals. I have shown that children as young as 4 and 5 expect babies to share more non-obvious physical properties with their parents than with unrelated adults, even when the babies have greater superficial resemblance to the unrelated individuals (Springer 1992; also see Weissman and Kalish, 1999). These expectations are implicit rather than explicit. In forced-choice tasks such as mine, children's responses are more sophisticated than when they respond to open-ended questions on similar themes (Horobin, 1997). That is, their ability to link kinship to shared physical properties has been observed only in my forced-choice tasks.

An informed child, who by definition knows where babies grow, has some basis for expecting physical resemblance between mother and offspring, at least, owing to the close proximity between baby and mother during prenatal growth. Here is one line of inductive reasoning that I have attributed to informed children (see Springer, 1995, for further details and other patterns of inference):

Premise 1: Babies grow inside their mothers prior to birth.
Premise 2: Close proximity between two individuals facilitates transfer of stable physical properties between them.

Conclusion: Babies share more stable physical properties with their mothers than with any other individual.

The conclusion embodies a somewhat incorrect prediction (or at least one that cannot be empirically falsified in any simple way), but the premises and conclusion together would nonetheless reflect a theory. A theory, according to most researchers, is a set of explanatory beliefs by which we make sense out of one domain of observable phenomena (Carey, 1985; Keil, 1989; Wellman, 1985). Theories allow us to explain and generate predictions about observable phenomena on the basis of our understanding of underlying, domain-specific mechanisms. In the line of reasoning represented above, a prediction about the phenotype is generated along with an explanation of why phenotypic properties should turn out a certain way. Notice, however, that by definition only informed children could accept the first premise. (Evidently, all children accept the broad second premise Springer, 1995.) If informed children actually do engage in the inductive reasoning outlined here, we would predict not only that they would be more likely than uninformed children to accept the conclusion, but also that no uninformed children would accept this conclusion. In other words, if the conclusion is generated by inductive inference, rather than by some other cognitive mechanism, then no child could appreciate the conclusion without prior awareness of the premises. This is exactly the pattern of findings that I have observed (Springer, 1995, 1996, 1997a, 1997b).

Attribution task

For example, in one study (Springer, 1995, experiment 1), twenty-three informed 4–7-year-olds and thirteen uninformed ones were shown a picture of a woman and two children. One child was noticeably more similar to the woman in surface appearance, but was described as belonging to a different family. The other child was less similar to the woman but described as belonging to her. Subjects were asked whether or not each child shares each of two properties with the woman, a stable, non-obvious physical property (gray bones), and a transitory, observable property (scrapes). I assumed that the mature, theoretical pattern of responses would be to say that the real baby shares the stable property with its mother but not the transitory one, while the other baby shares neither with the mother. Seventeen of the twenty-three informed children provided this pattern of responses, whereas only one of the uninformed children did so, thus providing evidence for the model of inference described above.[4]

Clarification of the model

Several aspects of this model of inference require further clarification. First, although the model is committed to the notion that inductive inference is what links the factual knowledge I am calling the "premises" to the so-called "conclusions," it is not committed to the idea that children who acquire the premises automatically generate the conclusions. In fact they do not. Six of the twenty-three informed children in the aforementioned study had not done so yet. In one study, I received permission from parents to teach premise 1 (see p. 50) and a related premise to uninformed children (Springer, 1995; experiment 2). Children's beliefs about kinship and inheritance were tested before and after training, and I found a significant increase in the extent to which they provided theoretical responses. (Unfortunately, this increase tended to be spread across children; successful training would have been more clearly implicated by a subset of children providing completely theoretical responses.)

Perhaps in order to understand when children will make the relevant inferences, it needs to be explained first why they choose to use knowledge about prenatal growth as a basis for inference in the first place. The fact that babies grow inside their mothers before birth is not intrinsically special; something about children's conceptual systems makes them give it special attention. It might be asked why children actually think about this knowledge rather than storing it away as they might the names of state capitals. Although I cannot provide a full answer, it is at least clear that this knowledge is particularly interesting to children, perhaps more interesting than any other simple factual knowledge about kinship and inheritance that they are capable of grasping. Children are highly curious about their origins, and the notion that they originate inside someone else's body seems especially remarkable to them. For example, many of the uninformed children in Springer (1995) who were taught about prenatal growth seemed fascinated by the idea, and various comments and questions were offered about how the baby got inside the mother, what it does for fun there, whether it can see outside the mother, and so on.

Another question that might be raised is whether informed children spontaneously generate inferences such as the one described above, or whether they did so only when presented with my stimuli. Given my assumption that the relevant knowledge is fairly implicit, this is a difficult question to address, since the mere act of testing for the prior existence of these inferences might elicit them. In a sense, it does not matter whether or not children's inferences were stimulus driven, just as it does not matter that not all informed children generate the relevant conclusions.

After all, participation in my experiments is not the only chance that informed children will have to reflect on kinship and inheritance. For example, discussion of family resemblances, and exposure to pregnant women are two arguably common events in young children's lives. It is not especially important whether events such as these, or my stimuli, are what spur the relevant inferences by a particular child. The point is that it is inference, not some other mechanism, that drives the acquisition of the child's theory, and that by age 4 or 5 some children have been exposed to circumstances that triggered these inferences.

One other question of importance is what constrains children's inductions. If a child knows that babies grow inside their mothers, and that this close proximity fosters transmission of properties between them, but happens to know little else, the child could infer an infinite number of irrelevant conclusions, such as the correct prediction that the fetus will be smaller than the mother, or the incorrect prediction that the mother's phenotype will change to resemble that of the fetus. Why does the child infer physical resemblance between fetus and mother? This feels like a very "natural" sort of inference, but what makes it natural is unclear. Perhaps a naive essentialism (e.g., Gelman and Hirschfeld, 1998) renders conclusions about family resemblance highly salient to children. It is conceivable that children are disposed to think of essence as transmitted from parent to offspring, and thus they expect a relatively high degree of resemblance among kin in both surface and, especially, underlying properties. Indeed, when children are asked to choose among a broad set of mechanisms of inheritance, they typically prefer ones in which an actual property directly passes from mother to offspring (Springer and Keil, 1991). For example, they reject genetic, intentional, and magical explanations for the acquisition of skin color in favor of a mechanism through which pieces of the mother's skin pass directly into the baby, as if skin color were an essential property passed from generation to generation with little alteration.

Prediction task

In the study just described, informed children expected babies to physically resemble their mothers more than unrelated individuals. However, the conclusion following the two premises (see p. 51) also indicates that babies will resemble their mothers more than their fathers. I refer to this prediction as a "mother bias," and have documented its existence in a series of studies in collaboration with Lawrence Hirschfeld (e.g., Springer and Hirschfeld, 1995; see also Johnson and Solomon, 1997).

In our basic task, we describe and/or present children with pictures of two parents who differ on one dimension (e.g., skin color). Children are then asked to choose which baby out of a small set belongs to the parents in question. The strength of the mother bias subsequently observed depends on the content of the set of babies presented to children. In some studies, three babies are presented: a baby who resembles the mother more, a baby who resembles the father more, and a baby who is intermediate between the two. In several studies, we have found that the intermediate baby is the modal choice among all children. Such a response could be based on either domain-specific or domain-general expectations about property blending. However, we have also looked at how children responded when they did not choose the intermediate. In such cases, we find that informed children choose the baby resembling the mother about three times more often than the baby resembling the father. This is a significant effect only among informed 4 and 5-year-olds, and only for physical properties.

The mother bias emerges more clearly when the set of babies is limited to two: one resembling the mother and one resembling the father. Now informed 4 and 5-year-olds clearly expect babies to resemble their mothers more than their fathers, but only on physical dimensions. In sum, informed children seem to infer from the fact that babies are close to their mothers during pregnancy the partially incorrect but theoretical prediction that babies will resemble their mothers more than any other individual.[5] This prediction is correct insofar as babies typically resemble their mothers more than unrelated adults, but incorrect in that babies do not simply resemble their mothers more than their fathers.

In the studies just described, informed children's inferences about parent–offspring resemblance were limited to physical properties and not, for example, non-physical properties such as beliefs and preferences. When biological and adoptive parentage was contrasted in some of these studies, children's inferences about physical resemblance were limited to offspring and biological parents. These findings suggest that ontological-level distinctions underlie children's reasoning. In these and other studies, children's specific theory of kinship is ontologically committed to distinctions between physical versus non-physical properties, and biological versus adoptive parentage, and these distinctions reflect the framework theory of biology that informs children's specific beliefs.

A theory of kinship embodies biological concepts of certain kin relations

Adults understand that relational terms such as "baby" can be defined on the basis of strictly biological properties. Although we recognize that babies tend to live with and receive nurturance from their biological parents, we also understand that proximity and nurturance are so to speak characteristic rather than defining features, and that being someone's baby is, in the biological sense, strictly a matter of shared genes. Although preschoolers have no knowledge of genetics, those who know that babies grow inside their mothers prior to birth can treat location of prenatal growth as the defining feature. That is, their concept of *mother* at least may be organized by a theory in which one particular feature has special precedence.

Although I shall develop the argument shortly that informed children do not consider surface resemblance an essential feature of kinship, I do not mean to imply that they fail to appreciate resemblance as a characteristic feature. Predicting physical resemblance between mother and offspring owing to the nature of prenatal growth does reflect theoretical competence, and even 4 and 5-year-olds, if informed, understand that kinship implies shared physical properties. For example, in Springer (1996, experiment 1) children heard stories in which a baby was adopted at birth, and were then asked whether the baby would resemble the adoptive or the biological parent as an adult. Informed preschoolers expected the baby to ultimately resemble the biological parents on physical dimensions such as size, but the adoptive parents on non-physical dimensions such as beliefs. These children understand that because the baby grew inside one particular mother, the baby will exhibit some degree of physical resemblance to her, whereas the baby would develop resemblances to an adoptive parent only on environmentally based properties.

However, babies do not necessarily have much observable physical resemblance to their biological parents. A mature understanding of kinship depends on the realization that kinship can be defined by genetic substrates (in adult theories) or by conditions of birth (in children's theories), regardless of phenotypic or social features. Although informed preschoolers expect intrafamily resemblance and proximity, some of these children also understand that being someone's baby is strictly a function of the conditions of birth. In short, they distinguish between what is necessarily versus only typically true of parent–offspring relations.

Belonging task

I have examined children's appreciation of this idea (Springer, 1996, experiment 2). My original motivation for the study was to look at what children think is meant when they hear that a baby "belongs" to a particular family, that a mother goes to a hospital to "have" a baby, or that Cecilia is "my" daughter. Such vocabulary does not unambiguously denote a biological connection. Only if children can recognize that such phrases implicate something about the location of prenatal growth can we conclude that they define the parent–offspring connection in biological terms. Again, the alternative is that when children hear such phrases, they think the speaker is referring only to characteristics such as proximity and resemblance. In this social construal, the sentence "Cecilia is my daughter" simply means Cecilia is a girl who lives with and physically resembles me.

I examined these possibilities by means of a task in which surface similarity and proximity were contrasted with information about where the baby grew prior to birth. Two story types were developed. In the first type, a baby does not look like or live with a husband and wife, but is described as having grown inside the wife. In the second story type, a baby looks like and lives with a husband and wife, but is described as having grown inside a different woman. The question in each case is whether the baby is "really" the baby of the husband and wife. Children who have a biological construal of the parent–offspring relation would answer "Yes" to the first story type, but "No" to the second. Here are some sample stories presented to informed children in the belonging task:

There are two people, Mr. and Mrs. Smith. They live in a big house. And there's a baby named Steven. He lives in a small house with a different family. So he doesn't live with Mr. and Mrs. Smith. And he doesn't look like them: he's got different color hair, different color eyes. But he grew inside Mrs. Smith's belly, and right after he was born he went to live in a different house with a different family. So Steven grew inside Mrs. Smith's belly, but he doesn't look like her and Mr. Smith and he never lived with them. Is Steven really Mr. and Mrs. Smith's baby?

There are two people, Mr. and Mrs. Jones. They live in a small house. And there's a baby named Joseph. He lives in the same house with Mr. and Mrs. Jones. So he lives with Mr. and Mrs. Jones. And he looks like them too: he's got the same color hair, same color eyes. But he didn't grow inside Mrs. Jones' belly. He grew inside another woman, and right after he was born he went to live with Mr. and Mrs. Jones. So Joseph grew inside someone else's belly, but he looks like Mr. and Mrs. Jones and he's always lived with them. Is Joseph really Mr. and Mrs. Jones' baby? (Springer, 1996, experiment 2)

Seventy-four informed 4–7-year-olds participated in this experiment (un-informed children were not interviewed, because information about where babies grow was given in the main task). Each child received four stories, two representing each type described above. Children could thus make anywhere from zero to four biological responses (a biological re-sponse is defined as answering "Yes" to an exemplar of the first story type, but "No" to an exemplar of the second one). For one set of

Table 3.1. *Frequencies of children making different numbers of biological responses, by age, in
belonging task*
(from Springer, 1996, experiment 2)

| | Numbers of biological responses | |
	3 or 4	0 to 2
Age		
4–5 (n = 38)	18	20
6 (n = 19)	14	5
7 (n = 17)	14	3

analyses, the frequencies of children in each age group who made three or
four biological responses were collapsed into a single category, as were the
frequencies of children who made between zero and two biological responses (see table 3.1). These collapsed frequency distributions were
compared to distributions expected by chance, by means of chi-square
goodness of fit tests.[6] Significant deviations from expected values for each
age group were found. In each case, the observed values for the three or
four biological response category were greater than expected values,
whereas the observed values for the zero to two biological response
category were less than would be expected by chance. Although 6- and
7-year-olds were more likely than 4 and 5-year-olds to make biological
responses, 38 percent of the 4-year-olds and 59 percent of the 5-year-olds
made primarily biological responses. The results were essentially the
same regardless of whether or not the stories were accompanied by
pictures.

In sum, some preschoolers define parent–offspring relations in terms of
where babies initially grow rather than where they subsequently live and
who they look like, and the extent of this understanding increases with
age. Although children understand that babies typically live with their
parents and physically resemble them, they also realize that these are
characteristic rather than essential features. Instead, the location of prenatal growth is often taken to be the defining property of the parent–
offspring relation. This tells us that the informed child's understanding of
concepts such as *mother* and *baby* will be very different from the uninformed child's, a point I shall return to in my conclusion.

One of the basic assumptions underlying my work is that the child's
first theory of kinship is primarily data driven. This brings me to a third
claim about a theory of kinship. This claim not only pertains to the
conceptual function that such a theory serves, but also focuses on an
important characteristic of such a theory.

A theory of kinship reflects individual differences in experience and knowledge

The content of primarily data-driven theories may differ in important ways as a result of differences in what children know, or in how they weight certain data. If the first specific theory of kinship emerges as a result of inductive inference, there may be individual differences in children's theories resulting from differences in the background knowledge that serves as premises. Having younger siblings, being adopted, and acquiring a step-parent may influence the content of children's specific theories, or at least determine the rate at which these theories are acquired.[7] Although I have not yet examined this variable, observing one's parents undergo divorce and subsequent remarriage is probably critical, given that it would tend to highlight the distinction between biological and non-biological forms of parentage, and given the relatively large number of children whose parents have undergone such an experience.

In recent work I have focused instead on a somewhat less common group: adopted children. Specifically, I have been studying children who know that they have been adopted by their two parents, and who know at least roughly what being adopted means. These children's experience is somewhat special in that at some point in their lives, they have been familiarized with a distinction between the parents who are living with them now and taking care of them, versus another set of parents with whom they have a different sort of connection pertaining to birth. In other words, these children have been exposed to an explicit distinction between social and biological forms of kinship.

In an ongoing set of studies (Springer, 1997a, 1997b) I have been comparing informed children who live with their biological parents to informed children who are adopted. I am examining two hypotheses about the conceptual effects of adoption. First, children who know they are adopted may develop a relatively coherent understanding of kinship owing to their unique experience – specifically, to a relatively salient distinction between biological and adoptive parentage. Initially, I shall use the term "coherence" in a narrow sense to mean consistency in appropriate responses to a task. A child who has a highly coherent understanding of the difference between kinship in the biological and social senses will recognize how to apply this distinction to a task, and will apply it consistently, without being swayed by superficial details of different task items. (Presumably, the extent of consistency also suggests something about children's conceptual system, a point I shall return to later.) Coherence in this sense is thus independent of what we might call sophistication. In the studies described earlier, I assumed that children who have a purely social construal of kinship are less sophisticated than children who have developed their first theory in which kinship is defined with reference to where babies grow. In other words, I assumed, and will continue to assume, that among North American children a partially biological construal of kinship is more advanced than a purely social one. But this is independent of coherence. Adopted children may have a more coherent biological construal of kinship than other informed children, which would indicate more coherent and more sophisticated thinking. Alternatively, they may have a more coherent *social* construal, which would reflect greater coherence but less sophistication.

In sum, one hypothesis predicts exceptional coherence in adopted children's thinking about kinship. A competing hypothesis is that owing to other unique aspects of their experience, adopted children possess a less coherent understanding of kinship than other children their age. There are a number of possible bases for this hypothesis. Despite their having been exposed to a salient distinction between biological and social forms of kinship, adopted children may also receive information that blurs this distinction. For example, most people would not want to emphasize to adopted children that the adults who raise them are not their "real" parents in some sense, and some individuals may deliberately downplay the distinction when interacting with them. Adopted children may also be motivated for personal reasons not to accept, or at least not to explicitly acknowledge, such clearcut distinctions.

In examining whether adopted children's reasoning about kinship is more or less coherent than that of children raised by their birth parents, I have sampled three groups of 4–7-year-olds so far:

1 *Control group*: thirty-two informed white children (sixteen 4 and 5-year-olds, sixteen 6 and 7-year-olds) of primarily middle- to upper-middle-class background who live with two biological parents.
2 *Within-race adoptees*: twenty-one informed white children (ten 4 and 5-year-olds, eleven 6 and 7-year-olds) who were adopted prior to age 1 year 7 months by white middle- to upper-middle-class families. Eight of these children live with the biological children of their adoptive parents. Five of these children live with other adoptive children of their adoptive parents.
3 *Transracial adoptees*: eighteen informed children (nine 4 and 5-year-olds, nine 6 and 7-year-olds) who were adopted prior to age 2 years 5 months by white middle- to upper-middle-class families. This sample was composed of fourteen black children, two Hispanics, and two Asians. Four of these children live with the biological children of their adoptive parents, four live with the adopted children of their adoptive parents, and two live with both kinds of siblings.

Adopted children were recruited by means of an advertisement in the local newspaper, and by word of mouth. They were interviewed only if adopted by two non-biological parents, and if these parents stated that they had explained the meaning of adoption to the children. All children in this study, including adopted children, were informed. Each child participated in a random ordering of nine different tasks over a period of two to three days. Here I shall describe the results of three tasks.

Definition task

The first task probed children's sense of what constitutes a valid definition of certain kin terms. In this definition task, children were asked how one could best explain the meanings of certain kin terms to aliens from another planet who do not possess referents for these terms. For each kin term, children responded by choosing one out of a pair of explanations. In each pair, one explanation refers exclusively to the social features of the kin term, while another one also refers to the biological basis (i.e., conditions of birth). The explanations are otherwise identical. These explanations were drawn from definitions given by a separate sample of children in an open-ended version of this task.[8] Children were shown how to use checkers to mark their preferred choice after the experimenter read each pair. Pairs of explanations are given in here:

A mother is a woman who loves you and does things for you. You grew inside her belly when you were very tiny, and she will always love you. (Biological)
vs.
A mother is a woman who loves you and does things for you. She took care of you when you were very tiny, and she will always love you. (Social)

A baby is a very small person. It lives with a mommy and a daddy, and it grew inside the mommy's belly. It doesn't have teeth, so it drinks milk. (Biological)
vs.
A baby is a very small person. It lives with a mommy and a daddy, and they take good care of it. It doesn't have teeth, so it drinks milk. (Social)

A family is a group of people who live together and take care of each other. It's a mommy, a daddy, and some children. The children grew inside the mommy's belly, and the mommy and daddy take care of each one. (Biological)
vs.
A family is a group of people who live together and take care of each other. It's a mommy, a daddy, and some children. The children grew up with the mommy and daddy, and the mommy and daddy take care of each one. (Social)

Since three kin terms were queried, each child could provide anywhere from zero to three biological choices. The number of biological choices each child made was divided by three and represented as a proportion. The proportions are given in figure 3.1.

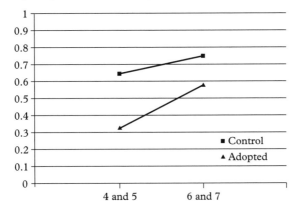

Figure 3.1 Proportions of biological choices in definition task, by subject group and age.

A between-subjects ANOVA conducted on these proportions after arcsine transformation revealed main effects of age and group. Older children made more biological choices than 4 and 5-year-olds, and control group children made more biological choices than each of the two adopted groups (with no differences among the latter). Analyses of individual response patterns showed that whereas only 44 percent of children in the control group made exclusively biological or non-biological choices for all three items, 69 percent of the children in the two adopted groups did so, and the difference was significant. In short, adopted children were more likely than controls to express a social construal of kin terms, but regardless of what construal they expressed, their responses were more consistent than those of the control group.

Belonging task

This task was identical to one reported earlier in this chapter in which children decided whether a baby belongs to a couple who lives with and resembles it, or to the biological parents with whom the baby neither lives nor shares resemblance (see p. 56; Springer, 1996, experiment 2; 1997a). The results were similar to those of the definition task (see figure 3.2). Control group children were more likely to say that the baby belongs to the birth parents, but adopted children were more consistent in linking the baby to either birth or adoptive parents. The only major difference between these results and the previous ones is that for reasons which are unclear, transracial adoptees were significantly more likely than within-

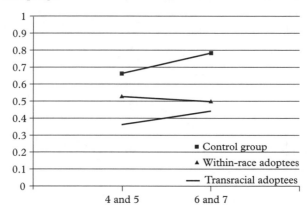

Figure 3.2   Proportions of biological responses in belonging task, by subject group and age.

race adoptees to say that the baby belongs to the adoptive parents.

The results of the definition and belonging tasks were consistent: in both tasks, adopted children were less likely than controls to relate kinship to prenatal growth, despite the fact that all children knew where babies grow. Adopted children were more likely to equate parent–offspring relations with nurturance and proximity rather than birth. On the surface, it would seem that for adopted children, terms like "baby" and "mother" tend to denote social rather than prenatal connections. However, in both tasks, adopted children were more consistent, so that even the minority who did feel that the location of prenatal growth defines the parent–offspring relation seemed relatively certain about this idea. Adopted children thus represent a more differentiated group than the rest of the population.

Phenotypic surprise task

This third task determines how well children can account for physical characteristics in babies that are not possessed by their parents. Children are told about phenotypic "surprises" and then asked to generate possible explanations. The question is whether children can generate kinship-relevant explanations (for example, stating that the surprising characteristic was possessed by the grandparents) as opposed to explanations unrelated to kinship, or no explanations at all. The phenotypic surprises presented to children listed here:

There's a red-haired baby. His hair is bright red. But his mom and dad both have black hair. How could that happen? How could two black-haired parents have a red-haired baby?

There's a brown baby. Her skin is a pretty brown color. But her mom and dad both have white skin. How could that happen? How could two white parents have a brown-skinned baby?

There's a baby with good hearing. She can hear really, really well. But both of her parents have bad hearing. How could that happen? How could two parents who hear badly have a baby with really good hearing?

There's a fat baby. He's really, really fat. But both of his parents are skinny. How could that happen? How could two skinny parents have a really fat baby?

The majority of adopted children and a handful of the control group proposed in response to whichever question they received first that the baby was adopted. These children were told that the baby was not adopted and were asked to guess again. The fat baby item was excluded from analyses because more than three-quarters of the children in each group proposed an obvious environmental cause: the baby ate a lot. This item served as a fortuitous control, in that the data show that children will not produce exclusively kinship-relevant explanations on this task. For the remaining items, children could provide anywhere from zero to three biological kinship-relevant explanations. The modal response in all groups was reference to grandparents. Two children referred to genes, two children referred to the notion of properties running in families, several children refused to guess, and there were a few silly responses as well. Each child's responses were coded as proportions (total number of kinship-relevant explanations divided by three), which are given in figure 3.3.

The proportions were arcsine transformed and submitted to a between-subjects ANOVA, which revealed main effects of age and group, and an interaction. Older children provided more kinship-relevant answers than younger children. Adopted children produced more kinship-relevant answers than the control group (with no differences between the two adopted groups). The difference between the control group and the two adopted groups taken together was significant among 4 and 5-year-olds but not among older children. Among all three groups, children tended to either provide the same sort of answer across all items, whether kinship-relevant or not. A distinctive pattern of responses to the question about surprising skin color was not observed among transracial, as opposed to within-race adoptees.

On the whole, adopted children were superior to controls at referring to

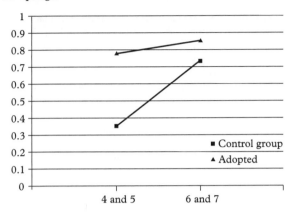

Figure 3.3   Proportions of kinship-relevant responses in phenotypic surprise task, by subject group and age.

kinship as a basis for explaining phenotypic surprises. Simple knowledge about family structure and inheritance seems to be more accessible to adopted children than to their peers. In a version of the attribution task described earlier, I found that children consider babies more similar to their grandparents than to unrelated adults (Springer, 1990), but the control group was not able to apply this idea here.

Perhaps, then, the results of this task show greater coherence in the thinking of adopted children, although in this case something about how children's conceptual knowledge is organized seems more directly implicated. Adopted children's knowledge about kin relations may be organized in such a way that this information is more accessible under certain conditions.

In other tasks, there were more similarities than differences among the three groups of children. In a switched-at-birth task, for example, all groups were equally facile at predicting that babies share more physical properties with their birth parents but more beliefs and preferences with the parents that raised them. In a task in which parents were described as differing on a dimension, and children were asked whether the baby would resemble the mother, the father, or be intermediate between them, performance across the three groups at each age was fairly similar. For example, the transracial adoptees did not show a distinct pattern of responses to an item in which one parent was black, the other was white, and children were asked what color the baby's skin would be. Differences in consistency were not observed in these tasks either.

Why were there no group differences on these tasks, while differences did emerge in the definition and adoption tasks reported earlier? Perhaps it is because these two tasks tap more directly into reasoning about the nature of kin relations, rather than requiring an application of this distinction to special cases. This of course raises the further question of why adopted children are more successful when dealing with special cases. Although I did not interview uninformed children, it appears that they would show the least sophisticated performance on these tasks.

The conceptual effects of adoption

The results of the three tasks reported here suggest several conclusions. First, adopted children are more likely to express a social construal of kin relations than other informed children. For example, they are more likely to express the idea that being a woman's baby means being raised by her rather than growing inside her. I am emphasizing the word "express" here, because all of the adopted children knew where babies come from, and it is possible that they were reluctant for some reason to apply this knowledge. (For example, they may feel that emphasis on linking birth to kinship is inappropriate because parents downplay the connection, because some people have told them kinship is purely a matter of love, because they feel pressure to assimilate, and so on.) In short, it is arguably unclear from my data whether adopted children are more likely to possess a social construal of kinship, or are simply more likely to express one.

A second conclusion is that adopted children are a more differentiated group than non-adopted children. Many adopted children possess or at least express a clearly social construal of kin relations, while a few express a clearly biological construal. It is unclear from my data and from discussions with the adoptive parents what aspects of children's experience were responsible for these differences, but certainly the messages that adopted children receive from their adoptive parents and other key adults may play a role.

The third conclusion, which flows from the second one, is that adopted children have a more coherent understanding of kin relations than non-adopted children. Whether their construal is social or biological, about two-thirds of adopted children responded in a completely consistent fashion to several tasks. In addition, the results of the phenotypic surprise task suggest that adopted children's knowledge about kinship is also more accessible than that of non-adopted children, perhaps owing to the way the knowledge is organized.

What then are the effects of adoption on children's understanding of the few aspects of kinship I have studied? On the whole, less sophistication, but greater coherence. Something about adopted children's experience increases the coherence of their theories, while contributing to differences in content.

Conclusions

What happens when children learn where babies grow? What I have argued in this chapter is that many informed children acquire a specific theory as a result of inductive inferences generated on the basis of this and other factual knowledge. This theory is implicit, domain-specific, on-tologically committed, appears among at least some 4 and 5-year-olds, and allows children to generate explanations of and predictions about phenotypic characteristics and mechanisms of inheritance. Although these explanations and predictions are somewhat incorrect, they are internally coherent and theoretical. They may reflect a framework theory of biology in which children's reasoning about kinship and inheritance is limited to living things, and in which there is an ontological commitment to the heritability of only physical properties. In addition, this first theory of kinship is based on a biological definition of mother–offspring relations which will be correct in the typical case. Traditionally, a baby's birth mother has always been its genetic mother as well. With the advent of surrogate motherhood in recent years, it is now possible for a baby to have no link to its birth mother. Only in such exceptional cases will links between the informed child's concepts of *mother* and *baby* and the conditions of birth be fallible.

In sum, my view of how children acquire a naive theory of kinship represents a hybrid of current views (in the terms of the introductory section, it is a "Type 3" view), but the central importance I impute to knowledge acquisition and inference are not intended to apply in all instances of theory building. Clearly, some theories are more data- and/or inference-driven than others. The acquisition of a theory of kinship in particular is associated with important conceptual changes, and I want to close with a discussion of one such change. It might be said that informed children's understanding of the term "mother" is incommensurable with that of uninformed children. Roughly, incommensurability in this case would mean that what one group of children means when they use the term "mother" cannot be represented coherently by any term or terms that the other group uses (Carey, 1991). Consider again children's conceptions of what mothers are. Informed children appear to think that a mother is an adult woman who has had (or currently has) a baby growing inside her, regardless of whether the woman actually lives with or cares for the baby. Uninformed children appear to think that a mother is any adult woman who lives with and nurtures a baby. Uninformed children would be surprised to note that informed children refer to some women as mothers, even when their putative babies live with different women. They would also be surprised that informed children deny that certain women are actually the mothers of the babies who live with them. Because uninformed children do not know about prenatal growth, they would have no basis for explaining these divergences in how informed children use the term "mother." Now consider informed children's perspective. Informed children would say (if they could) that uninformed children think of the term "mother" as referring to both real mothers as well as another kind of female caregiver. The informed child would say that the uninformed child's use of the term mother is correct in some cases, but incorrect in others. However, informed children do not have vocabulary yet for describing the uninformed child's various usages of the term "mother." At best they might be able to note that the uninformed child sometimes incorrectly expects mothers to physically resemble babies who did not grow inside them. Following Carey's (1991) analysis, informed and uninformed children's understandings of the term "mother" are not incommensurable merely because each child's use of the term refers to a somewhat different set of women, but also because of conceptual differences in their understanding of the relevant concepts. In sum, the first biological understanding of kinship that informed children acquire represents a fundamental conceptual change. Children will subsequently learn a great deal more about kinship and inheritance . Most 4 and 5-year-olds still know very little about the exact location of prenatal growth, what and how the father contributes to reproduction, a variety of kin terms and relations, and, of course, genetic concepts. Some kinds of new knowledge, such as the distinction between genetic and somatic tissue, will foster significant conceptual change. It remains to be seen how strongly such changes are driven by accumulation and reorganization of factual knowledge.

Acknowledgments: some of the research reported in this chapter was supported by grants to the author from the Ralph L. Smith Foundation and from the Hogg Foundation. Special thanks to Keehwa Hong for assistance in preparation of the manuscript. Address all correspondence to the author at Department of Psychology, Southern Methodist University, Dallas, TX, 75275–0442, USA. Email: kspringe@post.cis.smu.edu

NOTES

1 In the following discussion I assume a basic distinction between a small set of framework theories and the myriad specific theories they give rise to (Wellman, 1990; Carey, 1995). I shall be focusing on the acquisition of a specific theory

but shall note how it reflects the organizing principles of a framework theory of biology.

2 Although I assume that my claims have some cross-cultural generality, I am not prepared to argue that they apply to societies in which, for example, the nuclear family is not a salient characteristic of children's experience.

3 My method of determining whether children are informed or uninformed is to ask them initially "Do you know where babies come from?" or some comparable question. Children who simply answer "Yes" are asked to clarify. Children who do not provide clarification, or who say they do not know, are asked whether babies grow inside their mothers, or whether their mothers go somewhere to get them. More than half of the children labeled as informed spontaneously indicated that babies grow inside their mothers prior to birth.

4 Informed children generated other inferences from their knowledge about prenatal growth. For example, they seemed to infer from the premises listed on p. 50 that the mechanisms of inheritance involve direct transfer of material substrates of properties. The children were given descriptions of two mechanisms by which a baby could inherit hair on its arms and rough skin. One mechanism involved intentional processes (the mother wished for the baby to have such properties so it would resemble her) while the other involved material transfer (tiny pieces of skin and hair were transmitted to the fetus by a natural process). Informed 4–7-year-olds strongly preferred material transfer. (In earlier work, this mechanism was preferred over a variety of other options: Springer and Keil, 1991.)

5 At the same time, children seem to reject the possibility that the baby will look *exactly* like either parent. In an unpublished study in which I asked children which of a set of babies could belong to a particular parent, I found that most children rejected a baby that was perfectly identical to the parent in shape, color, and, probably most importantly, size.

6 Expected values were based on binomial calculations of the probabilities that a child would provide each of the possible numbers of biological responses by chance (with 0.5 as the probability of any given response being a biological one).

7 In one study, children's understanding of kinship was apparently unaffected by whether or not they had siblings (Springer, 1995).

8 In the open-ended version of the task, 4 and 5-year-olds often did not implicate birth or other biological features when defining the various kin terms. This is consistent with anecdotal evidence that children's conversation about kinship and family resemblances is not very "biological" (Callanan and Oakes, 1992), although it is in fact fairly easy to find exceptions to this. In any case, the theoretical competence I impute to children is implicit rather than explicit. Many of my subjects who defined the term "mother" as a nurturing female without noting, for instance, that a baby must have grown inside her at some point nonetheless indicated in other tasks that a baby belongs to whichever woman it grew inside, even if it does not resemble or live with that woman in surface features, and that if the baby no longer lives with that woman, it still shares underlying physical properties with her. That is, the very same subjects who seemed to have a social conception of motherhood in the open-ended

version of the definition task exhibited a biological construal in several forced-choice tasks. It is widely accepted that children's abilities can be underrepresented by open-ended question formats, and so I assume that the theoretical reasoning reflected in children's responses to my forced-choice tasks reflects their true competence.

REFERENCES

Atran, S. (1994). Core domains versus scientific theories. In L. A. Hirschfeld and S. A. Gelman (eds.), *Mapping the mind: Domain-specifity in cognition and culture* (pp. 316–340). New York: Cambridge University Press.

Au, T. K., and Romo, L. F. (1999). Mechanical causality in children's "folkbiology." In D. Medin and S. Astran (eds.), *Folkbiology*. Cambridge, MA: MIT Press.

Callanan, M. A., and Oakes, L. M. (1992). Preschooler's questions and parents' explanations: Causal thinking in everyday activity. *Cognitive Development, 7*, 213–233.

Carey, S. (1985). *Conceptual change in childhood*. Cambridge, MA: Bradford.
   (1991). Knowledge acquisition: Enrichment or conceptual change? In S. Carey and R. Gelman (eds.), *The epigenesis of mind: Essays on biology and cognition* (pp. 257–291). Hillsdale, NJ: Erlbaum.
   (1995). Cognitive domains as modes of thought. In D. R. Olson and N. Torrance (eds.), *Modes of thought: Explorations in culture and cognition* (pp. 268–302). Cambridge, UK: Cambridge University Press.

Gelman, S. A., and Hirschfeld, L. A. (1999). How biological is essentialism? In D. Medin and S. Atran (eds.), *Folkbiology*. Cambridge, MA: MIT Press.

Hatano, G., and Inagaki, K. (1994). Young children's naive theory of biology. *Cognition, 50*, 171–188.

Hirschfeld, L. (1989). Rethinking the acquisition of kinship terms. *International Journal of Behavioral Development, 12*, 541–568.
   (1994). Is the acquisition of social categories based on domain-specific competence or on knowledge transfer? In L. Hirschfeld and S. Gelman (eds.), *Mapping the mind: Domain-specificity in cognition and culture* (pp. 201–233). New York: Cambridge University Press.
   (1996). *The biology of race*. Cambridge, MA: MIT Press.

Horobin, K. D. (1997). Children's explanations of family resemblances. Poster presented at the biennial meeting of the Society for Research in Child Development, Washington, DC.

Inagaki, K. (1997). Emerging distinctions between naive biology and naive psychology. In H. M. Wellman and K. Inagaki (eds.), *The emergence of core domains of thought: Children's reasoning about physical psychological, and biological phenomena* (pp. 27–44). *New Directions for Child Development* no. 75, W. Damon (series ed.). San Francisco: Jossey-Bass.

Johnson, S. C., and Solomon, G. E. A. (1997). Why dogs have puppies and cats have kittens: The role of birth in young children's understanding of biological origins. *Child Development, 68*; 404–419.

Keil, F. C. (1989). *Concepts, kinds, and cognitive development*. Cambridge, MA: MIT Press.

(1992). The origins of an autonomous biology. In M. R. Gunnar and M. Maratsos (eds.), *Modularity and constraints in language and cognition: Minnesota symposia on child psychology*, vol. XXV (pp. 103–138). Hillsdale, NJ: Erlbaum.

Kelemen, D. (1998). The origins of teleological thought. In M. Corballis and S. Lea (eds.), *Evolution of the hominid mind*. Oxford: Oxford University Press.

Mayr, E. (1982). *The growth of biological thought*. Cambridge, MA: Belknap.

Solomon, G. E., Johnson, S. C., Zaitchik, D., and Carey, S. (1996). Like father, like son: Young children's understanding of how and why offspring resemble their parents. *Child Development*, 67, 151–171.

Springer, K. (1990). In defense of theories. *Cognition*, 35, 293–298.

(1992). Children's beliefs about the biological implications of kinship. *Child Development*, 63, 950–959.

(1995). How a naive theory is acquired through inference. *Child Development*, 66, 547–558.

(1996). Young children's understanding of a biological basis for parent–offspring relations. *Child Development*, 67, 2,841–2,856.

(1997a). Conceptual coherence in children's understanding of kinship. Invited paper presented at the Seventh Meeting of the European Association for Research in Learning and Instruction, Athens, Greece.

(1997b). The effects of within- and cross-race adoption on children's understanding of kinship and inheritance. Paper presented at the biennial meeting of the Society for Research in Child Development, Washington, DC.

Springer, K., and Keil, F. C. (1989). On the development of biologically specific beliefs: The case of inheritance. *Child Development*, 60, 637–648.

(1991). Early differentiation of causal beliefs appropriate to biological and nonbiological kinds. *Child Development*, 62, 767–781.

Springer, K., and Hirschfeld, L. (1995). The influence of age and ethnicity on reasoning about parent–offspring resemblance. Paper presented at the biennial meeting of the Society for Research in Child Development, Indianapolis.

Weissman, M. D., and Kalish, C. W. (1999). The inheritance of desired characteristics: Children's view of the role of intention in parent–offspring resemblance. Unpublished manuscript, University of Wisconsin.

Wellman, H. M. (1985). A child's theory of mind: The development of conceptions of cognition. In S. R. Yussen (ed.), *The growth of reflection* (pp. 99–135). New York: Academic Press.

(1990). *The child's theory of mind*. Cambridge, MA: MIT Press.

(1997). Knowledge acquisition in foundational domains. In D. Kuhn and R. Siegler (eds.), *Handbook of child psychology*, 5th edn, vol. II, *Cognition, perception, and language* (pp. 523–574). William Damon (editor-in-chief). New York: Wiley.

Wellman, H. M., and Gelman, S. A. (1992). Cognitive development: Foundational theories of core domains. *Annual Review of Psychology*, 43, 337–375.

4 Constructing a coherent theory: children's biological understanding of life and death

Virginia Slaughter, Raquel Jaakkola, and Susan Carey

Sophie stood on the gravel path, thinking. She tried to think extra hard about being alive so as to forget that she would not be alive forever. But it was impossible. As soon as she concentrated on being alive now, the thought of dying also came into her mind. The same thing happened the other way around: only by conjuring up an intense feeling of one day being dead could she appreciate how terribly good it was to be alive. It was like two sides of a coin that she kept turning over and over. And the bigger and clearer one side of the coin became, the bigger and clearer the other side became too.

(Jostein Gaarder, *Sophie's World*, 1995, p. 6)

The concept of death is emotionally charged and cognitively challenging. Understanding that all people die, that death is the inevitable end of the life cycle of each living individual, is fundamental to our understanding of ourselves as human beings. Conceptualizing and accepting death has consequences for how we live our lives as well as for how we manage our health. For these reasons, twentieth-century psychologists of many different theoretical persuasions – Freudians, Piagetians, educators, health psychologists – have described young children's grappling with the concept of death. These studies have documented in great detail the ways in which preschool children conceive of death differently from their elders, and the steps they take in approximating adult understanding.

Charting and explaining the emergence of the concept of death has importance beyond the intrinsic interest of the concept. Our understanding of conceptual development proceeds, by necessity, case by case, and case studies should be chosen because of the theoretical issues they address. An account of the acquisition of the concept of death during childhood bears on several controversies within current developmental theory. These include distinguishing conceptual change from knowledge enrichment and simple belief revision, establishing whether normal cognitive development involves conceptual change, sketching the mechanism underlying conceptual change, and explaining the origin of the intuitive theories that articulate adult thought. In this chapter, we explore

71

change within the concept of death in the late preschool years as this case study of conceptual development bears on these controversies.

A brief review of the literature

The earliest studies of preschoolers' concepts of death were carried out from a psychoanalytic perspective (Anthony, 1940; Nagy, 1948; Von Hug-Hellmuth, 1964). Diary records of children's questions about death, projective techniques (e.g., story completion), as well as some more structured interviews provided the major sources of data. Given their psychoanalytic point of view, it is not surprising that these authors concentrated on the emotional dimensions of the child's struggle to understand death. Nonetheless, the data from these studies paint a picture that is entirely consistent with the later, more systematic, Piagetian studies.

According to these writers, as the child first learns of death, its emotional significance derives from separation from the dead, as well as death's being seen as resulting from the ultimate act of aggression. Death is assimilated to departure. To die is to live on in some other place (under the ground; heaven) from which one cannot return (because the coffin is nailed shut; because of the weight of the dirt). Death is also assimilated to sleep, but a sleep from which one cannot wake. Some of these themes can be seen in a sample of the voluminous clinical interview material from this literature (Nagy, 1948, p. 10):

TP (age 4 years 10 months)
TP: A dead person is just as if he were asleep. Sleeps in the ground, too.
G: Sleeps the same as you do at night, or otherwise?
TP: Well – closes his eyes. Sleeps like people at night. Sleeps like that, just like that.
G: How do you know whether someone is asleep or dead?
TP: I know if they go to bed at night and don't open their eyes. If somebody goes to bed and doesn't get up, he's dead or ill.
G: Will he ever wake up?
TP: Never. A dead person only knows if somebody goes out to the grave or something. He feels that somebody is there, or is talking.
G: Are you certain? You're not mistaken?
TP: I don't think so. At funerals you're not allowed to sing, just talk, because otherwise the dead person couldn't sleep peacefully. A dead person feels it if you put something on his grave.
G: What is it he feels then?
TP: He feels that flowers are put on his grave. The water touches the sand. Slowly, slowly he hears everything. Auntie, does the dead person feel it if it goes deep into the ground? (i.e. the water).
G: What do you think, wouldn't he like to come away from there?

TP: He would like to come out, but the coffin is nailed down.
G: If he weren't in the coffin, would he come back?
TP: He couldn't root up all that sand.

In such materials, it is clear that children are conceiving of dead people as living on in some unusual way, the unusual form of living not being clearly or consistently understood. Death appears to be conceptualized in psychological or behavioral terms, that is, children see death as changing what the person does or can do, and what the person thinks. The psychoanalytic writers commented that preschoolers lacked a "biological" understanding of death, by which they meant that young children do not see death as inevitable or irreversible; nor do they see it as resulting from (or even related to) the breakdown of bodily functioning.

The Piagetian literature on the child's concept of death confirms and extends these observations (Kane, 1979; Koocher, 1973; White *et al.*, 1978; see Speece and Brent, 1985, for a review). These writers identified several sub-components of the target adult concept of death: (1) irreversibility, the understanding that the dead cannot come back to life; (2) cessation/non-functionality, the understanding that bodily and mental functions cease after death; (3) inevitability, the understanding that all living things die; (4) causality, the understanding that death is ultimately caused by a breakdown of bodily function. They developed standardized interviews that probed for understanding of each of these sub-components. Irreversibility is probed through the question: "Can dead people come back to life?" Cessation/non-functionality is probed through questions such as "Can a dead person eat/talk/dream?" Inevitability is probed through the questions "Does everybody die?" and "Will you die one day?" Causality is probed through the question "What makes things die?"

There is universal agreement that preschool children lack understanding of each of these sub-components of death. They say that dead people can come back to life, they think that dead people talk and dream, they say not all people die, and they offer distal causes as the causes of death – accidents, poison, guns. Further, they do not restrict death to animals and plants (Safier, 1964). Speece and Brent (1985) reported that the first three sub-components (irreversibility, cessation, inevitability) each emerge between the ages of 6 and 7, although elsewhere (Speece and Brent, 1992) they argued that a mature understanding of death, requiring the acquisition of all of the first three sub-components, is generally not seen until age 10. Similarly, this literature dates the acquisition of the fourth sub-component (causation) at age 10 at the earliest (Koocher, 1973; Orback *et al.*, 1985; Lazar and Torney-Purta, 1991).

Researchers working in the Piagetian tradition interpreted the developmental changes observed in children's understanding of death as reflecting transitions among preoperational, concrete-operational, and formal-operational stages of cognitive development. In the first stage (preoperational), children think of death as a temporary or reversible state, and tend to characterize death with respect to obvious perceptual features such as being still or having closed eyes. In the second stage (concrete-operational), children recognize that death is irreversible, but they still deny that all things must die, and consider death to be caused from without rather than viewing it as an intrinsic and natural part of the life cycle. In the final stage (formal-operational), children hold an adult view of death as an inevitable, universal final stage in the life cycle of all living things, characterized by the cessation of bodily function. The adult view is formal-operational, these authors claim, because it is abstract and reflects theoretical (biological) knowledge. Whereas one may question the utility of attempting to assimilate these developmental changes to Piagetian stages (Carey, 1985), the data from these studies are remarkably consistent.

The Freudian and Piagetian studies, taken together, provide a fairly detailed picture of the development of the concept of death during childhood. However, they all look at the concept of death as an isolated, albeit complex, concept. In general they do not address the question of the process that drives children's developing understanding of death. What allows children to go from thinking that death is a temporary, reversible state to recognizing that it is the inevitable final stage of the life cycle? How and when does the concept of death become for children essentially biological?

Death as a biological concept

The Piagetian authors, like the Freudians, commented that the preschool child's concept of death is not a biological one, whereas the adult's is. This observation seemed to them unremarkable, since it was a given that preschool children do not represent theories. Today, however, this is far from a given. Now it is widely agreed that *intuitive* theories are important cognitive structures even in the preschool years (Carey, 1985, 1988, 1995; Gopnik and Wellman, 1994; Wellman and Gelman, 1992; Keil, 1994). According to some authors, even infants represent intuitive theories (e.g., Gopnik and Meltzoff, 1997).

Intuitive theories, while not explicitly held as such (that is, young children are not aware that they hold theories), have many of the hallmarks of scientific theories. Intuitive theories are the conceptual structures that determine a person's deepest ontological commitments and causal schemata. They contain abstract concepts, richly interrelated and mutually determining, from which are derived predictions, inferences, and explanations concerning the phenomena in their domains. Whereas some might doubt that infants represent conceptual structures with all these properties (see Carey and Spelke [1996] for a discussion of this issue), it is clear that preschool children by the age of 4 represent at least one such theory – an intuitive theory of mind (Wellman, 1990; Perner, 1991; Gopnik and Wellman, 1992; Astington, 1993).

Research in this tradition makes two crucial assumptions about the nature of cognitive development. First, it is assumed that people's (both children's and adults') knowledge about the world is divided into distinct content domains, each of which is organized and structured according to a different intuitive theoretical framework. Second, it is assumed that the development of knowledge can best be described as a process of theory elaboration and theory change within domains. It is claimed that people's knowledge in various content domains including psychology, physics and biology exhibits properties characteristic of theories, including coherent structures, unique causal principles, and characteristic patterns of change (Carey, 1985; Wellman, 1990; Slaughter and Gopnik, 1996; Smith et al., 1985). One of the most important characteristics of intuitive theories is conceptual coherence. This refers to the way in which concepts within a given theory fit together: they tend to be closely interrelated, even interdefined. Wellman (1990, p. 6) describes coherence in the following way: "in theories it becomes impossible to consider a single concept in isolation because its meaning and significance are determined by its role in an interrelated web of other constructs and terms." The type of coherent structure evident in theories creates a productive system of concepts, capable of generating predictions and explanations for all sorts of relevant phenomena. Additionally, since each of the concepts gives meaning to the other concepts, when one concept changes, then the others do as well.

Given that preschool children can and do represent theories, the comment that their concept of death is non-biological becomes substantive and carries considerable explanatory weight. Consider the interrelated, sometimes interdefined, biological concepts that articulate the components of the concept of death studied by the Piagetians. One cannot understand death as the cessation of bodily function, and as resulting from the breakdown of bodily function, unless one *has* an understanding of bodily function. One cannot understand death as the inevitable end of each living thing's life cycle without the concepts of life and a life cycle. If this is so, investigations of developmental relationships between the concept of death and other biological concepts would provide important information not only about how the concept of death develops, but about how intuitive biology develops.

As described in the next sections (pp. 77–82), evidence is accumulating that children first construct a vitalistic biology, that is, an intuitive theory of biology organized around a core belief in a "vital" or "life" force, around age 6 (Inagaki and Hatano, 1993, chapter 2 in this volume; Jaakkola, 1997). Before this achievement, children lack the biological concept of life, and thus cannot unite animals and plants under a single category, "living thing," cannot conceive of animals in terms of a life cycle, and cannot understand the role of bodily functioning in maintaining life.

If it is true that preschool children lack the intuitive vitalism in which the concept of life first appears, then their concept of death differs from that of older children in the strong sense of incommensurability (for related analyses of incommensurability see Carey, 1988, 1999; Kuhn et al., 1988; Kitcher, 1988; Hacking, 1993). Examples of conceptual changes involving incommensurability include differentiations after which the previously undifferentiated concept no longer plays any coherent role in a theory, coalescences in which previously ontologically distinct categories are seen to be of a single kind, changes in a concept's core, in which new causal principles fulfil the role required by psychological essentialism (Medin and Ortony, 1989) and changes in a concept's kind (e.g., changes from a property to a relation).

Carey (1985, 1988, 1999) argues that the preschooler's concept of death is incommensurable with that of older children in each of these senses. The preschool child has undifferentiated concepts of both "life" (alive/active/real/existent) and "death" (not alive/inactive/unreal/absent), undifferentiated concepts which are incoherent once a vitalistic biology has been constructed. Further, she argues that the preschooler's concept of "animal" is incommensurable with a biological understanding of animals. The core of the concept "animal" derives from its role in the intuitive theory of psychology that is in place by age 4; for preschoolers, "animal" is essentially a psychological concept (i.e., behaving entity). The construction of a vitalistic biology allows the coalescence of animal and plant into a single category, with living being at its core. At the same time, the reanalysis of death, from living on in strange circumstances to the inevitable end of life, undergoes a change in kind. At the beginning it is merely *not alive*, the opposite of life; at the end it is a specific relation to life (its end).

On this analysis, the comment that the preschooler's concept of "death" is not biological, rather than being a side comment, as the Piagetian and Freudian literatures would have it, becomes essential to its characterization. If this analysis is correct, one would expect to find interrelations among children's conceptions of death and their mastery of other closely interrelated aspects of intuitive biology.

Studies of the development of the concept of death in relation to the development of other biological concepts

In general, there have been few published studies of the development of the concept of death that relate it to the development of other concepts. However, one notable exception is a study by Safier (1964) which investigated the relationship between children's levels of animistic thought and their concepts of death. Based on a Piagetian model of global stages in cognitive development, Safier reasoned that children's tendencies to appropriately attribute life (i.e., non-animistic thinking) would be related to their tendencies to appropriately distinguish those entities subject to death. From the intuitive theory perspective, we would also expect such a close relationship. As outlined above, young children know that to be dead is to be not alive, even though they have undifferentiated, non-biological concepts of each. Inanimate objects would be expected to be judged alive (e.g., useful things like buttons, active things like lamps) and subject to death (e.g., broken things, things that might disappear). Later, as death is reanalyzed as the end of the life cycle, only entities with life cycles should be subject to dying.

Safier (1964) tested boys of three different age groups (4–5, 7–8, 10–11) with a short animism/death interview. The interview asked about ten different entities, four living things (including both animals and plants), and six inanimate objects (both artifacts and natural kinds). For each entity, Safier asked the following questions: (1) Does an X live? (2) Does an X hurt when hit? (3) Does an X grow up? (4) Does an X die? She computed animism scores by adding the number of inanimate objects judged to live, hurt when hit, and grow up and she computed death scores by adding the number of inanimate objects judged to die. Thus she sought coherence in the applicability of children's concepts of life and death. She found that both animism and death scores decreased with age, and in a correlational analysis she found that for each age group there was a significant relationship between scores for non-animistic thinking and scores for appropriate attributions of death. She also carried out a further, non-structured interview about death, from which she established that only the oldest group of boys consistently conceived of death as both irreversible and inevitable.

Recent work on the development of children's intuitive biology has probed aspects of their understanding of death as well as other biological concepts. For instance, Inagaki and Hatano (1996, experiment 3) reported that 4–5-year-old preschool children in Japan recognize that animals and plants both die, as well as grow and need to eat. In their experiment, they tried to elicit children's recognition that animals and plants are similar, by asking the following question: "A squirrel or an alligator can die. Do you think anything similar to this occurs with a tulip or a pine tree?" They reported that 80 percent of preschoolers asserted that plants could die, compared to only 13 percent asserting that inanimate objects (a chair or a pay phone) could die. Of course, in the light of the literature reviewed above, one must ask what preschool children *mean* by the assertion "plants die." If the claims about incommensurability are correct, then they mean something different by this sentence than does an adult.

Similarly, Hatano *et al.* (1993) reported that kindergarten children aged 5–6 in three different cultures (Israel, United States, Japan) all attributed the biological properties "grow" and "die or wither" to people and not to inanimate objects. The children were less likely to judge plants as subject to those processes. Again, calling "dying" a biological process for 5–6-year-olds is possibly a theory-laden attribution (Carey, 1995). Just because dying is a biological process for adults does not mean it is for kindergarteners. At least, the literature reviewed above should raise doubts.

The study reported here bears on whether the preschooler's concept of death *is* indeed biological, as the above authors would have it. If so, it must be appropriately interrelated with the related biological concepts of life and of the bodily machine. Before turning to the present study, we briefly review research (some recent, some less so) which suggests that these concepts are emerging between the ages of 4 and 6.

The emergence of the concept of life

By far the most common method for studying children's concept of life is the Piagetian animism interview (e.g., Piaget, 1929; Klingensmith, 1953; Klingberg, 1957; Laurendeau and Pinard, 1962; Carey, 1985; Stavy and Wax, 1989; Hatano *et al.*, 1993). In this interview, children are typically asked to name some things that are alive and some that are not, and are then presented with a list of items and asked whether each is alive or not, and why. The results of these studies invariably show that young children over-attribute life to some inanimate objects, perhaps on the basis of motion (e.g., "A cloud is alive because it moves"), usefulness (e.g., "A table is alive because you can eat on it"), or activity (e.g., "A clock is alive because it goes tick-tock"). Indeed, it is not until approximately age 10 that children restrict their attributions of life to animals and plants, and justify their attributions by reference to biological criteria such as growth and the need for food or water.

A standard interpretation of the results of these animism studies is that children do not have a biological concept of life before the age of about 10 (e.g., Piaget, 1929; Laurendeau and Pinard, 1962). An alternative interpretation, however, is that before age 10, children simply do not understand that both animals and plants are living things (i.e., that they belong to the same category), and that children therefore – even if they have a concept of life – have difficulty finding a reasonable referent for the word "alive." Evidence for this view comes from Carey's (1985) life attribution task, in which she found two different patterns of response for children between the ages of 4 and 7. First, children who judged that both animals and plants are alive also attributed life to some inanimate objects. This pattern fits the traditional animism results. However, children who judged that animals are alive, but that plants are not, also correctly claimed that inanimate objects are not alive.

These data suggest that at least some preschool children have a concept of life restricted to animals alone. It is also possible that the demands of the Piagetian animism interview underestimate understanding, requiring as it does an explicit formulation of a criterion for life, and bringing attention, as it does, to the fact that animals and plants are both alive, which some children might know but might not yet understand. In other words, it is possible that all 4–7-year-olds have a biological concept of life, restricted to animals alone, and that some are misled by the animism interview. We find this latter possibility unlikely, given the literature on preschool children's understanding of death reviewed above. Recent studies establish that children do construct a biological theory between ages 4 and 6 in which the concept of life becomes the core of their understanding of bodily function. As suggested by the above analysis, many of these studies concern animals as living entities, for bodily function is first understood in terms of human and animal bodies.

In the first of these studies, Inagaki and Hatano (1993, and see chapter 2, this volume) tested the assertion that children in the early school years have a vitalistic theory of biology (the core of which is the concept of a "vital" or "life" force). In this experiment, 6 and 8 year olds were asked to choose among three types of causal explanations – intentional, vitalistic, and mechanistic – for a number of bodily phenomena. For example, for a question about why we eat, the intentional explanation offered was "because we want to eat tasty food", the vitalistic explanation was "because our stomach takes in vital power from the food", and the mechanistic explanation was "because we take the food into our body after its form is changed in the stomach and bowels." The 6-year-old children preferred vitalistic explanations, whereas the 8-year-old children preferred mechanistic explanations. From these data, Inagaki and Hatano argued that children's first biological theory – present by at least age 6 – is a vitalistic biology, and that between ages 6 and 8 there is a shift to a mechanist biology.

To investigate this proposal further, Jaakkola (1997) performed a similar study to that of Inagaki and Hatano (1993), but with several modifications. First, she made the three types of explanation more comparable in length and complexity. Second, she added a 4-year-old age group, adapting the procedure so that younger children could perform the task. Jaakkola found a dramatic change in children's bodily reasoning between the ages of 4 and 6. Specifically, 4-year-olds showed no preference among the explanations. (A control experiment using the same task structure, but questioning physical rather than bodily phenomena, showed that 4-year-olds could manage the explanation judgment methodology.) In contrast, 6-year-olds showed a marked preference for both vitalistic and mechanistic explanations. Jaakkola (1997) argues that the mechanistic explanations in both Inagaki and Hatano's (1993) and her own study actually also reflect a vitalistic biology, just one in which more details of the bodily processes have been filled in. Thus, while she supports Inagaki and Hatano's proposal that children have a vitalistic biological theory by age 6, she further contends that this theory is constructed by the child between the ages of 4 and 6.

Additional evidence that a biological theory based on the concept of life is constructed by children between 4 and 6 years of age comes from this study exploring children's beliefs about the functions of various bodily organs and processes (Jaakkola, 1997), where children between the ages of 4 and 10 answered a series of structured interview questions about the human body. Specifically, for a number of different body parts, children were asked what the function of each particular body part was, and also what would happen if a person were missing that body part (e.g., "What is the blood for? What would happen if someone didn't have any blood?"). In addition, children were asked about two bodily processes (eating food and breathing air).

In the analyses most relevant for the current discussion, children's answers were coded for appeals to life. For instance, in response to the question "What is the heart for?", life-answers included such statements as "so you can live", "if your heart stops beating then you die," or simply "your life." (Non-life responses included: "thinking," "to keep all your love," and "to drink and eat.") At the group level, there was a dramatic increase between the ages of 4 and 6 in children's tendency to appeal to

Table 4.1. *Percent of children classified as "life-theorizers" by age*

Age	Percent of life-theorizers
4	33
6	92
8	100
10	100

the goal of maintaining life. Children predominantly appealed to life for internal body parts (especially the heart, blood, lungs, brain, and stomach) and for food and air. In contrast, children almost never appealed to life for external body parts such as the eyes, hands, and teeth.

To examine children's individual patterns of response, Jaakkola (1997) classified children as "life-theorizers" if they mentioned the goal of maintaining life (or avoiding death) for more than one body organ or substance included in the interview. As shown in table 4.1, the developmental pattern revealed by this analysis was striking. Whereas only one-third of the 4-year-olds qualified as life-theorizers, virtually all of the 6–10-year-olds did so (the exception was a single 6-year-old). Moreover, this designation was found to be predictive of the level of sophistication of children's functional explanations of internal body organs. Specifically, among 4-year-olds (the only age at which there was variation in the life-theory classification), non-life-theorizers tended to give global and non-specific explanations (e.g., "the brain is for keeping your body good") or no explanation at all, while life-theorizers were more likely to give specific functional explanations (which may or may not have been "correct" explanations, e.g., "the heart is for breathing," "the brain is for thinking").

This study thus found that between the ages of 4 and 6, children begin to use the abstract concept of life to predict and explain biological phenomena related to the human body (Jaakkola, 1997). The striking increase in children who were classified as life-theorizers suggests that at this age, the concept of life becomes a central construct in the development of children's intuitive theory of human biology. Keep in mind, however, that there is nothing magical about referring to life exactly two times in an interview situation. This was simply an arbitrary cut-off point chosen in an attempt to catch the beginnings of the use of life in children's bodily reasoning. Still, this designation did seem to capture something real, as shown by the relation between the life-theorizer designation and a greater sophistication in explanations of organ function. Presumably, this is a reflection of "life" becoming the core of children's understanding of the bodily machine, in the sense that the ultimate goal of bodily functions is now the biological goal of maintaining life.

Children's knowledge of life and death

The data reviewed in the previous section suggest that preschool-aged life-theorizers have made "life" the core concept organizing their understanding of bodily function. The acquisition of this concept marks the beginning of a process of conceptual change within the domain of biology, which has important implications for further developments among related concepts. Specifically, our hypothesis is that the acquisition of the concept of "life" as the central construct of a vitalistic biological theory, is required for children to transform the concepts "alive" and "dead" into biological (as opposed to psychological/behavioral) concepts. Further, the development of the concept of "life" and its use as a vitalistic biological principle is required for children to differentiate the concept "not alive" (which for preschoolers means dead/inactive/unreal/absent) into "dead" and "inanimate." Finally, we suggest that the acquisition of the concept of "life" supports a restructuring of the concept "animal," such that the core feature becomes "living," rather than "behaving" (Carey, 1985, 1999).

We predicted that all of these related changes in children's biological knowledge would begin to be evident in children who could be classified as life-theorizers. Why? Because of the nature of the concepts that are developing. In adults' intuitive biology, the concepts of life and death are coherent with each other and with beliefs about body function. As children begin to acquire the vitalistic biological concepts "alive" and "dead," the interrelations among the relevant concepts and beliefs (e.g. animals are alive, living things have internal body parts that function to keep them alive, animals and plants can die, etc.) serve to constrain and structure the acquisition of new concepts and the differentiation of old concepts, so that they ultimately form an internally consistent, coherent intuitive theoretical structure. Therefore children who recognize life as the ultimate goal of body function are in a position to develop related concepts and beliefs that are coherent with that core knowledge.

We explored these predictions by examining the relationships between children's knowledge about (1) all of the sub-components of the concept of death; (2) body function; (3) life-theorizing. Given the findings discussed in the previous section, that the construction of a vitalistic biology and the transition to becoming a life-theorizer occurs between the ages of 4 and 6, the present study included a continuous sample of forty children aged between 4 years 1 month and 5 years 11 months. These children all participated in a twenty-five-minute interview session that included a version of the body interview described above, and a death interview. The final sample consisted of thirty-eight children, discarding the partial data from two children who did not complete the study.

Body interview

The body interview was taken from Jaakkola (1997) and asked a series of questions about bodily organs and bodily processes. The body parts included in this version of the body interview were heart, brain, eyes, lungs, blood, stomach, and hands. As in the study described above, children were asked three questions about each body part: (1) Where is X? (2) What is X for? (3) What would happen if somebody didn't have an X? Children were also asked questions about the bodily processes of eating food and breathing air: Why do we eat food/breathe air? What happens to the food we eat/air we breathe?

In the primary analysis, children were classified as life-theorizers using the criterion established in the previous study (Jaakkola, 1997), that is, if they mentioned staying alive, or not dying, at least two times in the course of the body interview. For instance, one life-theorizer provided the following responses: "If somebody didn't have any blood they would die" and "We breathe air to stay alive." It is worth noting that children very rarely provided life-answers in response to questions about the eyes or the hands; instead, both life-theorizers and non-life-theorizers almost always asserted that eyes were for "looking" or "seeing," and that hands were for "holding things," "touching," or "feeling." Thus there was no overall tendency to answer that the function of all body parts is to maintain life or avoid death. Further, preschoolers, both life-theorizers and non-life-theorizers, are capable of answering the question "What is X for?" with an appropriate, specific function; any difference between the two groups on the vital organs must be due to knowledge of the biology-relevant functions.

The sample of children was thus divided into life-theorizers and non-life-theorizers based on their complete body interview responses. In the final sample of thirty-eight, eighteen children were classified as non-life-theorizers, and twenty were classified as life-theorizers. These two groups were of fairly comparable ages, with the non-life-theorizers' ages ranging from 4 years 1 month to 5 years 11 months (average age 4 years 11 months) and the life-theorizers' ages ranging from 4 years 8 months to 5 years 10 months (average age 5 years 3 months). These results support the findings of Jaakkola (1997) discussed above, providing additional evidence that the transition between non-life-theorizing and life-theorizing occurs between the ages of 4 and 6.

The body interview was further analyzed with an examination of children's descriptions of the functions of the various body parts, following Jaakkola (1997). Children's responses to each of the questions "What is X for?" were coded according to the level of specificity of the response. The coding hierarchies conformed to the following general scheme:

Level 0: don't know; tautology (e.g. blood is for bleeding)
Level 1: general body function (e.g. heart is for life; for health; for your body)
Level 2: "incorrect" specific body function (e.g. heart is for walking; lungs are for eating)
Level 3: canonical function (e.g. stomach is for digesting food; lungs are for breathing).

Children were given credit for the highest level answer they provided for each body part function.

From this analysis of children's individual answers to the body interview questions, overall body scores were tabulated for each child. Body scores were computed as follows: for each question about a vital body part (e.g. heart, brain, lungs, blood, stomach), children were given one point for each "high-level" response on the interview. "High-level" answers were deemed those of Level 3, which indicated children's knowledge of the canonical bodily function of each body part (note that this criterion was stricter than that used by Jaakkola [1997] in the study described earlier). The body score then was computed by adding the number of scores (out of five body parts) of Level 3 for each child.

Given our argument that children who have a concept of "life" have begun to construct a biological theory of the human body and its function, we predicted that life-theorizers would differ from non-life-theorizers in their overall knowledge of body function. To test this prediction, we compared the mean body scores, based on the number of high-level responses on the body interview, of life-theorizers and non-life-theorizers. The difference was statistically significant: life-theorizers' average body score was 2.65, while the non-life-theorizers' average score was 1.33 ($t(36) = 3.42$; $p < 0.025$).

In sum, there is a significant difference between the two groups in canonical functional knowledge of the body, in spite of the fact that they were approximately of the same age. What distinguishes the groups is whether or not the children use "life" as a central construct in their understanding of the human body. Non-life-theorizers had almost no knowledge of canonical body function. Note also that the body scores for the life-theorizers were also well below the maximum of five high-level responses. The association between life-theorizing and knowledge of bodily function has two possible interpretations. First, it may be that learning about the canonical purpose of just a few specific vital organs provides a causal schema in which life is the ultimate teleological goal of bodily functioning, which is the beginning of the differentiated vitalistic concept of life, which in turn serves as a place-holder goal for other, as yet unknown, specific purposes of internal body parts. Alternatively, it is possible that there is some other source of life-theorizers' concept of life, which is needed for them to even begin to understand the body in vitalistic terms, as the strikingly low body scores of the non-life-theorizers might suggest. That is, without the concept of life to organize reasoning about the body, children might not have the conceptual resources to understand bodily organs in terms of their biological functions. It is not necessary to choose between these two alternative interpretations of the correlation we find here. The developments occur simultaneously and coherently, such that acquiring knowledge about the body and having "life" at the core of a vitalistic theory of the body are mutually defining.

The results of this study support the hypothesis that the vitalistic theory of biology reflects an entrenchment of the concept "life" as a central function of the bodily machine. Those children who have constructed the life-theory and therefore recognize that the ultimate goal of bodily function is to maintain life, are also the children who have begun to develop functional knowledge about the body and its vital organs. These results again support and extend the findings of Jaakkola (1997) discussed in the previous section, and provide further evidence for the construction of a vitalistic theory of biology in 4–6-year-old children.

Death interview

The data presented above, like those of Jaakkola (1997), support the hypothesis that between the ages of 4 and 6 children are constructing an understanding of some aspects of bodily function, and integrating these into a life-theory, such that the teleological goal of bodily function is to maintain life. We hypothesized that this development represents a conceptual change that should have ramifications for related biological concepts, and therefore predicted that there would also be differences between the life-theorizers' and non-life-theorizers' concepts of death. Specifically, we predicted that non-life-theorizers would be more likely to have a non-biological concept of death. Rather, they should be more likely to see death as living on in an altered state. Life-theorizers, in contrast, should be more likely to demonstrate a biological understanding of death as the endpoint of the life cycle and the cessation of bodily function.

To test these predictions, the thirty-eight children who completed the body interview were presented with the following interview about death:

1 Do you know what it means for something to die?
2 Can you name some things that die? (If people aren't mentioned) Do people sometimes die?
   (a) Does every person die?
   (b) What happens to a person's body when they die?
3 When a person is dead . . .
   (a) do they need food?
   (b) do they need to pee and poop?
   (c) do they need air?
   (d) can they move around?
   (e) do they have dreams?
   (f) do they need water?
   (g) If a dead person had a cut on their hand, would it heal?
4 How can you tell if a person is dead?
5 Can you name some things that don't die?
6 Can you think of something that might cause something to die?
7 Once something dies, is there anything anyone can do to make it live again?
8 Could a doctor make a dead person live again?

This death interview was designed to measure children's understanding of various sub-components of the concept of death, following from the previous research reviewed above. The sub-components of this death interview included: (1) *Applicability* (questions 2 and 5) that probed for the understanding that only living things can die; (2) *Inevitability* (questions 2a, 2b) that probed for the knowledge that death is a necessary part of the life cycle; (3) *Irreversibility* (questions 7 and 8) that probed for children's understanding that death is a permanent state; (4) *Cessation* (questions 3a–g) that probed for the understanding that death indicates a cessation of all bodily needs and functions; (5) *Signs and causes* (questions 4 and 6) that probed for children's understanding of how death ultimately comes about.

The cessation questions included in this interview are different from the typical cessation questions. Previous studies (reviewed above) probed this sub-component by asking children "Do dead people eat/walk/dream/ etc.?" That is, the earlier studies probed the cessation of mental and behavioral activity as well as activities that might be seen as biologically relevant (such as eating). We wanted to probe, as clearly as the child might be able to understand, whether preschoolers understood that the bodily functions that play a role in the earliest vitalism cease with death. Because many preschoolers assimilate death to sleep, some children might report that dead people do not eat, referring to inactivity, but they might not recognize that the dead no longer need food (because the body no longer requires sustenance). We included one question on which life-theorizers and non-life-theorizers might be expected to differ less than on the other question, namely, "Can a dead person move around?" since those non-life-theorizers who assimilate death to sleep and inactivity would be expected to reply "No."

The primary analysis of the death interview was to examine children's responses to each sub-component with respect to their status as life-theorizers or non-life-theorizers. It was predicted that life-theorizers would be more likely to demonstrate biological understandings of the various sub-components of the concept of death. In contrast, the non-life-theorizers were predicted to provide answers to the various death interview questions that would reflect a non-biological concept of death as a non-universal, reversible state of living on under altered circumstances. (Chi-square analyses at the 0.05 level were used to calculate the significance of the results reported below.)

Applicability Both life-theorizers and non-life-theorizers gave similar answers to the question of what types of things can die, with comparable numbers in each group naming people and animals as capable of dying. However, seven life-theorizers (35 percent) included plants (along with animals and people) as capable of dying, while only two (11 percent) of the non-life-theorizers listed plants among the things that could die. This difference was not statistically significant. It does suggest, however, that life-theorizers were more likely to have a biological category of "living thing" that included both plants and animals than were non-life-theorizers, and that children become life-theorizers with respect to animals before they incorporate plants into the domain (Jaakkola, 1997; see pp. 83–85 above).

When asked what types of things do not die, there was a significant difference in responses between the groups (see table 4.2). The majority of life-theorizers responded by naming only artifacts, such as buildings, books, or boxes. Non-life-theorizers, in contrast, if they named artifacts, often named them in conjunction with living things, for instance, one non-life-theorizer listed "kids, trees, books, people, chairs, houses, dolls, rings." This particular answer is interesting because it reflects this non-life-theorizer's lack of differentiation between the concepts "not alive"

Table 4.2. *Frequencies of responses to question: "Name things that don't die"*

	Life-theorizers	Non-life-theorizers
Living things only	4	5
Artifacts only	12	3
Living things + artifacts	1	4
Unreal entities (e.g., batman)/don't know[a]	3	6

[a] Answer types combined to increase expected frequencies: life-theorizers 2 don't know, 1 unreal entity; non-life-theorizers 4 don't know, 2 unreal entities.

and "inanimate," as well as the lack of recognition that death is inevitable.

Additionally, none of the life-theorizers listed people among things that do not die, while six (33 percent) of the non-life-theorizers did. This difference reflects the predicted difference between the two groups' understanding that death is inevitable.

Inevitability   In response to the question "Does every person die?" the two groups were again significantly different. Only seven (39 percent) of the non-life-theorizers asserted that every person dies, while seventeen (85 percent) of the life-theorizers did so. This difference reflects the life-theorizers' understanding of death in terms of the life cycle, and the recognition that living entities have finite life-spans.

Irreversibility   The two groups also differed significantly in their answers to the question about whether a doctor could make a dead person live again. Only three of the life-theorizers (15 percent) said that a doctor could revive a dead person, while nine (50 percent) of the non-life-theorizers made that assertion. Again, this difference suggests that the life-theorizers were more likely to conceptualize death as the unalterable cessation of life.

Cessation   In response to the series of questions about the bodily needs and functions of dead people, life-theorizers and non-life-theorizers again gave significantly different answers (see table 4.3). Asked whether people need food when they are dead, eight (44 percent) of the non-life-theorizers said yes, while only one (5 percent) of the life-theorizers did so. Similar differences were seen in the other questions about body functions, with the question about needing air also showing significant group differences: eight (44 percent) of the non-life-theorizers said that dead people need air, while none of the life-theorizers made that

Table 4.3. *Number of "Yes" responses to the questions "Do dead people ... ?"*

	Life-theorizers	Non-life-theorizers
Need food	1	8
Need to excrete	1	5
Need air	0	8
Move	0	1
Need water	2	5
Dream	2	6
Have cuts healed	8	10

claim. Looking overall, the life-theorizers were significantly more consistent in their answers to all seven cessation questions, with twelve (60 percent) life-theorizers answering "No" to every item, but only four (22.2 percent) of the non-life-theorizers showing the same consistent pattern.

These results provide unique evidence to support the claim that some young children conceptualize death as living on in altered circumstances, rather than as the cessation of the body machine. This is the first time that some of these questions have been presented to young children and it is striking that some children (in this case, primarily the non-life-theorizers) could assert that dead people need food, air, and water. In the interview, one non-life-theorizer stated that dead people need food because "all people need to eat healthy food." This interesting example reinforces the claim that in the pre-biological reasoning of young children, dead people are much the same as living people; the core of the concept "person" is not "alive" but "behaving." In contrast, the life-theorizers' answers to the cessation questions were more likely to demonstrate a recognition that once life is gone, then the body no longer functions, and thus no longer needs the materials that sustain life.

Two of the cessation questions failed to differentiate the two groups. As predicted, both groups said that dead people cannot move around (as being motionless is one of the signs of death, on both a biological and a behavioral view). Unexpectedly, both groups were equally likely to say that a dead person's cuts would heal. This answer is not surprising from the non-life-theorizers, of course. But from the life-theorizers it may suggest that they have made a distinction between bodily processes that support vital function, and in turn which require it, and some bodily processes which do not.

Signs and causes Finally, the groups demonstrated no discernible differences in their answers to the questions of how one can tell if a person is dead, and what are the potential causes of death. To the first question, both groups tended to give answers relating to external bodily symptoms or signs, such as "They don't wake up" or "They don't move." Similarly, both groups tended to list external causes of death such as "poison" or "an explosion," with "guns" the most popular answer in both groups.

Fate of the body With respect to the question about what happens to the body when people die, an unexpected difference between the groups emerged. Life-theorizers more often asserted that the body decomposes (ten of twenty children: 50 percent), compared to non-life-theorizers (one of eighteen children: 6 percent). Examples of this type of answer are "decomposes," "turns into grass," "rots," and "becomes a skeleton." This difference was not predicted. It may indicate that the life-theorizers were more likely to view the body as a biological entity, subject to biological laws such as decomposition (Springer *et al.*, 1996). It may also reflect the greater differentiation of "the body" and "the person" on the part of the life-theorizers. The person ceases to exist when he or she dies, and vital functions cease, but the body continues to exist. Without vital function, the body subsequently falls apart.

As a further step in analyzing children's responses to the death interview, an overall death score was computed that was based on children's answers to the various death questions, organized by sub-component. Children passed or failed each sub-component of the death concept listed above, which gave a range of scores from zero to six. The criteria for pass/failure were as follows:

> *Applicability*: pass if name only animals (or animals and plants) for "Name things that die" and name inanimate entities for "Name things that don't die."
>
> *Inevitability*: pass if correctly answer that all people die.
>
> *Irreversibility*: pass if answer "No" to both "Can someone live again?" and "Can a doctor bring a person back to life?"
>
> *Cessation*: pass if consistently answer "No" to series of questions about the bodily needs of dead people.
>
> *Signs and causes*: pass if give a body-function-relevant answer to either question "How can you tell if someone is dead?" (e.g. if they're not breathing they're dead) or "What could cause someone to die?" (e.g. when their heart stops because they get old).
>
> *Fate of the body*: pass if give answer regarding decomposition or cessation of biological function for question "What happens to the body after death?" (e.g. rots; the heart stops).

The overall death scores confirmed the differences found on the individual sub-components of the death interview. The average death score for life-theorizers was 3.60, compared to the average death score for non-life-theorizers of 1.28. This significant difference further supports our original prediction that children who have a concept of "life" would also be more likely to have a biological understanding of death as the inevitable, irreversible cessation of the working of the bodily machine.

It is worth noting that the death scores for both groups are well below ceiling, indicating that even those children who have the beginnings of the vitalistic theory (the life-theorizers) still have much to learn about death, in the same way that they still have much to learn about the biological functions of body organs (reported above). In particular, the sub-component "Signs and causes" of the death interview was rarely passed by children in either group, a finding that replicates previous reports that causality is the most difficult of the sub-components of death for children to understand (Speece and Brent, 1985; Orback et al., 1985; Lazar and Torney-Purta, 1991).

Our final analysis investigated the relationship between children's knowledge of body function and their knowledge of death. We computed Pearson correlations between children's body scores and their death scores. For all of the children combined, there was a significant relationship between knowledge of the body and knowledge about death: $r(36) = 0.543$, $p < 0.001$. Next, we looked at the correlations between body scores and death scores for the life-theorizers and the non-life-theorizers separately. For the life-theorizers, the correlation was not significant, $r(18) = 0.228$ (ns); for the non-life-theorizers, the correlation was significant, $r(16) = 0.475$ ($p < 0.05$).

This pattern was unexpected. What it appears to indicate is that for non-life-theorizers, those children who are accumulating biological knowledge about the body are also more likely to be accumulating a biological understanding of death. For the life-theorizers, in contrast, detailed biological knowledge of the body is not related to the understanding of death. Why would this be? We suggest that the life-theorizers have acquired the basic coherent structure of the vitalistic theory, for example that the maintenance of life is the goal of bodily function, and that death is the cessation of life, which is itself the cessation of body function. Beyond that, we suggest that the life-theorizers are individually acquiring various aspects of body or death knowledge, such that there is no longer a linear relationship between how much they know about the body and how much they know about death. That is, once children have constructed the coherent foundation of the working vitalistic theory, then the details of body function and death may develop in a piecemeal fashion depending on the particular interests and experiences of the individual children.

Conclusion

These data confirm the literature on preschool performance on the body and death interviews. Taken all together, the children in our study showed very little understanding of bodily function, and provided typical preschool responses on the death interview. Even life-theorizers were far from ceiling on each task; in particular, many of their responses were consistent with non-biological understanding of some of the components of the death interview.

These data go beyond those in the literature in two ways. We sampled a group of children of the ages (4 and 5) in which it appears a first vitalistic theory of the human body is being constructed, and more importantly, we tested for the coherence of children's understanding of three crucial aspects of a vitalistic biology: the emergence of the concept of "life" as a central organizing construct (as the teleological goal of bodily function), the acquisition of knowledge about the biological functions of the body, and the understanding of death as the end of the life cycle.

The data presented here replicated and extended those found in previous studies using each of these instruments. A vitalistic biology, organized around the concept of "life," is indeed emerging over these years. Roughly one-half of our sample of 4 and 5-year-olds were not yet life-theorizers. Similarly, all of the hallmarks of a non-biological understanding of death as living on in altered circumstances were observed in the overall sample. What is new in our study are the close relations we found among the three indices of vitalistic understanding – life-theorizing, knowledge of bodily function, and a relatively mature concept of death. This pattern supports the claim that the construction of a first vitalistic biology provides the structural basis for widespread change in children's biological concepts. Most importantly, the concepts of "life" and "death" themselves change radically. Children's concept of "life" transforms from an animistic notion focusing on movement, activity, or usefulness, to the ultimate biological goal of all living things. At the same time, children's concept of "death" changes, from the early, behavioral concept of death as living on in altered circumstances, to death as the inevitable end of the life cycle, the final cessation of life. It is no coincidence that these concepts change around the same time. This cluster of concepts – life-death-body function – forms a coherent, interrelated network of beliefs that, we propose, itself constitutes the basic structure of the first, vitalistic, intuitive biological theory.

Four details of the data provide hints about the process underlying conceptual change. First, the non-life-theorizers were near floor on the body and death interviews, but not at floor. Second, there was variation among them in their scores on each of these interviews, and further, their body function scores and death scores were correlated. Third, the life-theorizers, while performing markedly better than the non-life-theorizers on each of these measures, were far from ceiling. Fourth, there was variation among them in their scores on each of these interviews, and further, their scores on the two interviews were not correlated.

Apparently, the preschool child begins to learn about bodily function and components of an adult understanding of death in terms of concepts formulated over their non-life-based theory of people and animals. Inter-relations among these new facts learned support the differentiated concepts of life and death. For example, a child could learn that you would die if you did not have a heart, or that something goes seriously wrong without a heart. This fact adds to disequilibrating forces on the undifferentiated concepts of life and death, and supports restricting life and death to only those creatures that have hearts, i.e., animals and people. The correlation between bodily function scores and death scores among non-life-theorizers can be interpreted in terms of a process by which mutually reinforcing factual knowledge is being built up. Apparently, this process both supports the construction of a differentiated concept of life, and its entrenchment, until a certain threshold is reached, signified in these data and in Jaakkola's (1997), by becoming a life-theorizer. At this point, the differentiated concepts, embedded in a vitalistic biology, direct further learning. The structure is now available and further learning will accrue relatively easily and quickly, as opportunity affords, and further learning is no longer so closely correlated, as it is no longer playing the role of bootstrapping the new theory out of the old.

Further work could help to flesh out this picture. First, the pattern of results bears replication; especially the result that the body function scores and death scores are correlated only among non-life-theorizers. Second, the coherence between the concepts tested here and other aspects of early vitalistic biology should be probed. Third, and most important, are training studies (Slaughter and Lyons, forthcoming), for those would rule out potential confounds in the correlations we have found here. Training studies could test the prediction that life-theorizers will pick up new biological information much more readily than non-life-theorizers, and could delineate different routes to bootstrapping a vitalistic biology out of a conceptual structure that does not contain the differentiated concept of life.

Overall, this case study of the development of the concept of death supports the view of biological knowledge undergoing a process of conceptual change, beginning between the ages of 4 and 6. Children who have begun to construct a vitalistic biology, our life-theorizers, demonstrated concurrent development in a cluster of related concepts and beliefs. The concepts of life, death, and bodily function appeared to be developing coherently, so that each provides a structure and a context for the other, related concepts and beliefs.

Acknowledgments: much of the work reported in this chapter was supported by a postdoctoral fellowship to the first author from the James S. McDonnell Foundation program in Cognitive Studies for Education Practice. Portions of the data presented in this chapter were presented at the Society for Research in Child Development meetings in Indianapolis, IN, 1995 and Washington, DC, 1997.

REFERENCES

Anthony, S. (1940). *The child's discovery of death.* New York: Harcourt, Brace.
Astington, J. (1993). *The child's discovery of the mind.* Cambridge, MA: Harvard University Press.
Carey, S. (1985). *Conceptual change in childhood.* Cambridge, MA: MIT Press.
    (1988). Conceptual differences between children and adults. *Mind and Language,* 3, 167–182.
    (1995). On the origin of causal understanding. In D. Sperber, D. Premack, and A. J. Premack (eds.), *Causal cognition* (pp. 268–303). Oxford: Oxford University Press.
    (1999). Sources of conceptual change. In E. K. Scholnick, K. Nelson, S. A. Gelman, and P. Miller (eds.), *Conceptual development: Pigget's legacy.* Hillsdale, NJ: Erlbaum.
Carey, S., and Spelke, E. (1994). Domain-specific knowledge and conceptual change. In L. Hirschfeld and S. Gelman (eds.), *Mapping the mind: Domain-specificity in cognition and culture* (pp. 169–200). New York: Cambridge University Press.
    (1996). Science and core knowledge. *Philosophy of Science,* 63, 515–533.
Gaarder, J. (1995). *Sophie's world.* London: Phoenix House/Orion.
Gopnik, A., and Meltzoff, A. (1997). *Words, thoughts and theories.* Cambridge, MA: Bradford/MIT Press.
Gopnik, A., and Wellman, H. M. (1992). Why the child's theory of mind really is a theory. *Mind and Language,* 7, 145–172.
    (1994). The theory theory. In L. Hirschfeld and S. Gelman (eds.), *Mapping the mind: Domain-specificity in cognition and culture.* New York: Cambridge University Press.
Hacking, I. (1993). Working in a new world: The taxonomic solution. In P. Horwich and J. Thomson (eds.), *World changes* (pp. 275–310). Cambridge, MA: MIT Press.
Hatano, G., Siegler, R., Richards, D., Inagaki, K., Stavy, R., and Wax, N. (1993). The development of biological knowledge: A multi-national study. *Cognitive Development,* 8, 47–62.
Inagaki, K., and Hatano, G. (1993). Young children's understanding of the

mind–body distinction. *Child Development*, 64, 1,534–1,549.

(1996). Young children's recognition of commonalities between animals and plants. *Child Development*, 67, 2,823–2,840.

Jaakkola, R. (1997). The development of scientific understanding: Children's construction of their first biological theory. Unpublished Ph.D. thesis. Massachusetts Institute of Technology, Cambridge, MA.

Kane, B. (1979). Children's concept of death. *Journal of Genetic Psychology*, 134, 141–153.

Keil, F. (1994). The birth and nurturance of concepts by domains: The origins of concepts of living things. In L. Hirschfeld and S. Gelman (eds.), *Mapping the mind: Domain-specificity in cognition and culture* (pp. 234–254). New York: Cambridge University Press.

Kitcher, P. (1988). The child as parent of the scientist. *Mind and Language*, 3, 217–228.

Klingberg, G. (1957). The distinction between living and not living among 7–10 year old children, with some remarks concerning the so-called animism controversy. *Journal of Genetic Psychology*, 90, 227–238.

Klingensmith, S. W. (1953). Child animism: What the child means by alive. *Child Development*, 24, 51–61.

Koocher, G. (1973). Childhood, death and cognitive development. *Developmental Psychology*, 9, 369–375.

Kuhn, D., Amsel, E., and O'Loughlin, H. (1988). *The development of scientific thinking skills*. San Diego, CA: Academic Press.

Laurendeau, M., and Pinard, A. (1962). *Causal thinking in the child: A genetic and experimental approach*. New York: International Universities Press.

Lazar, A., and Torney-Purta, J. (1991). The development of the sub-concepts of death in young children: A short term longitudinal study. *Child Development*, 62, 1,321–1,333.

Medin, D., and Ortony, A. (1989). Psychological essentialism. In S. Vosniadou and A. Ortony (eds.), *Similarity and analogical reasoning*. New York: Cambridge University Press.

Nagy, M. (1948). The child's theories concerning death. *Journal of Genetic Psychology*, 83, 199–216.

Orback, I., Gross, Y., Glaubman, H., and Berman, D. (1985). Children's perception of death in humans and animals as a function of age, anxiety and cognitive ability. *Journal of Child Psychology and Psychiatry*, 26, 453–463.

Perner, J. (1991). *Understanding the representational mind*. Cambridge, MA: Bradford/MIT Press.

Piaget, J. (1929). *The child's conception of the world*. London: Routledge and Kegan Paul.

Safier, G. (1964). A study in relationships between the life and death concepts in children. *Journal of Genetic Psychology*, 105, 283–294.

Slaughter, V., and Gopnik, A. (1996). Conceptual coherence in the child's theory of mind: Training children to understand belief. *Child Development*, 67, 2,967–2,988.

Slaughter, V., and Lyons, M. (forthcoming). Teaching children about life to increase their understanding of death: Evidence for a coherent theory of biology in early childhood.

Smith, C., Carey, S., and Wiser, M. (1985). On differentiation: A case study of the development of the concepts of size, weight and density. *Cognition*, 21, 177–237.

Speece, M., and Brent, S. (1985). Children's understanding of death: A review of three components of a death concept. *Child Development*, 55, 1,671–1,686.

(1992). The acquisition of a mature understanding of three components of the concept of death. *Death Studies*, 16, 211–229.

Springer, K., Nguyen, T., and Samaniego, R. (1996). Early awareness of decomposition as a distinctive property of biological kinds: Evidence for a naive theory. *Cognitive Development*, 11, 65–82.

Stavy, R., and Wax, N. (1989). Children's conceptions of plants as living things. *Human Development*, 32, 88–94.

Von Hug-Helmuth, H. (1964). The child's concept of death. *Psychoanalytic Quarterly*, 34, 499–516.

Wellman, H. (1990). *The child's theory of mind*. Cambridge, MA: MIT Press.

Wellman, H. M., and Gelman, S. A. (1992). Cognitive development: Foundational theories of core domains. *Annual Review of Psychology*, 43, 337–375.

White, E., Elsom, B., and Prawat, R. (1978). Children's conceptions of death. *Child Development*, 49, 307–310.

Part II

Health issues

5   What young children's understanding of contamination and contagion tells us about their concepts of illness

Charles W. Kalish

Consider the range of theories and beliefs that people bring to bear when reasoning about illness. At a minimum, illness can be thought of in biological, social, psychological, moral/religious, and probabilistic terms. Various aspects of illness may be understood to be embedded in a number of explanatory contexts or theories. Any one "fact" about illness may involve a number of theories. For example there are several (partial) explanations for why sick children do not go to school. There is a biological rationale: sick people may be contagious and so may contaminate others they contact. There is also a social prohibition. It is a social norm that sick people are released from certain obligations and enjoined to others: one *gets* to stay home and *should* avoid making others ill. There also may be a psychological rationale: sick people feel bad and weak and so do not want to go to school.

Conceptions of illness provide researchers an excellent opportunity to study children's understandings of different domains of experience. To what extent, for example, do young children distinguish biological from social or psychological aspects of illness experience? This question has taken on particular importance in light of ongoing debates about the development of biological knowledge. Susan Carey and colleagues (Carey, 1985a, 1995; Solomon *et al.*, 1996) have argued that a differentiated notion of biology does not emerge until middle childhood. Other researchers suggest that some forms of biological knowledge are present much earlier (e.g., Simons and Keil, 1995; Wellman and Gelman, 1992). In this chapter I shall focus on children's reasoning about one central aspect of illness experience: contagion and contamination. How children think about contamination and contagion is an interesting and important question in its own right. Such an investigation also promises to shed light on larger issues within cognitive development.

Beliefs about contagion and contamination represent reasoning about causal relationships surrounding illness. At least for modern adults in western cultures, contagion and contamination, though separate concepts, are understood as components or aspects of a single model of disease transmission: an infection model of illness. Infection involves the idea of some agent of disease (a contaminant) being transmitted from an object or medium to a host who becomes ill as a result of this transmission (contagion). Because they may be parts of a model or theory of illness causation, conceptions of contagion and contamination are of great interest to researchers studying cognitive development. To what extent are children's ideas organized into a coherent model of infection? The coherence or organization of children's causal reasoning is a central issue within accounts of cognitive development based on the acquisition and elaboration of intuitive theories (see Wellman and Gelman [1992] for review). Particularly in the domain of biology, there is significant debate regarding the coherence of children's reasoning (e.g., Solomon and Cassimatis, 1999). Thus a central focus of this chapter will be a consideration of the degree to which children's ideas about contagion and contamination are organized into a coherent model of infection. Given this focus, and for ease of exposition, I shall often use the term "infection" to refer to the process (and conceptual model) involving contamination and contagion. By adopting this usage I do not mean to prejudge the issue of coherence.

Biological models and conceptions of illness

Contagion and contamination are likely to be the disease processes most familiar to young children. Most of the illnesses that affect children involve infection (e.g., colds, chicken-pox, measles). Many of the rules children know surrounding causes of illness relate to these processes (e.g., "Wash your hands before eating"). Further there is something cognitively compelling about contagion and contamination. Causal reasoning of this sort is pervasive. For example, cultures that lack a scientific understanding of disease transmission often nonetheless believe that disease, or other properties, may be transmitted from one person to another and that otherwise innocuous substances may become dangerous upon contact with contaminants (cf. Frazer, [1890]1981). Analogously, children extend infection beyond illness contexts, and beyond the range of (what adults understand to be) the underlying mechanism (e.g., the game of "cooties"). Since it is a virtual given that even quite young children think about contagion and contamination, in this chapter I shall explore some of the attributes and implications of these conceptions. In particular I shall focus on two questions. First, how do young children understand the processes of contagion and contamination? What kinds of models do they have of infection? The second focus will be on exploring how children's beliefs about infection figure in their conceptions of illness.

Do young children conceive of uniquely biological processes and entities? Contagion and contamination are prime candidates for such biological knowledge. As adults (at least as modern, western adults) our model of infection is grounded in biological conceptions of germs and the actions of pathogens in the body. However, a biological model is not the only way to conceive of infection. For example, we also seem to think about contamination and contagion in associational terms, as operating according to the principles of sympathetic magic (Frazer, [1890]1981; Rozin and Nemeroff, 1990). In the course of this review I shall outline four models or conceptions of infection: associational, physical, simple-biological, and differentiated-biological. I believe the evidence suggests that young children are not limited to associational models: they understand something of the physical nature of infection. However, we do not (yet) have compelling evidence that young children have biological conceptions of infection.

Children's models of infection are also important as sources of evidence about their conceptions of illness. Illness is a concept with significant and intriguing connections to theories of biology (cf. Reznek, 1987; Caplan et al., 1989) and so is relevant to the biology debate. Illness is also intrinsically important. We would like to know how children think about illness so we can communicate with them more effectively about prevention, treatment, consequences, etc. In addition, "illness" is part of a family of related concepts. As with conceptions of living things, conceptions of illness involve a hierarchy (for example, chicken-pox, infectious disease, illness; compare systematics with nosology). Discussions of conceptual representation often contrast kinds of living things with kinds of human-made objects (Gelman and Markman, 1986; Kalish, 1995; Keil, 1989). Kinds in the domain of illness provide a context for extending accounts of children's concepts. In particular, I shall argue that children's reasoning and inferences about infection provide important information about their concepts of illness. Children's, and adults', inferences about contagion (as well as other data) suggest that they represent illness as part of a kind-hierarchy (Shipley, 1989, 1993). This system of kinds is relatively unfamiliar within discussion of natural kinds of living things and prototypes/cluster concepts of human-made objects. Thus considering the implications of reasoning about contagion and contamination may also lead us to expand our ideas about the possible forms of conceptual representations.

Contagion and contamination

Definitions

The terms "contagion" and "contamination" have a venerable history and have developed many different meanings. For purposes of this discussion it is important to distinguish our familiar, commonsense, adult model of infection involving contamination and contagion from other possible conceptions. In particular, I would like to use a characterization of contagion and contamination that is broad enough to span a number of different models. In this definition, the core of both contagion and contamination is the idea that contact with an object may produce illness. Contamination refers to the idea that an otherwise innocuous object may be negatively affected by contact or mixture with some substance. Contagion refers to the idea of transfer of contamination from one object to another. The central cases of contagion are when the objects involved are people or other living things and the transmission involves a generative (potentially infinite) chain rather than a single, limited, instance. The central cases of contamination involve foods or other inanimate objects (e.g., a food becomes contaminated). However, in my characterization it is appropriate to describe people becoming contaminated (which results in illness) and inanimate objects being contagious. For example, consider the following chain: a fly falls into some juice and contaminates it. Person A drinks the juice. By a process of contagion Person A becomes contaminated (sick). Person A sneezes on Person B and passes the contamination on via contagion. The usage is not standard in this example, the terms "contagion" and "contamination" are applied more broadly than adult commonsense would warrant. Similarly, describing each part of this chain as involving a process of infection is also an extension of everyday usage. For example, we typically would not think of Person A as being contaminated, at least in the same way as the juice is; the person gets infected, the juice does not. However, I believe these distinctions are rooted in our underlying causal models. As adults we see an important difference between what is happening in the juice and in the person. With other models and conceptual schemes this distinction may not be motivated. I shall use the terms "contagion," "contamination," and "infection" in this broad sense and rely on the specifications of particular models to articulate distinctions (for example, the juice may be infected in a *physical* sense, the person in a *biological* sense).

The above definition, and the following discussion, captures only a limited perspective on contamination and contagion. The focus is restricted in limiting the effects of infection to illness, rather than, for example, including disgust as a possible outcome (Rozin, 1990). To the extent that infection is seen as involving biological relationships and is part of a coherent theory of illness, this distinction is well motivated. It remains possible that this distinction is artificial and at some points in development, infection involving illness is not differentiated from infection involving other effects (see below). It is also important to point out a second sense in which this discussion of infection is restricted. I shall focus on conceptions and developments only within a single cultural context – modern, western societies. Given that much of the input children receive in this culture reflects modern scientific findings, it is clear that universal claims would be inappropriate.

Associational infection

There is a long tradition of claims that preschool-aged (or preoperational) children's conceptions of infection involve only associations between two things or ideas. An associational conception of infection is very much like belief in sympathetic magic, described by Frazer ([1981]1890) as a mistaking of mental associations for real relations (Rozin and Nemeroff, 1990). For example, Bibace and Walsh (1981, p. 36) describe children's use of contagion in the following way: "The cause of illness is located in objects or people that are proximate to, but not touching, the child. The link between the cause and the illness is accounted for only in terms of mere proximity or magic." Similarly, Rozin *et al.* (1985) describe "associational contagion" where no physical processes are involved. For example, a piece of clothing worn by a disfavored person may evoke a disgust reaction despite the knowledge that no physical trace of the person remains on the clothing (Rozin and Fallon, 1987). While adults show associational contagion for judgments of disgust, they tend not to ascribe illness to associational contagion. It is not clear whether children make this distinction. They may not have a different model or conception of infection for illness and for emotional reactions.[1] This account of children's understanding of contamination and contagion as a cause of illness fits well with Piaget's description of preschoolers as thinking according to a transductive logic. However, more recent research has challenged claims that young children think about contagion and contamination in purely associational terms.

One piece of evidence cited in support of the contention that children have an associational understanding of contagion is that they view all illnesses as contagious (e.g., Kister and Patterson, 1980). Children predict an illness will be passed from one person to another simply because they associate the two people (e.g., the two people appear spatially close together). There are no limits on the conditions which may be associated this way. A mature understanding of contagion implies that only some conditions are contagious. Contagion involves a physical mechanism (germs, for example) present in some illnesses but not others.

More recent research suggests young children may understand something of the physical basis of contagion. Siegal (1988; Siegal et al., 1990) has argued that children limit their judgments of contagion (e.g., a scraped knee is not contagious; see also Kalish, 1996a). Similarly, Keil (1992, 1994) has argued that even young children recognize that behaviors are not contagious. Most directly, I (Kalish, 1996b) have argued that children's predictions of contagion are not based on simple associations, but rather involve some idea of intermediate mechanism. For example, children reliably judge that getting sneezed on by a person will make you sick. However, when provided information about a mechanism (in this case, that no germs were transferred) children no longer predict illness. Though the association between getting sneezed on and getting sick still holds, children no longer judge the illness to be contagious. In another study (Kalish, 1997) 3–5-year-old children were asked to predict whether story characters would get sick and how they would react emotionally to different types of contacts with contaminated foods. Children predicted emotional reactions (e.g., sadness) on the basis of associational contagion; it was what characters knew and thought that determined emotional reaction. However, illness was seen as the result of a physical process of contagion; it was what characters touched or ate, not what they knew, that determined whether they got sick. This pattern of predictions was clearer for older children in the study. There may be some developmental changes occurring between the ages of 3 and 5 in terms of an understanding of the physical basis of contagion. These data begin to suggest that young children may conceive of contagion in a fairly adult-like way, as physical processes. More details of this physical conception are being revealed by research on young children's understanding of contamination.

While evidence regarding associational contagion came from children's over-ascriptions, evidence for an associational understanding of contamination is said to come from children's under-ascriptions. Young children, unlike older children and adults, judge that foods are safe to eat (are uncontaminated) after all the large, visible portions of a contaminant are removed. So, for example, while young children will not drink juice with a grasshopper in it, they will drink the juice once the grasshopper is removed (see Rozin [1990] for a review, though see also Siegal and Share [1990] for conflicting results). This response is consistent with an associational conception of contagion. When the contaminant is visible, the associations are salient, when the contaminant is removed, the association is broken. Young children have been said not to understand that invisible particles of the contaminant may remain in the juice (e.g., Fallon *et al.*, 1984). Invisible particles (e.g., germs, toxins) are part of the mature understanding of the physical bases of contamination. More recent research with preschool-aged children suggests that by age 3 or 4 some understanding of invisible particles is present. They recognize that properties of visible matter (such as the sweetness of sugar) may remain when the matter is dissolved and no longer visible (Au *et al.*, 1993; Rosen and Rozin, 1993). These children often provide or endorse explanations for the persistence of tastes and contamination phrased in terms of invisible particles (Au *et al.*, 1993). Further understanding of the physical bases of contamination is demonstrated by children's insistence that physical contact between a contaminant and a food is necessary to render the food contaminated (Rosen and Rozin, 1993; Springer and Belk, 1994). However, a substantial minority of preschool-aged children accept that one object may contaminate another simply by being put in close proximity, but not touching. It is not clear if children think anything is transferred in this case. These data suggest (as does the contagion work described above) that an understanding of the physical bases of infection is developing during the preschool years.

Models of infection

Most recent research suggests that, at least by the end of the preschool years, children have a physical rather than associational view of infection. However, there remains dispute regarding just how close or comparable preschool-aged children's understanding is to that of older children and adults. This dispute concerns the coherence of infection as a model of illness causation. While young children may have some of the pieces, and roughly the correct ontology, have they put these elements together to form something like an integrated model of infection? For example, children may know that causes of illness are part of the physical world, and they may know many facts about how things get contaminated and how to avoid contagion, etc. These elements, though, may not be integrated into a unified explanatory structure (Solomon and Cassimatis, 1999). Part of the problem is that the (modern, western) understanding of infection is bound up with a germ theory of illness. It is our understanding of the action of germs that provides a coherent model of infection. It is not clear whether germs play this role for young children. A priori there is no reason to believe that an understanding of germs is necessary for a coherent, integrated model of infection – other models are conceivable. However, it is also conceivable that children just know a bunch of facts about contagion and contamination without having a model. Whether children have a germ-based model of infection, and whether their understanding of infection might be coherent in the absence of a clear understanding of germs, are issues of current debate.

At least for adults, infection is a coherent model of illness causation. The coherence comes in an understanding of underlying causal processes that provide a link between contamination and contagion. The way a person becomes sick (or an object becomes contaminated) determines whether or how they will be contagious. Contagion and contamination are seen as aspects of the same causal process. We often think about this process in terms of germs (which are taken to encompass viruses and bacteria, and possibly other micro-organisms). In some cases, germs are what contaminate food and make people sick. When germs are involved (and perhaps only in those cases) contamination and illness may be contagious – transferred from one object or person to another. There may be many other details to our commonsense model (e.g., reproduction and growth of germs, processes of decontamination) but an understanding of the role of germs in contamination and contagion seems central. Thus, in assessing the degree to which young children have a coherent model of infection it is important to examine their understanding of the causal basis of the phenomena.

A fundamental element of anything like our commonsense adult model of infection is that the mechanism which caused an illness or a case of contamination is crucial in determining whether that contamination is contagious. In previous research I have argued that cause is at least part of the basis for young children's judgments of contagion (Kalish, 1996a). In one study, children heard stories describing characters displaying a set of symptoms. Among other things, children were asked to judge whether that character was contagious ("Could you catch it if you played with that person?"). Of particular interest was comparing these judgments with those in a second condition in which children were presented the same stories with the addition of information about the causes of symptoms. When the cause of a character's symptoms was contagion (i.e., they caught the illness from someone else) characters were frequently judged to be contagious. Other sorts of causes (e.g., a headache resulting from a blow) were not predicted to result in contagious illness. In a second study, children judged all conditions said to be caused by germs to be contagious at the same rate despite variation in symptoms produced (e.g., positive vs. negative symptoms). This research demonstrates that children do focus on how a condition was caused (how someone became contaminated) when judging contagion.

This link between cause and contagion has been challenged in some recent research. Solomon and Cassimatis (1999) report that before age 10 children are relatively insensitive to the causes of conditions. For example, they judge conditions caused by germs, by poisons, and by "events" (e.g., sneezing because of pepper) to be contagious all at the same rates. To the extent that young children made differentiated predictions about contagion they seemed to do so on the basis of symptoms presented. For example, coughs were judged to be more contagious than tummy aches. The relationships between symptoms and contagion may be evidence of a set of empirical generalizations rather than any organized models.

Clearly these discrepant results need to be reconciled. Importantly, young children may have a different view of the range of causes of contagious illness. Agents other than germs, such as "cold air" (McMenamy and Wiser, 1997) or poisons (Keil, 1994), may be thought to mediate infection. Thus the question of whether children understand germs as agents of infection must be distinguished from the more general question of whether they have a model of infection. Young children may or may not realize the unique role that germs play. They may, however, understand that contagion and contamination are linked together as part of some coherent causal process. While important as a necessary component of a recognizable understanding of infection, knowing that the cause of contamination affects contagion is far from sufficient for providing a complete model. It remains to be demonstrated how young children conceive of the causes underlying infection. In particular, a central question is whether children have a biological, germ-based, model.

Physical infection Young children do see germs as a mechanism of infection (Kalish, 1995). For example, they recognize that events which often contaminate food will not do so if no germs are involved (e.g., a cookie that falls on the floor but gets no germs on it is not contaminated). Similarly, events which typically result in contagion will not do so in the absence of germs (e.g., playing with a sick child does not make you sick if no germs are transferred). However, children may not see germs as unique and distinctive agents of infection. McMenamy and Wiser (1997) find that preschool-aged children judge illnesses caused by "folk agents" (e.g., cold air) to be contagious. There is some suggestion that these young children saw folk agents as operating independently of germs.[2] One way the role of germs in infection has been addressed is by asking whether young children distinguish between germs and poisons. Young children are equally likely to judge as contagious illnesses caused by germs and illnesses caused by poisons (Keil, 1994; Solomon and Cassimatis, 1999). Moreover children may not see germs as living things and as different from chemical poisons. Keil (1992) found children more likely to attribute biological properties to germs than to poisons, however in some cases children were also given the information that germs (viruses) had purposes. The information about goals may have led them to ascribe other biological attributes. Solomon and Cassimatis (1999), in contrast, found that young children did not distinguish between germs and poisons and tended to treat both as non-living. The conservative conclusion may be that children do not see germs as a special kind of mechanism. This suggests they may have a physical, but not biological conception of infection.

Poisons and other chemical/physical entities can be viewed as mechanisms of contagion and contamination. Poison is clearly a contaminant. If one contacts poison one may become ill. Poison may also be a vehicle for contagion. For example, if someone gets a particularly virulent poison on the hand and then touches someone else, that second person may come to show the effects of the poison as well. This transfer of materials (and the effects of the materials) represents a coherent model of physical infection. This model seems consistent with what we know about young children's beliefs about infection. It is not associational, but rather based on material transfer. Further, it seems that young children's understanding of the role of germs may also fit within this physical model. Germs function like poisons, as physical agents of contamination.

Biological infection   A physical model of infection based on material transfer does differ from our adult commonsense biological understanding. A key feature of the adult model is generativity. Transfer of poisons strikes us as a marginal case; the process is too limited. Contagion and contamination are thought to be potentially infinite. This attribute is accounted for by our belief that the agents of infection, germs, reproduce and multiply. Similarly, a physical model of infection seems too static. In our biological model contamination spreads within the host. Contamination originally contacted by one part of the body (e.g., the mouth) may result in contagious transfer from other sites (e.g., mucus, saliva, feces). Again it is the living nature of germs, and the way germs interact with the biological host, that seems to account for these intuitions. Thus a biological conception of infection seems to require some additional knowledge over and above a physical model. Importantly, our core adult model of infection involves living things as both agents and hosts. While transfer of inanimate particles from one inanimate thing to another may be infection in "some sense" it is not the typical sense.

While there is little direct evidence, existing data suggest that young children do not hold a biological conception of infection. Au and Romo

(1997, see also chapter 9 in this volume) report that children's untutored explanations for contamination (e.g., rotting food) involve mechanical forces – movements of invisible particles. The possible physical conceptions of germs (and their conflation with poisons) discussed above would also be incompatible with a biological model of infection. Children have been held to be generally unaware of internal bodily processes (see Carey, 1985a). Yet it is what happens when a contaminant enters the body – how it reproduces, spreads, and causes reactions on the part of the host – that seem at the heart of a biological conception of the process. Most pre-school-aged children do not recognize that illness is a delayed effect of contact with germs (Kalish, 1997). Children think people become sick immediately upon contact with contaminants. This suggests some ignorance of the processes occurring inside the body in response to contamination. Clearly the understanding of the action of germs within the body is a complex matter. It is likely that many adults have only sketchy beliefs about these relationships. However, some understanding that more than simple material transfer is going on seems crucial to a truly biological model.

One way of characterizing a biological model of infection is that it is an elaborated, more complex, version of a physical model. In a physical model, the agents of infection are understood to be material entities. A biological model further specifies the nature of these entities: they are living things (e.g., that reproduce). A physical model requires that a contaminant must physically contact a host. A biological model further specifies what happens inside the host (bodily processes). However, an alternative criterion for identifying a body of knowledge as biological is the scope of phenomena or domain within which it is applied. Simons and Keil (1995) argue that young children may have only a skeletal or abstract notion of biological phenomena. What would identify a model of infection as biological on this conception would be how notions of infection interact with other biological knowledge. For example, infection may be seen as unique to living things, or be thought to have different properties when involving living and non-living things. One piece of evidence of this sort is Keil's (1992) demonstration that children limit contagion to physical/biological attributes. In Keil's work, preschool-aged children denied that behaviors (such as obsessive hand washing) may be caught from another person. Young children seemed to overextend contagion to all biological attributes: congenital conditions were thought to be just as contagious as acquired conditions. This suggests that children may identify infection with the domain of biological properties of living things. While more research is needed on the relationships between conceptions of infection and other elements of biological knowledge, the possibility of such relationships means that children may have a biological model of infection (of some sort) without understanding specific details.

In assessing young children's understanding of infection it is necessary to make distinctions between different types or models of infection. The first distinction drawn was between an associational and a material conception. Young children do not seem to be limited to an associational view, they can understand the material basis for contagion and contamination. A second distinction concerns whether children have an coherent model of infection or whether their knowledge is more fragmented and piecemeal. While children have been said to see infection as mediated by some underlying causal processes (e.g., transfer of material) there is some debate on this point. Assuming that children do have a causal model of infection the question arises, what sort of model? Here it is useful to make a distinction between physical and biological models of infection. While young children may understand that infection is based on material transfer, they may not have a particularly biological understanding. A biological model seems to involve more detail and specific knowledge than a physical conception For example, one crucial element seems to be the recognition that agents of infection act in particular ways inside the body (e.g., they reproduce). The existing evidence provides some suggestion that young children may hold a physical rather than a biological model.

This discussion of infection has focused almost exclusively on children in the preschool years. In part this reflects the focus of research in this area. However, it is also possible to make some conjectures about later developments based on data from early childhood. Many researchers believe that a biological understanding or way of viewing phenomena emerges from physical mechanical knowledge (Au, Romo, and DeWitt, chapter 9 in this volume; Kalish, 1997) or, perhaps, social knowledge (Carey, 1985a). This process requires some conceptual change and is thought to occur in middle childhood (Carey, 1985a) and/or in response to formal instruction (Au, Romo, and DeWitt, chapter 9 in this volume). Thus we might predict that children will be developing biological models of infection in middle childhood. Certainly as children grow older and are exposed to more information their knowledge about the specifics of germs and bodily processes increases. However, Simons and Keil (1995) argue we should not equate biological knowledge with knowledge of specifics. How much detail is required for a biological model remains a matter for further debate and research.

Conceptions of illness

Among the reasons that children's understanding of contagion and contamination has attracted so much attention is that children cite these processes as causes of illness. While there may be some debate surrounding the particular model children hold, infection does seem to play a central role in children's understanding of illness. Exactly how central is the next question taken up. For example, researchers have argued that at some points in development children think that all illnesses are contagious. This suggests that the model that children have of infection may also be their model of illness. What it is to be sick is to have a contagious ailment. While there are reasons to doubt this strong claim (see below), it does seem that children's reasoning about infection is quite informative regarding their more general conceptions of illness.

Infection as prototype for illness

One suggestion is that contagious illness is the prototypical case. A prototype is a probabilistic summary, or a best instance, and provides predictions about likely features (Rosch, 1975). The claim that infection is prototypical implies that when children think of illness they tend to think of a process involving contagion and contamination. Infection is thought to be the most typical, most likely, default sort of illness. There is some evidence that adults have prototype representations of disease and specific illnesses (cf. Bishop, 1991; Bishop and Converse, 1986; Reznek, 1987). Contagious ailments, specifically acute viral infections (e.g., colds, measles, chicken-pox), may be the prototypical or "best" cases of disease (Campbell et al., 1979). In fact, it has been argued that one of the changes that occurs in medical school is that students learn to give up this "cognitive bias" towards thinking about disease in terms of infection (Stefan and McManus, 1989).

To what extent might infection be the prototype of illness for young children? It does seem that adults have a notion of a "prototypical" contagious illness (Bishop, 1991). This prototype serves to organize thinking about many illness. However, adults also recognize non-contagious illnesses.[3] If infection is one among many causes of illness for adults, we might expect it to play a more dominant role for children. Most of the illnesses that most children experience are the acute viral infections, while adults may be familiar with more non-prototypical illnesses (heart disease, cancer). In fact, many of these best examples of contagious illness are often associated with childhood (e.g., chicken-pox, mumps, measles). Keil (1989) has argued that children's concepts develop from being organized primarily around characteristic features (prototypes) to an organization involving defining or causal features. For example, young children do not distinguish features which are merely associated with category memberships (e.g., that uncles are usually adults) from those features which are part of the definition or core of the category (e.g., that uncles are the brothers of a parent). Thus we might expect that children's earliest conceptions of illness are most heavily influenced by notions of prototypicality. One piece of evidence is that children often indicate that all illnesses are contagious (e.g., Hergenrather and Rabinowitz, 1991). Even congenital illnesses may be thought to have the prototypical property of being contagious (Keil, 1992). In the absence of other information, a prototype is the default. Kalish (1996a) found that children judged 72 percent of the conditions they identified as illnesses to be contagious (in the absence of information about the causes of the symptoms). Of those judged to be illnesses, 80 percent were predicted to involve a fever, a symptom usually associated with infections of some sort. To the extent that children's conceptions and identifications of illness are similar to adults (see Kalish [1996a] for arguments) this suggests that they too see some elements of infection as prototypical of illness. However, the role of prototypes in children's thinking about illness has not been directly addressed. Finding that infection is prototypical would provide information about how children might typically reason about illness but, in an important way, this finding would not be informative about the nature or structure of children's concept of illness. For example, any concept from nominal kinds (such as "even number") to natural kinds (such as "dog") may be associated with prototypes (Armstrong *et al.*, 1983; Rey, 1983). Thus many possible conceptions of illness are consistent with a claim that infection is a prototype. In particular, one possibility is that, more than just being a prototypical case, infection defines illness for young children.

Infection as the basis of a natural kind conception of illness

Taking infection as definitive of illness is to hold a "natural kind" conception of illness. A natural kind is a grouping or type that seems to have an objective basis; there is some fundamental identity that we discover (Mill, [1872]1973). For a kind such as "illness" the objective basis would be some particular biological process (Reznek, 1987). Contagion and contamination could provide a unitary underlying causal model for illness. For example, it has been reported that a germ-theory of illness was popular in Europe following the discoveries of Pasteur (Reznek, 1987). All illness was thought to involve germs and infection. This model would provide a natural kind conception of illness. Illness would have the

characteristics of other natural kinds (basic level animal kinds being the
central cases in the psychological literature). For example, there could be
anomalous cases, i.e., ailments which appeared to be illnesses but were
discovered not to be because they did not involve germs (see Gelman and
Coley, 1991; Markman, 1990, for further discussion). At least for modern western adults, illness is not a natural kind: there is no unifying
underlying biological process with which illness may be identified (cf.
Reznek, 1987). In particular adults recognize that some illnesses are
contagious and caused by contamination, but not all are (e.g., inherited
diseases, vitamin deficiencies, etc.). However, children may hold different views.

There have been several claims in the literature that children view all
illnesses as infections, and that infection is thought to be the only causal
processes underlying illness (Bibace and Walsh, 1980, 1981; Brewster,
1982; Hergenrather and Rabinowitz, 1991; Nagy, 1951; Perrin and
Gerrity, 1981). Importantly this position is different from the view associated with associational infection. The claim is not that all ailments or
conditions are judged to be contagious because of children's magical/
transductive thinking. Rather the argument is that once children have
grasped a causal mechanism underlying illness (germs and infection) they
overextend it (analogous to the nineteenth-century Europeans mentioned above). Thus it is often young school-aged children who are said to
hold this view; concrete operations are said to be a prerequisite for
conceiving underlying causes (e.g., Kister and Patterson, 1980). Demonstrations that these children do not view particular conditions as contagious – e.g., toothaches (Siegal, 1988) or aberrant behaviors (Keil,
1994) – do not tell against this claim unless the non-contagious conditions are also seen as illnesses (e.g., a person with a toothache is probably
not considered to be sick). Similarly, demonstrations that preschool-aged
children judge some illnesses to be non-contagious (Kalish, 1996a) do
not address the views of older children. However, arguments that
younger children can (and do) understand germs and mechanisms of
infection (Au et al., 1993; Kalish, 1996b; Springer and Belk, 1994)
militate against the developmental logic of the position. It is not that 7
year olds are just coming to understand germs. There are also reasons to
question the generalized claim that all illnesses are thought to be contagious. Studies have asked children how particular illnesses are caused
(e.g., "bronchitis": Hergenrather and Rabinowitz, 1991). It is an unwarranted inference from the fact that children say all the illnesses included
in a particular study are contagious to the conclusion that they think
contagion (and contamination) is the only cause of illnesses. Nonetheless, the conclusive demonstration, that young school-aged children will

deny that a condition they identify as an illness is also contagious, has not been produced. While preschool-aged children do not seem to identify illness with a particular causal model, it remains possible that older children do see all illness as involving infection. Younger children do not conceive of illness as a natural kind, older children may. However, if young school-aged children do hold a natural kind model of illness they eventually give it up in favor of a notion of illness that recognizes a variety of causes. This seems to be the adult view and is shared by children in early adolescence (Bibace and Walsh, 1980; Hergenrather and Rabinowitz, 1991).

An alternative model of illness

Discussions of concepts often posit three types of representation: concepts are natural kinds, nominal kinds, or property clusters (cf. Keil, 1989). If children's and adults' conception of illness is not a natural kind, and is not nominal (based on an analytic definition), then it must be a property cluster. Property cluster concepts are based on similarity and prototypes. Thus illness may have a prototype structure as well as showing prototype effects (see Lakoff [1986] for this distinction). However, there is a fourth alternative. Within a given domain the natural kinds might exist only at a low level of generality but be collected together into higher order kinds. Those higher order kinds need not themselves be natural kinds but might have some other structure. Shipley (1989, 1993) and Goodman (1955) have described a set of principles for this kind of organization – an organization involving "kind-hierarchies" and "over-hypotheses." A kind-hierarchy is consistent with prototype effects but posits more structure or specific relationships between concepts and attributes. In the remainder of this chapter I shall outline the notion of a kind-hierarchy and argue that this type of conceptual structure best matches children's and adults' thinking about illness. In particular, reasoning about infection will be a crucial piece of evidence in favor of a kind-hierarchy account of the illness concept.

Kind-hierarchies and over-hypotheses   As part of an account of induction, Goodman (1955) proposed the idea that people were sensitive to fairly abstract relationships between classes of categories and dimensions. These relationships he termed "over-hypotheses." An over-hypothesis is a proposition such as "Instances of the same kind of illness have the same cause." It is a hypothesis about a set of categories (the kinds of illnesses – chicken-pox, sickle-cell anemia, etc.) and a dimension (cause). It specifies that within a category the values on the dimension will be uniform (e.g., all instances of chicken-pox will have a common cause). Systems of concepts built out of over-hypotheses are called "kind-hierarchies" (Shipley, 1989). Higher order kinds (e.g., illness) involve over-hypotheses about subordinate level kinds (e.g., chicken-pox). One important point for the present discussion that the higher order kinds are characterized by over-hypotheses, rather than by features shared among instances of the higher order kind. On a kind-hierarchy view, there is no claim that illnesses share any qualities or that there are a particular set of properties unique to illnesses.[4] That is, there are not necessarily any laws that apply to all and only illnesses. However, "illness" is not simply an arbitrary or unstructured concept. The concept captures some important similarities shared by its members, each of which is a natural kind. To identify a kind as an illness is to say what type of natural kind it is.

Over-hypotheses and illness   There are some existing data suggesting that people's conceptions of illness are part of a kind-hierarchy. Illness is not a natural kind but it is a superordinate kind that identifies a set of natural kinds. The kinds of illnesses (which I shall refer to as "diseases") are natural kinds of a particular type. One piece of evidence comes from the analysis of experts' conceptions. In his exploration of the concept of "disease," Reznek (1987) suggests that particular diseases (such as chicken-pox) are natural kinds. There are characteristic biological processes underlying these particular diseases. Reznek argues that higher-level concepts of "disease" or "illness" are social constructs which exist for only peculiar historical reasons (e.g., professional disputes, technological limitations), though he does not consider that they may provide some organization for the natural kinds of diseases. While the claims about expert usage are suggestive, more direct evidence comes from accounts of lay adults' illness representations. In particular, Leventhal *et al.*'s (1980) theory of a dimensional representation is also consistent with a kind-hierarchy account.

An influential model of commonsense conceptions of illness (Leventhal *et al.*, 1980; also Lau and Hartmann, 1983) states that people think about illness in terms of values on dimensions. An example of a set of dimensions used to think about illness is presented in table 5.1. This model has been proposed for lay adults, and has also been said to characterize young children's representations of illness (Goldman *et al.*, 1991). One source of data for these claims comes from studies in which people are asked to describe a particular illness (e.g., their most recent illness). The finding is that statements can be classified into one of the five dimensions (e.g., statements about identity, symptoms, cause, cure, or time-course). Values on these dimensions are used to characterize

Table 5.1. *Five dimensions of illness representations*

Dimension	Content
Identity	What is the name (and symptoms) associated with the illness?
Consequences	What will happen as a result of having the illness?
Time-course	How does the illness progress? Is it acute or chronic or reoccurring?
Cause	What caused the illness?
Cure	What will cure the illness?

particular illness episodes. Similarly, knowledge about types of illness (e.g., colds) is also organized around these dimensions (Goldman *et al.*, 1991). What people know or want to find out about an illness is how it was caused, what will make someone better, etc. Importantly the claim is not that all illnesses have some features in common (e.g., all have the same cause) but rather that questions about cause are relevant in cases of illness. Thus the concept of illness involves beliefs about what kinds of information or features are relevant to instances. In this way the characterization of illness is very similar to Keil's (1979) description of an ontological level of knowledge representation. In Keil's terms, Leventhal's account is a hypothesis about a characteristic set of predicates that span illnesses.

While related to an ontological characterization, the suggestion that illness is part of a kind-hierarchy is a stronger claim. The supposition is not just that "illness" is associated with a particular set of spanning predicates, but also that values of the predicate/dimension will be shared within sub-types of illnesses. Similarly, a kind-hierarchy is a stronger constraint on conceptions of illness than that directly implied by Leventhal's account. From Leventhal's theory one could predict that upon encountering a novel illness ("lumenza") people would want to know (roughly) five things (its symptoms, consequences, time-course, cause, and cure). A kind-hierarchy account would further predict that people would generalize ("project": Goodman, 1955) these five pieces of information to all other instances of the same illness. This is because the concept of "illness" includes over-hypotheses such as "cause is shared across instances of the same kind of illness." For example, if told that one case of lumenza is contagious (or acquired via contamination) people will assume that other cases of lumenza are also contagious. Importantly, there are predicates that span illness (e.g., began in June) that are not part of over-hypotheses (and so not projected).[5] Thus the kind-hierarchy hypothesis is that the concept of illness specifies the types of features (dimensions) projectable across instances (cases) of particular diseases.

Some evidence Since a kind-hierarchy account involves stronger claims than a dimensional or ontological view, it is appropriate to ask for some more data in support of this account. One way to test this hypothesis is to study the projection of properties across instances of novel diseases. Given two pieces of information about a condition, first that it is an illness and second that some property is associated with the condition, over-hypotheses allow projection of the property to other cases of the same disease. If children's and adults' concept of illness includes over-hypotheses then they should be willing to project some properties of a novel disease based on a single instance. If these projections are based on over-hypotheses, rather than general inductive strategies, they should be limited to some properties. Not all properties of a novel disease will be projected. These predictions were borne out in a study of predictions of illness properties. This study is only a preliminary attempt to assess the kind-hierarchy hypothesis. While more work needs to be done, the results are suggestive.

Thirty-one adults and thirty children (5-year-olds) participated in the experiment. Participants were told stories about characters suffering from one of two novel diseases.[6] In one condition participants heard about two (training) characters; 12-year-old Johnny (sick with "lumenza") and 6-year-old Lisa (sick with something else). The characters were ascribed two opposite properties (e.g., one is contagious, the other isn't). The task was to rate which property another (test) character would have. The test character shared gender and age with one of the training characters but had the same disease as the other (6-year-old Julie – sick with lumenza). In this condition the phrasing of the question to the child was "Will Julie be X (e.g., contagious) like Johnny or will Julie be not-X (not contagious) like Lisa?" In the no-training condition, subjects were simply asked to predict the properties of the test character with no other information ("Will Julie be contagious or not?").

People were asked about two different kinds of properties. There were five sickness properties, which were expected to be shared within disease kind. These properties were chosen to express values on some of the five dimensions identified as components of lay illness representations (Goldman *et al.*, 1991; Leventhal *et al.*, 1980). There were also five social/psychological dimensions, which were expected to be shared within age/gender (or be randomly distributed). A list of properties is presented in table 5.2. There were two sets of stimuli (set A and set B). These sets differed in the properties ascribed to the sick characters. For example, in set A the training character who had the same illness as the test character was said to have a fever. In set B training character was said to not have a fever.

Table 5.2. Properties used in projection study

Illness dimensions	Symptoms	Duration	Cure	Cause	Cause/symptoms
Set A properties	No fever	Was sick for a short time	Did not need medicine from a doctor	The illness was caused by germs	The illness is contagious
Set B properties	Had a fever	Was sick for a long time	Needed medicine from a doctor	Illness not caused by germs	The illness is not contagious
Non-illness dimensions	Food preference	Transportation	Emotional reaction	Parental care	Entertainment preference
Set A properties	Wanted juice when sick	Rode bus to doctor	Happy to miss school	Dad brought soup when sick	Watched *Sesame Street* when sick
Set B properties	Wanted milk when sick	Rode car to doctor	Sad to miss school	Mom brought soup when sick	Watched Mr. Rogers when sick

One thing this experiment does is provide information about proto-types or default reasoning about illness. Illness properties were not pro-jected randomly in the absence of other information. Though only ten children participated in the no-training condition, there was a significant tendency to judge that someone suffering from an unfamiliar illness would have a fever, need medicine, and be contagious (eight or more judgments out of ten, $p = 0.05$, binomial theorem). This is consistent with prototype theory of illness representation. A prototype provides default information. However, this may not be the only way the general concept of illness provides prediction. In particular, the kind-hierarchy hypothesis specified that the concept of illness should guide inductions from cases of illnesses.

The main question was how people would use information about a single case of a novel illness to make inferences about future cases. Would properties be projected to the test character on the basis of the disease she shared with the training character or on some other basis (e.g., random-ly)? One way to address this question is to look at the differences between projections for set A and set B. If people judged that the test character would have the same property as the same-illness training character then their ascriptions would be reversed in sets A (where lumenza is said to be contagious) and in sets B (where lumenza is said to not be contagious). If properties were projected on some other basis (e.g., using base rate or prototypicality judgments, for example, that all illnesses are contagious) then there should be no differences in judgments across sets. Finally, if gender or age is used as the basis for projections sets A and B would differ but in the opposite direction (e.g., if lumenza is contagious then the test character is not because she is a girl and the other, training, girl was not contagious).

Figure 5.1 shows the patterns of children's and adults' property projec-tions. For illness dimensions (those predicted to be projectable from illness) there was a large difference between property judgments for set A and for set B. For non-illness dimensions the difference was small. Similarly, we can compare inferences in the training and no-training conditions. For illness dimensions, predictions in these two conditions are very different. For non-illness dimensions differences are small. Thus, the information that one case of a novel disease is associated with a particular property (e.g., is contagious) affected projection of that prop-erty to a second case of the novel disease for some properties but not others. Children and adults have intuitions about which properties are projectable within categories of illness and which are not. Properties projectable within illness categories were those identified as components

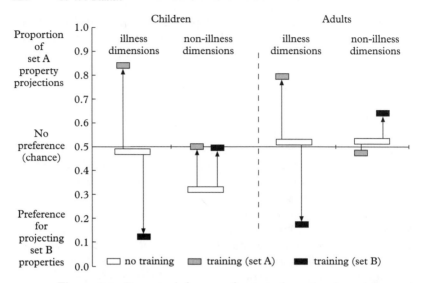

Figure 5.1 Property inferences for test characters in training and no-training conditions. The vertical axis represents the mean proportion of judgments that test characters would have properties from set A. Predictions of set B properties are the inverse of set A predictions (0 percent A predictions = 100 percent B predictions). The midline indicates no-preference for set A or set B properties (chance performance). Open boxes indicate how frequently set A properties were predicted in the no-training condition. Arrows from these boxes indicate the direction and magnitude of change between the no-training and training conditions. In the set A condition, the training character who shared disease with the test character was said to have set A properties. In the set B condition that character was said to have set B properties.

of lay illness representations in previous research (e.g., Leventhal *et al.*, 1980).

Children and adults have some important and consistent assumptions about the general properties of illnesses. In particular, knowing just that a character was suffering from an illness led people to make many other inferences. For example, a novel illness was predicted to lead to a fever and to be contagious. These judgments (in the no-training condition) are consistent with a prototype of illness based on acute infections and processes of contagion and contamination. However, people also have more assumptions. There is more to their concept of illness than a set of default expectations. In particular there also seem to be beliefs about which properties of a novel illness are projectable. These over-hypotheses specify what can be learned about a type of illness from experience with individual instances.

People judge that two instances of the same illness will be alike in symptoms displayed (having a fever or not), the time-course, cure (requiring medicine or not), and cause (involving germs or not, and contagious or not). This suggests that the concept of illness contains over-hypotheses for these dimensions (e.g., "cause is projectable within types of illnesses"). Importantly, not all properties are thought to generalize. People judge that two characters suffering from the same illness need not have similar preferences or emotional reactions. The concept of illness does not contain over-hypotheses for these dimensions. Contagion and contamination, for example, are important components of people's conceptions of illness in a way that preferences or emotions are not. However, it is not the properties themselves that form part of the illness concept. Rather it is beliefs about the consistency of properties that are part of the general notion. "Is contagious" is not a component of people's representation of illness. Something like "Is contagious or not" may be.

The results of the experiment described above suggest that children's and lay adults' conceptions of illness do include over-hypotheses about projectable dimensions. This is certainly one piece of evidence consistent with a kind-hierarchy representation of illness. Another element of the hypothesis is that the categories at a more specific level (types of diseases) are thought to specify common features. The results lend some support this hypothesis for a novel illness. People were willing to project properties, such as contagion, within categories of diseases. However, this is only suggestive of the stronger belief that these properties will be always shared across instances of the same disease. For example, people may have been establishing a prototype of the novel illness, rather than viewing it as a natural kind.[7] Part of the kind-hierarchy hypothesis was that illness is a general category which collects together a set of natural kinds; it says what kind of natural kind a specific disease is. Thus, one remaining question is whether or not conceptions of specific diseases are natural kinds.

Specific diseases and differentiated infection

One of the pieces of evidence used to support the claim that experts view diseases as natural kinds was that they see each disease as involving a characteristic underlying process (Reznek, 1987). At least for familiar, common illnesses, this seems to be the lay adult view as well. One of the indications that a category is organized around a characteristic underlying causal process is that it serves as a productive basis for induction (cf. Gelman and Coley, 1991; Keil, 1989; Markman, 1990). From the above study people did use disease categories as bases of induction (e.g., that if one case involves infection then another will). However, this is not definitive proof that people identify diseases with particular underlying process. For lay adults (again, modern western adults) this characterization does seem plausible (cf. Campbell et al., 1979). For example, most of us probably belief that a specific disease, say chicken-pox, is not defined by its symptoms (e.g., red spot, contagious) but rather what makes a case of illness chicken-pox is that it involves a particular biological process and disease agent (a chicken-pox virus which causes spots and contagion). Whether adults believe this to be true of all types of illnesses (or whether, for example, lay adults recognize some conditions to be syndromes – defined by symptoms) is a matter for future research. What is also unclear is whether young children (ever) have this essentialistic, natural kind, view of specific diseases.

While there is not much research on children's (or adults') conceptions of specific diseases, Keil (1992) reports some data suggesting that young children do not have natural kind representations of diseases. Keil presented subjects with cases of illnesses which shared either observable symptoms or shared origins/etiology, but not both. The question was whether children would identify types of illnesses on the basis of symptoms or on the basis of causal process (as indicated by the origins and developmental progress of the disease). Thus Keil asked children which cases of illness were the same kinds. What Keil (1992) found was kindergarten-aged children (5–6 years old) almost always judged that illnesses with the same symptoms were the same kind and ignored differences in origins. Second-graders (7–8 years old) paid some attention to origins, but not until fourth grade (9–10 years old) were children consistently using causal process to identify types of illnesses. This suggests that young children do not have a natural kind conception of specific diseases.

Why is it that children do not use causal process to identify diseases? It is not that they generally ignore causes. For example, Keil (1989) has found that quite young children recognize the importance of origins and causes in making the general distinction between biological (living things) and non-biological kinds. Similarly the results of Kalish (1996a) suggest that children attend to causes when judging whether something is an illness or not. It may be that it is level of detail of the distinction that leads children to ignore causes. Children's causal models may not be developed in enough detail to account for or represent distinctions at the level of specific diseases (or specific species: Keil, 1989; cf. Simons and Keil, 1995). In particular, their model of infection may be too general to account for specific diseases.

Children know that infection is a causal process that underlies some cases of illness. However, to understand how cause distinguishes one illness from another (e.g., chicken-pox from measles from mumps) one needs a specific, differentiated, understanding of infection. Our adult view is that infection is a superordinate level concept; there are many types of infectious processes, each of which involves a unique germ (or other agent). While both chicken-pox and measles are contagious, there are fundamental differences between the causal processes involved in these two diseases. If children do not understand that there are different germs which may be involved in cases of infection they could not use this causal model to distinguish particular diseases. For example from an undifferentiated model of infection it is not clear why it is measles that is caught from contact with a measles-sufferer rather than, say, chicken-pox or any other set of symptoms. Knowing that illness is contagious does not, necessarily, imply that type of illness is conserved.[8] Awareness of the specific nature of infection may be part of what it takes to really understand the uniqueness of particular diseases. In turn, awareness of the distinctive natures of particular diseases may prompt children to develop a more differentiated understanding of infection. If the initial results indicating that young children have a weak understanding of specific diseases are supported, this would be suggestive evidence for the possibility that these children have an undifferentiated view of infection. Thus, not only may children's understanding of infection inform us about their concepts of illness, but also their conceptions of illness may provide us some ideas about the models of infection they hold.

Summary

In the course of the above review of the literature on conceptions of contagion, contamination, and illness we can identify four models of infection.[9] First is an associational model: contagion and contamination are a mistaking of associations among ideas for associations between physical entities, akin to the principles of sympathetic magic (Frazer, [1890]1981; Rozin and Nemeroff, 1990). A second model treats infection as a physical relationship based on transfer of material particles. Third is a biological model where the agents of infection are understood to be living (e.g., reproducing) entities that infect and act on other living things (hosts). Fourth is a differentiated biological model. Here agents of infection are understood to come in distinct types, species, with unique attributes. Infection becomes a higher-order description of a set of related, but distinct, processes. A tentative conclusion from this review is that preschool-aged children hold something like the second of these models. There is good reason to believe they are not associationists, but we do not (yet) have compelling evidence they view infection in uniquely biological terms.

In the grand Piagetian tradition it is possible to describe a developmental progression of infection models, with subsequent models incorporating, elaborating on, and, at times, superseding the previous models. It would seem reasonable to predict an invariant sequence in the appearance of these models (to the extent they do appear it should be $1 \rightarrow 2 \rightarrow 3 \rightarrow 4$, rather than some other ordering). However, a crucial disanalogy may be the cognitive changes underlying the transitions between models. Rather than general changes in the organization of thought, it seems more likely that changes in models result from changes in specific knowledge or beliefs about germs, the body, and illness (cf. Carey, 1985a, 1985b; Simons and Keil, 1995). In particular, it does not seem appropriate to view model 2 as a product of an inferior logic or less sophisticated thinking than models 3 and 4. As discussed above, adults hold model 2 and use it to reason about interactions in the physical domain. If children lack models 3 and 4 it is likely because they lack the relevant knowledge about the biological specifics.

From this perspective of domain specific change, even the earliest form, associational infection, may not be adequately characterized as deriving from inferior logic or errors of thought. Rather, an early sensitivity to infection may represent a species-typical adaptation to the problem of food selection and illness avoidance (Rozin, 1990). This early (and perhaps universal?) conception is elaborated upon by individual experience and cultural forms of knowledge (e.g., magic, science). This interaction produces new forms of thinking about infection which are partially co-extensive with older forms. Different phenomena may come to be seen as illustrating (or being explained by) particular types of infection. For example, in western culture most adults probably see a biological model of infection involved in illness causation, rather seeing illness as mediated by associational or physical mechanisms. However, the assignment of phenomena to models need not be universally agreed upon. Moreover, as Rozin and colleagues have demonstrated (Rozin and Nemeroff, 1990), early models of contagion and contamination may coexist with later.

As models of infection are likely dependent on knowledge of biology and biological relationships, infection may be taken as an index of that knowledge. How children think about infection is diagnostic (and constitutive) of their general understanding of biology. More directly, thinking about infection is also informative about general conceptions of illness. Infection is not definitive of illness. Young children recognize illnesses that are non-contagious and cases of contamination which are not illness. This suggests illness is not a natural kind, based on a causal model of infection, for young children. While there have been some suggestions that older children see infection as underlying all illness, more data are needed to support this claim. Infection does seem to be part of children's and adults' prototype for illness (cf. Bishop, 1991). For example, in the absence of other information (e.g., in the study reported above) cases of a novel disease are assumed to be contagious. However, inferences about infection (and other properties of illness) also provide evidence for more structure to the concept of illness. In particular, children's and adults' conception of illness contains over-hypotheses about dimensions projectable within subtypes of illnesses (specific diseases). If told that one case of illness is contagious, people will infer another instance of same type is also. This pattern of inference is consistent with a kind-hierarchy conception of illness.

One general theme that emerges from the study of conceptions of infection and illness is the importance of identifying on the right level of generality to study children's thinking. For the study of conceptions of living things it is the folk-generic level of kinds (e.g., dog, cat, horse; cf. Atran, 1987) at which the most important identities and differences are conceptualized. In the sub-domain of illness the fundamental level is less clear. For adults, both "illness" and "contagious disease" are too broad. The most significant distinctions, the natural kinds, are more specific, at the level of types of diseases and micro-organisms. For children the level is less clear; "illness" seems too broad, but they may not see the significance of, and the basis for distinctions among, specific types of diseases. Perhaps it is at an intermediate level of generality, distinguishing between infection and other types of causal processes, that children's knowledge is organized. Certainly investigations of contagion and contamination have been informative about many issues regarding children's thinking. There is every reason to believe that future studies of beliefs about infection will continue to enlighten us about children's cognitive development.

NOTES

1 Of course the separation between biological (illness) and emotional reactions may not be clear-cut for adults either. Adults often do seem to behave according to associational infection. It may be only in justifications or explanations that associational and non-associational models of infection show a clear distinction. While our feelings of disgust, fear, and danger (of illness) may operate according to associational mechanisms, we justify those feelings in different ways. It is those justifications, or understandings, that are the focus of review and discussion in this chapter.

2 McMenamy (personal communication, May 1997). Older children in McMenamy & Wiser (1997) also endorsed folk agents as causes of illness and

as contagious. However, these older children explicitly mentioned germs as the mechanism underlying folk causes. While younger children may not believe germs were involved in these cases they also may simply have failed to mention germs.

3 There may be multiple prototypes rather than a single one underlying adults' thinking about illness (cf. Lakoff, 1986).

4 Just because "illness" is a higher order kind with natural kinds as members does not mean that "illness" cannot be a natural kind. There may be particular processes or properties unique to illnesses that could be discovered.

5 Presumably it is because the attributes of identity, consequence, time-course, cause, and cure are projectable that they are the salient dimensions of lay people's representations of illness.

6 Adults heard two novel illness labels; children heard only one novel label in order to make the items easier to understand. Thus children heard about a character who was sick with vemiton and one character who "is sick but doesn't have vemiton, she has something else." Another significant difference between the adult and child studies was that property reversal was a within-subjects manipulation for adults but a between-subjects manipulation for children. Adults made judgments about two test characters (children only one). One test character had the first illness, the other had the second. Thus each adult had the opportunity to project both values of a dimension (having a fever, not having a fever) to a new instance of an illness. Because children heard about one test character consistently (i.e., always a girl who had vemiton) balancing of properties was done between subjects. Half heard that vemiton was associated with fevers, half that it was associated with lack of fevers. Other procedural differences included the following: adults projected fifteen properties, children ten; adults responded on a nine-point rating scale, children gave yes/no responses; adults were tested on computer, children in interviews. Different wordings for some items were also used. In particular, adults were asked whether a person would be "contagious" or not. Children were asked whether people could get sick if they played with the person.

7 Strictly speaking both of these possibilities are consistent with a kind-hierarchy representation. Over-hypotheses need not be all-or-none. Probabilistic over-hypotheses would yield prototype effects.

8 A similar undifferentiated causal model may be the source of children's difficulties understanding the process of inheritance. While children know that species identity is conserved by inheritance and biological relatedness (Gelman and Wellman, 1991), they often have difficulties thinking about the role of inheritance in determining features within a species, such as whether a person will have blue eyes or brown eyes (Solomon et al., 1996; Weissman, 1997).

9 A fifth possibility is no model at all. Children know some facts about contagion and contamination but have not integrated these facts into a coherent model (cf. Solomon and Cassimatis, 1997).

Acknowledgments: preparation of this chapter was supported by a grant from the Graduate School of the University of Wisconsin-Madison and by a Spencer Foundation-National Academy of Education Postdoctoral Fellowship.

REFERENCES

Armstrong, S. L., Gleitman, L., and Gleitman, H. (1983). What some concepts might not be. *Cognition*, 13, 263–308.

Atran, S. (1987). Folkbiological universals as common sense. In S. Modgil and C. Modgil (eds.), *Noam Chomsky: Consensus and controversy* (pp. 247–268). London: Falmer.

Au, T. K., and Romo, L. F., (1997). Mechanical causality in children's "Folk Human Biology." Paper presented at the Society for Research in Child Development, Washington, DC.

Au, T. K., Sidle, A. L., and Rollins, K. (1993). Developing an understanding of conservation and contamination: Invisible particles as a plausible mechanism. *Developmental Psychology*, 2, 286–299.

Bibace, R., and Walsh, M. E. (1980). Development of children's concepts of illness. *Pediatrics*, 66, 912–917.

(1981). Children's conceptions of illness. In R. Bibace and M. E. Walsh (eds.), *New directions for child development: Children's conceptions of health, illness and bodily functions* (pp. 31–48). San Francisco: Jossey-Bass.

Bishop, G. D. (1991). Understanding the understanding of illness: Lay disease representations. In J. A. Skelton and R. T. Croyle (eds.), *Mental representations in health and illness* (pp. 32–59). New York: Springer-Verlag.

Bishop, G. D., and Converse, S. A. (1986). Illness representations: A prototype approach. *Health Psychology*, 5, 95–114.

Brewster, A. (1982). Chronically ill hospitalized children's concepts of their illness. *Pediatrics*. 69, 355–362.

Campbell, E. J., Scadding, J. G., and Roberts, R. S. (1979). The concept of disease. *British Medical Journal*, 29, 757–762.

Caplan, A. L., Engelhardt, Jr., H. T., and McCartney, J. J. (eds.) (1989). *Concepts of health and disease: Interdisciplinary perspectives*. London: Addison-Wesley.

Carey, S. (1985a). *Conceptual change in childhood*. Cambridge, MA: MIT Press.

(1985b). Are children fundamentally different kinds of thinkers and learners than adults? In S. Chipman, J. Segal, and R. Glaser (eds.), *Thinking and learning skills*, vol. II (pp. 485–517). Hillsdale, NJ: Erlbaum.

(1995). On the origin of causal understanding. In D. Sperber, D. Premack, and A. J. Premack (eds.), *Causal cognition: A multidisciplinary approach* (pp. 268–303). New York: Oxford University Press.

Fallon, A. E., Rozin, P., and Pliner, P. (1984). The child's conception of food: The development of food rejections with special reference to disgust and contamination sensitivity. *Child Development*, 55, 566–575.

Frazer, J. G. ([1890]1981). *The golden bough*. New York: Avenal.

Gelman, S. A., and Coley, J. C. (1991). Language and categorization: The acquisition of natural kind terms. In S. A. Gelman and J. P. Byrnes (eds.), *Perspectives on language and cognition: Interrelations in development* (pp. 146–196). Cambridge, UK: Cambridge University Press.

Gelman, S. A., and Markman, E. M. (1986). Categories and inductions in young children. *Cognition*, 23, 183–209.

Gelman, S. A., and Wellman, H. M. (1991). Insides and essences: Early understandings of the non-obvious. *Cognition*, 38, 213–244.
Goldman, S. L., Whitney-Saltiel, D., Granger, J., and Rodin, J. (1991).
Children's representations of "everyday" aspects of health and illness. *Jour-
nal of Pediatric Psychology*, 16, 747–766.
Goodman, N. (1955). *Fact, fiction, and forecast.* Indianapolis, IN: Bobbs-Merrill.
Hergenrather, J. R., and Rabinowitz, M. (1991). Age-related differences in the
organization of children's knowledge of illness. *Developmental Psychology*, 27,
952–959.
Kalish, C. W. (1995). Graded membership in animal and artifact categories.
Memory and Cognition, 23, 335–353.
   (1996a). Causes and symptoms in preschooler's conceptions of illness. *Child
   Development*, 67, 1,647–1,670.
   (1996b). Preschoolers' understanding of germs as invisible mechanisms. *Cognitive Development*, 11, 83–106.
   (1997). Children's understanding of mental and bodily reactions to contamination: What you don't know can hurt you but cannot sadden you. *Developmental Psychology*, 33, 79–91.
Keil, F. C. (1979). *Semantic and conceptual development: An ontological approach.*
Cambridge, MA: Harvard University Press.
   (1989). *Concepts, kinds, and cognitive development.* Cambridge, MA: MIT Press.
   (1992). The origins of an autonomous biology. In M. R. Gunnar and M.
   Maratsos (eds.),. *Modularity and constraints in language and cognition: Minnesota symposia on child psychology*, vol. XXV (pp. 103–138). Hillsdale, NJ:
   Erlbaum.
   (1994). The birth and nurturance of concepts by domains: The origins of
   concepts of living things. In L. A. Hirschfeld and S. A. Gelman (eds.),
   Mapping the mind: Domain-specificity in cognition and culture (pp. 234–254).
   New York: Cambridge University Press.
Kister, M. C., and Patterson, C. J. (1980). Children's conceptions of the causes
of illness: Understanding of contagion and use of immanent justice. *Child
Development*, 51, 839–846.
Lakoff, G. (1986). *Women, fire and dangerous things: What categories reveal about
the mind.* Chicago: University of Chicago Press.
Lau, R. R., and Hartman, K. A. (1983). Common sense representation of
common illnesses. *Health Psychology*, 2, 167–185.
Leventhal, H., Meyer, D., and Nerenz, D. R. (1980). The common sense
representation of illness danger. In S. Rachman (ed.), *Contributions to medical
psychology*, vol. II (pp. 7–30). New York: Pergamon.
McMenamy, J. M., and Wiser, M. (1997). *Germs and folk theories: Young children's
understanding of the causes, transmission and treatment of illness.* Paper pres-
ented at the Society for Research in Child Development, Washington, DC.
Markman, E. M. (1990) *Categorization and naming in children.* Cambridge, MA:
MIT Press.
Mill, J. S. ([1872]1973). *System of logic*, 8th edn. In J. M. Robson (ed.), *Collected
works of John Stuart Mill*, vols. VII and VIII. Toronto: University of Toronto
Press.

Nagy, M. H. (1951). Children's ideas of the origin of illness. *Health Education Journal*, 9, 6–12.

Perrin, E. C., and Gerrity, P. S. (1981). There's a demon in your belly: Children's understanding of illness. *Pediatrics*, 67, 841–849.

Rey, G. (1983). Concepts and stereotypes. *Cognition*, 15, 237–262.

Reznek, L. (1987). *The nature of disease*. New York: Routledge and Kegan Paul.

Rosch, E. (1975). Cognitive representations of semantic categories. *Journal of Experimental Psychology: General*, 104, 192–233.

Rosen, A. B., and Rozin, P. (1993). Now you see it, now you don't: The preschool child's conception of invisible particles in the context of dissolving. *Developmental Psychology*, 2, 300–311.

Rozin, P. (1990). Development in the food domain. *Developmental Psychology*, 26, 555–562.

Rozin, P., and Fallon, A. E. (1987). A perspective on disgust. *Psychological Review*, 94, 23–41.

Rozin, P., and Nemeroff, C. (1990). The laws of sympathetic magic: A psychological analysis of similarity and contagion. In J. Stigler, G. Herdt, and R. A. Shweder (eds.), *Cultural psychology: Essays on comparative human development* (pp. 205–232). Cambridge, UK: Cambridge University Press.

Rozin, P., Fallon, A., and Augustoni-Ziskind, M. (1985). The child's conception of food: The development of contamination sensitivity to "disgusting" substances. *Developmental Psychology*, 21, 1,075–1,079.

Shipley, E. (1989). Two types of hierarchies: Class inclusion hierarchies and kind hierarchies. *Genetic Epistemologist*, 17, 32–39.

(1993). Categories, hierarchies, and induction. *Psychology of Learning and Motivation*, 30, 265–301.

Siegal, M. (1988). Children's knowledge of contagion and contamination as causes of illness. *Child Development*, 59, 1,353–1,359.

Siegal, M., and Share, D. L., (1990). Contamination sensitivity in young children. *Developmental Psychology*, 26, 455–458.

Siegal, M., Patty, J., and Eiser, C. (1990). A re-examination of children's conceptions of contagion. *Psychology and Health*, 4, 159–165.

Simons, D. J., and Keil, F. C. (1995). An abstract to concrete shift in the development of biological thought: The insides story. *Cognition*, 56, 129–163.

Solomon, G. E., and Cassimatis, N. L. (1999). On facts and conceptual systems: Young children's integration of their understandings of germs and contagion. *Developmental Psychology*, 35, 113–126.

Solomon, G. E., Johnson, S., Zaitchik, D., and Carey, S. (1996). Like father, like son: Young children's understanding of how and why offspring resemble their parents. *Child Development*, 67, 151–171.

Springer, K., and Belk, A. (1994). The role of physical contact and association in early contamination sensitivity. *Developmental Psychology*, 30, 864–868.

Stefan, M. D., and McManus, I. C. (1989). The concept of disease: Its evolution in medical students. *Social Science in Medicine*, 29, 791–792.

Weissman, M. D. (1997). Preschoolers' beliefs about the role of intention in biological inheritance. Paper presented at the meetings of the Society for

Research in Child Development, Washington, DC, March.

Wellman, H. M., and Gelman, S. A. (1992). Cognitive development: Foundational theories of core domains. *Annual Review of Psychology*, 43, 337–375.

6   Children and pain

John E. Taplin, Belinda Goodenough, Joan R. Webb,
and Laura Vogl

The presence of pain is the single most common reason why people seek
help from doctors and other health professionals. Billions of dollars are
spent every year on pain-killing drugs and on various other treatments for
the relief of pain. Suffering due to chronic pain dominates the daily lives
of some people, seriously affecting their ability to function normally and
their overall quality of life.

Pain has a biological basis, reflecting the response by the body to a
nociceptive stimulus. This pain-producing event may have an external
origin (e.g., a skin cut or burn), or it may come from inside the body and
be related to a physical illness (e.g., a migraine headache or arthritic
joint). The pain response is potentially vital to the survival of the organism and thus serves an important evolutionary role.

Pain also has cognitive, affective, and behavioral components. The
perception of pain varies as a function of the psychological state of the
individual: it is likely to feel more intense when the person is anxious or
tense or focusing on the injury. People may learn to manage ongoing pain
through the use of various behavioral (e.g., relaxation) and cognitive
(e.g., distraction, positive imagery) coping strategies.

These physiological and psychological factors contributing to the perception of pain are implicated in the influential gate-control theory proposed by Melzack and Wall (1965, 1982). Central to this theory is a
gating mechanism located in the spinal cord that is controlled by ascending neural activity carrying messages from the periphery to the brain and
by descending neural impulses carrying information from the cerebral
cortex and brainstem. Both ascending and descending signals determine
how much the pain gate is opened and therefore how much pain is
experienced.

The investigation of how children interpret pain is important for several reasons. First, the development of their thinking in this respect may
bear a relationship to their understanding of cause-and-effect relationships in the world generally. More specifically, however, children's
understanding of the causality of pain is likely to be tied to their intuitive

131

comprehension of how their bodies work, and this in turn may be a function of their acquisition of a naive theory of biology. Second, it might be that the problem of measuring the amount of pain being experienced by a young child in a clinical context, would be easier to solve if we knew more about how they represented this experience. Third, how children interpret pain may well play an important role in its possible prevention. As children come to anticipate the pain that results from behaviors that lead to various types of injuries (cuts, burns, broken bones, etc.), this may contribute to a reduction in the number of health-threatening accidents that are a major concern with preschool and elementary schoolchildren especially. Fourth, given that some pain is unavoidable, children may be able to learn to use various cognitive and behavioral methods to minimize its debilitating effects, including the self-administration of analgesic medication.

Children's understanding of the causality of pain

Children's explanations for pain

Early research into children's concepts of pain typically assumed a Piagetian theoretical framework, and employed a quite similar approach to that used to study the development of their concepts of health and illness generally (e.g., Bibace and Walsh, 1979; Gaffney and Dunne, 1986). Thus, it was proposed that children's understanding of pain corresponds closely to their understanding of other related phenomena and is a manifestation of the particular stage to which they have progressed in the development of their thinking overall.

One contentious notion put forward here was that children at the preoperational stage attribute the states of pain and illness to some form of wrongdoing by the individual. That is, it was suggested that young children explain sickness and pain in immanent justice terms (Bibace and Walsh, 1981; Gaffney and Dunne, 1987), and that the negative feelings commonly associated with being unwell reflect their sense of guilt for not having done the right thing. More recent research into young children's causal understanding of illness has shown little or no evidence for this belief in immanent justice. Instead, it has been found that children typically attribute illness to the effects of germ transmission through contagion or contamination (Siegal, 1988; Kalish, 1996).

With respect to pain, empirical support for an immanent justice account by young children is also limited (e.g., Ross and Ross, 1984). The strongest indication comes from a study by Gaffney and Dunne (1987) who, on the basis of children's answers to open-ended questions about pain, suggested that children in the preoperational stage (aged 5 to 7 years) attribute it to a failure to comply with rules, as a result of misbehavior or carelessness. Older children, on the other hand, tended to adopt "more objective" physical explanations. A direct test of this hypothesis, that pain is believed by young children to be a consequence of inappropriate or disobedient behavior, has not been previously reported, however.

To investigate this question, therefore, we presented sixteen first-grade children (mean age 6 years 4 months) and sixteen fourth-grade children (mean age 9 years 8 months) with a series of sixteen brief scenarios. In each scenario, a hypothetical character suffered pain in a particular part of their body. For half of the scenarios, the pain was felt on the inside of the body, and for the other half on the outside of the body. The children were then asked to choose which of two alternative actions would have been the more likely cause of this pain.

Half of the test items contrasted a feasible explanation for pain with an immanent justice explanation; an example used was catching a cold versus telling lies to a friend, as explanations for pain due to a sore throat. The other half of the test items contrasted a plausible physical cause with one which was implausible; an example here was going for a walk in tight-fitting shoes versus swimming in a heated pool, as explanations for pain due to blistered feet.

Analysis of the number of items for which the participants selected the more plausible explanation in preference to the immanent justice or implausible alternative showed a significant effect of age, with the older children making more correct choices than the younger ones. However, the performance of the latter was still very significantly above the level that would be expected if participants were only guessing. Importantly, the rejection of the immanent justice alternative was even greater than was the rejection of the explanation considered to be physically implausible. These results suggest that even young children do not favor the view that pain experienced by a person is a consequence of that person doing something that is morally wrong.

Of course, the fact that young children did not choose the immanent justice explanation in favour of another simultaneously presented alternative does not mean that they would reject it altogether if it was presented by itself. To examine this possibility, a further experiment was conducted (Webb, 1997) in which the participants were thirty-two kindergarten children (mean age 5 years 7 months) and thirty-two fourth-grade children (mean age 9 years 9 months). Again, sixteen scenarios were presented in which a hypothetical character suffered pain in a certain part of their body; in half the cases the pain was internal and in the other half it was externally located. Each participant was then given a list of possible

134   *J. E. Taplin, B. Goodenough, J. R. Webb, L. Vogl*

reasons for the pain that was felt, and for each one they were asked to indicate "Yes" or "No" whether it could be the correct explanation for the pain; they were also asked to indicate whether they were sure or unsure about their answer on each occasion. For each scenario, the set of explanations comprised one that described the underlying biological mechanism, one that referred to a plausible physical/behavioral cause, one that involved an immanent justice explanation, and one that was intended to be plainly irrelevant and incorrect; the order in which these alternatives were presented was randomised across scenarios. Two of the scenarios presented and the accompanying explanations (with labels added showing the type of explanation) are shown below:

Cinead was playing football when she got a cramp in her leg. This made her leg hurt. Did Cinead feel a pain because:

> Her muscles weren't getting enough energy to keep working and they were letting her brain know this. (biological)
> She didn't warm up for the game and the muscles in her leg couldn't work properly. (physical/behavioral)
> She swore at the umpire. (immanent justice)
> She was wearing black shorts instead of blue shorts. (irrelevant)

Matthew was using a knife to get the vegetables ready for dinner when he cut his finger. Did Matthew feel a pain because:

> His brain was telling him that he had damaged the skin and nerves in his finger. (biological)
> The knife had slipped and cut his finger instead of the vegetables. (physical/behavioral)
> He had been complaining that he had to help with the dinner. (immanent justice)
> He had used the red knife instead of the blue knife. (irrelevant)

The results showed that both 5–6- and 9–10-year-old children accepted the biological and physical/behavioral explanations at levels well above chance. Older children were more inclined to accept the biological explanation than younger children, but there was no significant age effect with respect to the physical/behavioral explanation. The older children were also more likely than the younger ones to reject the immanent justice and the irrelevant answers; in fact, the younger ones did not consistently say "No" to these two spurious explanations.

Taken together, these findings provide a further indication that pain is less likely to be regarded as a form of punishment for wrongdoing than as due to a biological or physical/ behavioral cause, even by younger children. Whether the lack of outright rejection by the 5–6-year-olds of the immanent justice option was due to any doubts they had about the invalidity of this type of explanation or was simply a reflection of a general tendency towards affirmative responding commonly observed in yes–no testing situations such as this, is a question to be resolved by further research.

Understanding pain as a specific property of certain biological kinds

Since the mid-1980s, a considerable quantity of research has suggested that it is not only older children who have a basic understanding of biological kinds and biological processes. Even 5-year-olds have been shown to distinguish between living and non-living kinds in terms of the way they move (e.g., R. Gelman, 1990; R. Gelman et al., 1995; S. Gelman and Gottfried, 1996), their capacity for growth (Rosengren et al., 1991; Hickling and S. Gelman, 1995), their ability to regenerate and repair damaged parts (Backscheider et al., 1993), the resemblance between parents and their offspring due to inheritance (e.g., Springer and Keil, 1991; Springer, 1996), and so on.

In light of such findings, it has been proposed that by this age children have formed a naive theory of biology (Hatano and Inagaki, 1994; Keil, 1989, 1992). That is, by the time that they are in elementary school, young children have come to differentiate biological kinds from other kinds and to invoke causal explanations which apply specifically to this biological domain (Wellman and S. Gelman, 1992, 1997). According to this domain-specific account, conceptual development need not proceed in an identical fashion in every knowledge domain: rather the developmental process is assumed to be sensitive to the special features of the concepts being acquired and the causal mechanisms that are inferred to pertain to them.

In an important series of papers, Inagaki and Hatano (e.g., 1993, chapter 2 in this volume; Hatano and Inagaki, 1996) have suggested that young Japanese children engage in vitalistic causal reasoning with respect to the processes that occur in healthy living kinds. Recent research by Morris, Taplin, and S. Gelman (under review) has indicated that Australian children also subscribe to vitalistic causal explanations for biological phenomena, although they may not favour the organ-intentional component of this construct as strongly as their Japanese counterparts. The notion of vital force is represented in the Japanese language by the word ki, and the aim of traditional medicine in that culture has been "to enhance the organism's healthy vital force ... to overcome unhealthy forces" (Hatano and Inagaki, 1987, p. 123). A similar belief still seems to be found in elderly Korean women who suffer an abdominal syndrome

Hwabyung that is said to result from an interference in the harmony of the vital force (Pang, 1990).

Given the fact that pain too has a biological basis, the question must be asked therefore when it is that children associate the capacity to suffer pain with this domain. Following Hatano and Inagaki (1994), this recognition might be expected to have been formed by about 5 years of age. Indeed, one of the items used by Inagaki and Hatano (1993) in their demonstration of vitalistic reasoning in children of this age was "Why do we feel pain when we fall down and hurt our leg?" Likewise, in the experiment on children's evaluations of different explanations for pain that was described in the previous section of this chapter, we found that the biological account was strongly affirmed even by the 5–6-year-olds.

It is important to note that not everyone accepts that an autonomous theory of biology has been formed so soon in the development of the child. Carey (1985, 1995), in particular, has argued that a clearly differentiated theory of biology is not acquired until a few years later, and some support for this position has been put forward by Solomon *et al.* (1996) and Johnson and Solomon (1997) with respect to children's understanding of biological inheritance and genetic resemblance, for example. Moreover, with respect to the causes of illness, Solomon and Cassimatis (1995) have argued that young children fail to differentiate germs from other illness-inducing substances like poisons. Similarly, Finney and Taplin (1997) have shown that, although 5–6-year-olds know that germs can cause illness in humans and cannot cause illness in things that are non-living, they do not extend the illness-producing effect of germs to the entire domain of living kinds. Further, Finney and Taplin (1997) found that, unlike 9–10-year-olds, 5–6-year-olds tend to attribute to germs the properties of non-living kinds rather than those of living kinds.

With respect to pain, Carey (1985, 1995) would argue that, while 5-year-olds may have specific knowledge of this experience in humans, to be regarded as a distinctly biological property requires that it also be attributed to other relevant living kinds. Moreover, while they may connect pain with various behavioral antecedents, the criteria for a theory of biology have not been met until their causal understanding also reflects the involvement of some specifically biological mechanism. In the experiment on children's explanations for pain described earlier, we were able to show that 5–6-year-olds not only accept physical/behavioral explanations for human pain but also attribute pain to processes that involve the registration by the nervous system of some form of bodily damage. In other words, by this age children do indeed seem to be interpreting the occurrence of pain in biological terms. Still the question of children's beliefs about the ontology of pain has to be answered.

To find out whether children believe that pain is a phenomenon shared

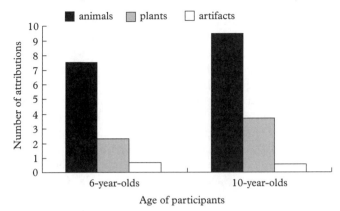

Figure 6.1   Mean number of instances of each kind (total = ten) which children in each age group said would feel pain

by animals, plants, and artifacts, or is restricted to some subset of these kinds, sixteen first-grade children and sixteen fourth-grade children were presented with a series of ten scenarios describing some action that occurred to each kind; ten different examples of animals, plants, and artifacts were referred to in these scenarios. The scenario was then followed by a yes/no question inquiring whether pain would be felt as a consequence of this action. For example, the action mentioned in one scenario was that of being cut, and the question then was whether the exemplar indicated (a dog, or a flower, or paper) would feel any pain as a result of this action.

As can be seen in figure 6.1, children clearly affirmed that animals would feel pain and rejected the possibility that this would be an outcome for artifacts. Their judgments with respect to plants were less clear-cut than for artifacts, but the mean number of affirmative responses was still significantly below chance. There was no effect of age, indicating that this pattern held for both the 6 and 10-year-olds who participated in this study.

Thus, we may draw the conclusion that, by 5–6 years of age, children have formed a causal understanding of pain as a distinctly biological phenomenon that occurs in both humans and animals, but not plants. Accordingly, for children of this age, pain would appear to be a property that coheres with some of the other biological properties identified within an intuitive theoretical account that is specific to this domain.

Understanding different types of pain

Not all pain is the same. Some pains are highly localized and of short duration, while others are more diffusely located and long lasting. Some pains affect the inside of the body, while others are felt on the outside surface. And the part of the body involved may be the head, or the trunk, or one of the limbs. It would be simplistic to assume that a single explanation could account for all these different types of pain.

Beales (1982) suggested that much of children's understanding of pain must be learned through experience and that any variation in when specific types of pain are understood is likely to reflect the opportunity to acquire this knowledge. Further contributing to this variability may be a factor related to the salience or ease of identification of the cause involved. For example, children may quickly come to associate visible tissue damage to the outer surface of the body with pain. On the other hand, understanding the cause of pain which originates from somewhere inside the body may be more difficult to achieve. According to the Piagetian account, pain originating internally may not be well comprehended until the formal-operational period, regardless of experience (cf. Bibace and Walsh, 1979). In support of this view, Beales et al. (1980) found that, prior to the age of 11 years, children suffering from chronic arthritis show little awareness or concern about internal pathology and instead seem to be preoccupied with the soreness of the skin in the vicinity of the affected joint. After 11 years of age, however, they display evidence of understanding the significance of these internal processes for pain.

Nevertheless, S. Gelman and Wellman (1991) have shown that even preschool children appreciate the importance of the insides of a living kind for its identity and functioning. Children of this age know that the members of a given category of living things are likely to have the same internal parts and substances as each other; for example, all dogs have "the same kinds of stuff inside" (S. Gelman and O'Reilly, 1988). In a similar vein, R. Gelman (1990) proposed that at a very early age children believe that animate beings move according to an "innards" principle. Findings such as these suggest that young children's thinking is not quite as dependent on external sources of information as Piaget surmised (cf. Simons and Keil, 1995).

In this regard, it is worth noting that in the first experiment described earlier in this chapter on children's preferred choice of explanation for pain, the internal versus external locus of the pain was found to interact with the age of the participant. Specifically, younger children made more correct responses when the pain had an external source, whereas there was little difference in the accuracy of identification of the cause of internal and external pains by children in the older age group.

A study by Harbeck and Peterson (1992) examined the development in children's understanding of three different types of pain: (1) due to injury (a skinned knee); (2) due to a medical intervention (an injection); (3) due to an illness (a headache). Subjects were asked a series of open-ended questions inviting them to describe each pain, to say why it hurt, and to state what good the pain might serve. Their answers to these questions were coded into Piagetian stages. The results were interpreted as indicating an overall developmental progression "from the child being unable to verbalize a reason why pain hurts, to verbalizing a general, usually external cause of the pain, to finally including physiological or psychological causes" (Harbeck and Peterson, 1992, p. 147). However, the level of understanding differed according to the type of pain: headache pain was the least well understood, pain due to a skinned knee was somewhat better, and needle pain was understood best of all.

We conducted a further experiment in order to determine how well children could predict the particular part of the body where pain would be felt, given information about the action which preceded that pain. The same sixteen first-grade and sixteen fourth-grade children who took part in the previous experiment were presented with twenty-four scenarios in which a hypothetical character suffered pain as a consequence of a given action. The participants were then asked to choose which of two alternative parts of the body was the more likely place where the pain would have been felt. Half of the scenarios were prejudged by a group of adults as producing pain internally (e.g., drinking very hot coffee and burning the inside of the mouth) and half as producing pain externally (e.g., burning one's back by going out in the hot sun without wearing a shirt). The anatomical region affected was either the head, the trunk, the upper limbs, or the lower limbs.

The results showed that pains on the outside of the body were identified correctly more often than those on the inside. However, children's predictions about internal pains were still well above the level that would be expected if they were only guessing. The interaction between age and the internal/external locus of the pain was not significant in this study. With respect to anatomical location, older children made more correct choices than younger children, although the latter nonetheless responded at a level significantly better than chance. In short, it was clear that even young children are sensitive to the differences between pains of different types.

The assessment and management of pain in children

Measuring children's own pain

In the absence of more objective measures, the measurement of pain in children is likely to depend largely on self-report (P. J. McGrath et al.,

1995). Hence, an understanding by the child of what pain is, is a prerequisite for its assessment. Knowing how the pain is caused may also contribute to this estimation process: for example, the magnitude of the pain experienced may be inferred perhaps from the salience of the cause (e.g., big needles hurt more than little needles). However, many other special characteristics of children impact as well upon the task of measuring their pain, especially by self-report methods. Given the variety of ways in which pain can be experienced and understood, the measurement of pain in clinical settings almost inevitably involves a considerable simplification, reducing a complex multidimensional construct to a single value. The degree to which such values provide a valid metric of a child's actual pain experience is the subject of ongoing research and, as we shall show from our own investigations and those of others, likely to depend on a number of factors. The most crucial of these appear to be connected either directly or indirectly with the child's level of cognitive development, as well as other situational and motivational variables associated with the measurement context.

Age-related differences in pain response have been frequently documented, especially in the case of acute pains (e.g., due to injections) for which younger children typically give higher intensity ratings than older children (Fowler-Kerry and Lander, 1987; Goodenough *et al.*, 1998; Goodenough *et al.*, 1997b). Although this might be attributed to poorly understood maturational factors affecting nociceptive sensitivity (e.g., Anand and Craig, 1996; Arts *et al.*, 1994; Goodenough *et al.*, 1997b), it is more likely that these age-related effects reflect developmental changes in the reporting of pain rather than in the underlying physiology *per se*. Several reasons can be given to support this view. First, the increase in cumulative experience of pain with age may well bring about some amendments to the ratings produced in response to the same painful stimulus (e.g., routine immunization injection) due to changes in the subjective reference points used to locate pain values along the self-report scale. Second, the development of pain coping strategies (see later) may partly account for why younger children tend to assign higher intensity scores than older children to the same set of pain descriptors (Abu-Saad *et al.*, 1990). Finally, cognitive maturation is likely to have an impact also, particularly in young children, because of the difficulties that they may encounter with rating scales in general, and specifically with the task of fractionating their experience of pain into degrees and projecting it onto a subjective continuum.

More than one-fifth of the presentations at the Third Symposium on Pediatric Pain held in 1994 were concerned with evaluating some fifty-nine different pain scales developed for children (Banos and Barajas,

1995; for a review of the extensive range of self-report pediatric pain scales, see Champion *et al.*, 1997). Thus far, no single scale has been found to be ideal for all applications or all age groups, even though children as young as 3 years of age do appear capable of reporting on their own pain (e.g., Arandine *et al.*, 1988). The bulk of pain scales for children currently focus on measuring pain intensity, with the sheer variety being a reflection of the inappropriateness of adult scales for pediatric use. The majority of adult self-report scales are derivatives of the visual analogue concept which, in its simplest form, requires the level of pain to be scored as a mark on a 10 cm line between the anchor points of pain and no pain. This method has been shown to be too abstract to yield a meaningful index for many children younger than 7 years of age, even when presented in the form of a toy (Goodenough *et al.*, 1997a), although an analogue scale employing changes in shape and color has shown promise in preliminary validation studies with 5–17-year-olds (P. A. McGrath *et al.*, 1996).

One age-appropriate alternative to the visual analogue scale seems to be the Poker Chip Tool (Hester, 1979; Hester *et al.*, 1990). Here, children rate their pain by choosing one to four poker chips, each representing "a piece of hurt," where four chips equates with the most hurt possible. There is reasonable consensus that this tool is practical for quite young children, and it was been recommended for use with 4–6-year-olds by the 1992 Task Force on Acute Pain set up by the International Association for the Study of Pain.

The largest amount of research has been devoted to developing self-report measures for children that are based on depictions of the facial reaction to pain. Even though more work is required on the ability of children of different ages to discriminate degrees of pain intensity through facial expressions, face scales appear to have particular advantages with young children because they are conceptually appealing and have minimal reliance on language. A child is asked to select the face from the series which shows how much pain (or distress due to pain) the child is feeling (see figure 6.2). The scaling properties of the majority of facial expression scales have not yet been well documented, but they are generally regarded as providing good measures of overall pain intensity. However, the contribution of the affective component to this measure remains contentious. Debate has focused on whether the scale should be anchored by a smiling "no pain" face at one end and an "extreme pain" face showing tears at the other end. In a review of ten published face scales (Champion *et al.*, 1997), only two did not appear to confound pain intensity with the mood dimension (see also Champion *et al.*, 1998). This confound could be important as it should not be assumed that the state of being pain-free is

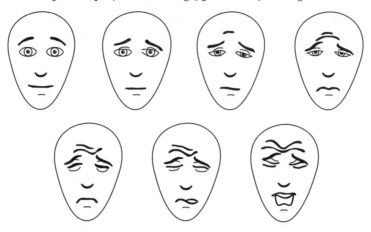

Figure 6.2   Faces Pain Scale (Bieri *et al.*, 1990)

the same as feeling happy, and children who do not cry with intense pain (especially older boys) may also be reluctant to select a face which shows tears.

The cognitive skills usually thought to be the most important determinants of whether young children can meaningfully use scales such as these to represent their pain are those involved in classification and seriation. That is, young children must be able to relate their present pain to other pains (including pains having very different qualities) that they have experienced in the past and to be able to arrange these painful experiences in order of their magnitude such that the present pain can be located at some point on this ordinal scale. To the extent that the pain scale is assumed to have interval or ratio properties as well, additional cognitive skills may perhaps be required.

Interestingly, these scales also appear to tacitly assume that children's ability to make relative judgments about pain is no more constrained than their ability to make similar judgments about non-painful experiences. That is, the number of levels that a child can attend to and differentiate on a pain scale is equivalent to the number that can be attended to and differentiated on a pain-unrelated (non-stressor) scale. This is in spite of other evidence suggesting that there is a narrowing of attention under conditions of stress, heightened anxiety, or arousal (e.g., Easterbrook, 1959). Anecdotally, medical staff report that young children, who were previously able to use a rating scale prior to the painful event, are often unable to report little more than the categorical distinction between pain and no pain during the recovery period following an operation – even when presented with a non-language-based measure such as a face scale.

It might be hypothesised that the self-report of pain should reflect an interaction between the intensity of the pain to be rated and age-related differences in the ability of children to utilize a subjective rating scale. When given a seriation task involving nine faces ranging from happy to distressed (cf. Facial Affective Scale: P. A. McGrath et al., 1985), a sample of 3–5-year-old children were able to discriminate between five different levels of pain-related affect; this ability was not associated with a separate measure of seriation ability, however (Shih and von Baeyer, 1994). This would suggest that seriation ability per se may be less important than the number of options or levels that a child can discriminate on a pain scale. Other evidence seems to indicate that for young children (i.e., 3 and 4 years of age), the self-report scale should comprise a maximum of three or four options, which may account for the success of the Poker Chip Tool for this age group. Thus, while existing facial expression scales appear to have many desirable features for use with children, it is still the case that such scales may present young children with too many choices: seven values in the case of the Faces Pain Scale (Bieri et al., 1990) and nine choices in the case of the Facial Affective Scale (P. A. McGrath, 1990a, 1990b). Presentation of too many choices may partly account for findings that the responses of younger children (especially 3 and 4-year-olds) are more likely than those of older children (7 to 13 years) to gravitate towards the end-points of pain scales, including face scales (Arts et al., 1994; Belter et al., 1988; Champion et al., 1993).

Given the large variety of scales available, there has been surprisingly little investigation into how the values obtained using different measures correspond with each other. Recent research (e.g., Champion et al., 1997) indicates that it cannot be taken for granted either that children understand scales to be measuring pain in the same way, or that different scales are equally susceptible to the influences of the same variable (e.g., pain type) and to the same degree. Indeed, children do not necessarily equate the categorical "no pain" and "extreme pain" end-points across different scales. For example, in a study asking 4–6-year-old children undergoing routine immunization injections to rate the pain of the needle on each of four measures (the Faces Pain Scale, the Poker Chip Tool, a visual analogue toy, and a verbal rating scale), a significant proportion of children who chose the "no pain" face on the Faces Pain Scale, failed to choose the corresponding "no pain" rating on the Poker Chip Tool and the verbal rating scale (Goodenough et al., 1997a).

Children's representation of their pain has been suggested to show a developmental trend from a unidimensional index of global severity towards an appreciation of its complex multidimensional nature that incorporates inter alia sensory and emotional components (Craig et al.,

1988). However, it is not known at what age children can meaningfully distinguish between these different components and report them independently. While there is no accepted definition of "pain affect" (this term has been used to imply and encompass general distress, mood, anxiety, unpleasantness, even boredom), recent data suggest that children may not be able to separately report on intensity and affect until at least 8 or 9 years of age: Thomas *et al.* (1997) asked children aged 3 to 15 years to report independently on the intensity and the unpleasantness of needle pain during venipuncture. The results showed that while intensity and unpleasantness ratings were highly correlated across the sample ($r = 0.78$), older children tended to give unpleasantness ratings that were higher than their intensity scores while younger children did not show this pattern; the divergence occurred from approximately 8 years of age. The issue has important clinical implications (Goodenough *et al.*, 1999) as it has been demonstrated, at least for adults, that the efficacy of various pain-relieving interventions is contingent on whether they have antinociceptive effects and/or alter the affective dimension of pain (see more on pain management later in this chapter).

In line with ratings of other internal states such as fear (Achenbach *et al.*, 1987), the correspondence between child self-report and parental estimates are generally low for pain, especially in the post-operative context (e.g., Beyer *et al.*, 1990). Even so, parents tend to provide estimates closer to the child's than do non-parents such as nurses (e.g., Manne *et al.*, 1992). Moreover, the relationship between ratings based on behavioral observations and on self-reports seems likely to depend on the type of pain involved. For children receiving routine immunization injections (Goodenough *et al.*, 1997a), observer ratings of verbal reactions (including "ouch") were not meaningfully related to self-ratings of pain. This result contrasted sharply with data from the post-operative pain context where verbal reactions correlated well with self-report (Champion *et al.*, 1991).

Factors affecting the pain reported by children

The correlation between self-reports of needle pain and behavioral observations related to that pain has been shown to decrease significantly with the increasing age of the child, at least in the situation where those observations are made by a person who does not know the child personally (Goodenough *et al.*, 1998). Younger children tend to give more overt behavioral responses to pain, and are less likely to engage in distraction behaviors such as looking away when receiving a needle (Goodenough *et al.*, 1997b, 1998). This finding may be contingent on the pain experienced (in this case, needle pain). To date, no parallel age-related effects have been reported for other types of pain, and there is no available data on potential interactions between age and pain type with respect to the correlation between self-report and observational ratings.

It is widely acknowledged that a child may deny pain if there is a fear of possible consequences, say, if the reporting of pain will lead to their having an injection (Lansdown, 1996). Alternatively, some children may feign or exaggerate pain (e.g., report a tummy ache to avoid school), or behave in ways that might favourably impress peers (e.g., ignore pain during sport or a playground fight). A child's pain rating may also be a vehicle for communication about non-pain issues, such as conveying dislike for a particular nurse when asked about their pain. Notwithstanding the influence of these variables, there are currently no methods for obtaining "true" estimates of a child's pain that allow for their impact.

With respect to situational factors, Johnson and Spence (1994) showed that a hospital environment can lead children with chronic pain to recall more pain-related words than a non-hospital context. Another relevant contextual factor is parental presence (Ross and Ross, 1988). While some clinicians apparently feel uncomfortable with parents present (e.g., Glasper, 1991), children prefer to have a parent present during medical procedures even though they tend to express greater distress in these circumstances. This latter paradox has been replicated many times and suggests that children feel more able to express distress with parents present, perhaps expecting comfort and protection. It remains to be determined whether the expression of more distress when a parent is present is reliably matched with higher self-report of pain, however.

Formally asking for a pain rating is an odd request to make, especially for children younger than school age. At least in western society, children learn about health and associated internal states in a predominantly binary categorical way (e.g., you are or are not hungry). Children are generally not taught or required to provide graded estimates of internal states like fatigue or hunger. Moreover, questions from adults are not usually neutral in their implications (Wilkinson, 1988), but often convey a message intended to lead the child to behave in a certain way (e.g., "Are you tired?" can mean "It's time to go to bed"). The potential importance of these social conventions and conversational implicatures when interviewing young children has been noted by Siegal (1991). Thus, being asked about pain, and to grade that pain, not only may be a foreign experience for a child with respect to the appraisal of an internal state, but also may be interpreted as a "loaded" question – particularly if it is perceived that acknowledgement of pain may result in, for example, confinement to bed or some medical procedure being performed.

Research is still in its infancy with respect to cultural differences in the response to pain, even though medical staff are replete with anecdotes on differences between children from various ethnic and socioeconomic backgrounds. The available literature focuses on the expression of pain-related behaviors and culture-specific pain descriptors (e.g., Abu-Saad, 1984; Abu-Saad *et al.*, 1990) rather than on potential differences in self-report. With regard to the latter, there is a respect for cultural variables with the development of different versions of existing scales using ethnic-specific language and pictures (e.g., Shapiro, 1997; Villareul and Deynes, 1991) and studies comparing the reliability of standard pain assessment measures across different ethnic groups (e.g., Adams, 1990), with calls for pain assessment to be "culturally sensitive" (Banoub-Baddour and Laryea, 1991; Berstein and Pachter, 1993).

Of similar importance are issues related to gender. While girls are more susceptible to some pain-related disorders than males (e.g., fibromyalgia: Malleson *et al.*, 1992), gender effects on the self-report of pain are far from robust. Some published studies have failed to find gender effects (e.g., Jay *et al.*, 1995; Zeltzer and LeBaron, 1982; LeBaron and Zeltzer, 1984; Arts *et al.*, 1994). Others, usually in the context of experimentally induced pain, report that boys give significantly lower ratings of pain or pain-related distress than girls (Katz *et al.*, 1980; LeBaron *et al.*, 1989), while a few report that gender differences, at least with respect to overt behavioral distress, change with age (Izard *et al.*, 1987). Abu-Saad *et al.* (1990) found that, when children 7 to 17 years of age were asked to select words from the McGill Pain Questionnaire to describe their pain, the girls tended to choose more words than the boys – a finding consistent with other research suggesting greater verbal fluency and emotional expressiveness in girls under conditions where boys may be encouraged to "grin and bear it" (P. A. McGrath, 1993).

Yet another factor that may be related to the amount of pain indicated by children is birth-order. There is evidence to suggest that firstborn children tend to report higher pain sensitivity than non-firstborn children (Goodenough *et al.*, 1997c; Johnston *et al.*, 1970; Schachter, 1959; Vernon, 1974). It is possible that these birth-order effects are related to temperamental differences between firstborn and later-born children, and that these in turn are associated with a preparedness to report pain.

Children's beliefs about whether pain is controllable

A fundamental question to ask of children with respect to pain is whether they believe that it can be modified or controlled in any way. Related to this, Inagaki and Hatano (1993) investigated young children's beliefs about the modifiability of various bodily characteristics. Their findings showed that 4–5-year-olds are aware that there are some characteristics that can be changed and some that cannot. For example, the participants in their experiment distinguished physically changeable attributes like weight and running speed from physically invariant features like eye color and gender. Moreover, children differentiated between physical and mental characteristics, in that the latter were judged to be generally more modifiable than the former. Extrapolating from this, it seems possible that these young children might also be prepared to accept that the amount of pain experienced by a person can be reduced to some extent at least.

We have conducted a study addressed to this question (Webb, 1997). The participants were the same thirty-two kindergarten and thirty-two fourth-grade children who were previously tested for their acceptance or rejection of different reasons for the occurrence of pain in sixteen different scenarios (see earlier in this chapter). Following their judgments about these explanations, the children were asked to indicate "Yes" or "No" whether anything could have been done so that the pain would not hurt as much; if they responded "Yes", they were then asked to say what they thought could be done. As figure 6.3 illustrates, both 5–6-year-olds and 9–10-year-olds believed that pain can be controlled; there was no difference due to age in this respect. External pains affecting the limbs were thought to be particularly manageable. The strategies mentioned for doing so included commonplace first-aid measures such as applying a cream or cold water to sunburnt skin, and putting a bandaid on a scratch or blister. It is doubtful whether the children in this study fully understood the causal mechanisms through which these actions might reduce the pain experienced, and more research is needed to follow up these findings. However, the significant point for now is that they did not regard the pain as immutable.

Beliefs about the meaning of a painful experience and about one's ability to cope are almost certainly related to how well a person adjusts to a pain stressor. In adults, pain-specific self-efficacy has been demonstrated to lead to a higher level of pain tolerance (e.g., Bandura et al., 1987; Dolce et al., 1986; Jensen and Karoly, 1991), lower anxiety (Martin et al., 1993), and more adaptive pain coping behavior (Schermellehengel et al., 1997). However, the role of pain self-efficacy in children has received somewhat less empirical attention, although the relationship between a child's beliefs about a pain stressor and their ability to cope with it has been accepted in theory (Peterson, 1989; Siegel and Smith, 1989, 1991; Rudolph et al., 1995). One study by Bennett-Branson and Craig (1993) on children's coping with post-operative pain found

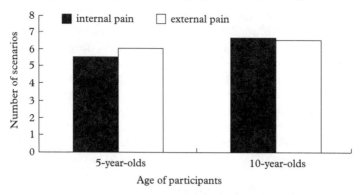

Figure 6.3   Mean number of scenarios (total = eight) for which children in each age group believed that the pain would be modifiable

self-efficacy to be a key determinant of distress ratings: the greater the self-efficacy, the lower the perceived intensity of the pain. Another study by Piira *et al.* (1998) using the cold-pressor test procedure with forty children aged from 7 to 14 years found not only that cold-pressor pain self-efficacy was correlated with self-efficacy for other types of pain (headache, stomach ache, grazed knee), but also that, when the effects of other variables like age, trait anxiety, and coping style were statistically controlled, cold-pressor pain self-efficacy was predictive of greater pain tolerance and lower rated pain intensity. No data are available on the significance of self-efficacy beliefs in children under 7 years of age at this stage.

Not surprisingly, a crucial factor affecting children's beliefs about whether they can cope with an anticipated painful episode is how well they have managed in the past. It is not the fact of having a previous experience *per se* that is important, but whether that experience was positive or negative (e.g., Dahlquist *et al.*, 1986). A particularly bad experience, for example, is one in which the child has had to be restrained during a medical procedure (Fanurik *et al.*, 1997). Negative experiences may lead a child to expect not to be able to cope with similar painful episodes in the future. Consistent with this, in a study of anticipated pain during voluntary ear-piercing, von Baeyer *et al.* (1997) found that, compared with "realistic" children, those who underestimated the pain that they would feel when their first ear was pierced, predicted significantly more pain prior to the piercing of the second ear.

Children's coping with pain

Individuals generally show considerable overlap in the types of pains experienced during childhood. There is, however, a class of extraordinary pains, typically associated with disease conditions (e.g., cancer, hemophilia, juvenile arthritis) and/or medical procedures (e.g., surgery, blood-sampling, lumbar puncture, burn debridement) which can be referred to as "special pain experiences" (Carter, 1994). While not all children will experience these "special pains," it is in this context that the bulk of research on coping styles and coping strategies has been conducted, usually in the form of clinical intervention trials; in large part, this is because of the ethical concerns associated with subjecting children to experimentally induced pain (P. A. McGrath, 1993). The topic of coping is a relatively new area of research in pediatric pain. To date, most studies have focused on children aged 7 years and older, especially in the context of managing brief acute pains related to medical procedures or recurrent complaints such as abdominal pain and headache (e.g., Engel and Rapoff, 1990).

Children are known to vary in the way that they attempt to cope with a particular type of pain and to prepare themselves for an upcoming painful event (Rudolph et al., 1995). Classification systems applicable to children have been developed both with respect to coping style, or trait-like dispositions for dealing with pain (e.g., Brown et al., 1986; Curry and Russ, 1985), as well as specific coping strategies (e.g., Branson and Craig, 1988; Ross and Ross, 1988; Tesler et al., 1981).

Regarding coping style, the most frequently investigated dichotomy is the repression-sensitization continuum, or behaviors concerned with information seeking versus information avoiding (e.g., Peterson and Toler, 1986; Smith et al., 1989). Research has shown that children with an "information seeking" disposition (i.e., children who are actively inclined to ask questions and to want to find out more about a painful procedure or stressor) tend to cope more successfully with these procedures than do "information avoiders" (Burstein and Meichenbam, 1979; Knight et al., 1979), although one study has found that the latter tend to protest less during minor surgery (Field et al., 1988). While positive effects have been generally observed when children are provided with information about a procedure (e.g., Månsson et al., 1993; Wolfer and Visintainer, 1979; Harrison, 1991; Huber and Gramer, 1991), the data are equivocal on whether providing information to an "avoider" has a detrimental pain coping outcome (e.g., Fanurik et al., 1993; Smith et al., 1989).

With respect to specific coping strategies, children need not be passive in their response to pain but may take active steps to reduce their suffering (Branson et al., 1990). As an adjunct to the strict pharmacological control of pain during medical procedures, children may spontaneously employ, or can be taught to use, a variety of cognitive and behavioral strategies (Anderson et al., 1993). These include cognitive methods such as thought stopping and listening to music or watching videos as forms of distraction (e.g., Zeltzer et al., 1989; Fowler-Kerry and Lander, 1987; Kachoyeanos and Friedhoff, 1993; Whitaker and Brereton, 1997) and behavioral strategies such as relaxation and controlled breathing (e.g., Blount et al., 1992; Manne et al., 1992; McDonnell and Bowden, 1989), plus a variety of combined cognitive-behavioral interventions (e.g., Jay et al., 1995).

Ample evidence attests to the prevalence and usefulness of these different pain coping strategies for adults, but there have been few data comparing the relative efficacy of such techniques, especially for children of different ages. As a start in this direction, we conducted a study with fifty children aged 6 to 16 years who were assigned to one of three skills training conditions (Vogl, 1996). The conditions differed as to the type of pain coping skills taught, namely, cognitive (e.g., thought stopping, positive imagery, and distraction), behavioral (e.g., progressive muscle relaxation and breathing), and a combined cognitive-behavioral condition. Children were exposed to cold-pressor pain three times – prior to being taught the coping strategy (baseline), immediately after being taught the coping strategy, and two weeks after the training session. The results showed that, irrespective of the age of the child, the three skills training conditions had significant positive effects on both pain tolerance and the affective response to pain (i.e., state anxiety). The degree of improvement in pain tolerance was greater in older children than in younger children. This improvement was related to the child's ability to recall the specific coping skills taught, and this too varied with age.

These findings seem to suggest that all three approaches to coping are equally beneficial. However, it remains to be determined whether some strategies will prove to be more helpful for children of different ages in the context of clinical pain, especially given the suggestion that children younger than 10 years may elect to use behavioral rather than cognitive strategies (Branson and Craig, 1988). Some of the processes involved in the spontaneous retrieval and use of cognitive coping strategies may be contra-indicated in young children also (Kuttner and LePage, 1989; Patterson and Ware, 1988).

Children's ability to cope with pain does not depend solely on the effectiveness of a specific coping strategy per se, but is influenced also by a wide range of situational, social, and emotional variables as well as the child's age, gender, and other characteristics (e.g., P. A. McGrath and Brigham, 1992; P. A. McGrath, 1993). Attempts to model these factors are necessarily complex, with the more useful accounts depicting how interactions between variables can lead to either adaptive or maladaptive coping outcomes (Rudolph et al., 1995).

Conclusion

It is disturbing to note that clinical researchers (e.g., Beyer *et al.*, 1983; Eland and Anderson, 1977; Gonzalez *et al.*, 1993; Mather and Mackie, 1983; Schechter *et al.*, 1986; Tesler *et al.*, 1994) have repeatedly drawn attention to the problem of under-treatment of pain in children. How could this be? Surely no one would wish to see children suffer needlessly. If in fact children from a relatively young age have acquired a basic understanding of pain as a biological phenomenon and already know a little about how it may be caused, as was argued in the first half of this chapter, then the claims about under-treatment are, if anything, even more disquieting. Further research is clearly needed to resolve this problem.

Two lines of investigation that may hold some of the answers to this dilemma were considered in the second half of this chapter. The first has to do with the attempt to find better ways to assess the pain that young children are suffering. The second concerns the need to help children to cope with their pain more effectively through the use of various medical, cognitive-behavioral, and other strategies. The findings being produced are not only relevant to the pursuit of these clinically important goals. They are likely to advance our fundamental knowledge of the development of children's thinking about pain as well. In this regard, then, the study of pain in children can be seen as a working example of the fruitful interaction that is possible between science and practice within the field of child health psychology.

Acknowledgments: preparation of this chapter was supported by grants from the Australian Research Council and National Health and Medical Research Council awarded to the first two authors.

REFERENCES

Abu-Saad, H. H. (1984). Cultural group indicators of pain in children. *Maternal and Child Nursing Journal*, 13, 187–196.
Abu-Saad, H. H., Kroonen, E., and Halfens, R. (1990). On the development of a multi-dimensional Dutch pain assessment tool for children. *Pain*, 43, 249–256.
Achenbach, T. M., McConaughy, S. H., and Howell, C. T. (1987). Child/adolescent behavioral and emotional problems: Implications of cross-informant correlations for situational specificity. *Psychological Bulletin*, 101, 213–232.
Adams, J. (1990). A methodological study of pain assessment in Anglo and Hispanic children with cancer. In D. C. Tyler and E. J. Krane (eds.), *Advances in pain research and therapy*, vol XV (pp. 43–51). New York: Raven.
Anand, K. J. S., and Craig, K. D. (1996). New perspectives on the definition of

pain. *Pain*, 67, 3–6.

Anderson, C. T. M., Zeltzer, L. K., and Fanurik, D. (1993). Procedural pain. In N. L. Schechter, C. B. Berde, and M.Yaster (eds.), *Pain in infants, children and adolescents* (pp. 435–458). Baltimore, MD: Williams and Wilkins.

Arandine, C. R., Beyer, J. E., and Tompkins, J. M. (1988). Children's pain perception before and after analgesia: A study of instrument construct validity and related issues. *Journal of Pediatric Nursing*, 3, 13–17.

Arts, S. E., Abu-Saad, H. H., Champion, G. D., *et al.* (1994). Age-related response to lignocaine-prilocaine (EMLA) emulsion and effect of music distraction on the pain of intravenous cannulation. *Pediatrics*, 93, 797–801.

Backscheider, A. G., Shatz, M., and Gelman, S. A. (1993). Preschoolers' ability to distinguish living kinds as a function of regrowth. *Child Development*, 64, 1,242–1,257.

Bandura, A., O'Leary, A., Taylor, C. B., Gauthier, J., and Gossard, D. (1987). Perceived self-efficacy and pain control: Opioid and nonopioid mechanisms. *Journal of Personality and Social Psychology*, 53, 663–671.

Banos, J-E., and Barajas, C. (1995). Assessment of pediatric pain: Time for an agreement. *Journal of Pain and Symptom Management*, 10, 181–182.

Banoub-Baddour, S., and Laryea, M. (1991). Children in pain: A culturally sensitive perspective for child care professionals. *Journal of Child and Youth Care*, 6, 19–24.

Beales, J. G. (1982). The assessment and management of pain in children. In P. Koroly, J. J. Steffen, and D. J. O'Grady (eds.), *Child health psychology: Concepts and issues* (pp. 154–179). New York: Pergamon.

Beales, J. G., Keen, J. H., Mellor, V. P., and Holt, P. J. L. (1980). Fantasies about the appearance of affected joints among children with juvenile chronic arthritis. *Annals of the Rheumatic Diseases*, 39, 603.

Belter, R. W., McIntosh, J. A., Finch, A. J. J., and Saylor, C. F. (1988). Preschoolers' ability to differentiate levels of pain: Relative efficacy of three self-report measures. *Journal of Clinical Child Psychology*, 17, 329–335.

Bennett-Branson, S. M., and Craig, K. D. (1993). Postoperative pain in children: Developmental and family influences on spontaneous coping strategies. *Canadian Journal of Behavioural Science*, 20, 402–412.

Berstein, B. A., and Pachter, L. M. (1993). Cultural considerations in children's pain. In N. L. Schechter, C. B. Berde, and M. Yaster (eds.), *Pain in infants, children and adolescents* (pp. 113–122). Baltimore: Williams and Wilkins.

Beyer, J. E. (1984). *The Oucher: A user's manual and technical report*. Evanston, IL: Hospital Play Equipment.

Beyer, J. E., DeGood, D. E., Ashley, L. C., and Russell, G. A. (1983). Patterns of post-operative analgesic use with adults and children following cardiac surgery. *Pain*, 17, 71–81.

Beyer, J. E., McGrath, P. J., and Berde, C. B. (1990). Discordance between self-report and behavioral measures in children aged 3–7 years after surgery. *Journal of Pain and Symptom Management*, 5, 350–356.

Bibace, R., and Walsh, M. E. (1979). Developmental stages in children's conceptions of illness. In G. C. Stone, F. Cohen and N. E. Adler (eds.), *Health psychology: A handbook* (pp. 285–301). San Francisco: Jossey-Bass.

(1981). Children's conceptions of illness. In R. Bibace and M. E. Walsh (eds.), *Children's conceptions of health, illness and bodily functions* (pp. 31–48). San Francisco: Jossey-Bass.

Bieri, D., Reeve, R. A., Champion, G. D., Addicoat, L., and Ziegler, J. B. (1990). The Faces Pain Scale for the self-assessment of the severity of pain experienced by children: Development, initial validation and preliminary investigation for ratio scale properties. *Pain*, 41, 139–150.

Blount, R. L., Bachanas, P. J., Powers, S. W., Cotter, M. C., Franklin, A., Chaplin, W., Mayfield, J., Henderson, M., and Blount, S. D. (1992). Training children to cope and parents to coach them during routine immunisations: Effects on child, parent and staff behaviors. *Behavior Therapy*, 23, 689–705.

Branson, S. M., and Craig, K. D. (1988). Children's spontaneous strategies for coping with pain: A review. *Canadian Journal of Behavioural Science*, 20, 402–412.

Branson, S. M., McGrath, P. J., Craig, K. D., Rubin, S. Z., and Vair, C. (1990). Spontaneous strategies for coping with pain and their origins in adolescents who undergo surgery. In D. C. Tyler and E. J. Krane (eds.), *Advances in pain research and therapy*, vol. XV, (pp. 237–253). New York: Raven.

Brown, J. M., O'Keeffe, J., Sanders, S. H., and Baker, B. (1986). Developmental changes in children's cognition to stressful and painful situations. *Journal of Pediatric Psychology*, 11, 343–357.

Burstein, S., and Meichenbaum, D. (1979). The work of worrying in children undergoing surgery. *Journal of Abnormal Child Psychology*, 7, 121–132.

Carey, S. (1985). *Conceptual change in childhood*. Cambridge, MA: MIT Press.
(1995). On the origin of causal understanding. In D. Sperber, D. Premack, and A. J. Premack (eds.), *Causal cognition* (pp. 268–308). Oxford: Clarendon.

Carter, B. (1994). *Child and infant pain*. San Diego, CA: Chapman and Hall.

Champion, G. D., Cairns, D., Gledhill, S., *et al.* (1991). Relationships between self-assessed post-operative pain and behavior in children. *Journal of Pain and Symptom Management*, 6, 199.

Champion, G. D., Arts, S. E., Abu-Saad, H. H., *et al.* (1993). Age-related responses to brief sharp physiological (needle) pain in children. Seventh World Congress on Pain (pp. 512–513). Seattle, WA: IASP Press.

Champion, G. D., Goodenough, B., von Baeyer, C. L., and Ziegler, J. B. (1997). Facial expression scales for self-report of pain by children: Rationale, validity and utility. Fourth International Symposium on Pediatric Pain, Helsinki, Finland.

Champion, G. D., Goodenough, B., von Baeyer, C. L., and Thomas, W. (1998). Self-report pain measures of pain in children. In P. J. McGrath and G. A. Finley (eds.), *The measurement of pain in infants and children* (pp. 123–160). Seattle, WA: IASP Press.

Craig, K. D., Grunau, R. V. E., and Branson, S. M. (1988). Age-related aspects of pain: Pain in children. In R. Dubner, G. F. Gebhart, and M. R. Bond (eds.), *Proceedings of the Fifth World Congress on Pain* (pp. 317–328). Amsterdam: Elsevier.

Curry, S. L., and Russ, S. W. (1985). Identifying coping strategies in children.

Journal of Clinical Child Psychology, 14, 61–69.

Dahlquist, L. M., Gil, K. M., Armstrong, F. D., DeLawyer, D. D., Greene, P., and Wuori, D. L. (1986). Preparing children for medical examinations: The importance of previous medical experience. In B. G. Melamed, K. A. Matthews, D. K. Routh, B. Stabler, and N. Schneiderman (eds.). *Child health psychology* (pp. 201–211). Hillsdale, NJ: Erlbaum.

Dolce, J. J., Doleys, D. M., Raczynski, J. M., Lossie, J., Poole, L., and Smith, M. (1986). The role of self-efficacy expectancies in the prediction of pain tolerance. *Pain*, 27, 261–272.

Easterbrook, J. A. (1959). The effect of emotion on cue utilisation and the organisation of behavior. *Psychological Review*, 66, 183–201.

Eland, J. M., and Anderson, J. E. (1977). The experience of pain in children. In A. K. Jacox (ed.), *Pain: A sourcebook for nurses and other health professionals* (pp. 453–473). Boston, MA: Little, Brown.

Engel, J. M., and Rapoff, M. A. (1990). Biofeedback-assisted relaxation training for adult and pediatric headache disorders. *Occupational Therapy Journal of Research*, 10, 283–299.

Fanurik, D., Zeltzer, L. K., Roberts, M. C., and Blount, R. L. (1993). The relationship between children's coping styles and psychological interventions for cold pressor pain. *Pain*, 53, 213–222.

Fanurik, D., Koh, J., Schmitz, M., and Brown, R. (1997). Pharmaco-behavioral intervention: Integrating pharmacologic and behavioral techniques for pediatric medical procedures. *Children's Health Care*, 26, 31–46.

Field, T., Alpert, B., Vega-Lahr, N., Goldstein, S., and Perry, S. (1988). Hospitalisation stress in children: Sensitizer and repressor coping styles. *Health Psychology*, 7, 433–445.

Finney, D. A., and Taplin, J. E. (1997). Children's understanding of germs as causes of illness. *Australian Journal of Psychology*, 49 suppl., 60.

Fowler-Kerry, S., and Lander, J. R. (1987). Management of injection pain in children. *Pain*, 30, 169–175.

Gaffney, A., and Dunne, E. A. (1986). Developmental aspects of children's definitions of pain. *Pain*, 29, 105–117.

(1987). Children's understanding of the causality of pain. *Pain*, 29, 91–104.

Gelman, R. (1990). First principles organise attention to and learning about relevant data: Number and the animate–inanimate distinction as examples. *Cognitive Science*, 14, 79–106.

Gelman, R., Durgin, F., and Kaufman, L. (1995). Distinguishing between animates and inanimates: Not by motion alone. In D. Sperber, D. Premack, and A. J. Premack (eds.), *Causal cognition* (pp. 150–184). Oxford: Clarendon.

Gelman, S. A., and Gottfried, G. M. (1996). Children's causal explanations of animate and inanimate motion. *Child Development*, 67, 1,970–1,987.

Gelman, S. A., and O'Reilly, A. W. (1988). Children's inductive inferences within superordinate categories. *Child Development*, 59, 876–887.

Gelman, S. A., and Wellman, H. M. (1991). Insides and essences: Early understandings of the nonobvious. *Cognition*, 38, 213–244.

Glasper, A. (1991). Parents in the anaesthetic room: A blessing or curse. In A. Glasper (ed.), *Child care: Some nursing perspectives* (pp. 238–243). London:

Wolfe.

Gonzalez, J. C., Routh, D. K., and Armstrong, F. D. (1993). Differential medication of child versus adult post-operative patients: The effects of nurses' assumptions. *Children's Health Care*, 22, 45–59.

Goodenough, B., Addicoat, L., Champion, G. D., McInerney, M., Young, B., Juniper, K., and Ziegler, J. B. (1997a). Pain in 4- to 6-year-old children receiving intramuscular injections: A comparison of the Faces Pain Scale with other self-report and behavioral measures. *Clinical Journal of Pain*, 13, 60–73.

Goodenough, B., Kampel, L., Champion, G. D., Nicholas, M. K., Laubreaux, L., Ziegler, J. B., and McInerney, M. (1997b). An investigation of the placebo effect and other factors in the report of pain severity during venipuncture in children. *Pain*, 72, 383–391.

Goodenough, B., Thomas, W., Laubreaux, L., Brouwer, N., and van Dongen, K. (1997c). Influence of family structure variables on ratings of needle pain in children. Eighteenth Scientific Meeting of the Australian Pain Society, Northern Territory.

Goodenough, B., Champion, G. D., Laubreaux, L., Tabah, L., and Kampel, L. (1998). Needle pain severity in children: Does the relationship between self-report and observed behaviour vary as a function of age? *Australian Journal of Psychology*, 50, 1–9.

Goodenough, B., Thomas, W., Champion, G. D., Perrott, D., Taplin, J. E., von Baeyer, C. L., and Ziegler, J. B. (1999). Unravelling age effects and sex differences in needle pain: Ratings of sensory intensity and unpleasantness of venipuncture pain by children and their parents. *Pain*.

Harbeck, C., and Peterson, L. J. (1992). Elephants dancing in my head: A developmental approach to children's concepts of specific pains. *Child Development*, 63, 138–149.

Harrison, A. (1991). Preparing children for venous blood sampling. *Pain*, 45, 299–306.

Hatano, G., and Inagaki, K. (1987). Everyday biology and school biology: How do they interact? *Quarterly Newsletter of the Laboratory of Comparative Human Cognition*, 9, 120–128.

(1994). Young children's naive theory of biology. *Cognition*, 50, 171–188.

(1996). Cognitive and cultural factors in the acquisition of intuitive biology. In D. R. Olson and N. Torrance (eds.), *The handbook of education and human development* (pp. 683–708). Cambridge, MA: Blackwells.

Hester, N. K. (1979). The preoperational child's reaction to immunization. *Nursing Research*, 28, 250–255.

Hester, N. O., Foster, R., and Kristensen, K. (1990). Measurement of pain in children: Generalizability and validity of the Pain Ladder and the Poker Chip Tool. In D. C. Tyler and E. J. Krane (eds.), *Advances in pain research and therapy*, vol. XV, *Pediatric pain* (pp. 79–84). New York: Raven.

Hickling, A. K., and Gelman, S. A. (1995). How does your garden grow? Early conceptualizations of seeds and their place in the plant growth cycle. *Child Development*, 66, 856–876.

Huber, H. P., and Gramer, M. (1991). Influence of age and pre-operative anxiety

156   *J. E. Taplin, B. Goodenough, J. R. Webb, L. Vogl*

on preparing children for surgery. *German Journal of Psychology*, 13, 213–221.

Inagaki, K., and Hatano, G. (1993). Young children's understanding of the mind–body distinction. *Child Development*, 64, 1,534–1,549.

Izard, C. E., Hembree, E. A., and Huebner, R. R. (1987). Infants' emotional expressions to acute pain: Developmental change and stability of individual differences. *Developmental Psychology*, 23, 105–113.

Jay, S., Elliott, C. H., Fitzgibbons, I., Woody, P., and Siegel, S. (1995). A comparative study of cognitive behavior therapy versus general anesthesia for painful medical procedures in children. *Pain*, 62, 3–9.

Jensen, M. P., and Karoly, P. (1991). Control beliefs, coping effort and adjustment to chronic pain. *Journal of Consulting and Clinical Psychology*, 59, 431–438.

Johnson, R., and Spence, S. H. (1994). Pain, affect and cognition in children: 2. Recall bias associated with pain. In G. F. Gebhart, D. L. Hammond and T. S. Jensen (eds.), *Proceedings of the Seventh World Congress on Pain* (pp. 877–884). Seattle, WA: IASP Press.

Johnson, S. C., and Solomon, G. E. A. (1997). Why dogs have puppies and cats have kittens: The role of birth in young children's understanding of biological origins. *Child Development*, 68, 404–419.

Johnston, J. E., Dabbs, J. M. Jr., and Leventhal, H. (1970). Psychosocial factors in the welfare of surgical patients. *Nursing Research*, 19, 18–29.

Kachoyeanos, M. K., and Friedhoff, M. (1993). Cognitive and behavioral strategies to reduce children's pain. *Maternal Care Nursing*, 18, 14–19.

Kalish, C. W. (1996). Preschoolers' understanding of germs as invisible mechanisms. *Cognitive Development*, 11, 83–106.

Katz, E. R., Kellerman, J., and Siegel, S. (1980). Behavioral distress in children with cancer undergoing medical procedures: Developmental considerations. *Journal of Consulting and Clinical Psychology*, 48, 356–365.

Keil, F. C. (1989). *Concepts, kinds, and cognitive development*. Cambridge, MA: MIT Press.

(1992). The origins of an autonomous biology. In M. A. Gunnar and M. Maratos (eds.), *Modularity and constraints in language and cognition, Minnesota symposia on child psychology*, vol. XXV (pp. 103–138). Hillsdale, NJ: Erlbaum.

Knight, R. B., Atkins, A., Eagle, C. J., Evans, N., Finkelstein, J. W., Fukushima, D., Katz, J., and Weiner, H. (1979). Psychological stress, ego defense, and cortisol production in children hospitalized for elective surgery. *Psychosomatic Medicine*, 41, 40–49.

Kuttner, L., and LePage, T. (1989). Face scales for the assessment of pediatric pain: A critical review. *Canadian Journal of Behavioural Science*, 21, 191–209.

Lansdown, R. (1996). *Children in hospital*. Oxford: Oxford University Press.

LeBaron, S., and Zeltzer, L. K. (1984). Assessment of acute pain and anxiety in children and adolescents by self-reports, observer reports, and a behavior checklist. *Journal of Consulting and Clinical Psychology*, 52, 729–738.

LeBaron, S., Zeltzer, L., and Fanurik, D. (1989). An investigation of cold pressor pain in children (part I). *Pain*, 37, 161–171.

McDonnell, L., and Bowden, M. L. (1989). Breathing management: A simple stress and pain reduction strategy for use in a pediatric service. *Issues in Comprehensive Nursing*, 12, 339–344.

McGrath, P. A. (1990a). *Pain in children: Nature, assessment, and treatment.* New York: Guilford.

(1990b). Pain assessment in children: A practical approach. In D. C. Tyler and E. J. Krane (eds.), *Advances in pain research and therapy*, vol. XV, *Pediatric pain* (pp. 5–30). New York: Raven.

(1993). Psychological aspects of pain perception. In N. L. Schechter, C. B. Berde, and M. Yaster (eds.). *Pain in infants, children and adolescents* (pp. 39–63). Baltimore: Williams and Wilkins.

McGrath, P. A., and Brigham, M. C. (1992). The assessment of pain in children and adolescents. In D. C. Turk and R. Melzack (eds.), *Handbook of pain assessment* (pp. 295–314). New York: Guilford.

McGrath, P. J., and Unruh, A. M. (1987). *Pain in children and adolescents.* New York: Elsevier.

McGrath, P. A., de Veber, L. L., and Hearn, M. J. (1985). Multidimensional pain assessment in children. In H. L. Fields, R. Dubner, and F. Cervero (eds.), *Advances in pain research and therapy*, vol. IX. New York: Raven.

McGrath, P. J., Unruh, A. M., and Finley, G. A. (1995). Pain measurement in children. *Pain: Clinical Updates*, 3, 1–4.

McGrath, P. A., Seifert, C. E., Speechley, K. N., Booth, J. C., Stitt, L., and Gibson, M. C. (1996). A new analogue scale for assessing children's pain: An initial validation study. *Pain*, 64, 435–443.

Malleson, P. N., Al-Matar, M., and Petty, R. E. (1992). Idiopathic musculoskeletal pain syndromes in children. *Journal of Rheumatology*, 19, 1786.

Manne, S. L., Jacobsen, P. B., and Redd, W. H. (1992). Assessment of acute pediatric pain: Do child self-report, parent ratings, and nurse ratings measure the same phenomenon? *Pain*, 48, 45–52.

Månsson, E. M., Bjorkhem, G., and Wiebe, T. (1993). The effect of preparation for lumbar puncture on children undergoing chemotherapy. *Oncology Nursing Forum*, 20, 39–45.

Martin, N. J., Holroyd, K. A., and Rokicki, L. A. (1993). The headache self-efficacy scale: Adaptation to recurrent headaches. *Headache*, 33, 244–248.

Mather, L., and Mackie, J. (1983). The incidence of post-operative pain in children. *Pain*, 15, 271–282.

Melzack, R., and Wall, P. D. (1965). Pain mechanisms: A new theory. *Science*, 150, 971–979.

(1982). *The challenge of pain.* Suffolk: Chaucer Press.

Morris, S. C., Taplin, J. E., and Gelman, S. A. (under review). How vital is vitalistic causality to children's biological thinking?

Pang, K. Y. C. (1990). Hwabyung: The construction of a Korean popular illness among Korean elderly immigrant women in the United States. *Culture, Medicine, and Psychiatry*, 14, 495–512.

Patterson, P. L., and Ware, L. L. (1988). Coping skills for children undergoing painful medical procedures. *Issues in Comprehensive Pediatric Nursing*, 11, 113–143.

Peterson, L. J. (1989). Coping by children undergoing stressful medical procedures: Some conceptual, methodological and therapeutic issues. *Journal of Consulting and Clinical Psychology*, 57, 380–387.

Peterson, L. J., and Toler, S. M. (1986). An information seeking disposition in child surgery patients. *Health Psychology*, 5, 343–358.

Piira, T., Taplin, J. E., and Goodenough, B. (1998). Determinants of children's pain tolerance using the cold-pressor test. Nineteenth Scientific Meeting of the Australian Pain Society, Hobart, Tasmania.

Rosengren, K. S., Gelman, S. A., Kalish, C. W., and McCormick, M. (1991). As time goes by: Children's early understanding of growth in animals. *Child Development*, 62, 1,302–1,320.

Ross, D. M., and Ross, S. A. (1984). Childhood pain: The school-aged child's viewpoint. *Pain*, 20, 179–191.

(1988). *Childhood pain: Current issues, research, and management*. Baltimore: Urban and Schwarzenberg.

Rudolph, K. D., Dennig, M. D., and Weisz, J. R. (1995). Determinants and consequences of children's coping in the medical setting: Conceptualisation, review and critique. *Psychological Bulletin*, 118, 328–357.

Schachter, S. (1959). *The psychology of affiliation*. Stanford, CA: Stanford University Press.

Schechter, N. L., Allen, D. A., and Hanson, K. (1986). The status of pediatric pain control: A comparion of hospital analgesic usage in children and adults. *Pediatrics*, 77, 11–15.

Schermellehengel, K., Eifert, G. H., Moosbrugger, H., and Frank, D. (1997). Perceived competence and trait anxiety as determinants of pain coping strategies. *Personality and Individual Differences*, 22, 1–10.

Shapiro, C. (1997). Development of the 'Oucher' pain assessment tool for Canadian Aboriginal children. Paper presented at the Fourth International Symposium on Pediatric Pain, Helsinki, Finland.

Shih, A. R., and von Baeyer, C. L. (1994). Preschool children's seriation of pain faces and happy faces in the Affective Facial Scale. *Psychological Reports*, 74, 659–665.

Siegal, M. (1988). Children's knowledge of contagion and contamination as causes of illness. *Child Development*, 59, 1,353–1,359.

(1991). *Knowing children: experiments in conversation and cognition*. Hove, UK: Erlbaum.

Siegel, L. J., and Smith, K. E. (1989). Children's strategies for coping with pain. *Pediatrician*, 16, 110–118.

(1991). Coping and adaptation in children's pain. In J. P. Bush and S. W. Harkins (eds.), *Children in pain: Clinical and research issues from a developmental perspective*. New York: Springer-Verlag.

Simons, D. J., and Keil, F. C. (1995). An abstract to concrete shift in the development of biological thought. *Cognition*, 56, 129–163.

Smith, K. E., Ackerson, J. D., and Blotcky, A. D. (1989). Reducing stress during invasive medical procedures: Relating behavioral interventions to preferred coping style in pediatric cancer patients. *Journal of Pediatric Psychology*, 14, 405–419.

Solomon, G. E. A., and Cassimatis, N. (1995). On young children's understanding of germs as biological causes of illness. Paper presented at the biennial meeting of the Society for Research in Child Development, Indianapolis.

Solomon, G. E. A., Johnson, S. C., Zaitchik, D., and Carey, S. (1996). Like father, like son: Young children's understanding of how and why offspring resemble their parents. *Child Development*, 67, 151–171.

Springer, K. (1996). Young children's understanding of a biological basis for parent–offspring relations. *Child Development*, 67, 2,841–2,856.

Springer, K., and Keil, F. C. (1991). Early differentiation of causal mechanisms appropriate to biological and nonbiological kinds. *Child Development*, 62, 767–781.

Tesler, M. D., Wegner, C., Savedra, M. C., Gibbons, P. T., and Ward, J. A. (1981). Coping strategies of children in pain. *Issues in Comprehensive Pediatric Nursing*, 5, 351–359.

Tesler, M. D., Wilkie, D. J., Holzemer, W. L., and Savedra, M. C. (1994). Postoperative analgesics for children and adolescents: Prescription and administration. *Journal of Pain and Symptom Management*, 9, 85–95.

Thomas, W., Goodenough, B., von Baeyer, C. L., and Champion, G. D. (1997). Influence of age and gender on children's ability to distinguish the intensity and unpleasantness of needle pain. Paper presented at the Fourth International Symposium on Pediatric Pain, Helsinki, Finland.

Vernon, D. T. A. (1974). Modeling and birth order in responses to painful stimuli. *Journal of Personality and Social Psychology*, 29, 794–799.

Villareul, A. M., and Deynes, M. J. (1991). Pain assessment in children: Theoretical and empirical validity. *Advances in Nursing Science*, 14, 32–41.

Vogl, L. (1996). The acquisition of pain coping skills by children. Unpublished Masters thesis, School of Psychology, University of New South Wales, Sydney, Australia.

Von Baeyer, C. L., Carlson, G., and Webb, L. (1997). Underprediction of pain in children undergoing ear piercing. *Behavior Research and Therapy*, 35, 399–404.

Webb, J. (1997). Children's understanding of the causality and controllability of pain. Unpublished Masters thesis, University of New South Wales, Sydney, Australia.

Wellman, H. M., and Gelman, S. A. (1992). Cognitive development: Foundational theories of core domains. *Annual Review of Psychology*, 43, 337–375.

(1997). Knowledge acquisition. In D. Kuhn and R. Siegler (eds.), *Handbook of child psychology*, 5th edn, *Cognitive development* (pp. 523–573). New York: Wiley.

Whitaker, B. H., and Brereton, K. E. (1997). Audiovisual cartoon distraction of children undergoing venipuncture: An adjuvant nursing intervention. Paper presented at the Fourth International Symposium on Pediatric Pain, Helsinki, Finland.

Wilkinson, S. R. (1988). *The child's world of illness: The development of health and illness behaviour.* Cambridge, UK: Cambridge University Press.

Wolfer, J. A., and Visintainer, M. A. (1979). Prehospital psychological preparation for tonsillectomy patients: Effects on children's and parent's adjustment. *Pediatrics*, 64, 646–655.

Zeltzer, L. K., and LeBaron, S. (1982). Hypnosis and non-hypnotic techniques for reduction of pain and anxiety during painful procedures in children and adolescents with cancer. *Journal of Pediatriacs*, 101, 1,032–1,035.

Zeltzer, L. K., Fanurik, D. and LeBaron, S. (1989). The cold pressor pain paradigm in children: Feasibility of an intervention model (part II). *Pain*, 37, 305–313.

7 Children and food

Leann Birch, Jennifer Fisher, and
Karen Grimm-Thomas

As young omnivores, children need to learn an enormous amount about food and eating. Fortunately, eating occurs frequently each day, providing many opportunities for learning to occur. From birth to 5 years, food intake patterns change dramatically, and change occurs in food selection as well as in the number and timing of meals. For example, during the first weeks of life, it is not uncommon for an infant to consume ten meals in a twenty-four-hour period. By the preschool period, children are consuming three regularly scheduled meals each day. The reduction in the number of meals reflects a shift from depletion-driven eating to eating meals on a culturally acceptable schedule. Regarding *what* is eaten, infants of all cultures begin life consuming an exclusive milk diet. During the second half of the first year of life, dramatic dietary changes occur as infants make the transition from consuming a single food to selecting foods that compose a modified adult diet. At weaning, the diets of children from different cultural groups begin to diverge, so that by the age of 4 or 5, children of different cultural groups may be consuming diets that share no foods in common.

To investigate how children's food acceptance patterns develop during these first years of life, multiple disciplinary perspectives must be adopted; cultural, social, psychological, and physiological factors all affect the developing child's food selection and the timing and size of meals. Unfortunately, although feeding is a crucial context for early parent–child interaction and is essential to children's growth and development, the research on children's understanding of the meaning of food and the causes and consequences of eating is very limited. However, the evidence regarding the role of learning in the developing controls of food intake is more complete.

Children's eating patterns can be characterized in terms of meal frequency and size, as well as by what foods are eaten. We shall see that learning has an impact on what to eat, when to eat, and how much to eat. For instance, children learn whether their eating should be controlled by internal cues of hunger and satiety, or by other cues, such as time of day, or the presence of food on the plate. These dimensions of children's eating are also shaped by culture and cuisine, the causes and consequences of eating, and the meanings of food and the purposes of eating. Although some of this learning occurs as a result of explicit teaching, much of it occurs via associative conditioning and social learning processes.

During the first five years of life, children are continuously provided with formal and informal nutrition education. For example, adults may impart more or less accurate information about foods and eating to young children, including where foods come from ("White milk comes from white cows, chocolate milk from brown ones"), the consequences of eating a particular food ("Eat your vegetables and you'll get big and strong"), whether particular foods are "good" or "bad" for us, and what constitutes acceptable or unacceptable cuisine rules ("You don't eat pizza for breakfast"; "Don't put ketchup on your apple slices"). Additionally, similar types of information regarding eating are conveyed to children through pervasive advertising targeted at this age group. For example, Jacobson and Maxwell (1994) suggest that a preschooler watching the average amount of TV probably sees 8,000 cereal commercials each year. The information and misinformation imparted by parents, caretakers, and TV undoubtedly shape children's understanding of foods and eating. We argue, however, that much of the important information that children are acquiring about food and eating is not primarily a product of the explicit transfer of information, but acquired indirectly as the result of repeated association of foods with social contexts and physiological consequences of ingestion.

For the infant and young child, who can not yet eat without help, eating is a social occasion, characterized by interactions with adult caretakers who may attempt to control what, when, and how much the child eats. The parent–child sharing of control of food intake is critical in determining the child's food acceptance patterns. Parents influence food selection by encouraging the intake of some foods, and restricting access to others. Findings indicate that the imposition of parental control does not always produce the effects that parents intend (Costanzo and Woody, 1985; Johnson and Birch, 1994). Further, there is wide variability across families in the extent to which caretakers are willing to share control with the child of when, what, and how much the child eats. Differences in the sharing of control are related to the child's level of development, and to parental dieting and weight history, and to the parents' concern about the extent to which the child is seen as "at risk" for subsequent health problems, such as obesity. Satter's (1986, 1987, 1990) clinical findings reveal that problems with shared responsibility between the parent and child are at the heart of many child feeding problems. As development progresses, the sharing of the control of feeding should provide opportunities for increased child control and autonomy, with a concomitant decrease in parental control.

Thus, children's experiences with eating are shaped by the environments and social interactions provided by parents and caregivers. These experiences provide the basis for the development of children's food acceptance patterns. Food acceptance refers to whether a food is ingested or not on a particular occasion and is influenced by a multiplicity of factors including: familiarity with that food, hedonic properties of the food (is it sweet?), nausea or illness associated with ingestion, food preferences (does it taste good?), ideas about where the food came from (animal or vegetable origin), or how it was prepared, and beliefs about the nutritional and health consequences of eating that food. This review that follows addresses how children's food acceptance patterns develop, and delineates the learning processes and contextual factors that influence food acceptance and rejection. While the review is focused primarily on food selection, evidence regarding how children's learning and experience can affect the timing and size of meals is also presented.

What foods are eaten? Factors influencing food selection

As omnivores, humans need to consume a variety of foods to obtain adequate diets, and our food acceptance patterns are a result of an interaction of genetic and experiential factors, with learning playing a central role. Omnivores have the advantage of being able to adapt their diets to environmental constraints, and come equipped with several predispositions that support this adaptive ability (Cowart, 1981). Omnivores have few innate preferences, and this implies many opportunities for learning and experience to affect food acceptance patterns. Human infants have an unlearned preference for the sweet taste; they reject sour and bitter tastes and have an unlearned preference for salt that emerges in the first months after birth. Omnivores are also predisposed to reject unfamiliar foods, which may serve to protect us from consuming potentially harmful toxic substances. We are also predisposed to learn associations between foods' flavor cues and the gastrointestinal consequences of eating. The ability to form these specific associations between flavor cues and gastrointestinal feedback may also serve a protective function, so that we can learn to avoid potentially toxic foods and to prefer foods associated with positive consequences, such as satiety and recovery from illness.

These predispositions were evolved over thousands of years in a very

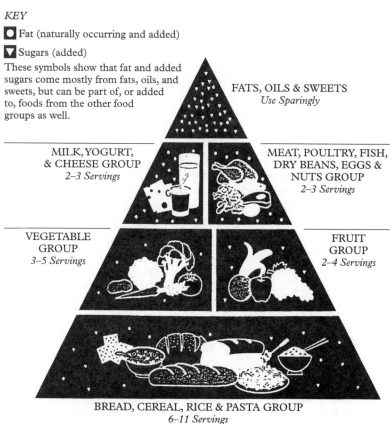

KEY

⚫ Fat (naturally occurring and added)

▼ Sugars (added)

These symbols show that fat and added sugars come mostly from fats, oils, and sweets, but can be part of, or added to, foods from the other food groups as well.

FATS, OILS & SWEETS
Use Sparingly

MILK, YOGURT,
& CHEESE GROUP
2–3 Servings

MEAT, POULTRY, FISH,
DRY BEANS, EGGS &
NUTS GROUP
2–3 Servings

VEGETABLE
GROUP
3–5 Servings

FRUIT
GROUP
2–4 Servings

BREAD, CEREAL, RICE & PASTA GROUP
6–11 Servings

Figure 7.1   USDA Food Guide Pyramid

different environment from our current one, an environment where food was scarce and Twinkies and Big Macs were as yet unknown. In that environmental context of food scarcity, our predispositions served an adaptive function (Galef, 1996).

Predispositions that were evolved under one set of conditions, however, may not prove to be adaptive under another set. In particular, these predispositions do not guarantee that today's children will select adequate diets and be safe from consuming harmful substances. In fact, we shall see that the predispositions which have evolved in a more sparse food environment may be maladaptive in our current dietary environment. For example, the unlearned preference for sweet and salty tastes and the predisposition to learn to prefer energy-dense foods would have

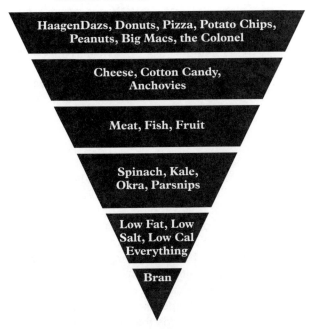

Figure 7.2   Hedonic Food Pyramid (Galef, 1996)

been adaptive in an environment where foods rich in these substances were scarce. In western society, people live in a context where foods high in sugar, salt, and fat are widely and readily available. The same predispositions that served us well in less affluent food environments can contribute to diets that are too high in sugar, fat, and salt.

In fact, in response to North American diets that are too high in sugar, fat, and salt, we now have dietary guidelines that provide us with information about how to compose a healthy diet by consuming the right balance of foods from among various categories (see Figure 7.1). Although the food pyramid mandates limiting consumption of sweets and fats, we are not predisposed to do so. Most of us consume diets that are not consistent with these guidelines, but would prefer to eat diets consistent with the hedonic pyramid shown in Figure 7.2 (Galef, 1996). It is our predispositions in combination with the ready availability of processed foods high in sugar, fat, and salt that make it so difficult for us to comply with current dietary guidelines which entreat us to limit our consumption of sugar, fat, and salt. The disparity that exists between what we *ought* to eat (Figure 7.1) and what we *do* eat (Figure 7.2) has origins in children's innate predispositions and in learning that occurs during the first years of life. The existence of these genetic predispositions does not mean that we should give up attempting to foster healthier diets by today's standards. Rather, the explicit recognition of these predispositions can suggest strategies that could be employed to attain that goal. For example, we could use what we know about exposure effects and associative conditioning to facilitate children's acquisition of preferences for nutritious foods that are not inherently palatable.

Effects of "mere" exposure on food selection

The unlearned preference for sweet and salty tastes implies that infants and children do not have to learn to like sweet or salty foods. In general, however, unfamiliar foods are initially rejected. This neophobic response is common to omnivores. As Rozin (1976) points out, the "omnivore's dilemma" is that although we need dietary variety to survive, expanding variety by trying new foods can be a risky business; the new substance may prove to be toxic. However, with repeated opportunities to consume a new food in the absence of illness following consumption, many new foods that were initially rejected will eventually be accepted. In fact, Kalat and Rozin (1973) conducted a series of experiments to provide evidence that the increased acceptance of novel foods that occurs with repeated exposure is a result of learning that the new food is safe to eat.

For the weanling child, who is just being introduced to the adult diet, all foods are initially novel and the young child's neophobic response can result in the child's rejecting many new foods. Further, if parents misinterpret the child's initial rejection to indicate a fixed and immutable response to the food, they may not continue to offer the food to the child. As a result, there is no opportunity to learn that the food is safe, and it certainly will not become a part of the child's diet. Additional problems can arise when parents are not aware that the rejection of new foods reflects a normal and adaptive response and they may misinterpret the child's neophobic response as symptomatic of a finicky, picky eater.

In a series of experiments, we have investigated the effects of repeated exposure to new foods on children's preferences for those foods; results indicate that many of the new foods that children initially rejected are ultimately accepted, although this change from rejection to acceptance may take several exposures (Birch and Marlin, 1982; Birch *et al.*, 1987a). The fact that repeated opportunities to eat new foods can change initial rejection to acceptance underscores the importance of early learning, and the critical role of parents in selecting the array of foods that are offered to their children. There is evidence that repeated exposure can modify even the unlearned preference for sweet and salty tastes (Sullivan and Birch, 1990). Via repeated experience with an initially unfamiliar food (tofu) that was prepared plain, or with added sugar or salt, children learned to prefer the version of the food that became familiar; it was as if they were learning cuisine rules for when it was appropriate to add sugar or salt to foods.

In her pioneering research on dietary selection among infants, Davis (1928, 1939) reported the dramatic changes that occurred in food acceptance as children were introduced to new foods and had repeated opportunities to sample them. The infants and toddlers in her research were offered a variety of simply prepared foods at each meal, and fed themselves in the absence of adult intervention. Data were obtained over several weeks or months, and Davis described how, with repeated opportunities to eat the foods, food preferences developed. As they had repeated opportunities to sample new foods, children began to avidly seek out some foods and reject others. When they were given the opportunity to self-select their diets, the infants grew well and had few illnesses and no feeding problems. This work has often been misinterpreted, and cited to support the view that infants and children, left to their own devices, will compose adequate diets. This is not the case. Davis herself was quick to point out that the "trick" of her experiment was the array of foods that were offered to the children: a set of healthy foods, simply prepared without added sugar or salt. These foods bear little resemblance to many of the foods available today, especially those high in sugar, fat, and salt that are marketed to children. Davis concluded (1939: 261): "leave the selection of the foods to be made available to young children in the hands of their elders where everyone has always known it belongs." She went on to indicate that within these constraints, children should be allowed a degree of autonomy in food selection.

Food selection: effects of associative conditioning to the contexts and consequences of eating

Neophobia and the opportunities for experience with new foods have a sizeable impact on young children's food acceptance patterns. Children's eating is also powerfully modified by its pairing with the positive or negative physiological consequences of eating, and the social context in which eating occurs. Rozin and Zellner (1985) have argued convincingly that associative conditioning plays a central role in the acquisition of food preferences. Associative conditioning, also known as Pavlovian conditioning, involves changes in response or attitude to stimuli (foods' sensory characteristics, which serve as conditioned stimuli [CS]), resulting from their contingent occurrence (temporally or spatially) with other, more potent stimuli (physiological, social, or environmental unconditioned stimuli [US]) (Rozin and Zellner, 1985).

Adults, siblings, and peers serve as models, and may attempt to exert control over what and how much the child eats, creating a social context for feeding that has either a positive or negative emotional tone. In general, associative conditioning processes have been shown to be central in the acquisition of evaluative responses (Martin and Levy, 1978). Probably the best known examples of the effects of associative conditioning on the formation of learned responses to food is the conditioned food aversion. A conditioned aversion is acquired when the flavor cues in a food are associated with negative physiological consequences of eating, particularly nausea and vomiting. Learning occurs rapidly; conditioned aversions are unusual in that they are typically formed with only a single pairing of the CS and the US (Domjan, 1977). Although quickly established, conditioned aversions are very long lasting and resistant to extinction. Bernstein's (1978) work has revealed that children form such conditioned aversions. In research with children receiving chemotherapy for cancer treatment, she reported that aversions were formed when novel ice cream flavors were paired with nausea and vomiting caused by drug treatment. While conditioned aversions are of practical importance and are of interest to students of learning, they probably contribute little to the food acceptance patterns of most people; most of us have only one or a very few conditioned aversions. Conditioned *preferences*, however, are more routinely encountered in the development of children's eating patterns. Such preferences result when food flavor cues are associated with positive physiological consequences, such as recovery from illness (Zahorik et al., 1974) or feelings of satiety that follow eating when hungry.

Because the pairing of food flavor cues with the positive post-ingestive consequences of eating occurs during normal meals, there are many opportunities for such learning to occur. Early work by Booth et al., (1974) indicated that rats form such conditioned preferences, learning to prefer energy-dense foods over more energy-dilute ones. These findings were observed whether the energy came from carbohydrate, fat, or protein. Booth and Toase (1983) also reported that adults formed a conditioned preference for flavors associated with high carbohydrate over those associated with low carbohydrate preparations. Similarly, in a series of experiments conducted in our laboratory, we have shown that children learn to prefer energy-dense (high fat or high carbohydrate) foods over less energy-dense versions of those same foods (see Birch [1992] for a discussion of this literature). The impact of associative conditioning processes on children's food preferences are most clearly seen when they are hungry (Kern et al., 1993). In these experiments, children were given two preparations of the same food, one high and one low in energy density (yoghurts, puddings, or soups have been used). Each version had a distinctive flavor cue added. Measures of preference were obtained before

and after several pairs of training trials in which the flavors were associated with high or low energy density. The results revealed that children
readily learned to prefer high energy over low energy paired flavors. Many
of the energy dense foods at the top of the hedonic pyramid have sweet or
salty flavors that are preferred prior to learning (see figure 7.2). The
evidence for learned preferences suggests that associative conditioning
can also potentiate our preferences for high energy, high fat, or high sugar
foods, and can produce preferences for other energy dense foods.

In contrast to the unlearned predisposition to accept sweet tastes,
however, there is no definitive evidence for an innate preference for fat.
Fat is difficult to identify in food, and imparts different flavor characteristics to different complex food systems: it can make foods crunchy,
creamy, greasy, or flaky. While many of the volatiles in foods that make
them inherently palatable are carried by fat, the data on learned preferences indicates that to some degree, children's preferences for fat may be
learned as a result of the consistent pairing of fat flavor cues with satiety
cues (Birch, 1992). Learned preferences for high fat foods would have
had adaptive value in the past in environments where food was scarce.
Given our current overabundance of energy-dense foods, however, these
learned preferences can be maladaptive, contributing to obesity by promoting preferences for and excessive intake of foods high in fat and
energy. There is a good deal of evidence that preferences for fat predict fat
intake (Fisher and Birch, 1995), and that high fat diets are associated with
greater body fatness in children (Fisher and Birch, 1995; Gazzagna and
Burns, 1993; Nguyen et al., 1996). Evidence for learned preferences for
energy-dense foods provides additional information regarding why it is so
difficult to adhere to dietary recommendations advocating limiting our
consumption of high energy, high fat foods.

Children can learn to adjust not only *what* they eat but also *how much*
they eat, based on foods' energy content. Using single meal protocols
similar to those described above, we have conducted a series of experiments revealing that children can learn to adjust the amount of food they
consume in response to the energy density of those foods. In these
experiments, children were fed two-course meals in which a fixed volume
of a first course preload was consumed. These first course preloads varied
in energy content. Results indicated that children adjusted their food
intake in a self-selected second course, eating more following the energy
dilute than following an energy-dense preload. This compensation for
energy is also seen across successive meals (Birch et al., 1991) over
twenty-four-hour periods, and there is evidence that over twenty-four-
hour periods, children can adjust their intake in response to the substitu-
tion of olestra for dietary fat for about 10 percent of the fat in the diet

(Birch et al., 1993). Olestra is a fat substitute that has the sensory characteristics of fat but is not absorbed by the body and hence has no calories, and can be used to reduce the fat and energy content of foods without altering their sensory characteristics and palatability.

In addition to forming associations between foods' flavors and physiological consequences of eating, children learn to associate foods with the social contexts in which they are presented, and that these social contexts can shape children's food preferences. We have shown that foods become more preferred when repeatedly associated with positive social contexts, such as when they serve as rewards or are paired with positive adult attention (Birch et al., 1980), and that these changes in preference persist for weeks after the presentations, even when the children have apparently forgotten about their experiences with the food. When the presentation context is more negative, the association of food cues with the social context produces dislikes for foods. For example, when foods were eaten in order to obtain rewards, they became more disliked (Birch et al., 1984b). This finding is reminiscent of Lepper's work on extrinsic motivation, which showed similar declines in liking as a result of rewarding children for performing a previously preferred activity (Lepper and Greene, 1978). In fact, Lepper suggested that it is in the context of food and eating that children in our culture first learn about contingencies, "If you eat your carrots, then you can have dessert." He demonstrated this in research in which children were told a story that involved children eating two hypothetical foods, "hupe" and "hule." In the story, children had to eat one food to get the other: "Eat your hupe and then you can have your hule." After hearing the story, young children were asked which food they would like better. Children indicated that the food in the reward component of the story was preferred over the food eaten to obtain the reward. This finding indicates that children learn about the relative value of foods based on the ways in which foods are presented to them.

Recent work from our laboratory on the effects of restricting children's access to food makes a similar point. Preschool-aged children were provided with two types of fruit bars of equal initial preference and consumption. Relative to the food offered in unlimited quantities, restricting access to a food increased children's behavioral response to that food. In particular, restricting children's access to a food resulted in more positive comments and behaviors about the food, in more requests for the restricted food, and more attempts to gain access to the restricted food. These findings suggest that children's experiences with restricted access to a food may cause them to attach value to those "forbidden" foods (Fisher, 1997).

The social context of children's eating: social learning and other learning processes impact food selection

Associative conditioning is an important contributor to the acquisition of food acceptance patterns, but there is also evidence that social learning plays a role. In a pioneering experiment to explore social influence effects, Duncker (1938, p. 489) investigated "the psychological mechanisms by which likes and dislikes were instilled into individual members of the group." He found that when children observed peers or adult models making food choices different from their own, the observers' food choices were altered in the direction of the models' choices. The evidence for social influence was clear, although the extent of influence varied with the absolute age of the children, the difference in age between the model and observer, and the relationship between the observer and the model. Subsequent research conducted in our laboratory revealed similar findings; after a child observed other children choosing and eating disliked vegetables, the observer's selection and consumption of the initially disliked foods increased significantly (Birch, 1980). In research exploring the effectiveness of adult models on children's food acceptance, Harper and Sanders (1975) noted that mothers were more effective than strangers at inducing child observers to try a new food. With respect to evidence for the impact of social influence on the food acceptance patterns of non-human omnivores, Galef has conducted an impressive series of experiments demonstrating the importance of social learning in both rat pups and adult rats, where the eating behavior of conspecifics has been shown to profoundly affect the food choices of observers (see Galef and Beck, 1991). Additional evidence for social influence effects on omnivores' food acceptance patterns comes from Rozin and Schiller's (1980) attempts to induce a preference in chimps for the hot flavor of chili pepper. They initially had no success with associative learning approaches. Only when the chimps observed their keepers eating the chili pepper flavored crackers did they begin to accept and eat the "hot" food.

Adult influence on children's food acceptance patterns involves interaction with the child, as well as modeling eating behavior. Child feeding practices, in addition to shaping preferences and regulatory predispositions, may be critical in providing children with information about which of the many cues in the environment should control eating. These cues include internal cues of hunger and satiety, as well as external cues, such as the presence of food, the time of day, the social context, and the amount of food remaining on the plate. As noted earlier, children can be responsive to the energy content of the diet and can use those cues to regulate energy intake in the absence of adult intervention. Children's responsiveness, however, can be readily disrupted by child feeding practices that interfere with their responsiveness to internal cues of hunger and satiety (Birch et al., 1987b; Johnson and Birch, 1994). For instance, restricting children's access to foods may highlight the salience of external eating cues by drawing children's attention to the availability of "forbidden" foods (Fisher, 1997). Ironically, the developmental literature on parental control and child outcomes, seems to indicate that the imposition of external control provides the child with few opportunities to develop self-control in the eating domain. Johnson and Birch (1994) found that controlling styles of child feeding were negatively associated with children's ability to regulate energy intake, suggesting that excessive parental control may diminish children's attention to internal cues in eating. In particular, practices which restrict children's access to foods may focus attention on "forbidden" foods and enhance children's intake of those foods, even when they are not hungry (Fisher, 1997). When observed following a meal, the degree to which mothers restricted their daughters' access to snack foods was closely linked to the girls' intake of those foods in an unrestricted setting.

We hypothesize that parental control over child feeding may play an important role in shaping individual differences in the controls of food intake among children. These differences among children may be defined in terms of the relative importance of internal and external cues in the control of food intake. Individual differences in the extent to which internal and external cues affect food intake may be precursors of later differences in the controls of food intake in adults. In particular, lack of responsiveness to internal cues of hunger and satiety are hypothesized to increase risk for chronic dieting, and high levels of dietary restraint and disinhibition.

Food selection: children's understanding of the taxonomy of reasons for food acceptance/rejection

There is a limited research base on the development of food acceptance patterns in children, but there is even less research on the development of children's understanding of the causes and consequences of eating. Two decades of anecdotal evidence from our laboratory suggest that most 3 year olds can indicate the foods they like, and that those preferences predict consumption. We were, however, unable to locate any published research on children's understanding of such causes and consequences of eating, with the exception of some research that examines the emergence of children's ideas about dieting and weight control during middle childhood.

The major contribution to our knowledge regarding children's understanding of reasons to accept or reject foods has been made by Rozin and colleagues (Fallon and Rozin, 1984; Fallon et al., 1984; Rozin and Fallon, 1980, 1981). They extended research on their taxonomy of reasons for food acceptance and rejection in adults to explore the development of this system during childhood. Their treatment of the development of children's understanding of reasons for accepting or rejecting foods is based on the premise that to understand food selection, physiology and individual factors must be considered, but we must also look at the cultural contribution to food acceptance patterns. In fact, Rozin (1984) has pointed out that if you want to know about an individual's food acceptance patterns, and can ask only one question, that question should be, "What is your cultural or ethnic group?"

From among the wide array of edible substances available within any ecological niche, the members of a cultural group consume only a relative few. For example, most US citizens do not eat sea worms or sea slugs, which are avidly consumed by members of some Asian cultural groups. Many Americans will enthusiastically eat pork chops, but orthodox Jews or Muslims would not, and would be disgusted at the thought of doing so. Cultures also have food taboos that can be age and sex specific, thereby restricting the food experience of these subgroups. For example, while children in several Central American countries regularly consume coffee, coffee is not seen as appropriate for children in the United States. Other food items, such as spicy foods, are not usually given to young US children. The French predilection for snails and frogs' legs is not generally shared by UK consumers. Culture also provides cuisine rules that indicate the appropriate time of day to eat certain foods; most of us eat pizza at lunch or dinner, not breakfast, and cereal at breakfast, not dinner. Research indicates that our preferences for foods vary with the time of day; we show the greatest preference for a food at the time of day when it is appropriate to eat that food. Furthermore, by as early as the preschool period, children have begun to acquire these preferences and cuisine rules (Birch et al., 1984a).

With respect to Rozin and Fallon's taxonomy, various potential edibles may be rejected (or accepted) as food for different reasons. They propose that there are three types of reasons for acceptance or rejection of edibles: sensory-affective factors, anticipated consequences, and ideational factors. Each category has a positive pole that motivates acceptance and a negative pole that motivates rejection. The individual's acceptance or rejection of a food will be based on one or more of these factors, as well as cultural factors, individual experience and physiological feedback.

With respect to sensory-affective factors, many foods are accepted or rejected in response to the food's sensory characteristics: flavor, texture, and appearance. Positive affect is produced by pleasant sensory characteristics, negative affect by bad ones. The affect generated may be due to an unlearned preference (e.g., for sweet or salty tastes) or via conditioned preferences or aversions. The second category, anticipated consequences, refers to the idea that some edibles are accepted or rejected because of the consequences they are thought to produce. These consequences may be immediate, as when you are hungry and eat a familiar food that you know will make you feel comfortably satiated. They can be more delayed, as when you eat something that is "good for you," or avoid a food that is believed to have negative consequences. This would be the case for a conditioned aversion, or a food that is believed to be "bad for you," such as a high fat food for someone on a low fat diet for weight control. Rozin and Fallon's third category deals with the ideational factors that can lead to acceptance and rejection, and addresses where foods come from and what they are. This knowledge operates to shape rejection to a greater extent than acceptance. Inappropriate substances are rejected because they are simply not food, e.g., grass or sand. The second subcategory includes disgusting items. Disgusting items, although usually never tasted, are thought to be bad tasting and may produce nausea just thinking about them. Disgust is ideational, and requires the knowledge of where the item came from; most items that elicit disgust are of animal origin. Some disgusting items are culturally specific; a Hindu might find the idea of eating beef disgusting, while many people would find the idea of eating horsemeat disgusting. In contrast, the disgust for feces appears universal, but does not appear developmentally until children are about 2 years old (Angyal, 1941).

The influence of television advertising on children's food preferences and selection

Television advertising and programming provides a great deal of information (and disinformation) to children about foods and eating. Children watch, on average, three or four hours of television per day, and estimates are that the average child sees about 350,000 commercials by the time he or she graduates from high school. In a review of the literature, Sylvester *et al.*, (1995) found that about 60 percent of the ads aired during children's programs are for food. A large proportion of the ads directed at children are primarily for cereals, candy, snacks, and fast foods (Jacobson and Maxwell, 1994; Sylvester *et al.*, 1995). By Jacobson's estimate, between one-fifth and one-third of all commercials targeted at children are for breakfast cereal; this means that for a child who watches 30,000 commercials a year, about 8,000 to 10,000 are for cereal alone. These ads include messages about the good taste of the advertised foods and how much fun it is to eat them. The nutritional messages given are frequently misleading or difficult to interpret (e.g., "part of a balanced breakfast"). Further, many ads manage to convey the impression that the advertised foods have positive nutritional qualities, although they are typically high in sugar or fat, and low in complex carbohydrates.

Despite the barrage of food advertising, there are relatively few studies investigating the impact of these ads on children's preferences, intake patterns, or their understanding of food and eating. Research has shown that in general, children under the age of 7 or 8 are incapable of recognizing a commercial's persuasive intent, and thus tend to express greater belief in commercials and more frequent requests to purchase advertised items (Kunkel and Roberts, 1991). There are a few well designed studies that explore the effects of television ads for foods on children's subsequent requests for the advertised foods, or their preferences for those foods, and this research shows clear effects (see e.g., Galst, 1980; Galst and White, 1976; Goldberg et al., 1978; Gorn and Goldberg, 1980), with children making requests for, selecting, and indicating preferences for the foods they have seen advertised on TV.

In addition to commercials, television programs also provide children with information about food and eating. In an analysis of the use of food in TV programs, Kotz and Story (1994) noted that TV programs can show children the most unhealthy aspects of an American diet, and they conclude that the prime-time TV diet is inconsistent with dietary guidelines for healthy Americans. They argue that one message conveyed by TV programs is that nothing bad happens to TV characters who eat high fat, high sugar diets and, in fact, characters seem to thrive on them. While 25 percent of television characters were overweight, young children and adolescents were never portrayed as being obese, and a mere 7 percent of teenagers were obese (Sylvester et al., 1995). Moreover, of the obese individuals depicted, none held leading roles (Sylvester et al., 1995). This under-representation of obese characters is inconsistent with the typical diet depicted on TV. Analysis of program content and advertisements revealed that non-nutritious foods were represented more often in both Saturday morning and prime-time programming than in the commercials aired at either time (Story and Faulkner, 1990; Sylvester et al., 1995). Though nutritious foods were presented as background props equally as often as non-nutritious foods, food-consumption situations, restaurant eating, and grocery-purchasing all contained less nutritious foods (Sylvester et al., 1995). Furthermore, snacking was depicted more often than regular meals (Sylvester et al., 1995).

Again, there is little research to indicate whether and how children incorporate such information into their understanding of food and eating. Studies investigating the representation of food in children's programming and its effect on children's consumption patterns and attitudes about food and nutrition have generated inconclusive findings (Sylvester et al., 1995; Williams et al., 1993). For example, Goldberg et al. (1978) found that having children watch a TV program that presented junk food as "bad for you" and fruit and vegetables presented as "good for you" reduced the number of sugared foods selected, even in the presence of ads for sugared foods. Peterson et al. (1984), however, reported contradictory findings based on their investigation of the influence of pro-nutrition television programming on kindergarten-aged children's nutritional knowledge, food preferences, and eating habits. They concluded that although children attended to and recalled pro-nutritional program messages, these messages failed to have an impact on children's preferences or consumption patterns (Peterson et al., 1984).

Though many of the advertising messages aimed at adults are for dieting and weight control products and programs, TV programs frequently seem to convey the message that we can eat "junk" diets and not get fat. Current demographics on obesity reveal that this does not reflect reality; the prevalence of obesity among adults and children continues to rise, despite an increased emphasis on slimness and dieting for weight control. Dieting has become normative among women and adolescent girls; recent information indicates that more than half of 9- and 10-year-old girls report that they have dieted and many are already dissatisfied with their weight and body shape (Collins, 1991; Thelen et al., 1992). The media images of an extremely thin Kate Moss body shape as the ideal of feminine attractiveness undoubtedly contributes to women's and girls' body dissatisfaction (Wardle and Marsland, 1990), but there are few studies on these effects, and whether they are moderated by subject or family characteristics. While the media's input is undoubtedly causally implicated in these trends, research is needed to assess their impact in the context of the influence on eating and weight control efforts provided by family members and peers.

Gender differences in the development of children's eating patterns

Especially for females in our society, physical attractiveness is equated with thinness, overweight is strongly stigmatized, and dieting is highly prevalent (Striegel-Moore, 1995). These factors may shape parental expectations, parental monitoring, and assessment of their daughters' eating. Child feeding practices aimed at the control of food intake may be particularly central to the eating experiences and development of young girls. We are currently conducting longitudinal research to examine the development of controls of food intake in young girls. We hypothesize that parents' own eating behaviors, and the types of child feeding practices generated by parents' own issues with eating and weight, may provide the basis for the transmission of problematic styles of eating from parent to daughter. In pilot work for this project, mothers' disinhibited eating styles mediated the relationship between mothers' and daughters' adiposity (Cutting and Birch, 1997). Further, mother–daughter similarities were noted in eating behavior pertaining to external cues in eating, such as the presence of palatable foods. This finding implies that parents' own lack of control in eating may serve as a formative template for their daughter's eating behaviors and consequent weight outcome. Alternatively, child feeding practices used by disinhibited mothers may produce similarities in eating and weight outcomes among mother and daughter.

Costanzo and Woody's (1985) obesity proneness model indicates that parents are not necessarily consistent in imposing control over children's behavior across domains and development. Rather, parents tend to impose control in areas (1) where they themselves are invested, or have a problem; (2) where they see the child as "at risk" for developing a problem; (3) where they see the child as being in need of parental intervention to prevent problems. In the feeding context, parental control may be elicited in response to parents' perceptions that the child is at risk for developing obesity or other chronic diseases. Currently, we are exploring the possibility that this "risk" is conferred by parents' own dieting and weight history as well as children's eating behavior and weight status. In a study from our laboratory, we examined these parent and child characteristics as predictors of the amount of restricted access to foods that mothers imposed in their children's eating (Fisher, 1997). Children's adiposity was a good predictor of maternal restriction. Additionally, parents' own restrained eating styles predicted the extent to which mothers restricted their daughters' intake. In related work, mothers' degree of overweight was related to disinhibited styles of eating which, in turn, predicted mothers' control of daughters' eating (Chhabra et al., 1997).

Finally, the manner in which children approach eating may be affected by social learning processes. We are currently pursuing work which examines the impact of parents' dieting behavior on young girls' understanding of the relationships between food selection, eating behavior, and weight outcomes. We hypothesize that the complexity of young girls' understanding of dieting will be closely aligned with their exposure to parental and peer dieting behaviors and weight control practices.

Summary and conclusions

Children's food intake patterns undergo enormous change during the first years of life as they make the transition from an exclusive milk diet to a modified adult diet. Change involves a reduction in the number of meals and their timing, and an increase in the number of different foods selected and consumed. Though little is known about the factors that influence children's knowledge about the meaning of food and the consequences of eating specific foods, research has shed some light on the role of learning in the development of food preferences and eating behaviors.

Though infants are born with innate predispositions to prefer sweet foods and reject sour and bitter foods, their relative lack of innate preferences means that they have abundant opportunities for experiences and learning to affect food acceptance patterns. Research has shown that children's emerging preferences for foods are based on internal cues such as the post-ingestive consequence of eating (Did it taste good? Did it make me sick? Did it make me feel full?). Furthermore, social and contextual cues (Is it time to eat breakfast? Does she have to reward me for eating this stuff? How much food is left on my plate?) also have an impact on children's food preferences and intake. Thus, the social context of children's eating contributes to the acquisition of food acceptance patterns. In this way, various influences from parents, siblings, peers, the media, and the larger culture all play important roles in how children learn to eat. Because children's social contexts and experiences vary, individual differences in food preferences and eating behaviors emerge.

Food acceptance patterns are formed as children encounter foods in environments provided by parents and caregivers. Presenting an accurate picture of children's developing understanding of food and eating will require an analysis of the sources of influence on children's food acceptance patterns, including cultural, social, psychological, and physiological levels. This is a necessary step in understanding how children are acquiring knowledge, attitudes, values, food preferences, and eating behaviors. Careful analysis of the child's early experience with food and eating reveals how children acquire food acceptance patterns, and why those patterns are often inconsistent with recommendations regarding healthy diets. Children's food acceptance patterns are critical to their growth and health and central to family interaction involving child feeding. Unfortunately, there is relatively little research on the causes and consequences of children's eating. Further, there are even fewer studies that address children's *understanding* of the meanings of foods and the purposes, causes, and consequences of eating. In addition to making an important contribution to our knowledge base regarding children's developing

understanding of health and nutrition, research in this area could make a
crucial contribution to the development of interventions designed to
reduce the prevalence of obesity and other problems of energy balance,
including chronic dieting and eating disorders.

REFERENCES

Angyal, A. (1941). Disgust and related aversions. *Journal of Abnormal and Social Psychology*, 36, 393–412.
Bernstein, I. L. (1978). Learned taste aversions in children receiving chemotherapy. *Science*, 200, 1,302–1,303.
Birch, L. L. (1980). Effects of peer models' food choices and eating behaviors on preschoolers' food preferences. *Child Development*, 51, 489–496.
  (1992). Children's preferences for high-fat foods. *Nutrition Reviews*, 50, 249–255.
Birch, L. L., and Marlin, D. W. (1982). I don't like it: I never tried it: Effects of exposure to food on two-year-old children's food preferences. *Appetite*, 4, 353–360.
Birch, L. L., Zimmerman, S., and Hind, H. (1980). The influence of social-affective context on preschool children's food preferences. *Child Development*, 51, 856–861.
Birch, L. L., Billman, J., and Richards, S. (1984a). Time of day influences food acceptability. *Appetite*, 5, 109–116.
Birch, L. L., Marlin, D. W., and Rotter, J. (1984b). Eating as the "means" activity in a contingency: Effects on young children's food preference. *Child Development*, 55, 432–439.
Birch, L. L., McPhee, L., Shoba, B. C., Pirok, E., and Steinberg, L. (1987a). What kind of exposure reduces children's food neophobia? *Appetite*, 9, 171–178.
Birch, L. L., McPhee, L., Shoba, B. C., Steinberg, L., and Krehbiel, R. (1987b). "Clean up your plate": Effects of child feeding practices on the conditioning of meal size. *Learning and Motivation*, 18, 301–317.
Birch, L. L., Johnson, S. L., Andresen, G., Peters, J. C., and Schulte, M. C. (1991). The variability of young children's energy intake. *New England Journal of Medicine*, 324, 232–235.
Birch, L. L., Johnson, S. L., Jones, M. B., and Peters, J. C. (1993). Effects of a non-energy fat substitute on children's energy and macronutrient intake. *American Journal of Clinical Nutrition*, 58, 326–333.
Booth, D. A., and Toase, A. M. (1983). Conditions of hunger/satiety signals as well as flavour cues in dieters. *Appetite*, 4, 235–236.
Booth, D. A., Stoloff, R., and Nicholls, J. (1974). Dietary flavor acceptance in infant rats established by association with effects of nutrient composition. *Physiological Psychology*, 2, 313–319.
Chhabra, J., Johnson, S. L., and Birch, L. L. (1997). Do parents' own eating practices influence their control of daughters' eating? Poster session at the biennial meeting of the Society for Research on Child Development, Washington, DC, April.

Collins, M. E. (1991). Body figure perceptions and preferences among pre-adolescent children. *International Journal of Eating Disorders*, 10, 199–208.

Costanzo, P. R., and Woody, E. Z. (1985). Domain-specific parenting styles and their impact on the child's development of particular deviance: The example of obesity proneness. *Journal of Social and Clinical Psychology*, 4, 425–445.

Cowart, B. (1981). Development of taste perception in humans: Sensitivity and preference throughout the life span. *Psychological Bulletin*, 90, 43–73.

Cutting, T. M., and Birch, L. L. (1997). Should children clean their plates? A look at fathers' control in the eating domain. Poster session at the biennial meeting of the Society for Research on Child Development, Washington, DC, April.

Davis, C. M. (1928). Self-selection of diet by newly weaned infants. *American Journal of Diseases of Children*, 36, 651–679.

    (1939). Results of the self-selection of diets by young children. *Canadian Medical Association Journal*, 41, 257–261.

Domjan, M. (1977). Attenuation and enhancement of neophobia for edible substances. In L. M. Barker, M. R. Best, and M. Domjan (eds.), *Learning mechanisms in food selection* (pp. 151–179). Waco, TX: Baylor University Press.

Duncker, K. (1938). Experimental modification of children's food preferences through social suggestion. *Journal of Abnormal Social Psychology*, 33, 489–507.

Fallon, A. E., and Rozin, P. (1984). The psychological bases of food rejections by humans. *Ecology of Food and Nutrition*, 13, 5–26.

Fallon, A. E., Rozin, P., and Pliner, P. (1984). The child's conception of food: The development of food rejection, with special reference to disgust and contamination sensitivity. *Child Development*, 55, 566–575.

Fisher, J. O. (1997). Forbidden foods and young children's eating in an unrestricted setting. Poster session at the biennial meeting of the Society for Research on Child Development, Washington, DC, April.

Fisher, J. O., and Birch, L. L. (1995). Fat preferences and fat consumption of 3-to 5-year-old children are related to parental adiposity. *Journal of the American Dietetic Association*, 95, 759–764.

Galef, B. G., Jr. (1996). Food selection: problems in understanding how we choose foods to eat. *Neuroscience and Biobehavioral Reviews*, 20, 67–73.

Galef, B. G., Jr., and Beck, M. (1991). Diet selection and poison avoidance by mammals individually and in social groups. In E. M. Stricker (ed.), *Handbook of behavioral neurobiology*, vol. X, *Neurobiology of food and fluid intake* (pp. 329–346). New York: Plenum.

Galst, J. P. (1980). Television food commercials and pro-nutritional public service announcements as determinants of young children's snack choices. *Child Development*, 51, 935–938.

Galst, J. P., and White, M. A. (1976). The unhealthy persuader: The reinforcing value of television and children's purchase-influencing attempts at the supermarket. *Child Development*, 47, 1,089–1,096.

Gazzaniga, J. M., and Burns, T. L. (1993). Relationship between diet composition and body fatness, with adjustment for resting expenditure and physical activity in preadolescent children. *American Journal of Clinical Nutrition*, 58, 21–28.

Goldberg, M. E., Gorn, G. J., and Gibson, W. (1978). T.V. messages for snack and breakfast foods: Do they influence children's preferences? *Journal of Consumer Research*, 5, 73–81.

Gorn, G. J., and Goldberg, M. E. (1980). Children's responses to repetitive television commercials. *Journal of Consumer Research*, 4, 421–424.

Harper, L. V., and Sanders, K. M. (1975). The effect of adult's eating on young children's acceptance of unfamiliar foods. *Journal of Experimental Child Psychology*, 20, 206–214.

Jacobson, M. F., and Maxwell, B. (1994). *What are we feeding our kids?* New York: Workman.

Johnson, S. L., and Birch, L. L. (1994). Parents' and children's adiposity and eating style. *Pediatrics*, 94, 653–661.

Kalat, J., and Rozin, P. (1973). "Learned safety" as a mechanism in long-delay taste aversion learning in rats. *Journal of Comparative and Physiological Psychology*, 83, 198–207.

Kern, D. L., McPhee, L., Fisher, J., Johnson, S., and Birch, L. L. (1993). The postingestive consequences of fat condition preferences for flavors associated with high dietary fat. *Physiology and Behavior*, 54, 71–76.

Kotz, K., and Story, M. (1994). Food advertisements during children's Saturday morning television programming: Are they consistent with dietary recommendations? *Journal of the American Dietetic Association*, 11, 1296–1300.

Kunkel, D., and Roberts, D. (1991). Young minds and marketplace values: Issues in children's television advertising. *Journal of Social Issues*, 47, 57–72.

Lepper, M., and Greene, D. (eds.). (1978). *The hidden costs of reward: New perspectives on the psychology of human motivation*. Hillsdale, NJ: Erlbaum.

Martin, I., and Levey, A. B. (1978). Evaluative conditioning. *Advances in Behavior Research and Therapy*, 1, 57–102.

Nguyen, V. T., Larson, D. E., Johnson, R. K., and Goran, M. I. (1996). Fat intake and adiposity in children of lean and obese parents. *American Journal of Clinical Nutrition*, 63, 507–513.

Peterson, P. E., Jeffrey, D. B., Bridgwater, C. A., and Dawson, B. (1984). How pronutrition television programming affects children's dietary habits. *Developmental Psychology*, 20, 55–63.

Rozin, P. (1976). The selection of foods by rats, humans, and other animals. In J. S. Rosenblatt, R. A. Hinder, E. Shaw, and C. Beer (eds.), *Advances in the study of behavior* (pp. 21–76). New York: Academic Press.

(1984). The acquisition of food habits and preferences. In J. D. Matarazzo, S. M. Weiss, J. A. Herd, and N. E. Miller (eds.), *Behavioral health: A handbook of health enhancement and disease prevention* (pp. 590–607). New York: Wiley.

Rozin, P., and Fallon, A. E. (1980). The psychological categorization of foods and non foods: A preliminary taxonomy of food rejections. *Appetite*, 1, 193–201.

(1981). The acquisition of likes and dislikes for foods. In J. Sohms and R. L. Hall (eds.), *Criteria of food acceptance: How man chooses what he eats* (pp. 35–48). Zurich: Forster Verlag.

Rozin, P., and Schiller, D. (1980). The nature of a preference for chili pepper by humans. *Motivation and Emotion*, 4, 77–101.

Rozin, P., and Zellner, D. (1985). The role of Pavlovian conditioning in the acquisition of food likes and dislikes. In N. Braverman and P. Bronstein (eds.), *Experimental assessments and clinical applications of conditioned food aversions* (pp. 189–202). New York: New York Academy of Sciences.

Satter, E. (1986). *Child of mine*. Palo Alto, CA: Bull.

     (1987). *How to get your kid to eat . . . but not too much*. Palo Alto, CA: Bull.

     (1990). The feeding relationship: problems and interventions. *Journal of Pediatrics*, 117, S181–S189.

Story, M., and Faulkner, P. (1990). The prime time diet: A content analysis of eating behavior and food messages in television program content and commercials. *American Journal of Public Health*, 80, 738–740.

Striegel-Moore, R. (1995). Psychological factors in the etiology of binge eating. *Addictive Behaviors*, 20, 713–723.

Sullivan, S. A., and Birch, L. L. (1990). Pass the sugar, pass the salt: Experience dictates preference. *Developmental Psychology*, 26, 546–551.

Sylvester, G., Achterberg, C., and Williams, J. (1995). Children's television and nutrition: Friends or foes? *Nutrition Today*, 30, 6–15.

Thelen, M. H., Powell, A. L., Lawrence, C., and Kuhnert, M. E. (1992). Eating and body image concerns among children. *Journal of Clinical Child Psychology*, 21, 41–46.

Wardle, J., and Marsland, L. (1990). Adolescent concerns about weight and eating; a social-developmental perspective. *Journal of Psychosomatic Research*, 34(4), 377–391.

Williams, J. D., Achterberg, C., and Sylvester, G. (1993). Target marketing of food products to ethnic minority youth. In C. Williams and S. Y. S. Kim (eds.), *Prevention and treatment of childhood obesity: Annals of the New York Academy of Sciences*, vol. 699 (pp. 107–114). New York: New York Academy of Sciences.

Zahorik, D. M., Maier, S. F., and Pies, R. W. (1974). Preferences for tastes paired with recovery from thiamine deficiency in rats: Appetitive conditioning or learned safety. *Journal of Comparative and Physiological Psychology*, 87, 1,083–1,091.

8 The ethics of emaciation: moral connotations of body, self, and diet

Carol J. Nemeroff and Carolyn J. Cavanaugh

Body and society

Throughout time and across cultures, the body and its primary form of material transaction with the environment, eating, have been the subjects of intense moral symbolism and attempts to regulate, restrict, and control (Douglas, 1966; Nemeroff and Rozin, 1989; Rozin, 1990, 1996). Modifications to the body serve a variety of functions, from simple ornamentation (e.g., earrings in modern western society) to rites of passage (e.g., subincision among Australian Aborigines), marks of group affiliation (e.g., circumcision among week-old Jewish males) or station in life (e.g., the dot on the forehead worn by Hindu Indian women or tattooing upon earning a master's rating among traditional Manx sailors). Jewelry, makeup, and fashions in clothing are ancient and more or less universal, as are religious and spiritual practices involving control over food and sex, abstentions and purges, and "mortifications of the flesh." Clearly, management of the body – its appearance, its boundaries, what goes in and what comes out – is a potent means of managing both the social and the personal image of self (Douglas, 1966; Nemeroff *et al.*, 1996).

Within the current western cultural context, thinness (and to a growing extent, fitness and healthiness) has come to represent virtue, success, and status. This is especially so for women. Many authors have speculated as to the exact nature of the symbolism involved. Thinness has been touted as the new virginity, claim to equal status with men through androgyny, rejection of femininity through rejection of the fertile "mother" form, or submission to the childlike role to which women are relegated through rejection of feminine secondary sexual characteristics such as breasts or hips (see, for example, Gilday, 1990; Kilbourne, 1998; Wolf, 1991). All agree, though, that thinness is seen as a mark of self-control and superiority (Brownell, 1991; Brownmiller, 1984; Nemeroff *et al.*, 1994; Stein and Nemeroff, 1995). Even the foods and practices that promote thinness are considered more positive in general, and more virtuous in particular (Chaiken and Pliner, 1987; Stein and Nemeroff, 1995). This sociocultural emphasis on thinness has been linked to multiple negative outcomes for women, including poor body esteem, rampant dieting behavior, and full-blown eating pathology (Pike and Rodin, 1991; Rodin et al., 1984; Stice, 1994; Stice and Shaw, 1994; Striegel-Moore et al., 1986). Dissatisfaction with one's body and weight is common enough to have been termed a "normative discontent" by Rodin et al. (1984); indeed, Polivy and Herman (1985) reported having difficulty identifying "normal" (that is, non-dieting) controls for their studies on effects of dieting. Ironically, all of these trends are occurring in the context of increasing levels of obesity, particularly in the United States (Gortmaker et al., 1987, 1990).

The majority of the theoretical and empirical literature on these issues focuses on adolescent and adult women. However, a number of investigations have shown similar trends among pre-pubertal children. Children learn the importance of appearance at a very early age, and what is valued and stigmatized; 6-year old children have been shown to be aware of the stigmatized status of obesity, attributing negative attributes such as laziness, naughtiness, dishonesty, and stupidity to overweight children (Staffieri, 1967). Children as young as 3 years of age categorize others on the basis of weight, preferring normal weight children to overweight ones (White et al., 1985). Females are becoming concerned about their own weight at ever younger ages (Boskind-White, 1991). In a study of London schoolchildren, Wardle and Beales (1986) found that a majority of girls aged 12 to 17 considered themselves overweight, in spite of actually being normal or even underweight, according to standard height and weight ranges for their ages. They engaged in dieting behavior and experienced guilt when not dieting. Salmons et al. (1988) reported over one-quarter of 11–13-year-old girls from a Birmingham (UK) school claiming "always" being terrified of gaining weight. Using a figure rating task, Collins (1991) found that 42 percent of girls as young as 6–7 years preferred body figures thinner than their own. Thompson et al. (1997) similarly reported that 41 percent of white and 39 percent of black fourth-grade females selected an ideal body size thinner than their current size, while Tiggeman and Wilson-Barrett (1998) found significant body dissatisfaction, specifically, desire to be thinner, among girls of all ages across third to seventh grades (8–13 years). Huon and Strong (1998) report that up to 80 percent of young females say they have dieted at some time. Gender differences in dieting frequency are also apparent: a survey of obese children revealed that only 49 percent of obese boys reported trying to lose weight in the previous year and 13 percent reported currently dieting, while 90 percent of obese girls reported a history of dieting and 72 percent reported currently trying to lose weight (Wadden et al., 1996).

These trends among adult women and female children are alarming, given the well-documented pathogenicity of over-concern with thinness and dieting. But they are not especially surprising given the centrality of appearance and thinness to the female gender role (e.g., Rodin *et al.*, 1984), and the primacy of food and the body in human psychology and experience (Nemeroff and Rozin, 1989; Rozin, 1990, 1996).

Body as "public self"

The physical or "bodily" self appears to be an especially important component of global self-concept, as indicated by the work of Harter and her colleagues (e.g., Harter, 1988). Harter reports that children are capable of making judgments about their global self-worth by the age of 8. Between 8 and 12 years, children consider five domains when evaluating their global self-worth and the number and type of domains considered increases and changes as people mature. Regardless of age, however, a domain that is *always* considered is physical appearance. Indeed, evaluation of one's physical self proves to be the *most* important contributor to global self-worth, for both genders, throughout the life span. Across samples of subjects ranging in age from 8 to 50 years, Harter and colleagues report correlations between physical appearance self-evaluations and global self-worth of approximately 0.65 (Harter, 1988). During the college years this correlation may be as high as 0.80 (Harter, 1988). Based on the magnitude and consistency of these correlations, Harter has speculated that physical appearance might be qualitatively different from other domains of self-concept, in that it is an especially pervasive aspect of the self, "a manifestation of the *outer self* [which is] always on display" (Harter, 1988, p. 21).

Based on this notion, Cavanaugh (1992) attempted to determine whether the enhanced importance of appearance for global self-esteem might be due to its generalized relevance to those other self-aspects as well. For example, although one might in theory distinguish social or professional self-concept from appearance self-concept, in practice both of the former might be influenced by the latter – as in the case of a dancer's professional self-evaluation, or a wife's self-evaluation as a spouse. Cavanaugh (1992) hypothesized that for women high in "self-complexity" (Linville, 1985, 1987) body esteem should be less highly correlated with global self-esteem, relative to women low in self-complexity. High self-complexity women are those who use a large number of relatively independent aspects to cognitively organize knowledge about themselves, while low self-complexity women use fewer independent aspects in thinking about themselves. The logic behind Cavanaugh's (1992) prediction was that, when self-descriptive aspects or domains are few in number, each will contribute more to global self-esteem than when there are more self-descriptive domains. Essentially, each comprises a larger or smaller slice of the self-esteem "pie" depending on how many servings it is divided into. Further, the more these domains overlap – in the sense that experiences that activate one also activate others – the more emotional "spillover" there should be from one domain to another (Linville, 1985). Thus to the extent that physical appearance overlaps with other self-descriptive domains, it should be more important to global self-esteem. But if a woman who has poor body esteem is highly self-complex, then negative affect regarding her body should be contained in a small number of self-aspects, and not unduly affect overall feelings about herself.

Female undergraduate students completed a series of questionnaires assessing demographic information, self-esteem (Rosenberg, 1965), and body esteem (Franzoi and Shields, 1984), and a trait-sort to assess self-complexity (Linville, 1985, 1987). Unlike Linville's original trait sort, the version used by Cavanaugh (1992) included adjectives related to the physical self, to allow calculation of both general self-complexity and of an alternative index: proportion of self defined in terms of body image traits, weighted by the importance of those self aspects. A hierarchical multiple regression tested whether, as hypothesized, self-complexity would moderate the relation between body esteem and global self-esteem. No moderation was found, indicating that high self-complexity offers no protection against the powerful impact of body esteem on global self-esteem. An identical regression using the alternative index of body-specific self-complexity, showed that it did no better at moderating the impact of body esteem on global self-esteem. The disturbing implication of these findings is that, by young adulthood, there may be an "unshakable" relation between body esteem and self-esteem – one which is not affected by the degree to which a woman's self-concept is complex, nor by the number of domains to which she feels physical appearance is relevant.

If the special status of physical appearance as an aspect of self is not accomplished via structural aspects of self-concept, then how can it be explained? The answer may lie in Harter's (1988) claim that physical appearance serves as a "public self" always on display: as such, it would powerfully affect how people respond to one. In fact, appearance has been documented to strongly influence how others perceive and treat an individual, with physically attractive people judged as kinder, more honest, more intelligent, and more talented; more likely to be hired for a job; and more likely to receive a higher salary than unattractive people (Cialdini, 1985). Stice et al. (1996) have demonstrated that perceived social pressures regarding appearance can have direct effects on behavior even without one's necessarily "buying in" to such thinking. In a test of the "dual pathway" model of bulimia, these authors found a (predicted) mediational path from perceived pressure to be thin, to internalization of the thin ideal, to body dissatisfaction, and finally to restrained eating (dieting). However, they also found two unpredicted *direct* paths: the first from perceived pressure directly to body dissatisfaction; and a second from perceived pressure directly to dieting behavior. Both paths bypassed "internalization" of the thin ideal, suggesting that social pressures regarding appearance can affect both self-esteem and behavior directly, without depending on an apparently critical aspect of appearance self-concept.

Gender differences in body esteem

During early adolescence, gender differences emerge in body esteem and its impact on self-esteem, and these remain throughout the life-span (Rodin *et al.*, 1984). In a survey of over 600 people ranging in age from 10 to 79 years, Pliner *et al.* (1990) found that women at every age level expressed significantly greater dissatisfaction than men in the areas of weight and appearance of their bodies. Fallon and Rozin (1985) reported similar results when they had college men and women select from a series of silhouettes the ones that best represented their current and ideal body shapes. They found a much larger discrepancy between ideal and actual body shape among females than males, with females perceiving their current body to be significantly bigger than their ideal.

This gender difference in body esteem seems likely to be due to the fact that physical appearance has traditionally been more central to the female gender role than it is to the male gender role (Rodin *et al.*, 1984). Thinner, more physically attractive women are perceived as more feminine than larger, less attractive ones (Polivy *et al.*, 1986; Guy *et al.*, 1980). The media's portrayal of the "model woman," for example, Miss America pageant contestants and Playboy centerfolds, has grown progressively thinner since the 1950s (Garner *et al.*, 1980; Wiseman *et al.*, 1992; Nemeroff *et al.*, 1994). It is important to note that while these "model" women have become strikingly thinner over this time-span, the average US woman's weight and body proportions have actually become larger, creating an increasing discrepancy between the culturally endorsed ideal and reality. The messages that women receive from the media not only tell them that they should be thinner, but also provide a variety of methods for (supposedly) becoming so. Surveys of men's and women's magazines have revealed dramatically more articles and advertisements on body size and shape, and for diet foods and methods, in women's magazines as compared with men's magazines (Silverstein *et al.*, 1986;

Nemeroff et al., 1994). It seems inescapable that the cumulative effect of these messages being continually presented by such omnipresent sources would be an increased likelihood for women to internalize these norms, and engage in dieting and other restrictive behaviors. The facts that Americans spend almost $33 billion annually on diets and diet-related products (Kilbourne, 1998), and that two-thirds of US dieters are women (Schlosberg, 1987), support this assertion.

The psychological context of food and its symbolism

Personal attractiveness concerns and social pressure to be thin and attractive undoubtedly play a major role in creating a high level of concern with body and eating in girls and young women, which in turn promotes disordered eating. However, it would be a grave mistake to stop here in an analysis of the sources of those concerns, for we would be overlooking both the powerful general symbolism associated with food and eating, and the fundamental psychological relations between self, body, and ingestion. Eating is, after all, the focus of the earliest social bond, the mother–infant feeding relationship. It is, further, a primary mechanism for socialization and potent marker of cultural identity (Rozin, 1990; Rozin and Fallon, 1981, 1987). Cultural rules govern what is eaten, how and when it is prepared and served, who eats with whom, and so on (e.g., Marriott, 1968; Rozin, 1996). Ingestion is a psychologically "loaded" activity on an individual level, too, inasmuch as for omnivores like humans (and rats and cockroaches), eating can be a particularly hazardous endeavor, and the mouth is the last checkpoint where substances can be identified and evaluated as food or toxin, and prevented from entering the body if necessary (Nemeroff and Rozin, 1989; Rozin and Fallon, 1981, 1987). The psychological importance of ingestion was acknowledged by Freud, who included "oral incorporation" as a fundamental concept in his theoretical formulations (Freud, [1913]1950; Nemeroff and Rozin, 1989); it is reflected also in the extreme potency of the orally based emotion of disgust (Rozin and Fallon, 1987; Rozin et al., 1995). Some subset of potential foodstuffs tends to be tabooed cross-culturally, although exactly which substances are prohibited obviously varies from culture to culture. By definition, though, things that are "taboo" are both powerful and heavily laden with moral value.

"You are what you eat"

An ingestion-related belief that is common in traditional cultures is that "you are what you eat," i.e., the notion that one will take on some or all of the properties of the foods one eats (e.g., Crawley, 1902; Frazer,

[1890]1959). This maxim is not unreasonable, psychologically speaking. Ingestion is a particularly potent form of contact, in which a substance is taken in and literally made part of one's body. In fact, this principle is occasionally true, as in the case of developing orange skin pigmentation from eating an overabundance of yellow fruits and vegetables, due to an excess of beta-carotene. But in general, the principles of digestion argue against the transmission of higher-level properties such as swiftness from eating rabbit or deer, for example. Biological training notwithstanding, however, Nemeroff and Rozin (1989) demonstrated "you are what you eat" beliefs to be operative at a covert level among college students in the United States. They had subjects read one of two versions of a description of a (fictitious) culture, in which typical members either regularly ate marine turtle, and hunted wild boar only for its tusk, or ate wild boar, and hunted marine turtle only for its shell. (Thus culture members in both versions presumably possessed skills relevant to procuring the animals; the only difference was in which they *ingest*.) Subjects then rated the typical culture member on an adjective checklist containing items relevant to boars and turtles. Marine turtle eaters were rated as more turtle-like than boar eaters – better swimmers, less facial hair, more phlegmatic, and so on. In a follow-up contrasting elephant eaters with vegetarians, elephant eaters were rated as more animal-like in general (e.g., interesting, loud) and more elephant-like, specifically (e.g., leathery skin, big build).

In a follow-up focusing on a more US-culture relevant version of "you are what you eat," which presumably might be operative at a more explicit level, Stein and Nemeroff (1995) explored the moral connotations of healthy and slimming foods, as opposed to unhealthy and fattening foods. The hypothesis that the moral significance of food in the United States is currently heavily bound up with its perceived contribution to healthiness and weight was based on everyday observations where one finds desserts described as "sinful" and people who successfully or unsuccessfully maintain their diets over a weekend morally commending or castigating themselves. Stein and Nemeroff (1995) began by having a small sample of subjects free-list five to ten foods that they thought of as "good" or as "bad," and then explaining briefly why they considered them so. Except for the (conceptually uninteresting) subset of responses for which explanations were based on taste factors alone, virtually all explanations were cast in terms of the healthiness and fatteningness (fat, sugar, and calorie content) of the foods. Based on this pilot test, two short lists were developed, one comprised of good or "virtuous" foods (e.g., fruit, chicken, potatoes, home-made bread), and the other of bad or "debauched" foods (e.g., double-fudge ice-cream sundaes, steaks, French fried potatoes). Subjects read a fictitious description of a college student who was of average height and weight, enjoyed tennis and running, and regularly ate either the good foods or the bad foods. Subjects then rated that student on a checklist including several moral adjectives, as well as adjectives geared to determining the mechanism of effects. Good food eaters were seen as substantially more moral than bad food eaters. Beliefs pertaining to both a "puritan ethic" (whereby hard work and self-control are virtuous and enjoyment is suspect) and to purity and pollution concerns were the major bases for the moral-food effect.

Scott-King and Nemeroff (1989) wondered whether such thinking about food might be present in young children, who are often presumed to be "magical thinkers" (e.g., Piaget, [1921]1959; Fraiberg, 1959). "You are what you eat" can be construed as a magical belief in two senses: first, it is characteristic of traditional societies, and second, it is likely to be based in one of the principles of sympathetic magic identified in the nineteenth century by anthropologists Tylor ([1871]1974), Frazer ([1890]1959), and Mauss ([1902]1972). Frazer in particular compiled thousands of examples of magical beliefs and practices from cultures worldwide, and concluded that three basic principles underlay most if not all of them. The principle of relevance here was named the "magical law of contagion" and it holds, briefly, that when two entities come into contact with each other, properties are transmitted between them; this transfer may be permanent. Contact may be very brief, and may be direct (as in a handshake) or indirect (i.e., transmitted through some medium object, as when a contagious source wears a sweater or touches an object later worn or touched by the recipient).[1] Inasmuch as ingestion is a particularly potent form of contact, it should be an excellent means of transmitting contagious properties – hence "you are what you eat."

Children are generally held to be "magical thinkers" and to outgrow this tendency as they mature. However, in one of the earliest studies investigating "magical contagion" beliefs, Rozin et al., (1986) concluded that contagion-thinking is not present in its full-blown form prior to approximately age 7. Thus magical contagion may be a type of magical thinking that is grown into, to some extent, rather than grown out of.

In an attempt to evaluate whether the "you are what you eat" principle is operative in young children, Scott-King and Nemeroff (1989) developed a series of stories involving twin children and twin animals who did not wish to be told apart. Children were asked to help the adults in the stories choose the best "test" to tell them apart, from several options presented. One option was based on the "you are what you eat" principle – each twin was described as liking to eat different foods, and the adult tested them on some property characteristic of that food (e.g., of two cats, one likes to drink milk, and the other likes to eat grasshoppers; the adult considers giving them a jumping test – implicitly based on the assumption that the grasshopper-eater should be a better jumper). Other options included a "magical non-mechanism" (e.g., think really hard); a general health option based on the presumptive nutritional values of the foods (take the cats to a veterinarian to see which is healthier); an adult-type "rational" option (put both foods in front of both animals when they are hungry and see who eats which); and a nonsense option. Subjects were thirty-six children between the ages of 3 and 6 years, divided into three age groups.

There was no clear evidence of "you are what you eat" thinking in children of any of the three age groups, not all that surprising in light of Rozin et al.'s (1986) failure to find contagion fully developed at such early ages. What was surprising about children's responses was threefold: first, while the youngest age group showed no preference for any option, the middle age group clearly preferred the rational adult-type option – they were perfect little rationalists. Second, by the third age group, the children shifted away from the so-called adult-type option, and instead considered the healthiness option to be the best choice and clearly thought of some foods as being healthier than others. While this was not originally intended as an alternative "rational" response, Scott-King and Nemeroff (1989) put a 16-year-old subject through the identical protocol – and she too selected the healthiness option as the best strategy. Finally, a few children spontaneously commented on the fatteningness of the foods! What all this might seem to suggest is that children are absorbing parental and/or societal messages regarding the connections between food, health, and perhaps thinness, well before their own symbolic capacities generate a notion of moral-food contagion.

Food as a vehicle for contagion

In addition to acting as a potential *source* of contagion, food can also act as a *vehicle* or carrier for attributes or pollution from other sources. The Hua of Papua New Guinea believe, for example, that food hunted, prepared, or contacted in various other ways by a given individual can become a vehicle for transfer of that person's qualities or intentions to whomever ingests that food (Meigs, 1984; Nemeroff and Rozin, 1989). Along similar lines, rules delimiting who may interact – and in what ways – with foods which will be ingested by people of a given caste, play a major role in maintaining and signifying social relations and distinctions in Hindu India (Appadurai, 1981; Marriott, 1968). This principle too appears to be operative in modern western culture at least at an implicit level: surely tea or soup made by a cold sufferer's own mother would be more welcome than the very same tea or soup prepared by their despised neighbor. Indeed, Rozin *et al*. (1989) demonstrated just such effects among a college student sample, finding that people prefer an apple bitten by a friend to one bitten by a disliked peer or stranger, and so on.

The symbolism of body and self

Eating obviously involves allowing external "stuff" to gain entry into the physical self and, as noted above, the mouth is a critical checkpoint in this risky process. But the mouth is not alone in its status as a place where the boundary between inside and outside, and hence self and world, is blurred. The bodily self is defined by a "sheath" of skin (Goffman, 1971) which is punctuated by several apertures (nostrils, ears, eyes, etc.), all of which tend to be seen as places of special vulnerability relative to other areas of the sheath, and all of which are guarded from intrusions (Rozin *et al*., 1995). In general, the degree of perceived vulnerability of an aperture corresponds approximately to the extent to which that aperture is considered intimate, or part of the self (Rozin *et al*., 1995). As Douglas (1966) suggested, we seem to think of these orifices as "gates" at the "borders" of the body, and of the bodily sheath as a somewhat permeable container for the self. Because of this, what gets into the body can have powerful implications for the sense of self since, psychologically speaking, what enters the body, enters the self. Cross-culturally, physical purification rituals (including fasting and purging) are used to cleanse oneself of sin and regulate personal moral integrity. Such practices are particularly common in cultures characterized by what has been termed an "ethics of divinity" (Haidt *et al*., 1997; Rozin, 1990). In such cultures the self is considered as a spiritual entity which strives for purity and avoids pollution, and the body is the temple which houses it. This type of conflation of physical and non-physical realms, and of body with self or spirit, is not unique to traditional cultures, however. As we have seen, purity and pollution concerns and beliefs are common in the modern United States (albeit at a more implicit level). Not only are foods considered virtuous or evil depending on health value and caloric content (Stein and Nemeroff, 1995), but also immoral people are seen as polluting, and their residues and possessions avoided, while contact with good or holy individuals is seen as uplifting, or at times even healing or curative (e.g., Nemeroff and Rozin, 1994; Haidt *et al*., 1997). Food is just one type of potential source or carrier of contagion in a broadly contagious world-view.

Within this broad context, food can represent not only nourishment or toxin, but also nurturance or threat, purity or pollution, elevation or debasement. Because entry into the body *is* entry into the self, control over the body – over what enters and leaves it, through its various apertures but especially through the all-important mouth – *is* control over the self.

Magico-moral thinking in the eating disorders

We believe that the current societal context of overwhelming pressure to be thin interacts with the general symbolism associated with ingestion, to create the unprecedented level of eating pathology that we are currently seeing among young women. Both anorexia and bulimia nervosa have been steadily on the rise since the 1960s (Wilfley and Rodin, 1995; Lucas, *et al.*, 1991; Fairburn and Beglin, 1990) and while they once appeared more or less limited to young Caucasian women of relatively high socioeconomic status, this is no longer the case (Wilfley and Rodin, 1995). Eating disorders are now rampant throughout the western world (American Psychiatric Association [APA], 1994); they are increasingly common among African-American, Hispanic, and other once-protected minority groups in the United States and elsewhere (Hsu, 1987; Lee, 1995, 1996); even rates among males are on the rise (Andersen, 1995).

Description of syndromes

According to the fourth edition of the *Diagnostic and statistical manual of mental disorders*, (DSM-IV: APA, 1994), anorexia nervosa is characterized by four major criteria: (1) refusal to maintain body weight over an expected minimum for age and height, such that body weight is at least 15 percent below expected weight (or in children, failure to make appropriate weight gains); (2) intense fear of gaining weight or becoming fat, in spite of being underweight; (3) disturbance in the way in which one's body weight, size, or shape is experienced; (4) in post-menarcheal females, the absence of at least three consecutive menstrual cycles when otherwise expected to occur. In the "restricting type," weight loss is accomplished through dieting, food refusal, and exercise, while in the "bulimic type," the individual purges via use of laxatives, diuretics, enemas, and/or self-induced vomiting. Both have approximately the same long-term prognosis; however, bulimic anorexia has been associated with relatively more difficulties with impulse control, including behaviors such as stealing, suicide attempts, and substance use (APA, 1994). The mean age of onset for anorexia is approximately 17 years, and the death rate is approximately 10 percent, whether from the effects of starvation or due to suicide (APA, 1994).

In contrast to anorexia, bulimia nervosa is diagnosed in women of normal weight or more. Criteria include (1) recurrent episodes of binge eating, defined as eating an inordinately large amount in a discrete period of time and feeling a lack of control during the episode; (2) recurrent inappropriate compensatory behavior to prevent weight gain, including use of laxatives, diuretics, enemas, or other medications, self-induced vomiting, and/or excessive exercise; (3) two binges per week for at least three months (on average); (4) self-evaluation unduly influenced by body shape and weight. In the "purging subtype," compensatory behaviors involve vomiting, laxatives, or diuretics, as opposed to the "non-purging subtype." Average age of onset is slightly later than for anorexia, and the mortality rate is substantially lower. However serious psychological, social, and physical complications are common, including dental erosion and esophageal damage as a result of chronic vomiting, and severe electrolyte imbalances (APA, 1994).

Etiological accounts of the eating disorders

A plethora of models have been put forth in attempts to explain the development of eating disorders, from diverse theoretical orientations. Biological accounts typically focus on hypothetical hypothalamic dysfunction or other disturbances of the hypothalamic–pituitary axis in anorexia (see Hsu [1987] for a review). Reid's (1990) biological account of bulimia is based on models of substance abuse, proposing that the release of endogenous opiates (endorphins) that typically follows binging and purging actually results in a form of addiction to these behaviors. While intriguing, such explanations have equivocal empirical support at best, and appear to do better as accounts of effects and/or maintaining mechanisms of anorexia and bulimia, rather than of etiology (Marx, 1994).

Psychodynamic approaches began with Freud's and Janet's descriptions of anorexic girls as attempting to avoid womanhood and heterosexuality, by preventing bodily maturation through starvation; these scholars also discussed the role of disgust, and the use of food in a contest of wills and/or attempt at self-mastery (Masson, 1985). Although these early themes were later revisited by psychosocial theorists, including Bruch (1962), Crisp (1980), and Minuchin et al. (1978), later psychodynamic approaches shifted focus, speculating elaborately about unconscious sexual symbolism and the wish for, or rejection of, oral impregnation by the father – a view often erroneously attributed to Freud himself (e.g., J. V. Waller et al., 1940, as cited in Blinder and Chao, 1994). With the development of object relations theories, early problems in separation-individuation were held culpable, supposedly resulting in impairments in object constancy and subsequent use of the body to achieve fusion with a "sensori-motor mother," as represented by food (Sugarman and Kurash, 1982; Johnson and Connors, 1987).

Currently, though, the most influential models are the "psychosocial" or "sociocultural" models. Beginning with Hilde Bruch's (1962) astute observation that societal changes and pressures on young women appeared to contribute to the genesis of anorexia, these models have taken as their starting point the cultural ideal of feminine beauty. They describe eating disorders as doomed and misguided attempts to achieve an impossibly thin ideal. But Bruch herself focused on the issue of identity in this process, concluding that anorexia was a misguided exercise of will in a desperate attempt at individuation (Bruch, 1973). Minuchin and colleagues (e.g., Minuchin et al., 1978) explored the family context that set the stage for this struggle for self-identity, by failing to provide privacy and thus to allow for the development of boundaries. Feminist-based sociocultural theories agree on the issue of identity deficits, although they focus attention and blame squarely on pervasive sociocultural messages and pressures regarding thinness (e.g., Boskind-Lodahl, 1976).

There is no question that the media in western societies have run amok with an increasingly, and at the moment, impossibly thin ideal for women (e.g., Garner et al., 1980; Nemeroff et al., 1994; Wiseman et al., 1992), and with antifat prejudice (Brown and Rothblum, 1989). There is also a great deal of evidence, both indirect and direct, to support the idea that the thin ideal contributes to the development of eating symptomatology (e.g., Stice, 1994; Stice and Shaw, 1994). The fact that not all young women succumb, however, would seem to indicate that individual characteristics are also important. Along these lines, various theories have taken an integrative approach, suggesting that sociocultural pressures interact with individual characteristics such as coping skills (e.g., Weiss et al., 1985), or are mediated by individual factors such as degree of internalization of the thin ideal and body dissatisfaction (e.g., Stice et al., 1996, 1998). These forces are thought to culminate in some combination of restrictive dieting (which presumably predisposes to binges: Polivy and Herman, 1985) and negative affect (which can both result from dieting as described in Stice's work, and lead to binges as a means of coping with stress), the end result being eating disorders.

While the diversity of models is daunting, one theme runs through them with striking constancy: the theme of a vulnerable self with an impoverished sense of identity. Food, these models generally claim, becomes a medium for seeking emotional regulation and/or a sense of autonomy and mastery. The body takes on exaggerated importance in the face of an impoverished sense of psychological self and/or overwhelming societal forces dictating that one must be thin and beautiful. Smolack and

Levine (1994) added a developmental diathesis-stress component, speculating that the self is particularly vulnerable during periods of developmental transition. It is noteworthy that the peak age of onset of the eating disorders coincides with the age at which Erikson and others (e.g., Erikson, 1963) claim adolescent identity formation takes place.

Oddly, identity concerns are addressed only indirectly in the current diagnostic criteria, which describe only exaggerated concern with, and distorted perception of, body shape or weight. Furthermore, with the exception of occasional references to food as symbolizing pregnancy or maternal nurturance (e.g., J. V. Waller *et al.*, 1940; Lehman and Rodin, 1989; Sugarman and Kurash, 1982), the powerful and probably universal symbolism connected with food and eating as described earlier in this chapter are ignored. Lacking as well is any discussion of the nature and potential relevance of symbolic relations between body, self, and ingestion.

The role of magico-moral symbolism in the eating disorders

Schupak-Neuberg and Nemeroff (1993) took the notions of identity deficit and emotional regulation as starting points, and attempted to elucidate exactly how it is that a weak sense of self can be bolstered by, and negative emotions managed by, eating symptoms, be they fasting, binging, or purging. Our hypothesis was that when the psychological self-concept is tenuous, one is more likely to fall back on the bodily sheath – the concrete, physical self – to represent the whole of oneself. Thus the always common tendency to conflate self with body would be heightened in such individuals, leading to an exaggerated degree of concern with bodily boundaries in general, such as sensitivity to physical contact and intrusions, and regulation of what enters and leaves the body. For the restricting anorexic, rigid guarding of bodily boundaries from any and all intrusions could be construed as protecting a vulnerable self from external influences, perhaps creating a clear space in which a fragile self could arise or exist; or alternatively the attention to the boundaries might *constitute* a sense of self (i.e., "I am my boundaries" or even "I am my self-control"). Interestingly, anorexics tend to be extraordinarily resistant to therapeutic interventions geared to get them to eat even if they are at a point where they say they want to gain weight. If our model is accurate, then ingestion is not merely a matter of gaining weight, but actually implies intrusion and obliteration of a fragile self.

In bulimia, the hypothetical case is somewhat different; here, collapse of self-regulation in a binge might be construed as serving the purpose of obliterating painful self-awareness. For an individual with a negative self-image, painful affective states, and perhaps lacking the iron control of the anorexic, this would undoubtedly be experienced as a relief, if only a temporary one. With the return of awareness at the end of the binge, the food ingested would be likely to easily take on the role of a concrete source of negative self-feelings, which could then be conveniently expelled via purging.

We wish to point out that this approach is not incompatible with those reviewed earlier; rather it supplies a broad symbolic context that explains just how it is that the specific eating behaviors could accomplish the things that others have suggested they accomplish – a sense of self for the anorexic, and regulation of negative affect for the bulimic. We note as well that the existence of bulimic (purging) anorexics, and the frequency with which young women switch back and forth between the two disorders, suggests that it is not necessarily an either-or path. One can apparently combine and switch motivations and metaphors.

In an initial study, Schupak-Neuberg and Nemeroff (1993) compared bulimics with binge-eaters and normal controls, to explore three core aspects of this symbolic account of bulimia: the presence of identity deficits in bulimics relative to the other two groups; the use of the binge to escape self-awareness and of the purge to more or less literally expel a sense of pollution or negativity; and finally, exaggerated concern with bodily boundaries in general, as opposed to just ingestion. Our comparison of twenty-six bulimic women with twenty-five binge-eaters and thirty-one normal controls showed that bulimics reported the highest degree of identity confusion, and normal controls the lowest, with binge-eaters in between. Furthermore, bulimics differed from binge-eaters in the extent to which they experienced "escape from self" during a binge, and degree of identity confusion significantly predicted the extent to which binging accomplished this escape from self. While only bulimics answered questions about purging, obviously, their responses indicated that the purge does indeed serve to regulate negative affect. Furthermore, they endorsed items indicating that an expulsion metaphor was key to the effect (e.g., "Purging helps throw out feelings of frustration") as opposed to distraction or relaxation mechanisms. Open-ended responses also supported this conclusion. For example, one bulimic young woman stated, "As I binge, I think of the food being all my problems. As I devour them, they go down inside." Finally, bulimics showed significantly less willingness to engage in various forms of "contagious" contact, such as sharing clothes and hugging, with positive others (e.g., mother, friends) relative to binge-eaters and controls. Once again, degree of identity confusion significantly predicted the degree of avoidance of such contacts.

In a follow-up study in progress, by Nemeroff, Schupak-Neuberg, and

Graci, anorexics are being compared with restrained eaters (dieters) and non-eating symptomatic controls, exploring three core aspects of the metaphorical account of anorexia: identity deficit; exaggerated sensitivity to contact with others as a function of identity confusion; and use of fasting as a means of establishing a sense of self. (In the absence of binging or purging, no escape from self-awareness or expulsion of negative affect should occur, therefore fasting was not predicted to serve any affect-regulation function.) Based on data thus far from ten anorexic women (restricting subtype), seven dieters, and nine controls, identity deficits are significantly greater among anorexics, and anorexics derive more of a sense of control from fasting relative to restrained eaters. (Interestingly, the two groups do not differ in the extent to which fasting makes them feel more pure and less contaminated; this is because both groups report feeling less polluted when restricting intake.) Finally, once again degree of identity confusion significantly predicts degree of discomfort with contagious contacts with positive others.

Some of the open-ended responses given by anorexics are intriguing with regard to the notion of a sense of self being established through fasting. As one anorexic stated, "I feel as though I am strong and special from other people because I don't have to eat." Furthermore, while anorexics describe fasting in glowing, positive terms (e.g., "I love feeling empty..."), dieters report feeling grumpy, irritable, tired, and deprived while dieting, and are uniformly clear that weight loss is their goal. No anorexic spontaneously mentioned weight loss as the goal of fasting.

Accounting for differential vulnerability by gender

Anecdotal reports from many sources suggest that rates of eating disorders are on the rise among males. Societal pressures concerning appearance and even thinness (or perhaps, rather, leanness) are clearly increasing for men (Mishkind et al., 1986; Nemeroff et al., 1994; Prybock, 1997). Some years ago, Anderson and DiDomenico (1992) demonstrated that the ratio of dieting ads and articles in popular women's magazines to those in popular men's magazines exactly mirrored the ratio of female to male eating disorders: both were ten to one. The obvious implication is that, as social pressures to be concerned with appearance and particularly to diet, increase for males, eating disorders should increase accordingly (Nemeroff et al., 1994).

Yet there are several reasons why we would be surprised to see anorexia and bulimia reach the same levels among young men as they have attained among young women. First, while emphasis on male body and appearance are undoubtedly increasing at least among some subgroups, the messages regarding just how young men should strive to look may be far more heterogeneous than they are for women. Although football coaches may now be shown on television drinking diet-aid milkshakes, the general idealized prototype tends to be large, muscular, and warrior-like (e.g., Petrie *et al.*, 1996) rather than slight and willowy. Not surprisingly, Prybock (1997) notes that in studies assessing body image concerns and body dissatisfaction among males, subjects are about equally likely to report feeling underweight as they are feeling overweight – which might provide an artifactual explanation for why males have on average appeared to be satisfied with their bodies. Approximately half would be more likely to engage in attempts to gain weight, and "bulk up" with muscle, rather than to diet. Based on this logic, Prybock (1997) claims that obligatory exercise and use of anabolic-androgenic steroids might be male equivalents of eating disorders among women, and cites clinical reports of "reverse anorexia" in which male clients fear weight loss as intensely as anorexic women fear weight gain.

There is an additional reason why we think anorexia and bulimia seem unlikely to reach epidemic proportions among males: in general, we find gender differences in contagion-based thinking, with females being significantly more sensitive to both intrusion and contagion (i.e., contamination) concerns, as well as to disgust *per se* (Haidt *et al.*, 1994; Rozin *et al.*, 1995). This may be related to our physical differences: women, after all, have one important and extremely personal aperture that men do not have, which is involved in a major form of transaction between self and world, namely, sex. We have found that for men, the mouth is unequivocally the most sensitive and protected aperture; indeed many men are shocked to discover that women consider the vagina to be at least as sensitive and personal as the mouth. (Women, of course, are shocked to discover men's shock on this point.) Indeed, we have speculated that this may be one basis for some of the tragic sexual misunderstandings that end in rape (Rozin *et al.*, 1995). There is evidence to suggest that sexual abuse predisposes to eating disorders (see G. Waller [1994], for a review) and that eating disordered individuals have substantial difficulties concerning sexuality. Thus it may be that, as Erik Erikson (1968, p. 285) claimed, "anatomy is destiny" where the eating disorders are concerned, and that societal pressures (and even gender differences in sexual abuse) aside, women are more predisposed to manifesting identity issues via eating behavior because of the relatively more "incorporative" physical nature of being female.

All of the foregoing is highly speculative. Our bulimic data await replication, the anorexic study awaits completion, and much of the thinking presented about males and body image is thoroughly conjectural at best. Still, the symbolic account of eating disorders that we have described makes obvious the path whereby physical violation gives rise to eating symptoms. It also adds a new dimension to explanations of gender differences in these disorders.

Conclusions

We began by demonstrating that very young children already know that it is unacceptable and both pragmatically and morally bad to be fat in modern western culture. Body concerns are being documented at ever-younger ages, as are dieting behaviors and eating symptoms, primarily among young women. We reviewed evidence suggesting the special importance of physical appearance self-concept in determining overall self-esteem, and the failure of complexity of self-structure to moderate this relationship. We also described some of the powerful general symbolism associated with food and eating, both in terms of the magico-moral "you are what you eat" principle and the attendant "moral-food effect," and in terms of its broader progenitor, the "magical law of contagion." We have suggested that although such symbolic-moral thinking is not fully developed in young children, they nevertheless seem aware of some of the conclusions of such thinking even at very early ages. We have linked both societal pressures and magico-moral symbolic thinking to anorexia and bulimia nervosa, and provided preliminary data to support our speculations. Finally, we discussed the implications of changes in societal pressures, and gender differences in intuitive symbolism, with regard to what trends we might expect to see over the next few years concerning male body image and attempts to manage it.

We conclude that the eating disorders constitute a phenomenon in which current cultural and enduring human symbolism regarding body-as-self converge, at a critical point in self-development, to produce what is arguably the iconic psychopathology of our time for young women. And we invite theorists and researchers to further explore this approach, as well as to consider increasing their attention to the possible manifestations of bodily expectations and body dissatisfaction among men.

NOTE

1 Although germ theory is a scientifically validated subcase of magical contagion, the range of things seen as transmissible is far broader in the magical version than in its scientific counterpart.

REFERENCES

American Psychiatric Association (1994). *Diagnostic and statistical manual of mental Disorders*, 4th edn. Washington, DC: APA.

Andersen, A. (1995). Eating disorders in males. In K. Brownell and C. Fairburn (eds.), *Eating disorders and obesity: A comprehensive handbook* (pp. 177–182). New York: Guilford.

Andersen, A. E., and DiDomenico, L. (1992). Diet vs. shape content of popular male and female magazines: A dose–response relationship to the incidence of eating disorders? *International Journal of Eating Disorders*, 11, 283–287.

Appadurai, A. (1981). Gastro-politics in Hindu South Asia. *American Ethnologist*, 8, 494–511.

Blinder, B. J., and Chao, K. H. (1994). Eating disorders: A historical perspective. In L. Alexander-Mott and D. B. Lumsden (eds.), *Understanding eating disorders* (pp. 3–36). Washington, DC: Taylor and Francis.

Boskind-Lodahl, M. (1976). Cinderella's stepsisters: A feminist perspective on anorexia nervosa and bulimia. *Signs: Journal of Women in Culture and Society*, 2, 342–346.

Boskind-White, M. (1991). Gender and eating disorders. Paper presented at the Eating Disorders Conference, Tempe, AZ, February.

Brown, L. S., and Rothblum, E. D. (1989). *Overcoming fear of fat.* New York: Harrington.

Brownell, K. D. (1991). Personal responsibility and control over our bodies: When expectation exceeds reality. *Health Psychology*, 10 (5), 303–310.

Brownmiller, S. (1984). *Femininity.* New York: Linden.

Bruch, H. (1962). Perceptual and conceptual disturbances in anorexia nervosa. *Psychosomatic Medicine*, 24, 287–294.

(1973). *Eating disorders: Obesity and anorexia nervosa, and the person within.* New York: Basic Books.

Cavanaugh, C. J. (1992). Moderating the effect of body esteem on self-esteem: The role of self-complexity. Unpublished manuscript.

Chaiken, S., and Pliner, P. (1987). Women, but not men, are what they eat: The effect of meal size and gender on perceived femininity and masculinity. *Personality and Social Psychology Bulletin*, 13(2), 166–176.

Cialdini, R. (1985). *Influence.* Glenview, IL: Scott Foresman.

Collins, M. E. (1991). Body figure perceptions and preferences among preadolescent children. *International Journal of Eating Disorders*, 10,199–208.

Crawley, E. (1902). *The mystic rose: A study of primitive marriage.* London: Macmillan.

Crisp, A. (1980). *Anorexia nervosa: Let me be.* London: Academic Press.

Douglas, M. (1966). *Purity and danger.* London: Routledge and Kegan Paul.

Erikson, E. H. (1963). *Childhood and society*, 2nd edn. New York: Norton.

(1968). *Identity, youth and crisis.* New York: Norton.

Fairburn, C. G., and Beglin, S. J. (1990). Studies of the epidemiology of bulimia nervosa. *American Journal of Psychiatry*, 147, 401–408.

Fallon, A., and Rozin, P. (1985). Sex differences in perceptions of desirable body shape. *Journal of Abnormal Psychology*, 94, 102–5.

Fraiberg, S. H. (1959). *The magic years.* New York: Charles Scribner's Sons.

Franzoi, S., and Shields, S. (1984). The body esteem scale: Multidimensional structure and sex differences in a college population. *Journal of Personality Assessment*, 48(2), 173–178.

Frazer, J. G. ([1890]1959). *The new golden bough: A study in magic and religion (abridged)*. T. H. Gaster (ed.). New York: Macmillan.

Freud, S. ([1913]1950). *Totem and taboo.* New York: Norton.

Garner, D., Garfinkel, P., Schwartz, D., and Thompson, M. (1980). Cultural expectations of thinness in women. *Psychological Reports,* 47, 483–491.

Gilday, K. (director). (1990). *The famine within* (film). Direct Cinema Limited.

Goffman, E. (1971). *Relations in public.* New York: Harper and Row.

Gortmaker, S., Dietz, W., Sobol, A., and Wehler, C. (1987). Increasing pediatric obesity in the United States. *American Journal of Diseases in Children,* 141, 535–540.

Gortmaker, S., Dietz, W., and Cheung, L. (1990). Inactivity, diet, and the fattening of America. *Journal of the American Dietetic Association,* 90, 1,247–1,255.

Guy, F., Rankin, B., and Norville, M. (1980). The relation of sex-role stereotyping to body image. *Journal of Psychology,* 105, 167–177.

Haidt, J., McCauley, C. R., and Rozin, P. (1994). A scale to measure disgust sensitivity. *Personality and Individual Differences,* 16, 701–713.

Haidt, J., Rozin, P., McCauley, C. R., and Imada, S. (1997). Body, psyche, and culture: The relationship between disgust and morality. *Psychology and Developing Societies,* 9, 107–131.

Harter, S. (1988). Causes, correlates and the functional role of global self-worth: A life-span perspective. In J. Kolligan and R. Sternberg (eds.), *Perceptions of competence and incompetence across the lifespan* (pp. 67–97). New Haven, CT: Yale University Press.

Hsu, L. K. G. (1987). Are the eating disorders becoming more common in blacks? *International Journal of Eating Disorders,* 6(1), 113–124.

(1990). *Eating disorders.* New York: Guilford.

Huon, G. F., and Strong, K. G. (1998). The initiation and the maintenance of dieting: Structural models for large-scale longitudinal investigations. *International Journal of Eating Disorders,* 23, 361–370.

Johnson, C., and Connors, M. E. (1987). *The etiology and treatment of bulimia nervosa: A biopsychosocial perspective.* New York: Basic Books.

Kilbourne, J. (1998). *Killing us softly: Romance and rebellion in advertising.* New York: Henry Holt.

Lee, S. (1995). Self starvation in context: Towards a culturally sensitive understanding of anorexia nervosa. *Social Science Medicine,* 41, 25–36.

(1996). Clinical lessons from the cross cultural study of anorexia nervosa, *Eating Disorders Review,* 7, 1–3.

Lehman, A. K., and Rodin, J. (1989). Styles of self-nurturance and disordered eating. *Journal of Consulting and Clinical Psychology,* 57, 117–122.

Linville, P. (1985). Self-complexity and affective extremity: Don't put all your eggs in one basket. *Social Cognition,* 3, 94–120.

(1987). Self-complexity as a cognitive buffer against stress-related illness and depression. *Journal of Personality and Social Psychology,* 52(4), 663–676.

Lucas, A. R., Beard, C. M., O'Fallon, W. M., and Kurland, L. T. (1991). 50-year trends in the incidence of anorexia nervosa in Rochester, MN: A population-based study. *American Journal of Psychiatry,* 148 (7), 917–922.

Marriott, M. (1968). Caste ranking and food transactions: A matrix analysis. In

M. Singers and B. S. Cohn (eds.), *Structure and change in Indian society*, (pp. 23–64). Chicago: Aldine.

Marx, R. D. (1994). Anorexia nervosa: Theories of etiology. In L. Alexander-Mott and D. B. Lumsden (eds.), *Understanding eating disorders: Anorexia nervosa, bulimia nervosa, and obesity* (pp. 123–134). Washington, DC: Taylor and Francis.

Masson, J. M. (1985). *The complete letters of Sigmund Freud to Wilhelm Fliess: 1887–1904*. Cambridge, MA: Belknap.

Mauss, M. ([1902]1972). *A general theory of magic*. R. Brain (trans.). New York: Norton.

Meigs, A. S. (1984). *Food, sex, and pollution: A New Guinea religion*. New Brunswick, NJ: Rutgers University Press.

Minuchin, S., Rosman, B., and Baker, L. (1978). *Psychosomatic families: Anorexia nervosa in context*. Cambridge, MA: Harvard University Press.

Mishkind, M. E., Rodin, J., Silberstein, L. R., and Striegel-Moore, R. H. (1986). The embodiment of masculinity: Cultural, psychological, and behavioral dimensions. *American Behavioral Scientist*, 29, 545–562.

Nemeroff, C., and Rozin, P. (1989). "You are what you eat": Applying the demand-free "impressions" technique to an unacknowledged belief. *Ethos: Journal of the Society for Psychological Anthropology*, 17, 50–69.

(1994). The contagion concept in adult thinking in the United States: Transmission of germs and of interpersonal influence. *Ethos: Journal of Psychological Anthropology*, 22, 158–186.

Nemeroff, C., Stein, R., Diehl, N., and Smilack, K. (1994). From the Cleavers to the Clintons: Role choices and body orientation as reflected in magazine article content. *International Journal of Eating Disorders*, 16(2), 167–176.

Nemeroff, C., Schupak-Neuberg, E., and Graci, G. (1996). Je (ne) suis (que) mon corps: pensée magique et troubles du comportement alimentaire (My body, my self: magical thinking and eating disorders). In C. Fischler (ed.), *Pensée magique et alimentation aujourd'hui (Magical thinking and nutrition today)*, (pp. 86–100) CIDIL, Cahiers de l'OCHA, no. 5. Paris: CIDIL.

Petrie, T. A., Austin, L. J., Cowley, B. J., Helmcamp, A., et al. (1996). Sociocultural expectations of attractiveness for males. *Sex Roles*, 35, 581–602.

Piaget, J. ([1929]1951). *The child's conception of the world*. London: Routledge and Kegan Paul.

Pike, K. M., and Rodin, J. (1991). Mothers, daughters, and disordered eating. *Journal of Abnormal Psychology*, 100, 198–204.

Pliner, P., Chaiken, S., and Flett, G. (1990). Gender differences in concern with body weight and physical appearance over the lifespan. *Personality and Social Psychology Bulletin*, 16(2), 263–273.

Polivy, J., and Herman, C. P. (1983). *Breaking the dieting habit*. New York: Basic Books.

(1985). Dieting and binging: A causal analysis. *American Psychologist*, 4, 193–201.

Polivy, J., Garner, D., and Garfinkel, P. (1986). Causes and consequences in the current preference for thin female physiques. In C. P. Herman, M. P. Zanna, and E. T. Higgins (eds.), *Physical appearance, stigma and social behavior: The*

Ontario symposium, vol. III (pp. 89–111). Hillsdale, NJ: Erlbaum.

Prybock, D. (1997). Body dissatisfaction and its behavioral manifestations among males. Manuscript in preparation.

Reid, L. D. (ed.) (1990). Opioids, bulimia, and alcohol abuse and alcoholism. New York: Springer-Verlag.

Rodin, J., Silberstein, L., and Striegel-Moore, R. (1984). Women and weight: A normative discontent. In T. B. Sonderegger (ed.), Nebraska symposium on motivation, vol. XXXII, Psychology and gender (pp. 267–307). Lincoln, NB: University of Nebraska Press.

Rosenberg, M. (1965). Society and the adolescent self-image. NewYork: Basic Books.

Rozin, P. (1990). Social and moral aspects of food and eating. In I. Rocks (ed.), The legacy of Solomon Asch: Essays in cognition and social psychology (pp. 97–110). Hillsdale, NJ: Erlbaum.

    (1996). Towards a psychology of food and eating: From motivation to model to meaning, morality, and metaphor. Current Directions in Psychological Science, 5, 1–7.

Rozin, P., and Fallon, A. E. (1981). The acquisition of likes and dislikes for foods. In J. Solms and R. L. Halls (eds.), Criteria of food acceptance: How man chooses what he eats. A symposium (pp. 35–48). Zurich: Forster.

    (1987). A perspective on disgust. Psychological Review, 94, 23– 41.

Rozin, P., Fallon, A. E., and Augustoni-Ziskind, A. (1986). The child's conception of food: The development of contamination sensitivity to disgusting substances. Developmental Psychology, 21, 1,075–1,079.

Rozin, P., Nemeroff, C., Wane, M., and Sherrod, A. (1989). Operation of the laws of sympathetic magic in the interpersonal domain in American culture. Bulletin of the Psychonomic Society, 27 (4), 367–370.

Rozin, P., Nemeroff, C., Horowitz, M., Gordon, B., and Voet, W. (1995). The borders of the self: Contamination sensitivity and potency of the body apertures and other body parts. Journal of Research in Personality, 29, 318–340.

Salmons, P., Lewis, V., Rogers, P., Gatherer, A., and Booth, D. (1988). Body shape dissatisfaction in schoolchildren. British Journal of Psychiatry, 153 (supp. 2), 27–31.

Schlosberg, J. (1987). The demographics of dieting. American Demographics, 9(7), 34–37.

Schupak-Neuberg, E., and Nemeroff, C. J. (1993). Disturbances in identity and self-regulation in bulimia nervosa: Implications for a metaphorical perspective of "body as self." International Journal of Eating Disorders, 13, 335–347.

Scott-King, K., and Nemeroff, C. (1989). Developmental aspects of magical cognitions about food. Unpublished dataset.

Silverstein, B., Purdue, L., Peterson, B., and Kelly, E. (1986). The role of the mass media in promoting a thin standard of bodily attractiveness for women. Sex Roles, 14 (9/10), 519–532.

Smolack, L., and Levine, M.P. (1994). Critical issues in the developmental psychopathology of eating disorders. In L. Alexander-Mott and D. B. Lumsden (eds.), Understanding eating disorders (pp. 37–60). Washington, DC:

Taylor and Francis.

Staffieri, J. (1967). A study of social stereotypes of body image in children. *Journal of Personality and Social Psychology*, 7(1), 101–104.

Stein, R., and Nemeroff, C. (1995). Moral overtones of food: Judgments of others based on what they eat. *Personality and Social Psychology Bulletin*, 21, 480–490.

Stice, E. (1994). A review of the evidence for a sociocultural model of bulimia nervosa and an exploration of the mechanisms of action. *Clinical Psychology Review*, 14, 633–661.

Stice, E., and Shaw, H. (1994). Adverse effects of the media portrayed thin-ideal on women and linkages to bulimic symptomatology. *Journal of Clinical and Social Psychology*, 13(3), 288–308.

Stice, E., Nemeroff, C., and Shaw, H. (1996). A test of the dual-pathway model of bulimia nervosa: Evidence for dietary-restraint and affect-regulation mechanisms. *Journal of Social and Clinical Psychology*, 15, 340–363.

Stice, E., Shaw, H., and Nemeroff, C. (1998) Dual pathway model of bulimia nervosa: Longitudinal support for dietary restraint and affect-regulation mechanisms. *Journal of Social and Clinical Psychology*, 17, 129–149.

Striegel-Moore, R. H., Silberstein, L. R., and Rodin, J. (1986). Toward an understanding of risk factors for bulimia. *American Psychologist*, 41, 246–263.

Sugarman, A., and Kurash, C. (1982). The body as a transitional object in bulimia. *International Journal of Eating Disorders*, 1, 57–67.

Thompson, S. H., Corwin, S. J., and Sargent, R. G. (1997). Ideal body size beliefs and weight concerns of fourth-grade children. *International Journal of Eating Disorders*, 21, 279–284.

Tiggeman, M., and Wilson-Barrett, E. (1998). Children's figure ratings: Relationship to self-esteem and negative stereotyping. *International Journal of Eating Disorders*, 23, 83–88.

Tylor, E. B. ([1871]1974). *Primitive culture: Researches into the development of mythology, philosophy, religion, art, and custom*. New York: Gordon.

Wadden, T., Steen, S., Foster, G., and Andersen, R. (1996). Are obese adolescent boys ignoring an important health risk? *International Journal of Eating Disorders*, 20, 281–286.

Waller, G., Everill, J., and Calam, R. (1994). Sexual abuse and the eating disorders. In L. Alexander-Mott and D. B. Lumsden (eds.), *Understanding eating disorders*, (pp. 77–98). Washington, DC: Taylor and Francis.

Waller, J. V., Kaufman, M. R., and Deutsch, F. (1940). Anorexia nervosa: A psychosomatic entity. *Psychosomatic Medicine*, 2, 3–16.

Wardle, J., and Beales, S. (1986). Restraint, body image and food attitudes in children from 12 to 18 years. *Appetite*, 7, 209–217.

Weiss, L., Katzman, M., and Wolchik, S. (1985). *Treating bulimia: A psychoeducational approach*. New York: Pergamon.

White, D., Mauro, K., and Spindler, J. (1985). Development of body-type salience: Implications for early childhood educators. *International Review of Applied Psychology*, 34, 422–433.

Wilfley, D., and Rodin, J. (1995). Cultural influences on eating disorders. In K. Browenell and C. Fairburn (eds.) *Eating disorders and obesity: A comprehensive handbook* (pp. 78–82). New York: Guilford.

Wiseman, M., Gray, J., Mosimann, J., and Ahrens, H. (1992). Cultural expectations of thinness in women: An update. *International Journal of Eating Disorders*, 11, 85–89.

Wolf, N. (1991). *The beauty myth: How images of beauty are used against women.* New York: William Morrow.

Part III

Applications

9 Considering children's folkbiology in health education

*Terry Kit-fong Au, Laura F. Romo, and
Jennifer E. DeWitt*

A prevalent approach to health education is to focus on dos and don'ts.
We are advised to exercise more; eat more fruit and vegetables; take
vitamins, folic acid, zinc, and whatever the latest health studies suggest
that we should take; reduce our intake of saturated fat, salt, alcohol, and
so forth; refrain from smoking; use condoms; wash hands frequently and
avoid touching our faces during the flu season; always finish the full
course of antibiotics prescribed by our doctors; cook chicken thoroughly;
wash hands with soap after handling raw eggs and meat. Even though it is
easier to remember things that make sense than to remember a number of
unconnected facts (Dooling and Lachman, 1971), health educators typically try to help us remember lists of recommendations by nagging (i.e.,
sheer repetition) rather than by helping us make sense of the dos and
don'ts.

Consider the current approach to AIDS education. In schools as well as
the public media, the basic messages in AIDS education are simple
(perhaps to a fault): AIDS is deadly, and there is no cure; the best
documented ways of getting AIDS are through sharing a needle, sexual
intercourse, or getting contaminated blood in a transfusion. Such a list of
seemingly unconnected facts about AIDS probably serves more as "food
for memorization" than "food for thought." So, children and adults alike
might simply learn and then stow away these facts, much as they do with
the names of the capital cities of nations around the world. It should come
as little surprise that such superficial knowledge does not translate well
into useful actions in AIDS prevention (e.g., Au and Romo, 1996; Keller,
1993; Keller *et al.*, 1991).

Moreover, knowing only a few facts about AIDS can be frightening.
For instance, we are told that one cannot get AIDS through casual
contact. But what counts as "casual contact?" We are told that holding
hands, hugging, kissing on the cheek, and the like count as casual contact;
that sharing an intravenous needle, having sex, or getting someone's

blood through a transfusion are definitely not casual contact. But what about the many, varied kinds of human contact less casual than holding hands but more casual than sharing a drug needle? For example, what about breast-feeding, French kissing, tattooing, body piercing, being bitten by the same mosquito, sharing a shaving razor, sharing a bath towel, sharing a toothbrush, sharing a lipstick, sharing a glass of milk, sharing a plate of scrambled eggs, sharing eating utensils, or a mother picking scabs off herself and then picking scabs off her baby?

To reason sensibly about the AIDS risk of various behaviors, including those just listed, simply knowing a few highly publicized positive and negative exemplars of AIDS risks will not do. Even knowing more positive exemplars might not do. To illustrate this point, let us point out that there is at least one documented case of HIV transmission for each of these behaviors: breast-feeding, French kissing, sharing a shaving razor, and picking scabs off two people without washing hands properly in between. Tattooing and ear/body piercing with shared needles are also considered by health experts to carry AIDS risk. What, then, does knowing a few more positive exemplars of HIV transmission buy us? The obvious answer is that the knowledge could steer us away from these risky behaviors. But the bigger challenge remains. Namely, what are we supposed to make of many other varied behaviors not explicitly discussed in current AIDS education programs? Note that whether a certain kind of contact is "casual" or "risky" depends on whether the HIV can be transmitted. It would take more than memorizing a list of dos and don'ts – indeed it would take some understanding of the causal mechanism for HIV transmission – to do the job.

We would like to propose a new approach to health education (including AIDS education) that offers children and adults a tool to reason about infectious diseases sensibly and coherently. It capitalizes on and respects the learners' intellectual and natural curiosity about the why's and how's of the biological world. Our approach is inspired by recent research on conceptual development suggesting that children spontaneously and actively build intuitive foundational theories about the world (e.g., Au, 1994; Carey, 1985, 1995; Carey and Spelke, 1994; Gelman, 1996; Wellman and Gelman, 1992, 1997). One such foundational theory is folkbiology, a commonsense theory about living things. Like scientific theories, these foundational theories outline the ontological/fundamental categories and basic causal devices in their respective domains, thereby offering coherent bases for reasoning about relevant phenomena. Because children, and apparently adults as well, rely on their folkbiology to reason about everyday biological phenomena including health and illness, building health education programs on the learners' folkbiology seems like a reasonable thing to do. This is the approach that we have adopted. But before we discuss our experimental health education curricula, a quick review of what we know about the nature of children's folkbiology – on which our curricula are built – is in order. Because more comprehensive reviews are available elsewhere (e.g., Au and Romo, 1999; Gelman, 1996; Wellman and Gelman, 1997), here we shall focus on children's beliefs about germs and biological processes that are relevant to the design of our health curricula.

Understanding the nature of children's folkbiology

Basic ontology

Children begin to distinguish plants and animals from human artifacts by age 3 or 4 (e.g., Backscheider et al., 1993; Hickling and Gelman, 1995; Keil, 1994); some children can apply their inchoate understanding of the biological–non-biological distinction to novel entities (e.g., germs) as well as familiar ones by age 5 (Au and Romo, 1996; see also Keil, 1992). In other words, even before reaching school age, children begin to sort out the ontological categories "biological kinds" and "non-biological kinds" (see also Gelman, 1996; Wellman and Gelman, 1997).

Basic causal devices/mechanisms

In addition to outlining the ontology in a domain, however, a foundational theory should also specify basic causal devices or mechanisms unique to that domain in order to offer coherent bases for reasoning about relevant phenomena (e.g., Au, 1994; Brewer and Samarapungavan, 1991; Wellman, 1990; Wellman and Gelman, 1992, 1997). Causal mechanisms/devices are crucial to theory building because they help us understand how observable events might be causally related (Koslowski, 1996). For instance, we can easily observe that leaving a piece of raw fish at room temperature overnight (an input event) will result in the fish turning smelly and unfit for eating (an output event). The causal chain of events that links up such input and output would include imperceptible (or not readily perceptible in everyday life) events such as: some bacteria in the fish use the fish as nutrients to reproduce; the bacteria produce smelly waste products; the multiplication of illness-causing bacteria results in enough germs to render the fish unfit for eating. In other words, causal mechanisms can help us understand observable input–output causal relations, providing conceptual glue (or coherence) to complex networks of input–output causal relations represented in our belief systems about the world.

To date, there is little evidence that an understanding of any biological causal mechanism is something children pick up intuitively in everyday life (see also Au and Romo, 1996, 1990). Much of the research on children's causal understanding of biological phenomena has focused on biological processes, observable input–output relations, and causal agents, rather than causal devices or mechanisms *per se*. Some studies, for instance, revealed that preschool children seemed to know that "growth" and "self-healing" are unique to plants and animals (Carey, 1985; Rosengren *et al.*, 1991; Backscheider *et al.*, 1993). From age 6 on, some children spontaneously attribute "can grow bigger" to novel entities such as germs (Au and Romo, 1996). Preschoolers also know about constraints on growth and development: animals get bigger not smaller and become structurally more complex not simpler (e.g., from caterpillar to butterfly and not vice versa: Rosengren *et al.*, 1991).

In the domain of illness, preschool children appreciate that illness and contamination can be caused by germs. By age 6, children manage to construct rather sophisticated beliefs about germs: germs exist despite absence of perceptible evidence; germs can live, die, and grow bigger; germs can make people sick (e.g., Au and Romo, 1996; Au *et al.*, 1993; Kalish, 1996). In general, children's inchoate understanding of phenomena seems to include causal input–output relations (e.g., input = a glass of milk was left in a warm room for a few days; output = the milk turned sour). How the input is turned into the output (i.e., the causal mechanism) however, remains unspecified (Au and Romo, 1996, 1999; Carey, 1995).

Mechanical causality

In several studies, our research team asked over 300 children from ages 5 to 14 years to explain in their own words a range of biological phenomena: food spoilage, incubation of an infectious disease, inheritance of hair color, HIV/AIDS transmission (Au and Romo, 1996, 1999). Our results suggest that mechanical causality is the mechanism of choice for children in their attempts to make sense of various biological phenomena. For instance, children explained that a piece of fish would have more germs if left on a table overnight because germs in the air fell onto the fish, or because bugs might carry germs to the fish. Few children, even among fifth to seventh graders (10 to 13 year olds), invoked a biological causal mechanism such as reproduction/multiplication of germs. In other words, children focused on the movement of (or the mechanical path traversed by) germs rather than the biology of germs. Similarly, when asked why it took a day to feel the symptoms of a cold after the child had been sneezed on and coughed at by a sick friend, the causal mechanism of choice was that it took time for more cold germs to get into the child's body or for the germs to travel to different parts of the child's body. Few children mentioned that it took time for the cold germs to multiply in the child's body (i.e., incubation). When asked why a baby has the same hair color as the mother, children typically explained that some stuff from the mother (e.g., blood, parts of her body) went into the baby's body. Only 1 out of the 260 5–14-year-olds who were asked about inheritance of hair color mentioned that the stuff being transmitted carries instruction to the baby's body for making hair of a certain color (Au and Romo, 1999). When asked about the AIDS risk of swimming with someone who has the AIDS virus, children tended to focus on whether there was blood (as a mechanical carrier of the virus) rather than whether the virus would die instantly in water and become harmless (Au and Romo, 1996).

Our findings are consistent with some suggestive evidence from Inagaki and Hatano's (1993) and Springer and Keil's (1991) studies, in which children favored mechanical explanations when asked to choose among several kinds of causal mechanisms (e.g., biological, vitalistic, intentional, mechanical) to explain some biological phenomena. Inagaki and Hatano (1993, chapter 2 in this volume), for instance, asked children why we eat food everyday. Children were asked to choose among three explanations: "Because we want to eat tasty food" (intentional); "Because our stomach takes in vital power from the food" (vitalistic); "Because we take the food into our body after its form is changed in the stomach and bowels" (mechanical). In this study, 6-year-olds chose vitalistic explanations as most plausible most often (54 percent of the time), while 8 year olds chose vitalistic explanations only 34 percent of the time; they generally preferred mechanical explanations (62 percent). Adults overwhelmingly preferred mechanical explanations (96 percent). Springer and Keil (1991) also found that 6 and 7-year-olds favored mechanical causality over other kinds of causal mechanisms (e.g., genetic, intentional) in explaining why, for instance, how a baby flower may get its blue color. Children in this study were offered three kinds of possible explanations: "The mother flower wanted her baby to be blue just like her. Because she wanted the baby to be blue, she gave it some very tiny things that went into the seed and turned the baby flower blue" (intentional); "Some very tiny blue pieces went from the mother to the baby flower. These tiny blue pieces went into the seed and got all over the baby flower. Because they got into the baby flower's petals, the baby flower turned blue" (mechanical); "Some very tiny colorless things went from the mother to the baby flower. These tiny things put the blue color together in the baby flower. Even though these tiny things aren't any color, they could make the baby flower blue" (genetic). The mechanical account (or the "gemmulic account" in Springer and Keil's term) was judged best by the 6-year-olds nearly 80 percent of the time. An important difference between the winner and the losers is that the mechanical account specifies a simple mechanical transfer of color pigment, whereas the genetic and the intentional accounts did not.

Why do children favor mechanical causal mechanisms in explaining biological phenomena? For one thing, from infancy on, children know and rapidly learn quite a lot about how objects and substances behave in terms of mechanics. Their naive mechanics allows them to appreciate that physical entities will move according to principles such as cohesion, solidity, contact, and continuity (e.g., Carey and Spelke, 1994; Spelke and Hermer, 1996; Wellman and Gelman, 1992, 1997). So, before children understand any uniquely biological causal mechanisms, it makes sense for them to apply their naive mechanics – a rather well worked-out foundational theory – to reason about living things because it has served them well in reasoning about non-living things. From this quick sketch of children's folkbiology, we would like to zoom in on children's beliefs about a class of illness of considerable significance in children's everyday life, namely, infectious diseases.

How do children explain infectious illness?

One way children can explain how people get sick is to focus on people's behaviors in observable events linked to illness episodes. Indeed, when we (Au and Romo, 1999) asked 260 children (ages 5 to 14 years) to explain why a child named John had a sore throat the day after he had played with another child, Mary, who already had a cold, many children (36 percent), especially kindergarteners and first graders, gave responses such as "John had a sore throat because he had gone out into the cold and didn't wear a jacket," or "Because he had played too much with Mary." What young children are likely to do then, as Carey (1985, 1995) noted, is to give explanations invoking people's behaviors in everyday observable events.

Another way children explain illness events is to talk about germs. In the study just mentioned, almost half of the children (45 percent), regardless of ethnic (Anglo, Latino, Asian) and socioeconomic backgrounds, named Mary's cold germs as the cause of John's sore throat. This should not come as a surprise given the research literature revealing young children's rather sophisticated beliefs about germs. For example, around age 4 or 5, children believe that germs are causal agents of illness (Kalish,

1993; Keil, 1992; Springer and Ruckel, 1992). By age 6 or so, children know that germs have biological attributes such as "can grow bigger" and "will die someday" (Au and Romo, 1996; Keil, 1992). Young children also know that germs can cause symptoms (Kalish, 1996, chapter 5 in this volume), and that germs cause illness by getting inside people and using parts of people's body (Keil, 1994). Moreover, children will name germs as a cause of bodily ailments but not mental ones (Keil *et al.*, 1999).

But knowing that germs are biological kinds that can cause illness is far from knowing *how* germs make people sick. Young children typically do not *spontaneously* use biological causal mechanisms to explain illness (Au and Romo, 1996, 1999). So, when children talk about germs, they may just be stating learned facts about illness events without understanding any biological causal mechanism, however crude and simple, for how germs affect the body (see also Carey, 1995; Solomon and Cassimatis, 1995). No doubt, one could argue that although children do not spontaneously use biological mechanisms to explain illness when asked open-ended questions, they might nonetheless endorse such mechanisms over less appropriate ones when given a choice between the two. One methodological concern: it is very difficult to make different explanation types comparable with respect to the informativeness of the explanation and familiarity with the information it contains. So, as Carey (1995) pointed out, when children chose one type of explanation over another, it is not always clear why they did so. This methodological concern aside, it is worth noting that Springer and Keil (1991) did ask children to choose among several possible mechanisms for biological inheritance, rather than to generate one on their own. In that study, as summarized earlier, the biological causal mechanism (i.e., the genetic account) was not favored.

Are we being too harsh in judging children's knowledge in the domain of illness, or more generally, biology? As a matter of fact, by age 5 or 6, children know that germs are biological entities that can cause illness (e.g., Hatano and Inagaki, 1994; Keil, 1992). If, pondered Hatano (1997), children can come up with some kind of causal mechanism – be it biological or mechanical or even psychological – to explain how germs are involved in illness, can children be credited with understanding a biological causal mechanism? To put it simply, this question can be expressed as: biological kind(s) + any causal mechanism = a biological causal mechanism. For example, suppose a child offers this causal explanation for food poisoning: a living fly landed on some food and deposited some living germs; a person later ate the food, the germs entered the person's body, and caused illness. Because biological entities (e.g., a fly, a person, germs) play a role in this causal chain of events, Hatano (1997) argues that the child has demonstrated knowledge about a biological causal mechanism for food spoilage.

With all due respect, we disagree. Consider, if you will, this causal chain of events: an elephant (undeniably a biological entity) accidentally sat on a snail (another undeniably biological entity) and caused the snail to die (an undeniably biological event). It seems fair to say that the cause of this unfortunate death was mechanical (i.e., due to the mechanical force exerted by the elephant's body on the snail) rather than biological. Our point is that any biological entity by necessity is also a physical entity; it can thereby participate in causal events as a physical/mechanical being. The accidental fact that it is also a biological being does not automatically turn a mechanical causal mechanism into a biological one.

Let us return to the main question of interest: do children understand any biological causal mechanism that can help them reason coherently, deeply, and sensibly about infectious diseases? To date, the answer seems to be, "Not sure." For one thing, it remains unclear whether children reason about biological germs any differently than they do about non-biological poison (Solomon and Cassimatis, 1995; see also Au and Romo, 1996). Keil (1992) points out that kindergarten children may think that germs cause illness because germs are foreign matter that can get inside people's bodies. Nothing about the "biological machinery" of germs, perhaps, is understood to be the cause of disease. Quite probably, children know only about causal input-output relations (e.g., input = germs enter a person's body; output = the person gets sick), leaving how the input is turned into the output unexplained (Au and Romo, 1996; Carey, 1995).

Why do we care so much about whether children understand any truly biological causal mechanism? First, as we have discussed elsewhere (Au and Romo, 1996, 1999), a crucial element of any theory, including foundational theories, is the specification of basic causal devices/ mechanisms unique to that domain (Wellman and Gelman, 1992). So, if children do not understand any biological causal mechanisms, they cannot be credited with an autonomous foundational theory in the domain of biology. This issue also has important applied implications. Earlier we noted that one way to reason coherently and sensibly about the AIDS risk of many, varied forms of human contact is to rely on an understanding of a biological causal mechanism for HIV transmission. Simply memorizing a list of AIDS risks and non-risks will not do because such a list does not provide a good enough basis for reasoning about novel situations. So, if children (or adults for that matter) do not already understand a biological causal mechanism for HIV transmission, it might be useful to help them develop such an understanding. More generally, biological causal mechanisms should perhaps feature more prominently in health education because they might provide coherence (or conceptual glue) to the learners' numerous, and at times seemingly disjoint beliefs about illness and health.

Developing a coherent understanding of health and illness

Grounded in children's entrenched belief-system

Although children's folkbiology does not seem to include explicit biological causal mechanisms, it does have several virtues. First, it has made the important ontological cut between biological kinds (e.g., plants, animals, germs) and non-biological kinds (e.g., artifacts, minerals). Second, it represents a complex network of input–output relations by and large based on accurate observations (e.g., eating well leads to growth; leaving a piece of uncooked fish out overnight renders it smelly and slimy; being around someone who sneezes and coughs leads to catching a cold). Third, children's folkbiology grows out of their curiosity, keen observations, and painstaking sense-making – rather impressive intellectual endeavors. Health educators would do well to respect children's hard work by helping them build on their folkbiology in developing an understanding of health and illness.

Filling conceptual gaps

To say that children do not spontaneously develop an intuitive understanding of biological mechanisms is not the same as to say that children cannot learn them readily. Quite the contrary, children can readily learn biological causal mechanisms explicitly taught to them. In two studies to be reported in this chapter, we found that grade school children (8 to 12 year olds) who received our experimental curricula readily learned biological causal mechanisms for food spoilage and transmission of AIDS and other infectious diseases. More importantly, their grasp of such mechanisms seemed to help them reason about novel illness-related biological phenomena and enhance their prudent caution without engendering unwarranted fear about various kinds of illness (see also Au and Romo, 1996; Au et al., 1996).

Biological causal mechanisms as the core of the curricula

In our AIDS education study (to be reviewed shortly), the experimental curriculum included three lessons that focused on the biology of HIV to help children understand a basic causal mechanism for AIDS transmission. The mechanism can be summarized as follows: the AIDS virus is a living thing, and so it can reproduce, stay alive, and will die in various environments. For instance, it can reproduce rapidly in a person's fresh blood; it can stay alive and perhaps reproduce very slowly in human saliva; it will die instantly in air and water. Importantly, the AIDS virus is harmful (i.e., it can infect people to make them sick) only when it is alive; the dead virus is harmless. Note that this curriculum is grounded in children's folkbiology because some of the concepts invoked in this causal mechanism (e.g., germs are living things that can reproduce, stay alive, and die) are in most children's conceptual repertoire by age 5 or 6. What our experimental curriculum aimed at accomplishing was to help children fill a conceptual gap by explicitly teaching them about a biological causal mechanism for HIV transmission. Grasping this causal mechanism could help a child figure out, for instance, that one cannot get AIDS by sharing a swimming pool with someone who has the AIDS virus because the virus instantly dies, and thereby becomes harmless, in water (see also Au and Romo, 1996; Au et al., 1996).

Think Biology: a new approach to AIDS education

To see if our experimental curriculum module was feasible and more effective than existing AIDS education programs offered in schools, we compared it to a published AIDS curriculum recommended by the National Catholic Educational Association (1992), which was favored by the school in which this study was conducted. The instruction in both the experimental group and the comparison group was led by our research team. This study included eighty-seven 9 to 14 year olds (roughly half girls and half boys, in fourth, sixth, and eighth grades) enrolled in a middle-class, predominantly Latino, parochial school. Over 90 percent of the parents who had children enrolled in these three grades consented to their children's participation. Individual children were randomly assigned to either the experimental or comparison group. For each grade, the lessons for the two groups were conducted in separate rooms. Table 9.1 presents the "Think Biology" AIDS curriculum offered to the experimental group. Table 9.2 presents an existing curriculum offered to the comparison group.

The effectiveness of the "Think Biology" AIDS curriculum

On our post-test, we asked children, "Is the AIDS virus dangerous only when it is alive?" About 75 percent of the fourth graders, 93 percent of sixth graders, and 83 percent of the eighth graders in the experimental

Table 9.1. *The "Think Biology" AIDS curriculum for the experimental group*

Lesson 1 Germs are microscopic
Children saw color-slides of germs (viruses, bacteria, fungi), including the HIV. The narration emphasized that (1) germs come in all shapes and sizes; (2) some germs are good (e.g., certain yeast cells for making bread), and some germs are bad (e.g. disease-causing germs); (3) germs are so small that we cannot see individual germs with the naked eye; (4) when germs are in large numbers (e.g., in colonies), we can see them; (5) although extremely small, germs are nonetheless tiny organisms basically similar to other bigger and more familiar living things. To convince children that germs are living things, we asked them to get their hands dirty and then touch or spit into several petri dishes containing nutrient agar. The petri dishes were then covered and kept warm in a Styrofoam cooler with a small light bulb at roughly 95°F for a week.

Lesson 2 Germs can reproduce and die
Children examined the bacteria colonies and moldy spots on their agar culture from the previous week. We discussed how certain places are suitable or friendly environments for germs to live and reproduce in. For example, many bacteria live and reproduce best in a warm and moist environment where there is plenty of food for them (e.g., nutrient agar gel kept in an incubator). That was why we found colonies of bacteria on the nutrient agar. We showed children color-slides of different modes of reproduction for germs (with narration): mold spores, yeast cells budding, bacteria dividing, and HIV bursting out of a human white blood cell. We also demonstrated how chlorine bleach can kill germs by putting a few drops of bleach on the germ colonies in the petri dishes. We talked about the notion that germs, like other living things, can die as well as reproduce.

Children participated in a discussion on environments where the HIV can: (1) reproduce/multiply quickly (e.g., fresh human blood); (2) die almost instantly (e.g., air, water); (3) live and possibly reproduce very slowly, if at all (e.g., human saliva). We told children that the story with saliva is still unclear, and they should not worry about contact with saliva that has been exposed to air or water, since the AIDS virus dies in these environments very quickly. For instance, even if someone who has the AIDS virus sneezes tiny droplets of their saliva into the air, the virus will be dead on arrival if it travels through the air to another person.

Lesson 3 Relating the ecological environments for HIV to AIDS risk for people
We discussed how different kinds of bodily fluids vary in how friendly they are to the AIDS virus. We tried to help children link information about ecological environments for the AIDS virus (i.e., friendly, hostile, or neutral environments) to the likelihood of transmission for various human behaviors or events. For instance, someone should not worry about getting AIDS from sharing a toilet seat with a person who carries the AIDS virus because the AIDS virus will die in the air quickly. We asked children to come up with some safe and unsafe behaviors with respect to AIDS transmission. Children were encouraged to use the concepts of "friendly," "hostile," or "neutral" environment for the AIDS virus to reason about the AIDS risk of each behavior brought up in the class discussion.

group answered "yes" compared to only chance-level performance in the comparison group (43 percent, 53 percent, and 53 percent for the three grades, respectively). Children in the experimental group seemed to have learned this important fact quite well. More importantly, they were also

Table 9.2. *An existing AIDS curriculum for the comparison group*

Lesson 1 Germs are microscopic
This lesson was similar to that of the experimental group, except that we did not invite
these children to prepare germ cultures. Instead, we played a "traveling germ" game with
the younger children, illustrating the concept of how germs can be spread from one person
to another. This game was found in their AIDS education curriculum guidelines. We
asked the older children to discuss the different ways that cold germs could be spread from
one person to another and to compare and contrast such behaviors to the different ways
that a person could contract HIV.
Lesson 2 Coping with AIDS
Children watched a videotape called *What's in the news: Coping with AIDS* (Swartz, 1989).
The topics included: What does the acronym "AIDS" stand for? What are the most
common ways of getting the AIDS virus? In what ways do people infected with the AIDS
virus have to suffer socially (e.g., losing rights to choose where to live, attend school, and
work) as well as physically? Children discussed the topics raised by the video and talked
about their fears related to being exposed to AIDS.
Lesson 3 Ethical issues and high-risk behaviors
Children talked about ethical issues related to AIDS such as "Is it right to ban children
with AIDS from schools? From sports?" We ended the lesson with a discussion about
various risky behaviors associated with AIDS transmission.

---

better at reasoning about AIDS risks in novel situations. We asked
children to consider whether a person could get AIDS by engaging in
these five behaviors (with our biomedical consultants' responses in par-
entheses): tattooing (yes), ear-piercing (yes), wiping an infected person's
bleeding nose (yes), swimming in a small pond with an infected person
(no), sharing a toothbrush with an infected person (no). We found that
children who had received the experimental curriculum gave reliably
more correct responses about the AIDS risks in these novel situations
than their peers in the comparison group.

We also asked children to explain their yes/no answers concerning
these five novel situations. A main finding was that children in the
comparison group were more likely to offer irrelevant explanations (e.g.,
"You cannot get AIDS by ear-piercing because it doesn't affect the AIDS
virus at all") or no explanations at all. By contrast, children in the
experimental group were more likely to offer thoughtful explanations
than their peers in the comparison group (e.g., "No, because the saliva on
the toothbrush bristles connected with air, so the AIDS in the saliva are
dead").

When we looked at how often children thought about the biology of
HIV (i.e., environments in which it can reproduce, survive, and die) when
they reasoned about AIDS transmission, there was a marked difference
between the two groups. On average, children in the experimental group

invoked the biology of HIV in their reasoning at least once or twice (out of five chances); their peers in the comparison group rarely did so.

Moreover, there was a clear benefit of thinking about the biology of HIV. When children mentioned the biology of HIV in their explanations for their judgments of AIDS risks in novel situations, they decided correctly about the AIDS risk of a behavior about 90 percent of the time. When they did not mention it, they decided correctly about 45 percent of the time, which was no better than randomly guessing a behavior being "safe" or "unsafe." (In these analyses, children's responses for all five novel situations in both the experimental and comparison group were pooled together.) These findings suggest that children in the experimental group reasoned better about AIDS transmission in novel situations, i.e., making more correct judgments about AIDS risk of a behavior and giving more meaningful explanations for their judgments, probably because they made use of what they had learned about the biological causal mechanism of AIDS transmission in the experimental curriculum. The benefit of the experimental curriculum over the comparison curriculum seems to be attributable to our experimental curriculum's focus on biology, rather than to some peripheral variables such as differences in hands-on activities (e.g., culturing germs with nutrient agar in the experimental condition) or our enthusiasm in leading class discussions.

In short, children readily learned a biological causal mechanism for HIV transmission introduced in our experimental curriculum. Their grasp of the biological mechanism seemed to provide children with a coherent basis for thinking about HIV transmission, thereby helping them reason about novel situations. Furthermore, the experimental curriculum may have motivated children to think about AIDS more deeply, as evidenced by children in the experimental group giving meaningful justifications for judgments of AIDS risks in novel situations more often than children in the comparison group. (For a more complete report of the findings, see Au and Romo, 1996.)

Educating children about infectious disease transmission and prevention

In one of our studies on children's knowledge about food spoilage, we asked middle-class children in first, third, fifth, and seventh grades whether a piece of fish would have more germs if it were left out on the table overnight and to explain why (Au and Romo, 1999). Virtually none of the first, third, or seventh graders talked about germ reproduction/multiplication. Instead, they typically talked about movement or transfer of additional germs onto the fish (e.g., "The piece of fish would have more germs because bugs can get in and spread germs"). The story with the fifth grade children was very different. Roughly 75 percent of them explained that if the fish was left out on the table all night, the environment would be just right for germs to reproduce on the fish. As it turned out, they had recently seen a film in their science class about food contamination. The film discussed the kinds of environments that germs will reproduce and die in. Apparently the children readily learned about the role of germ biology in food spoilage, and they then used this information to answer our questions weeks later. Together with our finding that children readily learned a biological causal mechanism for HIV transmission, this unexpected twist in our research story encouraged us to think that school-aged children can readily learn biological causal mechanisms for contamination and contagion.

Interestingly, the fifth graders were limited in how far they could stretch what they had learned from the film on food contamination to other illness phenomena involving germ reproduction (e.g., incubation period and spreading of symptoms over the body). When we asked them, in a story-like scenario, why John had a sore throat the day after he played with Mary, who had a cold, only 32 percent of the children talked about the biology of germs in explaining why it took so much time for John to feel sick (e.g., "It takes time for the germs to reproduce"). When asked why John felt worse that night – not only did his throat hurt, but also his whole body felt sick all over – only 24 percent of the children talked about the biology of germs as a cause for worsening and spreading of symptoms (e.g., it took time for germs to multiply enough to make John feel worse). So while the film helped these children understand the role of germ reproduction in food spoilage, the knowledge did not transfer to illness events involving incubation and the time-course of an infectious disease. We wanted to do a better job. We challenged ourselves to design an infectious disease curriculum that could help children focus on biology not only for reasoning about food spoilage, but also for reasoning about a wider range of phenomena related to infectious disease transmission and prevention. Moreover, because we believe in early health education, our study was aimed at teaching children as young as 8 to 11 years of age (in third and fourth grade).

One hundred and two 8–11-year-olds enrolled in four mixed third and fourth grade classrooms in the university lab school at UCLA participated in this study. Two teachers at the school were each responsible for teaching science to two of these four classrooms. For each teacher, one of her classes was randomly chosen to receive our five-lesson experimental curriculum module. The other class served as a comparison group and was taught the regular physiology science curriculum at the school.

Table 9.3. *The "Think Biology" infectious disease curriculum for the experimental group*

Lessons 1 and 2 Germs are microscopic organisms
Same as lessons 1 and 2 of our "Think Biology" AIDS curriculum. Briefly, the main points were that germs are micro-organisms that can reproduce in favorable environments, will die in hostile environments, and can survive in neutral environments.
Lesson 3 Relating the ecological environments for germs and infection prevention
The lesson began with a discussion that germs are everywhere. We can find them in moist places like sinks, bathrooms, clothes, and people's bodies. The teacher then led a discussion about hostile environments for germs, places where germs will die. She demonstrated how chlorine bleach, Lysol, Listerine, and antibiotics can kill germs, by putting a few drops of each liquid on the germ colonies in the petri dishes.

After talking about different ways to kill germs, the class talked about how to prevent germs from entering the body and causing illness. The focus was on the cold virus, its characteristics, and relevant behaviors to avoid catching a cold. For example, they learned that the cold virus is a kind of germ that lives and reproduces very fast in saliva. It does not die immediately outside of the body. So children should wash their hands frequently and avoid touching their faces – especially during the cold/flu season – to avoid picking up cold germs from doorknobs, people's hands, and most other places that children are likely to touch.
Lesson 4 Prevention of infection and food contamination
An expert on infectious diseases visited the classes and talked about different kinds of germs and their linkage to particular kinds of diseases. He also talked about germs and bodily infections, namely where you can get them (e.g., cuts on hands or feet) and how to avoid them (e.g., cleaning wounds). He discussed relevant behaviors for preventing food contamination. For example, he told children to store eggs or milk in the refrigerator because bacteria cannot grow rapidly in cold environments.
Lesson 5 Review
The teacher reviewed concepts such as what are friendly environments for germs to reproduce in and how people can kill germs or prevent them from reproducing. The main focus of the lesson was on preventing food contamination. Children reviewed concepts about the need to refrigerate and cook some foods.

There were fifty children in the experimental group (average age = 10 years 0 months). There were fifty-two children in the comparison group (average age = 9 years 8 months). In reporting what we found in the post-test, the number of children varies slightly from question to question because some children left a few questions unanswered.

The "Think Biology" infectious disease curriculum

The "Think Biology" infectious disease curriculum included five weekly forty-five-minute lessons. It was taught by the children's science teachers to help them understand the biology of germs as a basic causal mechanism for common illnesses. Table 9.3 presents a summary of the lessons.

Table 9.4. *Classification of children's answers to the food spoilage questions on the post-test*

---

1 Biology of Germs
E.g., "It is good to put meat, milk, and cheese in the refrigerator because it also is a germ killer and it keeps it from getting spoiled." And (there will be more germs on the piece of fish because) "germs will grow on it and it will smell."
2 Movement or transfer of germs (explicit mechanical transfer)
E.g., (It's good to put meat, milk, and cheese in the refrigerator) "so bacteria and germs don't get in the food and make you sick." Or (there will be fewer germs on the piece of fish) "because the plastic bag does not let any germs in"; "The sealing keeps whatever germs on either the inside or out, would stay inside or out."
3 Sources of additional germs (implicit mechanical transfer)
E.g., (It's good to put meat, milk, and cheese in the refrigerator) "so bugs won't get to it." Or (there will be more germs on the piece of fish) "because there would still be germs from the air in the bag."
4 Observable events
E.g., (It's good to put meat, milk, and cheese in the refrigerator) "so it will stay fresh." Or (there will be more germs on the piece of fish) "because the fish starts to smell bad and it gets older everyday."
Other/irrelevant/uninformative/no explanations

Note: An explanation mentioning any biological process of germ would be classified as a category 1 (biology of germs) explanation. Such a response supersedes a category 2 (movement of germs) explanation, which supersedes a category 3 (sources of additional germs) explanation, which in turn supersedes a category 4 (observable event) response. All explanations given by children in the post-test were coded by two coders independently; they agreed on 89 percent of the cases and discussed the disagreed-upon cases to resolve their differences.

Crucial concepts included: (1) germs are living things and so they can reproduce, stay alive, and will die in various environments; (2) a germ is harmful (i.e., it can infect people to make them sick) only when it is alive, and a dead germ is harmless. This mechanism is inherently biological because the biology of germs (e.g., reproduction, survival, death) is at its core. This causal mechanism can potentially serve as a coherent basis for deciding about which behaviors are safe or unsafe with respect to common illness events. For example, we should brush our teeth often because our mouths are friendly environments (i.e., warm, moist, has food) for germs to reproduce in.

The effectiveness of the "Think Biology" infectious disease curriculum

About two weeks after the last lesson, the children were given a forty-five-minute post-test in class. The post-test was a paper-and-pencil test; the teacher or a researcher read each question aloud for the children, and the children wrote down their answers. Two research assistants walked around the room to help children with spelling.

What have children learned about food spoilage? We began the post-test by asking about food contamination. We asked children to write down their answers in detail. Table 9.4 explains how we classified children's answers.

1 "Why is it good to put meat, milk, and cheese in the refrigerator?"
2 "There are a few germs on a piece of fish inside a plastic bag. What will happen to the germs in a couple of days? Will there be more germs, will there be fewer germs, or will the number of germs stay the same? Why?"

The refrigeration question Children in the experimental group were reliably more likely to give biological causal explanations than children in the comparison group: 38 percent of the forty-seven children in the experimental group discussed the importance of putting food in the refrigerator so bacteria could not grow or reproduce; only 8 percent of their fifty-two peers in the comparison group did so ($p < 0.001$, Fisher's Exact test). Most of the children in the comparison group (87 percent) talked instead only about observable events related to food storage, compared to just 38 percent in the experimental group.

The fish-in-a-plastic-bag question Children in the experimental group (67 percent of forty-eight children) were reliably more likely to mention germ reproduction/death in explaining why there might be more/fewer/the same number of germs on the fish in the plastic bag than those in the comparison group (37 percent of fifty-one children), although this was the most prevalent kind of explanation in both groups. Interestingly, out of the fifty-one children (both groups combined) who gave a biological explanation, 90 percent of them also correctly stated that the fish would have more germs in a couple of days, compared to only 55 percent of children who gave non-biological explanations. Recall that, in our AIDS education study, children who mentioned the biology of germs in explaining their judgment of AIDS risk of a novel situation were more likely to give a correct AIDS risk judgment than those who did not mention biology in their explanation. The present finding for the "fish-in-a-plastic-bag" question converges with the finding in the AIDS education study to suggest that thinking about the biology of germs – the core of our experimental curriculum, rather than some extraneous factors – accounts

Table 9.5. *Percentage of children giving various kinds of explanations for food spoilage*

Food in refrigerator Explanation type	Experimental group (n = 47)	Comparison group (n = 52)
Biology of germs	38	8
Explicit movement of germs	19	2
Sources of additional germs	0	2
Observable events related to food storage	38	87
Fish in a plastic bag Explanation type	Experimental group (n = 48)	Comparison group (n = 51)
Biology of germs	67	37
Explicit movement of germs	6	20
Sources of additional germs	6	4
Observable events related to food storage	17	27

for the better health risk judgment by children in the experimental group than those in the comparison group.

Table 9.5 presents the percentages of children giving various kinds of explanations about food spoilage. Overall, children in the experimental group did well in using germ biology to reason sensibly about food spoilage. But this was not surprising, given that our experimental group received quite a lot of information about this phenomenon in our curriculum. The next section of the post-test goes beyond food contamination to see whether children could use the biology of germs to reason about a rather different illness phenomenon, namely, the clinical time course of a cold/flu episode.

Does thinking about the biology of germs help children reason about other illness phenomena?   We presented children with the following scenario: "See this girl? (picture of girl). Some bad germs got inside her body. She felt okay for a day. But then the next day she started to feel sick all over her whole body. Her head ached and her stomach hurt and her throat hurt – all at the same time." We then asked,

1 Why did it take a whole day for her to feel sick after the germs got inside her body?
2 How did the germs make her feel sick in so many parts of her body at the same time?

Table 9.6. *Classification of children's answers to cold/flu questions on the post-test*

---

1 Biology of germs
E.g., "The germs had to multiply a lot before they spread into the rest of her body before it started to hurt." Or "The germs took long to reproduce and make the germs spread."
2 Movement or transfer of germs (explicit mechanical transfer)
E.g., "Because the germs had to settle in." Or "Because the germs take time to go through the body."
3 Observable events
E.g., "She didn't take medicine."
4 Other/irrelevant/uninformative/no explanations

Table 9.6 shows how we classified the children's answers. When asked about the delay between the germs entering the girl's body and the onset of cold/flu symptoms, children in the experimental group (59 percent of forty-six children) were reliably more likely than those in the comparison group (8 percent of the forty-nine children) to explain that it took time for the germs to reproduce/multiply. This considerable training effect aside, mechanical causality explanations (e.g., it took time for the germs to move around and settle in the girl's body) were quite popular for both the experimental group (26 percent) and the comparison group (35 percent) – attesting to the prominence of mechanical causality in children's conception of infectious disease transmission.

The findings were similar for the question "How did the germs make her feel sick in so many parts of her body at the same time?" Briefly, biological explanations were reliably more prevalent in the experimental group (26 percent) than the comparison group (10 percent, $p < 0.04$, Fisher's Exact test). Again, mechanical causality was frequently invoked by children in both groups; they talked about, for instance, the physical movement or transfer of germs (48 percent and 55 percent, respectively). Table 9.7 presents the percentages of various kinds of explanations given by the two groups for the questions concerning the time course of a cold/flu episode.

These findings suggest that children could learn and use the biological causal mechanism taught in our curriculum to reason about a range of phenomena. Although the experimental curriculum covered biological attributes of cold viruses and cold transmission, it did not include a discussion of reasons for an incubation period and multiple symptoms spreading all over the body. Nonetheless, the third and fourth graders in the experimental group managed to make use of their understanding of the biology of germs to reason about these illness phenomena.

Thus far, we have focused on children's ability to appeal to

Table 9.7. *Percentage of children giving various kinds of explanations for illness*

Incubation period of colds	Experimental group	Comparison group
Explanation type	(n = 46)	(n = 49)
Biology of germs	59	8
Explicit movement of germs	26	35
People's behaviors	7	27
Spreading of symptoms to different parts of the body Explanation type	Experimental group (n = 46)	Comparison group (n = 49)
Biology of germs	26	10
Explicit movement of germs	48	55
People's behaviors	17	10

imperceptible biological causal mechanisms – specifically germ reproduction and death – to explain germ-related health threats such as food spoilage and infectious diseases. Beside helping children make sense of illness phenomena, can thinking about the biology of germs help children decide which behaviors are relevant for avoiding particular infectious diseases?

Can thinking about the biology of germs help children figure out how to prevent novel infectious diseases? We asked children to think about how to avoid being infected with two particular kinds of germs. One kind of hypothetical infection was similar to a fungus infection such as athlete's foot; the other kind was similar to a blood-borne infection such as hepatitis or AIDS. Children heard these two descriptions:

1 "There is a bad germ that can infect the skin under your arms or the skin on the inside of your elbow. This germ reproduces in wet or damp places. In dry places, this germ doesn't die, but it doesn't reproduce either. What should you do to avoid getting this infection?"
2 "There is a bad germ that can make you sick all over your whole body. This germ reproduces only in blood. This germ doesn't die in saliva, but it doesn't reproduce either. This germ dies everywhere else (like in the air or in the water). What should you do to avoid getting this infection?"

For each kind of hypothetical germ, children were asked to consider a list of "dos and don'ts." They were to place a check mark next to the behaviors they thought were relevant to avoid getting that infection (see

Table 9.8. *Yes/no pattern of behaviors related to avoiding infection or illness*

Relevant behavior?	Skin infection	Blood-borne infection
Don't share a bath towel	Yes	No
Keep your skin dry	Yes	No
Wash yourself with soap	Yes	No
After playing, wash your hands right away	Yes	No
Don't touch a tooth that has fallen out of someone's mouth	No	Yes
Don't touch someone's cut	No	Yes
Don't touch other people's blood	No	Yes
Brush your teeth twice a day	No	No
Eat healthy foods	No	No

Table 9.8 for the checklist and the appropriate check-off patterns). For preventing the skin infection, there were four relevant hygiene behaviors: (1) Don't share a bath towel; (2) Keep your skin dry; (3) Wash yourself with soap; (4) After playing, wash your hands. The remaining six behaviors were quite irrelevant. For preventing the blood-borne infection, there were only three relevant behaviors: (1) Don't touch a tooth that has fallen out of someone's mouth; (2) Don't touch someone's cut; (3) Don't touch other people's blood.

For avoiding the hypothetical skin infection, children in the experimental group on average correctly identified 74 percent of the relevant preventive measures. Their performance was not reliably different from that of the children in the comparison group (73 percent). However, in recognizing irrelevant behaviors for preventing the skin infection and not checking them off, the experimental group (59 percent) did somewhat better than the comparison group (49 percent).

For avoiding a blood-borne infection, the experimental group (94 percent) outperformed the comparison group (83 percent) in identifying relevant preventive measures. The experimental group also outperformed the comparison group in identifying irrelevant behaviors and not checking them off (71 percent and 46 percent, respectively).

Overall, children in both groups were quite good at endorsing relevant preventive measures. Nonetheless, the experimental group managed to outperform the comparison group in endorsing relevant behaviors for preventing the blood-borne infection. What distinguishes these two groups better, however, is children's ability to recognize *which* behaviors were relevant for preventing *which* infectious disease. Learning to think about the biology of germs seemed to help the experimental group classify relevant and irrelevant behaviors for preventing each hypothetical infection. By contrast, children in the comparison group tended to make more false alarm errors – endorsing any or all behaviors that seemed like good hygiene practice, regardless of the biological characteristics of the germs (e.g., the ecological environments in which a specific germ might flourish or perish). This training effect is rather impressive. Recall that in the experimental group, the teachers used the biology of cold/flu viruses (e.g., they can survive outside the human body for a few minutes on hot, dry days and up to several hours on cool, wet days) as the rationale for cold/flu preventive measures (e.g., wash hands with soap frequently; do not touch your face because eyes, nose, and mouth are easy points of entry for live cold/flu germs). When confronted with agents of novel infections, children in the experimental group were able to apply this strategy to identify relevant and irrelevant behaviors for preventing the unfamiliar infection. That is, they were able to use information about the biology of the specific infectious agent to reason about pertinent preventive measures.

Learning and motivation

One goal of our "Think Biology" curriculum is motivating children to learn and think deeply about infectious disease transmission and prevention. Indeed, children in the experimental group seemed interested and enthusiastic. They asked many thoughtful questions in every lesson, some pertaining to the biology of germs, some about the why's and how's of infectious disease transmission, and some about both. Here is a sample of their questions:

- Are germs living in the water?
- Do germs live in dust?
- Can little viruses take over our cells?
- Do the agar plates smell funny because of mold in the air?
- Why can scrubbed hands still have germs?
- Why are germs on wet towels and clothes if they like warm places?
- How do some vitamins keep germs away?
- How do the little shapes work (virus shapes)?
- How do shots (vaccines) prevent disease?
- Why do we get some sicknesses only once (e.g., chicken-pox)?

Conclusion

The study of conceptual development has made enormous strides since the 1970s, in no small part because of the fruitful approach to think of children – and adults for that matter – as intuitive theory builders. Children as well as adults seem to use such intuitive foundational theories to organize and seek information about the world in everyday life, to make sense of their observations, and to reason about novel situations. One such foundational theory is folkbiology. Perhaps because illness and health figure so prominently in everyday life, children have rather sophisticated and rich beliefs in this domain from quite early on. It makes sense to capitalize on such a rich store of knowledge in helping children reason about illness causation and prevention. The two studies reported in this chapter constitute a modest first step in this endeavor.

In both the AIDS education study and the infectious disease education study, we found that children did not spontaneously invoke biological causal mechanisms to explain biological phenomena such as contagion and food contamination. Children in the comparison condition tended to talk about observable events, especially people's behaviors, and/or mechanical causal mechanisms (e.g., movement or transfer of germs). This is consistent with our research revealing that children from kindergarten through seventh grade (5 to 13 year olds) are unlikely to talk about biology spontaneously in explaining a range of biological phenomena (Au and Romo, 1999). But why should this come as a surprise? After all, it took centuries for scientists to discover biological causal mechanisms for phenomena such as contagion and contamination.

The good news is that concepts about biological causal mechanisms can easily be taught. Our experimental curricula seemed to help children as young as 8 or 9 years of age to fill a major conceptual gap in their belief system about biological kinds. Specifically, they seemed to help children use ideas about biological causal mechanisms to reason about novel as well as familiar phenomena in the domain of illness and health. Moreover, children seemed to enjoy the challenge to their intellectual curiosity and the respect for their ability to think deeply about illness and health. Such an active interest in this domain may stand a better chance than memorized "dos and don'ts" to translate into sensible health practices.

Acknowledgments: the two senior authors contributed about equally; the order of their authorship is alphabetical. We thank the children, staff, and parents of UCLA Seeds University Elementary School for their support and cooperation. We are particularly grateful to several teachers at the school: Janice Cohn and Merilyn Buchanan for implementing our experimental curriculum in their classrooms; Muriel Ifekwunigwe and Ann De la Sota for their input to the curriculum. Two biomedical experts on campus, Marcus Horwitz and Jeffrey Ohmen, taught us much about infectious diseases. Remaining misconceptions are of course ours. We

thank Albert DeLeon, Gabriela Fajardo, Wendy Francis, Karla Iz-
quierdo, Marlene Martinez, Lauralyn Miles, Sharon Peri, and Denise
Piñon for their invaluable assistance in data collection and coding. This
work was supported in part by the UCLA AIDS Institute and the UCLA
Urban Education Studies Center.

REFERENCES

Au, T. K. (1994). Developing an intuitive understanding of substance kinds.
    Cognitive Psychology, 27, 71–111.
Au, T. K., and Romo, L. F. (1996). Building a coherent conception of HIV
    transmission: A new approach to AIDS education. In D. Medin (ed.), *The
    Psychology of Learning and Motivation*, vol. XXXV (pp. 193–241). New York:
    Academic Press.
    (1999). Mechanical causality in children's "folkbiology." In D. Medin and S.
    Atran (eds.), *Folkbiology*. Cambridge, MA: MIT Press.
Au, T. K., Sidle, A. L., and Rollins, K. B. (1993). Developing an intuitive
    understanding of conservation and contamination: Invisible particles as a
    plausible mechanism. *Developmental Psychology*, 29, 286–299.
Au, T. K., Romo, L. F., DeWitt, J. E., De la Sota, A., and Ifekwunigwe, M.
    (1996). Talking about AIDS in science education. *Connections* (a newsletter
    for teachers in the Los Angeles area and beyond), Fall 1996, 3–9. Los
    Angeles: UCLA Urban Education Studies Center.
Backscheider, A. G., Shatz, M., and Gelman, S. A. (1993). Preschoolers' ability
    to distinguish living kinds as a function of regrowth. *Child Development*, 64,
    1,242–1,257.
Brewer, W., and Samarapungavan, A. (1991). Children's theories vs. scientific
    theories: Differences in reasoning or differences in knowledge? In R. Hoff-
    man and D. Palermo (eds.), *Cognition and the symbolic processes* (pp. 209–
    232). Hillsdale, NJ: Erlbaum.
Carey, S. (1985). *Conceptual change in childhood*. Cambridge, MA: MIT Press.
    (1995). On the origin of causal understanding. In D. Sperber, D. Premack, and
    A. J. Premack (eds.), *Causal cognition* (pp. 268–302). Oxford: Oxford Uni-
    versity Press.
Carey, S., and Spelke, E. (1994). Domain-specific knowledge and conceptual
    change. In L. A. Hirschfeld and S. A. Gelman (eds.), *Mapping the mind:
    Domain-specificity in cognition and culture* (pp. 169–200). New York: Cam-
    bridge University Press.
Dooling, D. J., and Lachman, R. (1971). Effects of comprehension on retention
    of prose. *Journal of experimental Psychology*, 88, 216–222.
Gelman, S. A. (1996). Concepts and theories. In R. Gelman and T. K. Au (eds.),
    Handbook of perception and cognition, 2nd edn, Perceptual and cognitive
    development (pp. 117–150). New York: Academic Press.
Hatano, G. (1997). Children's understanding of illness. Paper presented at the
    biennial meeting of the Society for Research in Child Development, Wash-
    ington, DC.
Hatano, G., and Inagaki, K. (1994). Young children's naive theory of biology.

Cognition, 50, 171–188.

Hickling, A. K., and Gelman, S. A. (1995). How does your garden grow? Evidence of an early conception of plants as biological kinds. *Child Development*, 66, 856–876.

Inagaki, K., and Hatano, G. (1993). Young children's understanding of the mind–body distinction. *Child Development*, 64, 1,534–1,549.

Kalish, C. (1993). Preschoolers' understanding of germs as causes of illness. Paper presented at the biennial meeting of the Society for Research in Child Development, New Orleans.

(1996). Preschoolers' understanding of germs as invisible mechanisms. *Cognitive Development*, 11, 83–106.

Keil, F. C. (1992). The origins of an autonomous biology. In M. R. Gunnar and M. Maratsos (eds.), *Modularity and constraints in language and cognition: Minnesota symposia on child psychology*, vol. XXV (pp. 103–137). Hillsdale, NJ: Erlbaum.

(1994). The birth and nurturance of concepts by domains: The origins of concepts of living things. In L. A. Hirschfeld and S. A. Gelman (eds.), *Mapping the mind: Domain-specificity in cognition and culture* (pp. 234–254). New York: Cambridge University Press.

Keil, F. C., Levin, D., Gutheil, G., and Richman, B. (1999).Explanation, cause and mechanism: The case of contagion. In D. Medin and S. Atran (eds.), *Folkbiology*. Cambridge, MA: MIT Press.

Keller, M. L. (1993). Why don't young adults protect themselves against sexual transmission of HIV? Possible answers to a complex question. *AIDS Education and Prevention*, 5, 220–233.

Keller, S. E., Bartlett, J. A., Schleifer, S. J., Johnson, R. L., Pinner, E., and Delaney, B. (1991). HIV-relevant sexual behavior among a healthy inner-city heterosexual adolescent population in an endemic area of HIV. *Journal of Adolescent Health*, 12, 44–48.

Koslowski, B. (1996). *Theory and evidence: The development of scientific reasoning*. Cambridge, MA: MIT Press.

National Catholic Educational Association AIDS Education Task Force (1992). *AIDS: A Catholic education approach to HIV (human immunodeficiency virus)*. Teacher's manual. Washington, DC: National Catholic Educational Association.

Rosengren, K. S., Gelman, S. A., Kalish, C. W., and McCormick, M. (1991). As time goes by: Children's early understanding of growth in animals. *Child Development*, 62, 1,302–1,320.

Solomon, G. E. A., and Cassimatis, N. L. (1995). On young children's understanding of germs as biological causes of illness. Poster presented at the biennial meeting of the Society for Research in Child Development, Indianapolis.

Spelke, E. S., and Hermer, L. (1996). Early cognitive development: Objects and space. In R. Gelman and T. K. Au (eds.), *Handbook of perception and cognition*, 2nd edn, *Perceptual and cognitive development* (pp. 71–114). New York: Academic Press.

Springer, K., and Keil, F. C. (1991). Early differentiation of causal mechanisms appropriate to biological and non-biological kinds. *Child Developmental*, 62, 767–781.

Springer, K., and Ruckel, J. (1992). Early beliefs about the causes of illness: Evidence against immanent justice. *Cognitive Development*, 7, 429–443.

Swartz, T. E. (producer and director) (1989). *What's in the news: Coping with AIDS* [video]. Center for Instructional Design and Interactive Video. Philadelphia, PA: Pennsylvania State University.

Wellman, H. M. (1990). *The child's theory of mind.* Cambridge, MA: MIT Press.

Wellman, H. M., and Gelman, S. A. (1992). Cognitive development: Foundational theories of core domains. *Annual Review of Psychology*, 43, 337–375.

    (1997). Knowledge acquisition. In D. Kuhn and R. Siegler (eds.), *Handbook of child psychology*, 5th edn, *Cognitive development* (pp. 523–573). New York: Wiley.

10 Young children's understanding of the physician's role and the medical hearsay exception

Melody R. Herbst, Margaret S. Steward,
John E. B. Myers, and Robin L. Hansen

The study described in this chapter was prompted by the report of a decision of the United States Federal Eighth Circuit Court of Appeals in St. Louis (Woo, 1992).[1] In this decision, a child molestation conviction was overturned because the appellate court determined that the presiding trial judge had erred in allowing a 3-year-old child's hearsay statements to a physician to be admitted as testimony under the medical diagnosis and treatment exception. The Federal Court of Appeals ruled that the exception does not apply when the patient is too young to understand the importance of telling the truth to the physician.

When children, especially young children, are excluded from giving testimony, the physician's report of the child's statement given during a physical examination can be of great importance. The child's statements to the physician are known as hearsay, which is a statement made out of court and later used in court to "establish the truth of what was said earlier" (Myers, 1986). While the hearsay rule exists in all English-speaking countries, different countries have different exceptions to the hearsay rule. In several countries, hearsay is more liberally admissible in civil cases (e.g., England, Scotland). In the United States, there has long been a hearsay exception for hearsay statements to health care providers. This exception is based on the premise that patients have an incentive to be truthful with a health care professional, thus rendering the hearsay reliable. Although certain hearsay statements to health care professionals are admissible in other countries, our research did not locate statutes elsewhere premised on the patient's incentive to be truthful. Generally, statements termed hearsay are "not admissible because it is difficult to determine whether they are trustworthy: [the statements] are not made under oath, there is no opportunity to cross-examine the child, and the jury is unable to observe the child's demeanor" (Bulkley and Whitcomb, 1992). Risks of hearsay are possible insincerity, miscommunication,

235

memory loss, and misperception. Without testimony in court, the speaker cannot be tested regarding these risks (Myers, 1986).

The medical hearsay exception can be an important legal tool in cases of both sexual and physical abuse because the child's narrative given to a physician may corroborate existing physical findings. For example, in a review of 115 consecutive child sexual abuse felony cases, De Jong and Rose (1991) found that successful prosecution depended on the quality of verbal evidence as well as the effectiveness of the child victim's testimony, yet no difference was found in the rate of conviction between cases with and without physical evidence. Frequently, in sexual abuse cases, often neither medical or laboratory findings exist, and there are no bystander witnesses. Thus the child's report to the physician is the only evidence to support a claim of sexual abuse (De Jong *et al.*, 1983; Enos *et al.*, 1986; McCann *et al.*, 1990). Therefore, in child maltreatment cases, whether or not physical evidence exists, the collection, preservation, and presentation of the child's corroborating verbal evidence in the form of a medical hearsay exception is often essential.

While the Eighth Circuit Court of Appeals has viewed the capacity of a 3-year-old child as quite limited, a review of the research literature since the late 1980s highlights the conceptual and cognitive strengths of very young children (Siegal, 1997). Of specific relevance to the medical hearsay exception is the documentation of the content, consistency, and coherence of early autobiographical memory (Fivush, 1993; Fivush and Shukat, 1995) and interest in young children's spontaneous reports of their everyday experiences (Nelson, 1988, 1993; Peterson, 1990), including reports of accidental injury (Howe *et al.*, 1994; Peterson *et al.*, 1993). There has been special focus on techniques that interviewers can employ to elicit additional information from young children, because their initial spontaneous reports of an event are often sparse (Ornstein *et al.*, 1992; Saywitz *et al.*, 1992; Steward *et al.*, 1993; Warren *et al.*, 1996; Wood *et al.*, 1996; Yuille *et al.*, 1993). It is clear that the types of questions asked, and the selection and use of props and dolls, can confuse (Boat and Everson, 1996; Ceci and Bruck, 1995) or enhance (Boat and Everson, 1993; Goodman and Aman, 1990; Pipe *et al.*, 1993; Saywitz *et al.*, 1991; Sternberg *et al.*, 1996; Steward and Steward, 1996) the accuracy and completeness of children's reports. During the course of the physical examination, the physician's touch may also cue memory of a previous touch experience and prompt the child patient's report. In fact, the touch events that have been most often studied in children are medical diagnostic or treatment procedures, because of the compelling analogue that medical touch holds for physical and sexual abuse and the ethical limitations on experimental researchers (Steward and Steward, 1996). However, there is little research literature on what children report to doctors about touch from others. Our pediatric colleagues tell us that although children rarely volunteer information about an injury, when a doctor observes and comments on a bruise, scratch, or injury on a child's body, the child usually does tell how it occurred.

Ross and Ross (1988) asked nearly a thousand 5–13-year-old school-children whom they would tell about a physically painful event. Children reported that they would describe different facets of that experience to different audiences. For example, they would report concise factual information of painful injury or accident to their parents, share the stress and emotion of the painful experience with their peers, and report both factual information and emotional distress associated with the painful experience to their doctors. This differential reporting may function to get parental attention and appropriate care for an injury, while friends may provide sympathy. The information the children said they would give to a physician was elicited in response to a question about advice-giving to medical students who are learning to be doctors and had never experienced a migraine headache.

How young children understand the physician's role has not been explored; however, findings of how children understand adult authority and role-associated knowledge are available. Children increasingly equate social position and authority with age. They believe that their parents hold epistemic authority or "know best" from 4 to 9 years of age. Laupa (1991) has found that children from around ages 6 to 13 weigh social position (for example, teacher) and knowledge more heavily than adult status in legitimizing obedience to authority. The concept of legitimate authority is tied to children's developing understanding of social organization and social position. First graders chose knowledge attributes to legitimize authority. For children in middle childhood, authority required both knowledge and social position. Adolescent children chose social position and excluded other attributes. Based on Laupa's (1991) findings, it appears young patients may respond to the physician's role during interview and examination with perceptions which vary with age. Perhaps 6–7 year olds see the physician as having important knowledge, the middle childhood group perceive the knowledge and social position associated with the role, and the early adolescent group focuses on primarily on social position.

Children's perception of legitimate authority related to knowledge source and knowledge area becomes increasingly defined with age as well. Raviv et al. (1990) studied kindergarten, first and third graders (4–5, 6–7, and 8–9 year olds) and found that with age, children perceive more differences in epistemic authority between four roles or knowledge sources (mother, father, teacher, friend) regarding seven knowledge areas including social relations, rules and laws, personal feelings, science and future planning. Unfortunately, health care, illness, and trauma knowledge areas were not included in this study; in the category of personal feelings, however, parents were consistently rated as higher in authority than teachers or friends.

Numerous researchers have examined children's understanding of social roles with varying results. Piaget's (1928) estimate of social role understanding at 10 years is much later than that of Watson and Fischer (1980), who found children to understand the behaviors associated with various roles at 3 years and social role understanding at 5 years. In a study of parental social role understanding, Watson and Amgott-Kwan (1983) found mean ages similar to those at which children attain steps parallel to doctor–patient role-playing. The close synchrony in parent and physician role comprehension suggests a generalized process of social role understanding. Watson and Fischer (1980) used real-life tasks without complicated verbal demands to tap young children's social role understanding of specific concrete scenarios, whereas Piaget (1928) used purely verbal means to examine the level at which children understand social role concepts. Perhaps less verbally demanding tasks are needed, especially to study young children's understanding of these concepts.

Fu *et al.* (1987) interviewed preschool, first and fourth grade children regarding family and social roles. Findings were similar to those of Piaget in 1928 – that relational qualities and multiple roles were more often described by older children, fourth graders in this sample. Again, their interview method with its verbal task demands may have overburdened preschool and first grade children and limited the younger children's ability to respond optimally. In methodological contrast, Steward and Regalbuto (1975) asked 5–6 and 8–9 year olds to demonstrate what a doctor does with a syringe and stethoscope. The children performed a behavioral role enactment as they used the instruments. While the focus of the study was to understand children's comprehension of medical procedures, their easy and skillful use of the medical equipment constituted effective physician role-play.

Young children perceive few role differences among legal personnel such as the judge, lawyers, bailiff, witnesses, and jury present in the courtroom. However, not all young children believe that all of the adults in the courtroom have the same role. Warren-Leubecker *et al.* (1989) described a charming confounding of authority and social role assignment made by one young child who reported that if the judge was not in the courtroom, a doctor would be in charge. However, even 4 year olds understood that a witness in court must be truthful (Saywitz, 1989) and they also discriminated between intentional and accidental wrongdoing (Warren-Leubecker et al., 1989).

What children report in the context of a medical examination depends not only on the role and authority of the physician but also upon their own social role as a patient and the complementary doctor–patient relationship. An important means for children to construct understanding of the social world is through participation in ongoing dynamic activities such as daily caretaking routines (Nelson, 1981) and in other familiar but less frequent events such as birthday parties, meals in restaurants, and health care visits (Bearison and Pacifici, 1989). Nelson (1986) has demonstrated that young children create general, sequentially organized models of familiar and recurring events as "scripts." In memory tasks, children recall routine events better through increased experience with the particular event; for younger children, recall and participation in discussion or play about a routine event is more dependent on specific cues such as props (Nelson, 1988). Children are better able to respond to logical tasks presented in terms of familiar experiences (Donaldson, 1978).

Fischer's (1980) finding that children understand role complementarity by about 6 years (the doctor role functions as a complement to the patient role) and role intersection by 7 years (the person in a doctor role can be physician, parent, and spouse to other persons' patient, child, and spouse roles simultaneously) suggests that children may understand the practical or functional nature of specific roles with sufficient detail to realize the physician's special knowledge or beneficent authority role by this time as well.

However, Warren-Leubecker et al. (1989) note that some young children assume that adults who question them about an event already know what has happened. They suggest that this has implications regarding testimony in that children may assume they are providing only corroboration for an event the adult already understands. This idea is pertinent regarding children's report to a physician as well. Thus one should exercise caution in estimating the facility with which a child coordinates doctor–patient communication. Without adequate understanding of the doctor's role, the child may not appreciate the fact-finding nature of the interview, participate effectively, or serve their own self-interest.

In sum, empirical study of children's report of physical touch finds young children to be very terse but truthful informants especially when reporting painful, but necessary medical procedures to an interviewer. The discrepancy between accuracy and completeness may be influenced by children's limited understanding of adult authority and conversational rules where young children assume that their role is merely to corroborate what adults already know, especially the answers to questions they ask children. While theory and research regarding social role understanding have identified both knowledge and social position as components of children's understanding of the authority related to social role, studies of school-aged children's understanding of family roles and relationships have predominated. The assumption underlying the medical hearsay exception, that of young children's understanding of the physician's role, has not been empirically tested. We do know that by age 3 children are able to imitate some of the physician's activities using common medical equipment; by age 4 children know that truth-telling is expected in court and by age 6 they can imitate and coordinate two social roles such as doctor and patient. By about 8 years, children increasingly perceive authority as linked to social role and special knowledge, with social role eclipsing knowledge as most important in adolescence. However, there has been no direct assessment of children's understanding of the knowledge and social position of physicians or of what children expect in reciprocal doctor–patient relationships regarding telling the truth. Methodologically it is important to note that most studies to date have relied heavily on verbal question-response formats, and often report little or no use of stimulus materials to enhance communication between the researcher and the child.

Based on the review of the research literature presently available, a series of questions can be asked to evaluate the appropriateness of extending the diagnosis and treatment exception to young children: when children have experienced abusive touch, whom, if anyone, do they tell, and why? For example, do they tell other children but assume it is not necessary to report the incident to parents, teachers, or physicians in their lives because adults are all-knowing? When children report body touch, do they discriminate different kinds of contact, such as negative and positive touch? It should be noted that touch judged by a society to be abusive may range from gentle fondling to that which is excruciatingly painful. Are young children as likely to report self-injury as to tell about touch inflicted by others? Finally, what kind of touch do young children believe they should report to their doctor? These questions are nested within young children's understanding of the physician's role, activities and beneficence.

To begin exploring these questions, an interview was designed and materials were selected to enhance communication between the interviewer and the child and to maximize the child's opportunity to report what the child knew and believed. We posed a series of questions to forty healthy children ranging in age from 3 years 6 months to 6 years 11 months. In order to assess developmental differences we decided to compare the responses of the younger group of children (mean age of 4 years 2 months) with the responses of the older group of children (mean age of 5 years 11 months). Each of the groups included ten boys and ten girls. The children attended preschool or after school day care. Reflecting the population of the university community in northern California in which they lived, the majority of the children's parents had completed their college education and some postgraduate level work. Ethnic membership also paralleled the community and included 83 percent Caucasian, 7.5 percent Hispanic, 7.5 percent Asian, and 2.5 percent African-American children. A brief questionnaire completed by the parents confirmed that all children were currently healthy, that both the younger and older groups of children had similar health histories, and provided the name of each child's pediatrician.

The senior author, who conducted all interviews, met with each child in a quiet room at the child care site for two meetings of approximately twenty-five minutes each. To begin, the interviewer introduced herself, noted parent and teacher consent, and stated, "I want to learn your ideas about the jobs grown-ups do." To reduce possible anxiety, children were told their "ideas were the most important," and that "answers aren't right or wrong." To enhance interest and participation, children were told that they would receive a sticker at the end of each part of the interview and that the interviewer would "write down their ideas so [she] can remember them better."

A four-part structured interview was developed. The first and last sections presented were composed of warm-up and truth and lie items respectively. The orders of the two middle sections, touch events and social role items, were counterbalanced so that half the children of each age responded to touch questions first, and half responded to adult role items first.

To acclimate children to interaction with us and to informally assess receptive language level, each child was initially asked a total of six questions about three picture cards showing two to four familiar objects. With each card, the interviewer named the objects shown and then asked questions related to object function. Although no verbal responses were required, over 80 percent of children matched or embellished their pointing responses with single words or comments.

To learn what young children could tell us about the experiences of body touch they might report to a physician, questions were asked about four touch events with a positive or neutral valence (a light tap on the head, a hug, a tickle on the neck, and a soft shoulder touch), and four events with a negative valence (a bruise, a skinned knee, a scraped elbow, and a stubbed toe). To present these touches in a recognizable way, we asked about the events as part of a regular head-to-toe well child check-up using a child model and props. An 18-inch, soft-body doll, matching the child's gender, was marked with the requisite bruise, scabs, and an adhesive bandage to illustrate negative touch events. With the subject's assent, the doll was given the child's name and the examining physician in the scenario was given the subject's physician's name. An ophthalmoscope, patellar hammer, and stethoscope were used as props for the examination.

For both touch event and social role sections, a rogues' gallery of four faces was created to represent possible message receivers and social role representatives. Possible touch report receivers were shown using pictures to represent mother, physician, teacher, and same-sex peer. For the social role section gallery, a police officer replaced the same-sex peer choice. We tried to suggest the people who fill these roles for each subject by selecting pictures to match them by sex and race. Parents provided us with the name and gender of the child's personal physician.

As each touch event was presented, the subject was asked, "Do you need to tell someone about the (touch/injury)?" Negative responses were probed with the follow-up question "Why don't you need to tell about (name event)?" Affirmative responses were probed with the question "Whom do you tell?" to which children responded verbally or used the pictures to indicate their choices. Next, subjects were asked what they would report about the event, why they would report the event to specific receivers and what would come of their making this report.

If a child did not spontaneously volunteer that he or she would report a negative touch item to the physician, the child was asked specifically, "At a check-up, do you need to tell (physician's name) about (the injury)?" with appropriate follow-up probes. In addition, for minor injury events, children were asked, "At a check-up, do you need to tell (physician's name) if you got (injury) by yourself?" and "Do you tell if another person hurt you?"

Finally we asked to hear of an injury the child had experienced personally. We probed for a detailed description of the injury and whether the child had told anyone when the injury occurred.

A series of open-ended questions was designed to learn children's ideas about the adult social roles of mother, doctor, teacher, and police officer. Each face shown in the rogues' gallery was briefly identified by role and the child was asked if he or she were personally acquainted with a person in each of the roles and if so, the name of the person they knew.

To explore each role with the child, the interviewer used the name of the role exemplar, saying, "Now you said (name) is a (role)" and then, "What is the job of a (role)?" If the child hesitated we probed, "Where does (name) do his or her job?" or "When you visit (name), what does he or she do?" To probe overlapping duties, and role purpose and knowledge we asked "Does anyone else do that, what does a (role) know about, and does anyone else know about that?" To further probe special knowledge, we asked, "Is there something only (roles) know about?" and especially, "Do doctors know special things?" To probe role overlap, we asked if the child's physician "is a mom or dad" or if "he or she could be a mom or dad?"

We also asked sixteen questions regarding epistemic or knowledge-based authority. We posed these questions in four settings (e.g., home, school, hospital, jail) to probe for the accompanying role and followed with twelve items about role knowledge which began, "Who knows best about" and continued with tasks such as "giving people tickets if they drive too fast" and "how to get better if you are very sick."

To explore the concepts of truth and lie, we asked the open-ended questions, "What does the truth/a lie mean?" and probed "Tell me what it's like when people tell the truth/a lie." When the child's response included either an appropriate example or definition, we probed the consequences of telling a lie by asking, "What would happen if a boy/girl tells a lie to a doctor?" To probe valence we asked, "Is telling the truth bad or good?" and "Is telling a lie bad or good?"

The total number of possible touches which children could report had a range from zero to eight. The number of positive or negative touches had a potential range of from zero to four. The content of children's open-ended reports of a personal injury was coded categorically for descriptive and affective information. The number of potential social role receivers ranged from zero to thirty-two.

Social role knowledge data were coded as number of correct responses to multiple choice items, with a potential range of zero to sixteen. Responses to the physician's role description were coded categorically as concrete, idiosyncratic, or functional. Concrete responses included use of medical equipment (e.g., "checks your ears" or "looks in your ears with a little light"). Idiosyncratic responses included describing an action performed by the physician which was not a part of the medical role such as talking on the telephone. Functional behaviors included describing a goal such as maintaining health or assessing illness. Answers regarding physician's special knowledge were coded for presence or absence of a relevant descriptor such as "makes you well," or "gives you the right medicine."

The definition of truth and lie concepts and consequences were coded using a three-point scale with 2 assigned for an accurate definition, 1 assigned for an appropriate example, and 0 assigned for an irrelevant or inaccurate example or definition. The valence of truth and lie were coded for accuracy; one point was given for each correct response. The consequences of lying to a doctor were coded 2 for an appropriate example or description, 1 for vague negative consequences, and 0 for no understanding or an idiosyncratic response. Coding reliability was assessed by randomly selecting 25% of protocols for coding by a second rater. Inter-rater agreement for open-ended questions ranged from 88–100%, with a mean of 97%. Inter-rater agreement for questions with predetermined discrete response choices ranged from 96–100%.

To evaluate our findings, we first examined the dependent variables of training trial score, total receivers, number of events reported, valence, injury source, epistemic authority score, and truth and lie definition. These outcomes were analyzed for order effects and sex differences. Because no statistically significant differences were found for either the order in which touch and social role questions were asked, or for the sex of the subject, data were combined across those two variables.

We coded children's open-ended descriptions of the physician's role for concrete and conceptual descriptors and examined them for differences by subject age. The majority of children in both age groups included concrete descriptors such as mentioning use of a medical equipment item in telling us what a physician does. A significantly greater number of older children than younger children also provided conceptual descriptors of the doctor's role.

Older children gave significantly more correct responses to sixteen multiple-choice questions regarding special knowledge components associated with adult roles than did younger children. When asked specifically about the physician's role, significantly more older children described the physician as having special knowledge in general terms such as "makes you well." Older children also offered significantly more descriptors of the physician's special knowledge, e.g., "knows about medicines."

However, age was not a statistically significant factor in determining children's ability to name their personal physician. In fact, 80 percent of older children and 68 percent of younger children were able to do so.

Children were queried regarding self or other as agent of injury. Our data suggest that their report to the physician did vary accordingly. Older children were significantly more likely to respond that they would tell their doctor about an injury caused to them by another person than did younger children. The difference between age groups for self-injury was not significant.

Regarding the question of corroboration, our data do not suggest that younger children feel that there is no need to report an injury event to a physician because they assume that physicians already know the answers to questions they ask during an office visit. Of twenty-three children who responded to this interview item, only one of ten children from the younger group, and none of thirteen children in the older group affirmed that a doctor knew how a presented injury was caused without being told.

Regarding the concepts of truth and lie, older children gave significantly more accurate responses to open-ended questions asked of them than did younger children. In addition, significantly more older children reported that it was both good to tell the truth and bad to tell a lie. Separate chi-square analyses of truth and lie by age revealed no significant difference for truth, and a trend for lie. Most older and younger children agreed that telling the truth is desirable (95 percent and 82 percent respectively). Most older and somewhat fewer younger children agreed that telling a lie is undesirable (95 percent and 75 percent respectively).

Children who showed some understanding of truth and lie concepts were probed regarding the consequences of lying to a physician. Approximately half of the younger group responded to this item (9 of 20) and nearly all of the older group (19 of 20) did so. There was a statistical trend for more older than younger children to understand the potentially negative consequences of lying to a physician. Younger children achieved only vague understanding at best and half the older children suggested realistic potentially negative consequences of lying to a physician.

Who is your doctor and what is the doctor's job?

Most of the children we interviewed were able to name their personal physician. In fact, 80 percent of the 5 and 6-year-olds and 68 percent of the 3 and 4-year-olds were able to do so. All of the children were able to tell us something about the doctor's job. The differences we found in the descriptions of physician's role by the 3–6-year-old children in our study were focused on conceptual descriptors. In response to structured multiple-choice questions beginning with the expression "Who knows best," we found that older children were significantly better able than younger children to select the appropriate role associated with specific knowledge areas. Most children mentioned the doctor's use of medical equipment or procedures such as use of stethoscopes and giving immunizations. Both are descriptions bound by perception and concrete personal experience and consistent with Steward and Regalbuto's (1975) earlier findings regarding preschool children. One subject commented, "first [doctors] check [patient's] hearts to make sure their hearts are still beating" (KW, 4 years 10 months). A significantly greater number of older subjects gave conceptual descriptors as well when describing what physicians do. They nearly always mentioned "help or helping people." At times treatment was implied, "to make them not sick so they won't die" (SH, 6 years 1 month) and more specifically, "[to] help ... when they're hurt or have an ear infection or cold or something like that. They tell you the right way to help the sickness, the inside of your body [to] fight the little bugs" (KN, 6 years 1 month). This treatment comes in the form of "a shot or . . . with medicine." In this sample of healthy children, health maintenance was included in several children's descriptions, for instance, "make sure people are okay, aren't sick" (TQ, 6 years 7 months). This safeguarding and confirmation of health was accomplished through the use of "special tools" (TN, 6 years 1 month). Causality was implied by a few older children through the mention of "little bugs" and diet. The younger children's preoperational self- and body-centered role descriptions and the older children's more differentiated role-specific understanding are consonant with the dimensions described by Steward and Steward (1981).

When asked what doctors know, significantly more 5–6-year-olds, in both general and specific terms could describe the kinds of special knowledge that physicians have. In general terms, younger children again mentioned concrete activities, for example "giving shots." Older children mentioned safety and caretaking and knowledge of effective medicines as well as knowledge of a healthy diet and body systems. These findings are in accord with Raviv et al. (1990). Using a structured approach, they found children did not begin to differentiate areas of specific knowledge associated with various roles until they became school aged.

Do doctors already know what children know?

To tap the child's sense of whether or not doctors already know the answers to the questions they pose, we probed reports of the child's own injury with the question, "Does (physician's name) know what happened when you hurt yourself if you don't tell?" Only one subject, a 4 year old, thought the physician knew this without being told by the child. Our findings were in contrast to the suggestion by Warren-Leubecker et al. (1989) that young children may assume adults seek corroboration, and Siegal's (1997) work cautioning that prolonged or unconventional questioning may violate children's understanding of conversational rules and the interrogator's sincerity. The children who spoke with us responded as if the physicians genuinely seek information. Alternatively, in response to structured event questions, a 6-year-old boy commented that the doctor might know what happened because his mother has told the doctor. In fact, children in US society do not independently present for examination or treatment but are brought for care by a responsible adult.

Table 10.1. *Mean report of touch event to receiver by valence and age group*

	3–4 years (n = 20)		5–6 years (n = 20)	
	Valence			
Receiver	Positive	Negative	Positive	Negative
Mother	0.45[de]	1.55[b]	0.74[bcde]	3.05[a]
Doctor	0.15[e]	1.30[bc]	0.05[e]	0.53[cde]
Teacher	0.35[de]	0.95[bcde]	0.11[e]	1.21[bcd]
Peer	0.50[de]	0.35[de]	0.21[de]	0.37[de]

Note: Means that do not share a common letter designation differ at the $p < 0.05$ level.

Reporting body touch: what do you tell and to whom?

In order to answer this question, we evaluated the children's reports regarding body touch events by total number of reports, type of touch (whether the touch was positive or negative), and receiver (doctor, parent, teacher, or peer). Children said they would report approximately five of the eight touch events to others. Children said they would report negative touch events more than twice as often as they would report positive events. They were nearly three times as likely to report touch events to their mother than to a doctor, teacher, or peer. Inspection of the significant cell means in table 10.1 reveals a developmental difference in report of negative touch: the older children said they would tell their mother about negative touch events significantly more often than the other adults or a peer, while the younger group made only the discrimination between reporting to adults rather than peers. In striking contrast, children from both the older and younger groups rarely reported positive touch, and they did not make differential reports to adults or children.

Thus our data indicate that young children are more likely to report painful than benign touch and that they understand the necessity to provide an accurate narrative to persons in authority. This suggests that, compared to younger children, older children were better able to distinguish what kinds of events merit possible concern and need an adult's attention or acknowledgment. They often mentioned the presence of blood as a reporting criterion. The older children, in determining whether or not to tell a doctor, also made the discrimination between self-inflicted injury and injury caused by another – and were more likely to report the latter. These findings parallel research on children's highly accurate reports of painful medical procedures (Goodman *et al.*, 1994; Merritt *et al.*, 1994; Steward and Steward, 1996) and suggest that even some very young children have the capacity to meet the medical hearsay exception.

As we mentioned above, in our structured touch items, mothers received far more reports of body touch, positive or negative, than any other receiver. This is consistent with the primacy of the maternal role and the amount of contact children have with their mothers. In this healthy sample, most children visited a physician perhaps twice a year, generally for well child care or for minor illnesses or treatment which occurs in the presence of a responsible adult, usually the mother. Peterson *et al.* (1993) interviewed 8–11-year-old children and their mothers independently every two weeks about children's daily injury events. They found that mothers knew of and recalled their children's daily injuries that were characterized by higher negative affect, need for medical treatment, and those involving unusual circumstances or novel behavior. One of the children we interviewed explained his rationale for reporting touch events as follows: for everyday pleasant touches, you "don't have to [tell] if you don't want to" or "unless it's a bad stranger" and for minor injuries, you "don't tell if you don't cry" (KW, 4 years 10 months).

However, adults were more likely to hear about children's injuries than were the children's peers. The child's understanding of epistemic authority, that is the role knowledge associated with parent, physician, teacher, and police officer roles, was more strongly linked to receiver by valence interaction than was age. This suggests that response to epistemic authority items is a stand-in variable for age in the age × receiver × valence interaction. For purposes of this study, the epistemic authority score may be a better measure of developmental level than age. Perhaps children who responded more knowledgeably or carefully to structured role knowledge items were better able to attend to and understand touch and injury items as well.

Unlike the findings of Ross and Ross (1984), no subject reported that he or she would give different message receivers different kinds of information when reporting their injuries. When telling us to whom they would report a given injury, all children provided only factual or concretely descriptive information. No child included affective information in describing their report for structured events. In addition, when children were invited to report their personal experiences of injury, only two children of thirty-seven included affective information. The majority of children interviewed by Ross and Ross (1984) were older than those in our study, and perhaps were better able to tailor messages to varying receivers in order to elicit specific desired responses.

Our findings regarding agent of injury are similar to the findings of Lollar *et al.* (1982) regarding the impact of setting on children's perception of pain. Our data suggest agent-of-injury influences report to the physician as older children were significantly more likely to tell their physician if they were hurt by another person than if they had injured themselves. Younger children told us they would report self-injury to the doctor more so than injury by another. Responses among younger children were much more variable than among older children; standard errors and standard deviations for the younger group were more than twice those of the older group.

You "don't tell if you don't cry"

Peterson and her colleagues (1993) found that mothers reported only 42 percent of the daily injury events their children had independently reported to interviewers. Thus parents may never hear about a substantial proportion of the injuries children experience. When we asked children to tell us about an injury they had experienced, five children described pain or injury they had kept from adults. One child, GI (6 years 11 months) evaluated the need to report an injury based on the duration of the problem. She hit her knee swimming in a friend's pool and "it got all swollen," but she didn't tell anyone because, before long, "it got better." Intensity of pain is also a consideration. When UT (5 years 0 months) hurt his knee while running, he reported, "[I] didn't need to tell because I didn't cry." A precocious younger subject (SY, 4 years 3 months) expressed pride as she told us, "One day I got an owie on my knee and I did not cry because I'm already a big girl." SY told "all my friends" but no adults. A sense of shame motivated KM (6 years 7 months) to keep a playground mishap to himself. KM was playing when a peer "took his foot and pushed my foot." KM fell, but "didn't want anybody to know." He reported he "was embarrassed and thought, like I can't play this game without hurting myself."

In response to all eight touch events, IN (3 years 11 months) claimed that she would not report any of them "because I don't want to" or because "I'm a little bit scare[d]." A few months previously she had cut her lower lip in a fall and was very upset when sutures were placed to close the wound. In light of her recent experience, this preschooler's coping strategy to avoid any possible adult intervention is suggestive of results found by Altshuler and Ruble (1989) in which schoolchildren of ages 5–12 years used avoidance tactics to cope with conditions of uncontrollable stress.

Truth and lies: "You're in big trouble now!"

Most older and younger children agreed that telling the truth is desirable (95 percent and 82 percent respectively) and that telling a lie is undesirable (95 percent and 75 percent respectively). As we had anticipated, older children were significantly better able to define and give appropriate examples of truth and lie concepts than younger children. However, we need to qualify this statement because many respondents in both groups assigned the correct valence to both terms; a ceiling effect limited the difference between group means. From these findings, it appears that younger subjects have little ability to define truth and lie but were often able to recognize and label the words "telling the truth" positively and less often to label "telling a lie" negatively. These findings are in accord with those of Bussey (1992) who studied preschool, second and fifth grade children (mean ages of 4 years 9 months, 7 years 8 months and 11 years respectively) and found that those in second grade and older were more able to identify truth and lies correctly and that lies were seen as "worse than truthful statements" in all age groups who participated.

In addition to observing how children define and appraise truth and lies, we also asked our participants about the consequence of lying to a doctor. A trend in group differences was found. Characteristic of the younger children were vague negative responses such as "You're in big trouble now" or punishments such as a time-out or a loud reprimand from the doctor. Older children often thought that the doctor would become angry; eight children understood that the doctor would not be able to be helpful or would prescribe inappropriate treatment. Missing data may have impacted the outcome of this item, as only nine responses were available for the younger group.

As with social role definitions, the children's responses were consonant with the order of conceptualization proposed by Steward and Steward (1981). Younger children's responses were characterized by centration and showed concern with possible punishment for lying. Older children were beginning to express a discriminated perception wherein lying prevents the physician from being helpful or results in possible harm from inappropriate treatment.

Methodological notes

It is not an easy task to interview young children and elicit meaningful responses from them. Young children lack skill in responding to study items and some have difficulty responding to questions even with props provided to clarify our queries or enhance the interview process. Between age groups and within individual children the range of their ability both to engage with the interviewer and to attend to the task during the course of the interview was markedly variable. Some children consistently responded tersely or stated "I don't know." Others seemed to enjoy this time with an interested adult, expanded their responses, asked about the interview itself and made conversational bids such as, "Do you have a mom or dad?" The occurrence of missing data was greater among younger children, who were generally more difficult to engage and also more rapidly declined in their ability to effectively participate. In addition, responses elicited in the research setting may not be comparable to what children experience in genuine well child or treatment office visits or in diagnosis and treatment of sexual abuse.

The children who spoke with us for this study lived with well-educated parents. Child interview participants from homes where they are seldom spoken to or not listened to by caretaking adults may have less practice with the rules of verbal intercourse and therefore less facility with the conversational structure used in an interview such as ours. This was found to be the case by another study (Steward and Steward, 1996).

We introduced a same-sex doll as a prop to describe four positive and four negative touch events. The doll was identified as a child of the subject's age and gender and, with the child's agreement, given the child's name as well. All children agreed with this premise although one older subject found the suggestion that the doll child's physician have the same name as his own physician to be humorous and suggested an alternative. When describing personal injuries, the children used their own bodies to describe or illustrate their experiences, not the doll, as did the children participating in other studies (Steward and Steward, 1996). Although it is counter-intuitive to many adults, we would agree with DeLoache and Marzolf (1995), who have noted some limitations to the use of dolls as illustrator props or models when interviewing children younger than $3\frac{1}{2}$ years. Neither our group of children or those interviewed by DeLoache and Marzolf used the doll as a self-representation.

Recommendations

While we do not recommend that physicians assume the role of investigative interviewer, if during a medical visit a child offers a statement describing an abusive event, or if the physician's touch elicits a negative or fearful response from a child, it is important for the physician to inquire. It is important for the physician to pay close attention to a young child's spontaneous statement especially because the findings of Peterson et al. (1993) underline the fact that mothers – the pediatrician's most common source of information about a child's injuries – may not always know what has happened to their own children. Another potential real-world complication is that if an injured child is brought to the physician by an abusive parent, or a parent whose partner is the perpetrator of the injury, the accompanying parent may discourage the child's cooperation with the physician. Even if the parent will not cooperate, it is important that the physician pursue the child's narrative explanation in order to assess risk, to determine whether suspicion of abuse exists, and if so, to make mandated reports.

Siegal's (1997) work on children's conversational competence implies that a child may respond positively to physicians, stating their fact-finding role, the need for truth, and the child's self-interest in reporting truthfully. Additionally, because pediatricians are trained to talk to children at the child's developmental level and to listen carefully to their young patients, we believe that they can be the "right person in the right place at the right time" to speak for the child in court if a child does disclose abuse during a medical visit. Medical staff can increase the child's understanding of the need to be candid by informing the child of the purpose of the visit by introducing themselves and remarking "I'm going to do a check-up to see how strong you are, how healthy you are, and if there's anything that needs to be done" (Myers, 1992). The professional can further emphasize the importance of being accurate and complete.

Those who diagnose and treat possible victims of abuse need to document factors related to how reliable the child's statements would be considered by a judge including spontaneity, whether leading or non-leading questions are used in information gathering, consistent statements regarding core details rather than peripheral details, the child's state of mind and emotion when statements were made, concurrent play and gestures, developmentally unusual knowledge of sexual acts or anatomy, idiosyncratic detail, use of developmentally appropriate terminology, child's belief that disclosure may lead to punishment, possible motive to fabricate, and the child's correction of the interviewer (Myers, 1997). If children describe the sensations and feelings experienced during the specific alleged activities, this detail will bolster the credibility of their statements (Seidl, 1992).

In sum, the original impetus for this study was to address how young children understand what physicians do and know and what the impact of a report or telling a lie to a physician may have on treatment. Based on our work with 3–6-year-old children in a low stress, non-traumatic interview setting, we found that children said that they would report more injuries than positive touches, and that mother was most likely to hear about these injuries. Older children, 5–6-year-olds, were less likely to report self-injuries to a physician than those caused to them by another person. Both the 3–4-year-olds and the 5–6-year-olds could concretely describe what a physician does: older children were better able to describe concepts such as treatment and prevention functions and to identify the special knowledge associated with the physician's role than younger children. Neither group expected that the physician would know the cause of an injury without being told. Both age groups identified the truth as positive and older children tended to more reliably identify lying as negative. Older children were significantly better than younger children at describing the concepts of truth telling and lying and could also better understand potential consequences of lying to a physician. While generalizability is limited, we are concerned that for children in incestuous families, positive touch such as sexual fondling will not be reported. We are also concerned that when children who live in neglectful families report an injury to their mother or other caregiver, their report may not be appropriately acted upon. Further naturalistic research of children interacting with their physicians would be valuable and increase the ecological validity of our findings.

Acknowledgments: the authors are grateful to the directors, classroom staff, students, parents, and children at Russell Park Child Development Center, La Rue Park Children's House, North Davis School-Age Day Care Center, and the Child and Family Study Center at the University of California at Davis for their participation in the study. Thanks also to Carol Rodning for ongoing consultation and support, to Lianne Friedman for assistance with data analysis, and to Michael G. Shafto for help with post-hoc data analysis.

NOTE

1 The research presented in this chapter is based on a thesis submitted by Melody R. Herbst in partial fulfilment of the requirements for a Master of Science degree at the University of California, Davis.

REFERENCES

Altshuler, J. L., and Ruble, D. N. (1989). Developmental changes in children's awareness of strategies for coping with uncontrollable stress. *Child Development*, 60, 1,337–1,349.
Bearison, D. J., and Pacifici, C. (1989). Children's event knowledge of cancer treatment. *Journal of Applied Developmental Psychology*, 10, 469–486.
Boat, B., and Everson, M. (1993). The use of anatomical dolls in sexual abuse evaluations: Current research and practice. In G. S. Goodman and B. L. Bottoms (eds.), *Child victims, child witnesses: Understanding and improving*

254   M. R. Herbst, M. S. Steward, J E. B. Myers, R. L. Hansen

testimony (pp. 47–69). New York: Guilford.
(1996). Concerning practices of interviewers when using anatomical dolls in child protective services investigations. *Child Maltreatment*, 1, 96–104.

Bulkley, J., and Whitcomb, D. (1992). Admissibility of children's statements of abuse under the confrontation clause and recent Supreme Court cases. *Journal of Interpersonal Violence*, 7, 8–10.

Bussey, K. (1992). Lying and truthfulness: Children's definitions, standards and evaluative reactions. *Child Development*, 63, 129–137.

Ceci, S. J., and Bruck, M. (1995). *Jeopardy in the courtroom*. Washington, DC: American Psychological Association.

De Jong, A. R., and Rose, M. (1991). Legal proof of child sexual abuse in the absence of physical evidence. *Pediatrics*, 88, 506–511.

De Jong, A., Hervada, A., and Emmett, G. (1983). Epidemiological variations in childhood sexual abuse. *Child Abuse and Neglect*, 7, 155–162.

DeLoache, J. S., and Marzolf, D.P. (1995). The use of dolls to interview young children: Issues of symbolic representation. *Journal of experimental Child Psychology*, 60, 155–173.

Donaldson, M. (1978). *Children's minds*. New York: Norton.

Enos, W. F., Conrath, T. B., and Byer, J. C. (1986). Forensic evaluation of the sexually abused child. *Pediatrics*, 78(3), 385–398.

Fischer, K. W. (1980). A theory of cognitive development: The control and construction of hierarchies of skills. *Psychological Review*, 87(6), 477–531.

Fivush, R. (1993). Developmental perspectives on autobiographical recall. In G. S. Goodman and B. L. Bottoms (eds.), *Child victims, child witnesses: Understanding and improving testimony* (pp. 1–24). New York: Guilford.

Fivush, R., and Shukat, J. (1995). Content, consistency and coherence of early autobiographical memory. In M. S. Zargoza, J. R. Graham, G. C. N. Hall, R. Hirschman, and Y. S. Ben-Porath (eds.), *Memory and testimony in the child witness* (pp. 5–23). Thousand Oaks, CA: Sage.

Fu, V. R., Goodwin, M. P., Sporakowski, M. J., and Hinkle, D. E. (1987). Children's thinking about family characteristics and parent attributes. *Journal of Genetic Psychology*, 148(2), 153–166.

Goodman, G., and Aman, C. (1990). Children's use of anatomically correct dolls to recount an event. *Child Development*, 61, 1,859–1,871.

Goodman, G. S., Quas, J. A., Batteman-Faunce, J. M., Riddlesberger, M. M., and Kuhn, J. (1994). Predictors of accurate and inaccurate memories of traumatic events experienced in childhood. *Consciousness and Cognition*, 3, 269–294.

Howe, M. L., Courage, M. L., and Peterson, C. (1994). How can I remember when "I" wasn't there: Long-term retention of traumatic experiences and emergence of the cognitive self. *Consciousness and Cognition*, 3, 327–355.

Laupa, M. (1991). Children's reasoning about three authority attributes: Adult status, knowledge and social position. *Developmental Psychology*, 27, 321–329.

Lollar, D. J., Smits, S. J., and Patterson, D. L. (1982). Assessment of pediatric pain: An empirical perspective. *Journal of Pediatric Psychology*, 7(3), 267–277.

McCann, J., Wells, R., Voris, S., and Voris, J. (1990). Genital findings in prepubertal girls selected for nonabuse: A descriptive study. *Pediatrics*, 86, 179–193.

Merritt, K. A., Ornstein, P. A. and Spiker, B. (1994). Children's memory for a salient medical procedure: Implication for testimony. *Pediatrics*, 94, 17–23.

Myers, J. E. B. (1986). Role of physician in preserving verbal evidence of child abuse. *Journal of Pediatrics*, 109(3), 409–411.

(1992). *Legal issues in child abuse and neglect*, 1st edn. Newbury Park, CA: Sage.

(1997). *Evidence in child abuse and neglect cases*, 3rd edn. New York: Wiley Law.

Nelson, K. (1981). Social cognition in a script framework. In J. H. Flavell and L. Ross (eds.), *Social cognitive development* (pp. 97–118). Cambridge, UK: Cambridge University Press.

(1986). *Event knowledge: Structures and function in development*. Hillsdale, NJ: Erlbaum.

(1988). The ontogeny of memory for real events. In U. Neisser and E. Winograd (eds.), *Remembering reconsidered: Ecological and traditional approaches to the study of memory* (pp. 244–276). New York: Cambridge University Press.

(1993). Events, narratives, memory: What develops? In C. A. Nelson (ed.), *Memory and affect in development: Minnesota symposia on child psychology*, vol. XXVI (pp. 1–24). Hillsdale, NJ: Erlbaum.

Ornstein, P. A., Gordon, B. N., and Larus, D. H. (1992). Children's memory for a personally experienced event: Implications for testimony. *Applied Cognitive Psychology*, 6, 49–60.

Peterson, C. (1990). The who, when and where of early narratives. *Journal of Child Language*, 17, 433–455.

Peterson, L., Moreno, A., and Harbeck-Weber, C. (1993). "And then it started bleeding": Children's and mothers' perceptions and recollections of daily injury events. *Journal of Clinical Child Psychology*, 22(3), 345–354.

Piaget, J. (1928). *Judgement and reasoning in the child*. M. Warden (trans.). London: Routledge and Kegan Paul.

Pipe, M.-E., Gee, S., and Wilson, C. (1993). Cues, props and context: Do they facilitate children's event reports? In G. S. Goodman and B. L. Bottoms (eds.), *Child victims, child witnesses: Understanding and improving testimony* (pp. 25–45). New York: Guilford.

Raviv, A., Bar-Tal, D., Raviv, A., and Houminer, D. (1990). Development in children's perceptions of epistemic authorities. *British Journal of Developmental Psychology*, 8, 157–169.

Ross, D. M., and Ross, S. A. (1984). The importance of type of question, psychological climate and subject set in interviewing children about pain. *Pain*, 19, 71–79.

(1988). *Childhood pain*. Baltimore: Urban and Schwarzberg.

Saywitz, K. J. (1989). Children's conceptions of the legal system: "Court is a place to play basketball." In S. J. Ceci, D. F. Ross, and M. P. Toglia (eds.), *Perspectives on children's testimony* (pp. 131–157). New York: Springer-Verlag.

Saywitz, K. J., Goodman, G. S., Nicholas, E., and Moan, S. F. (1991). Children's memories of a physical examination involving genital touch: Implications for reports of child sexual abuse. *Journal of Consulting and Clinical Psychology*, 59(5), 682–691.

Saywitz, K., Geiselman, R. E., and Bornstein, G. K. (1992). Effects of cognitive interviewing and practice on children's recall performance. *Journal of Applied Psychology*, 77, 744–756.

Seidl, T. (1992). Special interviewing techniques. In S. Ludwig and A. E. Kornberg (eds.), *Child abuse: A medical reference* (pp. 279–293). New York: Churchill Livingstone.

Siegal, M. (1997). *Knowing children: experiments in conversation and cognition*, 2nd edn. Hove, UK: Psychology Press.

Sternberg, K. J., Lamb, M. E., Hershkowitz, I., Esplin, P. W., Redlich, A., and Sunshine, N. (1996). The relationship between investigative utterance types and the informativeness of child witnesses. *Journal of Applied Developmental Psychology*, 17, 439–451.

Steward, M. S., and Regalbuto, G. (1975). Do doctors know what children know? *American Journal of Orthopsychiatry*, 45, 146–149.

Steward, M. S., and Steward, D. S. (1981). Children's conceptions of medical procedures. In R. Bibace and M. Walsh (eds.), *New directions for child development: Children's conceptions of health, illness, and bodily functions*, no. 14 (pp. 67–83). San Francisco: Jossey-Bass.

(1996). Interviewing young children about body touch and handling. *Monographs of the Society for Research in Child Development*, no. 248, vol. 61 (4–5), 1–186.

Steward, M. S., Bussey, K., Goodman, G. S., and Saywitz, K. (1993). Implications of developmental research for interviewing children. *Child Abuse and Neglect*, 17, 25–37.

Warren, A. R., Woodall, J. S., Hunt, J. S., and Perry, N. W. (1996). "It sounds good in theory, but...": Do investigative interviewers follow guidelines based on memory research? *Child Maltreatment*, 1, 231–245.

Warren-Leubecker, A. J., Tate, C. S., Hinton, I. D., and Ozbek, I. N. (1989). What do children know about the legal system and when do they know it? First steps down a less traveled path in child witness research. In S. J. Ceci, D. F. Ross, and M. P. Toglia (eds.), *Perspectives on children's testimony* (pp. 158–183). New York: Springer-Verlag.

Watson, M. W., and Amgott-Kwan, T. (1983). Transitions in children's understanding in parental roles. *Developmental Psychology*, 19, 659–666.

Watson, M. W., and Fischer, K. W. (1980). Development of social roles in elicited and spontaneous behavior during preschool years. *Developmental Psychology*, 16, 483–494.

Woo, J. (1992). Child–doctor confidences are often banned in court. *Wall Street Journal*, July 17, p. B6.

Wood, J. M., McClure, K. A., and Birch, R. A. (1996). Suggestions for improving interviews in child protection agencies. *Child Maltreatment*, 1, 223–230.

Yuille, J., Hunter, R., Joffe, R., and Zaparniuk, J. (1993). Interviewing children in sexual abuse cases. In G. S. Goodman and B. Bottoms (eds.), *Child victims, child witnesses: Understanding and improving testimony* (pp. 95–115). New York: Guilford.

11 Cognitive development and the competence to consent to medical and psychotherapeutic treatment

Candida C. Peterson and Michael Siegal

Questions regarding the ages at which children and adolescents are likely to become capable of granting informed consent for medical or psychotherapeutic treatment provide new avenues for the interface between research in developmental psychology and applications in legal and health settings. An increasing emphasis upon voluntary choice and the active role of the individual in determining treatment outcomes has opened the way for greater consultation between health professionals and patients before, during, and after medical, dental, therapeutic, and psychiatric care. At the same time, advancement in the understanding of the benefits and risks associated with standard health procedures, together with the proliferation of alternative therapies, has meant that the range of treatment options open to patients has broadened immensely.

Dilemmas in the interface between law, health, and psychology

In keeping with innovations in health care, children's legal status has undergone dramatic change since the 1980s. In this respect, evidence on children's competency in legal settings has accumulated (see Cashmore and Bussey [1996] for a review). These studies suggest that, under appropriate circumstances, even some children as young as 3 or 4 years can demonstrate their understanding of the distinction between truthfulness and lying in specialized domains of knowledge (Siegal and Peterson, 1996) and of the necessity for truthfulness in court (Peterson, 1991). When questioned in a manner that respects their assumptions about the purpose and relevance of conversations about the social world, even preschoolers can often resist misleading suggestions under cross-examination (Newcombe and Siegal, 1997; Siegal et al., 1998). In relation to this research, there has been an increased willingness to allow very young witnesses to testify in court accompanied by law reform in many

258   C. C. Peterson and M. Siegal

jurisdictions aimed to facilitate this process (see also Herbst et al., chapter 10 in this volume). Children who are victims of abuse and other crimes are now allowed to give evidence in criminal trials under circumstances that formerly would have precluded their courtroom appearance (Spencer and Flin, 1990). At the same time, divorce custody cases are increasingly taking the opinions and preferences of legal minors into account (Scott, 1992).

These changes are relevant to the continuing debate over whether a family autonomy or state interventionist approach should be taken in reforming laws that concern the welfare of children (Eekelaar, 1984; Wald et al., 1983). On the one hand, respect for family life can be seen as requiring the right of parents to make key decisions for their children free of external constraints imposed by society. On the other hand, it can be maintained that there are cases when legislation and applications made to courts should permit the bypass of parental authority. In this connection, exponents of "children's rights" (Scott, 1992; Limber and Flekkoy, 1995) have advocated that in all legal and societal settings, the young person's dignity and freedom to choose must be accorded greater consideration than has been feasible under existing "paternalistic" and "protectionist" legislation that has traditionally enshrined the right of parents to guard the welfare of their children. Extended into the arenas of health care and therapy, recent social and legal trends have raised important questions about children's status as medical decision-makers. As will be outlined in more detail later in this chapter, legal barriers in most contemporary English-speaking jurisdictions presently curtail the opportunities that are given to legal minors under the age of 18 years for making serious health choices independently. Would-be reformers of this legislation have argued that laws requiring informed parental consent for most non-emergency, invasive forms of medical, dental, and psychotherapeutic treatment of children and adolescents create situations in which young people may be denied access to necessary and beneficial treatments, owing to a reluctance to consult their parents or inform them accurately about health conditions they consider to be their private concern. At the same time, it is argued, positive therapeutic outcomes would be facilitated if young patients could become more actively involved in medical decisions involving their own health. Directly consulting the wishes of the patient can enable the therapist to take account of idiosyncratic personal factors that will facilitate compliance, cooperation, and adherence to the treatment regime. Young patients who are accurately informed about their health conditions and therapeutic options and allowed to make autonomous choices can also be more likely to gain stronger feelings of optimism, personal control, and mature self-confidence, quite apart from the direct benefits of their active involvement in the treatments themselves.

Balanced against these considerations, however, are doubts that are often shared by lawyers, doctors, and developmental psychologists alike (Scott, 1992) over the capabilities of children and adolescents to assume responsibility for health outcomes that may be controversial, irreversible, slow-acting, or life-threatening. Do teenagers or even younger children possess the foresight to recognize that health risks taken today (e.g., uptake of tobacco, or having sexual intercourse without a condom) may exert adverse consequences over their well-being in the distant future? How old does a patient need to be in order to possess the cognitive skills both for accurately assessing probabilistic risks and benefits and for weighing these against one another in a systematic and future-oriented manner? Once these cognitive capacities are achieved, might a young person's medical judgment still be clouded by inexperience, naivety, or the social and emotional immaturity of adolescence?

In this regard, despite the cognitive competence of young persons to make informed judgments, a number of socioemotional phenomena are apt to influence their everyday decision-making. Those seen as most relevant to medical and therapeutic treatment include the preadolescent's unilateral respect for authority figures (Piaget, 1932), the early adolescent's magical sense of personal invulnerability as a consequence of the imaginary audience syndrome (Elkind, 1985), the moodiness of the teenager in the throes of hormonal changes of puberty (Steinberg, 1990), and the intransigence of late adolescents striving to establish independence from their parents. Steinberg and Cauffman (1996) have concluded that the level of psychosocial maturity that should ideally constitute the minimum standard for permitting young people to make autonomous medical decisions without their parents' knowledge or consent incorporated three elements, each involving both cognitive and personal/experiential components. These elements are: "(1) responsibility (i.e., healthy autonomy, self-reliance, and clarity of identity); (2) temperance (i.e., the ability to limit impulsivity, avoid extremes in decision making, and to evaluate a situation thoroughly before acting, including seeking the advice of others when appropriate); (3) perspective (i.e., being able to acknowledge the complexity of a situation and to frame a specific decision within a larger context)" (Steinberg and Cauffman, 1996, p. 252). When it comes to choosing or rejecting treatments with serious health consequences, the social situation and physical environment may contribute along with psychosocial maturity to the quality of young persons' decision-making. Those anxious over the risks of granting autonomy to adolescents prematurely have expressed the concern that young people may be even more vulnerable than adults to situational distortions of their judgments in the daunting medical settings where many health care choices are made. Even adult patients are inclined to find the unfamiliar atmosphere of a hospital or psychiatry clinic intimidating. Children with less first-hand experience of medical situations may find them so aversive and anxiety provoking as to preclude the asking of questions, the consideration of alternatives, or the overt expression of wishes, doubts, and concerns. The stresses associated with many difficult health care choices in the aftermath of illness or accidental injury can selectively impair their capacities to make rational judgments, and the immediate desire to escape pain, fear, or the restraint of a hospital ward may motivate impulsive choices or blind compliance (Scherer and Repucci, 1988).

Considerations like these have tempered moves towards the granting of mature health care autonomy to legal minors while at the same time highlighting the intricate linkage of the issues that pertain to making difficult treatment choices by, or on behalf of, young people. Some of this complexity can be glimpsed in the following examples. The first two cases are drawn from actual medical records and interviews reported by Shields and Johnson (1992, p. 311) and Alderson (1993, pp. 25–26) respectively. The third is a fictitious case compiled from information in Luetke-Stahlman (1995), Marschark (1996), and Moores (1995). None of the children's names is genuine.

Kate: An academically-able 14-year-old junior high school student in the USA, Kate, had been referred to a psychotherapist by her school counsellor. Kate had been found in the school locker room slashing her leg with a razor blade. Previously, her teachers had noticed an abrupt decline in the quality of her written work, which had formerly been above average. They also noted that she was no longer making contributions to class discussions or interacting as much as formerly with her peers at recess and after school. Kate's teachers described her at present as listless, depressed, and withdrawn. After two assessment sessions, the therapist the school referred her to had told Kate that it would be necessary to contact her widowed mother, Kate's legal guardian, to obtain her permission to undertake treatment. Kate had adamantly and emotionally refused to allow this, explaining that her mother, a Charismatic Christian, believed Kate's self-mutilating behaviors to be "caused by Satan" and to be curable only through prayer. While admitting that there were additional reasons why her mother should not be told that she had been asked to see a therapist, Kate refused to divulge these. Any attempts by the therapist to probe were, like offers to contact her mother, greeted by the claim by Kate that she was "all better," "fine now," and in no need of further counselling appointments. Though giving the lie to these words through her listlessness, apathy, and sadness, Kate made it clear that she would not return for psychotherapy as long as there was any possibility that her mother might be contacted. But, in view of her age, Kate was legally barred from consenting to treatment independently.

Helen: A 7-year-old cystic fibrosis patient, Helen, had been admitted to a London hospital to be assessed for a possible heart-lung transplant. In evaluating her awareness of the probable risks and outcomes associated with having versus refusing the operation, the nursing sister in charge of her case reported that Helen had competently articulated a simple cost-benefit analysis. She said that she knew the transplant would be very unpleasant, might not work, and that she might die. On the other hand, she was aware that she could eventually die of her cystic fibrosis, and that the operation might make her well enough to ride her pony. So she said she wanted to have it. The doctor took these arguments as evidence that, notwithstanding her age, Helen comprehended enough of the intended treatment and its risks and consequences to have provided valid consent.

Valerie: The profoundly deaf daughter of a hearing mother and signing deaf father, 11-year-old Valerie uses sign language fluently at the Total Communication school she attends, and is doing well both academically and socially in a signing deaf peer group with whom she socializes at school and on weekends. The medical dilemma that first faced Valerie's parents and now Valerie is whether she should have surgery to install a cochlear implant. These sophisticated, surgically implanted, hearing aids enable the reception of sound even by individuals like Valerie who became profoundly deaf before acquiring language. In an effort to decide whether she should have the implant, Valerie's parents read the available literature on the topic and consulted with a group of deaf adults and teenagers who had had implants fitted. The evidence, they concluded, is mixed. Most well-controlled studies of prelingually deafened adults show little or no benefit from cochlear implants, though adults who became deaf later in life generally gain a great deal. There is still a dearth of reliable evidence about children, though individual case histories document extremes of success and failure. The success stories are persuasive to Valerie's mother, who hopes that with the aid of an implant her daughter might be able to acquire spoken language and with it full adult participation in the hearing world. Her father opposes the implant. Not only is he concerned about medical complications through "the risks of invasive surgery and the placement of a foreign object in the head for a condition – deafness – that is certainly not life-threatening" (Moores, 1995, p. 246) but also he worries that both the implant and the extensive oral training required for its success might limit Valerie's access to the social support that she presently gains from her deaf peers and the adult deaf community into which both she and her father are presently firmly integrated. Since her parents cannot agree, they decide the decision should be Valerie's.

Cases like these highlight the complex range and interconnections of the psychological attributes to be desired in a fully autonomous medical decision-maker, and raise questions for developmental researchers about the ages at which such attributes are likely to emerge. Within the cognitive domain, these questions center around not only the development of children's abilities to understand abstract health concepts but also their decision-making abilities to weigh probabilistic outcomes, choices, and alternatives rationally into an effective cost-benefit analysis. For example, is it likely that an intelligent 7-year-old child like "Helen" could understand the finality and irreversibility of death (see Slaughter *et al.*, chapter 4 in this volume)? How accurately will she be able to assess the threat to her life entailed by the proposed surgery relative to that entailed by the progress of her disease if surgery were refused? Similar developmental research questions surround the abilities of a preadolescent such as "Valerie" to ignore the future consequences of her proposed cochlear implant surgery, owing to a cognitive bias in favor of immediate, concrete information. To what extent do unrealistic, magical conceptions (for example, about the benefits likely to accrue from being able to hear speech) detract from the logical reasoning skills of 11-year-old children like "Valerie"? Even a 14 year old like "Kate" can be expected, based on her age, to have some distance yet to go before attaining full cognitive-emotional maturity. To what extent is this immaturity likely to restrict her likelihood of benefiting from therapy, especially if it is undertaken against her mother's wishes? Can an adolescent of this age be expected to evaluate her mother's explanations for her health condition rationally compared to those likely to be offered by her counsellors or psychotherapists? The biological upheavals of early adolescence may also influence the responsiveness of a girl of Kate's age to any treatment choices or decisions that may be offered. To what extent can information about chronological, mental, or menarcheal age be used to guide decisions over Kate's appropriate mode and level of involvement in therapeutic decision-making?

These are all questions that reflect the need for research not only into individual decisions such as those illustrated in case histories but also into the general arena of policy recommendations and legislative reform. However, before going on to consider recent research findings and how these may shed light on informed consent policies, it is appropriate to overview the current legal position of young people under the age of 18 years in contemporary English-speaking jurisdictions.

Legal definitions of competency to make treatment decisions

The cases cited above illustrate how complex and uncertain decisions over children's health care issues can sometimes prove to be. For this reason, legislation has been introduced in most parts of the English-speaking world to provide guidelines on the circumstances under which the consent of a parent or legal guardian, acting with the child's best interests, should be required to substitute for the patient's own choice. Despite a shared recognition of the need for some form of special protection for minors in health care settings, however, legal systems differ enormously in their specific provisions for different age groups and different health conditions. Furthermore, recent law reforms in a number of jurisdictions have changed these provisions; reforms are, or have been, contemplated in many others.

Historically, legislation on behalf of children's consent in most English-speaking courts can be traced back to the Common Law of England in the nineteenth century that prescribed the age of majority as a necessary precondition for independent health care decisions. Apart from emergencies, it was then illegal to treat patients under the age of 21 years (later 18) whose parents did not know, or refused to give their consent. In 1969, the Family Law Reform Act in the UK amended this provision so as to specifically allow "surgical, medical or dental treatment" upon the consent of a patient "16 years or older." Such a consent was deemed as effective as the consent of an adult, though the position regarding psychotherapy and other forms of health care remained unclear, and no special provisions existed for any patients under the age of 16. Subsequently, in 1986 the widely publicised case of *Gillick versus West Norfolk and Wisbech Area Health Authority* [1986, 1AC 112 at 116 to 150] modified the English position and set a precedent which continues to govern medical consent for minors not only in Britain but also in Australia (Devereux, 1991), Canada (British Columbia Supreme Court, 1993), and other jurisdictions with a Common Law tradition at the present time (Queensland Law Reform Commission, 1995).

The Gillick case was initiated by the mother of five daughters under the age of 16 years who wished to legally establish her parental right to forbid health professionals from offering contraceptive advice or birth control medication to any of her children until they reached the age of 18. On appeal, the House of Lords established the Common Law precedent known as "Gillick competency" (Queensland Law Reform Commission, 1995). Under this ruling, a child of any age can make a case for competency. Provided the court is satisfied that the minor fully understands the nature and consequences of the proposed treatment, a legally binding consent can be granted without parents' involvement. According to the Gillick decision "the parental right to determine whether or not their minor child below the age of 16 will have medical treatment terminates if and when the child achieves a sufficient understanding and intelligence to enable him or her to understand fully what is proposed. It will be a question of fact whether a child seeking advice has sufficient understanding of what is involved to give consent valid in law" [1986: 1 AC 112 at

188–189]. In other words, a child's medical competency in the wake of the Gillick decision is viewed as a purely cognitive attribute that can be established in court on an individual basis by passing the so-called "Gillick test." In theory, a child of any age could pass this test by displaying to the court's satisfaction that he or she is both intelligent and well informed enough to fully comprehend the proposed treatment and its consequences. Thus, for example, a child like 7-year-old "Helen" in the above example might be capable of legally qualifying as competent to give or withhold her own consent for a life-threatening operation in opposition to her parents' wishes if she articulated a clear understanding of the nature and likely consequences of the surgery proposed. In practice, however, the requirement to establish Gillick competency in a court of law for each minor patient individually renders this particular definition of competency a very difficult one to apply. Furthermore, if a literal interpretation is given to the Gillick criterion to "to understand fully what is proposed," it is doubtful whether even many adults could satisfactorily pass the Gillick test. Partly for this reason, a number of law reform initiatives (e.g., Queensland Law Reform Commission, 1995) have sought to replace the Gillick provision by specified chronological age boundaries, though what the actual age limits should be for different kinds of health decisions remains unclear and controversial, highlighting the need for further input from research findings.

The legal position in the United States is somewhat different, though arguments for closer consultation between law makers and developmental researchers have been articulated just as persuasively in the USA as in Australia and Britain (e.g., Melton et al., 1983; Scherer and Repucci, 1988; Scott et al., 1995; Weithorn, 1985). Steinberg and Cauffman (1996, p. 249) state the present position under United States law as simply that "Adolescents have been deemed unable to provide informed consent for most health care procedures." Specific provisions do vary in fine detail from state to state and legislation has been enacted in some jurisdictions to enable adolescents (usually aged between 14 and 18 years) to be treated for particular health problems that are deemed to pose unique personal or public health risks to their age group (e.g., substance abuse, venereal disease) without parental knowledge. Basic family planning services (usually excluding sterilization and abortion) are likewise available to legal minors above certain specified chronological ages in a number of US states. But such provisions are the exception rather than the rule. Furthermore, where such exceptions do exist, they have been described as a "patchwork" of limited rights and specific, non-uniform exceptions such as access to contraceptives that have been prompted by economic and political considerations.

Owing to the inherent ambiguity of reaching social, political, and legal decisions regarding minors' competency in the absence of scientific evidence, further research urgently needs to be conducted into the development of medical decision-making capacities in children and adolescents as a basis for law reforms to regularize, and supply a knowledge base for, the legal positioning of minors in health care. As Scott (1992, p. 1,669) has remarked, "The challenge is to deepen and broaden empirical understanding and replace intuition with insight."

Research evidence on the development of the capacity to grant informed consent

When applied to individual cases of medical decision-making, recent studies such as those reported in this volume by Kalish (chapter 5) and by Au, Romo, and DeWitt (chapter 9) suggest that even children younger than the cases of "Helen" or "Valerie" described above can be made to understand causes of illness that would enable rational processing of specific information about their particular conditions. Similarly, children do not necessarily conceptualize the outcomes of their proposed surgical treatments in a purely magical or supernatural light and a child like "Kate" might not accept her mother's account of her depression solely in terms of a punishment by Satan.

However, accurate knowledge of the causes and cures of illnesses are only one of the elements involved in a child's cognitive competency to make medical decisions. Another entails the rational ability to weigh choices, probabilities, and alternatives against one another in evaluating treatment choices. For Piaget (1970, 1972), mature decision-making capacities arise with the transition from concrete-operational to formal-operational thinking during late adolescence or early adulthood. The development of formal operations equips the decision-maker with the high-level cognitive skills that are needed in order to systematically consider all possible combinations of present and future costs and benefits. The scientific logic underpinning formal operations includes an awareness of correlational and probabilistic connections among variables, along with the notion of systematic deduction under controlled conditions. Formal-operational thinkers can also think flexibly about abstract and relativistic concepts. Consequently, assuming that they have been fully and accurately informed, children or adolescents who have developed Piagetian formal operations would have the cognitive capacity to pass the Gillick test of medical decision-making competency by displaying a complete understanding of both long-term and immediate benefits and risks of any treatment proposed.

Thus Piaget's highest stage of formal-operational thought might appear to be the ideal minimum standard of cognitive competencies for individual patients faced with complex treatment decisions. Nevertheless, there are two important obstacles that are likely to limit the effectiveness of such an approach in practice. First, the legal determination of whether or not any individual young patient was a competent decision-maker would require that a cognitive assessment of that person be undertaken, since there is no specific chronological age at which the development of formal operations can be assumed to be universal, even among individuals of average or above average intelligence (Connell et al., 1975; Piaget, 1972). Indeed, the results of one ambitious study of several thousand Australian adolescents aged 12 to 20 years (Connell et al., 1975) revealed that only one 16 year old in four had attained Piaget's formal-operational stage. By age 18, approximately 65 percent of university-entrance students had done so. But less than 25 percent of the employed Australian 18-year-olds who had no plans to attend university had achieved formal operational reasoning and, even by age 20, the proportion of the employed group who could reason at this level remained less than half. These figures, confirmed by studies conducted in Europe and the United States, indicate that no binding legal age prior to attaining majority could safely be set as the uniform boundary for medical decision-making on the assumption that most teenagers should have reached formal operational stage by this time. This same empirical evidence also highlights a second practical problem with the use of Piagetian cognitive development as the legal criterion of Gillick-style competency: many adults would also fail this test. Yet few courts would wish to disqualify large proportions of intellectually normal adults from having the legal right to make self-determining health care choices.

If Piaget's (1970, 1972) developmental theory of the maturation of decision-making competence is deemed to set too stringent a standard for the determination of cognitive maturity in the context of medical and psychotherapeutic decision-making, a more valid research approach may be to assess directly the decision-making processes of children and adolescents when faced with hypothetical treatment choices. In one of the first studies to adopt this method, Weithorn and Campbell (1982) compared four groups of young people ranging in age from 9 to 21 years on a set of hypothetical dilemmas involving treatment for epilepsy, depression, diabetes, and enuresis. The task was to select a treatment option for each patient and then give a detailed justification for the choice. The 9-year-olds did less well than subjects over age 14 and over on all response measures. In line with Piaget's (1970) theory of concrete-operational thinking, they seemed incapable of considering the multiple factors relevant to each treatment option and displayed poorer factual understanding of the medical information than older groups. The 14-year-olds did better, though there were still some significant differences between their performance and that of the legal adults aged 18 and 21 years. The young teenagers had particular problems with the epilepsy dilemma which involved treatments entailing minor adverse effects on body image. The researchers therefore concluded that: "Competency, as defined by certain legal tests, may depend to some degree upon the dimensions of the specific decision-making context" (Weithorn and Campbell, 1982, p. 1,596).

In another study that addressed children's competency to give consent, Lewis *et al.*, (1978) questioned whole classroom groups of primary school children orally about their willingness to participate as "guinea pigs" in a research trial of a new swine flu vaccine. Though the views and competencies of individual children were not systematically assessed, the group results revealed a surprisingly high level of understanding over the period from 6 to 9 years. Even the youngest raised issues that revealed a sophisticated awareness of many elements needing to be considered when making a valid decision about an experimental form of treatment. Children questioned the researchers about likely side-effects of the vaccine, including queries about the frequency of adverse outcomes. They also displayed an awareness through their questions of the need to balance the relative risk of the proposed treatment as compared with the illness it was designed to prevent.

More recently, Mulvey and Peeples (1996) compared the comprehension, reasoned inferences, and decision-making processes of groups of normal and at-risk teenagers in response to hypothetical vignettes involving treatment choices about mental health problems including depression, refusal to attend school, and pyromania. The at-risk teenagers, especially the males, were overall less capable of weighing the risks and benefits associated with different options than their peers from the normal community. However, the variability among individuals within each group was high. When it came to a comparative evaluation of the advantages and disadvantages of several treatment options, the teenagers with a history of behavior problems did poorly overall, earning average scores of only 50 percent on a reasoning scale. But some were able to express levels of reasoning that were on a par with those of the normal comparison group. Furthermore, even this latter group had problems with a number of the dilemmas, especially when it came to evaluating likely treatment outcomes in relation to one another. According to Mulvey and Peeples (1996), their study showed that at-risk status was a powerful factor when the adolescents were asked to weigh risks and benefits of particular treatment approaches, but that it was not as influential as other variables when the subjects were asked to recall information or make inferences about likely outcomes of treatment involvement. If this differential capacity is found in future investigations, it would seem that competency might be best thought of as an ability that varies with the type of decision posed to the disordered adolescent. (Mulvey and Peeples, 1996, p. 285)

In summary, children and adolescents appear to possess some awareness of factors that need to be incorporated into a valid decision about treatment (for a review, see Melton and Stanley, 1996). However, in line with studies using Piagetian measures of formal-operational thinking, the results of these more "ecologically valid" health decision studies are not yet sufficiently clear-cut to answer the pressing practical questions that have been raised by members of the legal and health professions regarding children's competency (Scott, 1992). Furthermore, as Mulvey and Peeples (1996) have noted, important questions remain to be answered about the role of individual differences in cognitive maturity and other treatment-relevant variables among young people of similar chronological age.

Relation of cognition development to perceptions about decision-making competencies

To investigate these issues, we carried out a study in which adolescents and young adults were asked to respond to dilemmas involving decisions about health. We explored the relation between their perceptions about the competency to make health decisions and cognitive development. The participants were ninety-three first-year university students ranging in age from 16 to 25 years. Of these, 24 percent were below 18 years which, aside from a legal Gillick test, is the minimum age for independent consent for non-emergency medical, dental, and psychotherapeutic care in Queensland (Australia). Thus the students had not reached the legal age of competency in their local jurisdiction to consent independently to treatment in taking health care decisions such as those depicted in the hypothetical dilemmas used in this study.

As a basis for assessing cognitive maturity according to Piaget's (1970, 1972) stage model, each student completed Connell et al.'s (1975) paper-and-pencil adaptation of three of Inhelder and Piaget's (1958) tests of formal-operational reasoning. We administered and scored this test exactly as described by Connell et al. (1975). In brief, respondents were asked to respond to three stories that contained incomplete and ambiguous information. Questions at the end of each story required an inference to be backed up by a detailed justification. These rationales were scored for the presence of three Piagetian criteria of formal-operational thinking: (1) drawing inferences beyond the information supplied by the examiner; (2) articulation of hypothetical or probabilistic possibilities; (3) systematic evaluation of these alternatives using hypothetico-deductive reasoning. Students who met each of these criteria in response to at least two of the three stories were categorized as formal-operational. Those who never did so were deemed to be concrete-operational, and those who gave a formal-operational justification in response to only one story were categorized as transitional between concrete and formal operations. Of the total sample, 44 percent were scored as concrete-operational on this measure, 20 percent as formal-operational, and 36 percent as transitional between the two stages. The frequency of concrete operational reasoning in the subgroup of legal minors under the age of 18 (43 percent) did not differ significantly from that observed among the adults over age 18 (45 percent).

Respondents also completed measures of their knowledge of the legal requirements for minors' consent to treatment in Queensland, along with a set of questions relating to dilemmas contained in vignettes on the themes of depression, contraception, cosmetic surgery, and anorexia nervosa that are shown in the appendix. After reading each vignette, subjects were asked to indicate the minimum age that they believed the normally intelligent patient in the dilemma would need to have reached in order to make an independent treatment decision without her parents' knowledge or consent. Response options on a seven-point scale offered choices of 9, 12, 14, 16, 18, 21 years, and "never." (This latter was coded as 25 years for the statistical analyses.) In addition, in response to each of the four dilemmas, subjects were asked whether any criteria for independent consent should be required in addition to chronological age. The multiple-choice response options for these items were drawn from the legal literature and represented the criteria for minors' consent that have been used in various English-speaking jurisdictions, or suggested in law reform documents. Specifically the choices were: (1) she fully understands her choices and their consequences; (2) she has demonstrated her independence from her parents (e.g., lives away from home); (3) she is intellectually and educationally mature (e.g., has successfully completed high school); (4) the doctor believes that the option she wants is in her best interests; (5) she has reasons for not wanting her parents to know of her treatment that the doctor considers are valid ones; (6) she is financially independent (e.g., she can cover the costs of therapy without her parents' help). Respondents were encouraged to select as many of these criteria for each dilemma as they considered to be relevant to a decision

Table 11.1. *Mean minimum recommended ages for independent treatment decision-making as a function of health problem and respondents' cognitive maturity and the mean number of additional consent criteria over and above chronological age that were deemed to be prerequisite before dispensing with parental consent*

	Type of problem			
	Medical		Psychotherapeutic	
	Contraception	Cosmetic surgery	Depression	Anorexia
Concrete-operational (n = 41)				
Mean minimum age				
required	15.58	15.53	15.44	17.08
% requiring 18 or older	16	13	18	37
Mean additional criteria	3.00	1.97	4.38	2.64
Formal-operational or transitional (n = 52)				
Mean minimum age				
required	16.87	17.25	17.84	18.50
% requiring 18 or older	44	59	59	69
Mean additional criteria	3.59	3.18	4.30	3.39
Total group (n = 93)				
Mean minimum age				
required	16.17	16.10	16.54	17.73
% requiring 18 or older	29	39	37	51
Mean additional criteria	3.32	2.62	4.33	3.04

about the patient's competency. If they chose more than one, they were also asked to rank their chosen criteria in order of subjective importance.

Table 11.1 shows the mean ages nominated by respondents as the minimum consent boundary for each health condition. Compared to transitional and formal-operational subjects who were combined together into a single "cognitively advanced" group for purposes of analyses, the concrete-operational group gave significantly earlier ages for autonomous decision-making. For the vast majority of concrete-operational subjects, the age boundary of 18 years (the present minimum age of legal consent in Queensland) was too high. By contrast, a majority of the advanced group nominated either 18 years or an older age as the minimum requirement to take health conditions apart from the case of contraceptive protection. There were no significant differences between the responses of males and females.

When asked whether additional criteria besides chronological age should enter into the decision about the consent competencies of the patients depicted in these vignettes, the respondents' own levels of cogni-

Table 11.2. *Most important criterion besides age for independent treatment decision-making according to concrete-operational and formal-operational respondents (percentages)*

	Type of problem			
	Medical		Psychotherapeutic	
	Contraception	Cosmetic surgery	Depression	Anorexia
Concrete-operational (n = 41)				
No added criteria	32	56	15	44
Understands her options	45	34	54	35
Family independence	7	0	2	0
Cognitive maturity	2	2	5	5
Doctor endorses her choice	5	2	5	14
Valid grounds to exclude parents	7	5	19	2
Financial independence	0	0	0	0
Formal-operational or transitional (n = 52)				
No added criteria	23	15	9	30
Understands her options	44	50	52	34
Family independence	2	4	2	6
Cognitive maturity	8	8	10	10
Doctor endorses her choice	6	6	10	10
Valid grounds to exclude parents	15	12	15	8
Financial independence	2	6	2	2

tive maturity was significantly related to their judgments. Subjects who reasoned at the concrete-operational level were likely to feel that age alone was a sufficient criterion for consenting to cosmetic surgery, without a parent's knowledge or approval in contrast those in the advanced group who significantly more often nominated conditions in addition to age which should be satisfied before allowing independent surgical consent. In fact, 56 percent of the concrete-operational group as deemed age sufficient in this instance compared with only 15 percent of those in the advanced group. However, in the case of depression, the vast majority of respondents in both cognitive groups indicated that there were additional consent criteria over and above age that would need to be satisfied before dispensing with parental consent.

Table 11.2 shows the percentages of respondents in the two groups who ranked each of the proposed competency criteria as highest in

272   C. C. Peterson and M. Siegal

importance when it was felt that some additional proof of competency was required beyond that of chronological age. For each of the dilemmas, the criterion of Gillick-style understanding ("she fully understands her choices and the consequences") was the preeminent response of both groups. A small minority viewed the existence of valid grounds for the exclusion of patients as the most important non-chronological criterion. But even for the dilemma about depression where this occurred most often, three times as many respondents placed understanding of the treatment options highest on their list. This response pattern clearly illustrates perceptions of the importance of the Gillick criterion in a case where a patient's decision-making competency may be impaired by mental illness.

Of course the students' own age and legal status might have influenced their evaluations of the dilemmas. To investigate this possibility, scores were allocated to reflect (1) the sum of the age boundaries that each student had nominated for each of the four dilemmas (age score) and (2) the total number of criteria over and above chronological age that had been specified by the student in response to the second question across the four vignettes (additional-criteria score). Then students were grouped as either "legally competent" (aged 18 years or older) or "legally incompetent" (aged 17 years or under). No significant differences emerged between legally competent and incompetent subjects in their recommendations as the minimum chronological boundary for independent consent. Nor did the two groups differ in their additional-criteria scores. Thus in contrast to level of cognitive development, students' own legal status was not significantly associated with their responses to the dilemmas. Legal knowledge also did not influence the number of criteria that were recommended in addition to age. The 41 percent of subjects who were aware of the current legislation in Queensland regarding minors' competency did not differ in their recommendations about the age of consent from the 59 percent who were legally ignorant or misinformed.

Overall, one of the most striking results to emerge from this study was the clear indication of the extent to which respondents' own levels of cognitive maturity shaped their recommendations regarding legal criteria for granting autonomy in health situations. This relationship was somewhat paradoxical. Young people who themselves possessed the advanced cognitive skills that would have equipped them in health settings to make their own valid treatment choices autonomously were the ones least likely to endorse autonomy for the young patients in our hypothetical dilemmas. Though chronological age had no effect on judgments of competency, the cognitive maturity was associated with recommendations of later ages at which independent health decisions could be competently taken. Possibly those reasoning at a formal-operational level are liable to be more aware of the multiplicity of factors needing to be considered in a valid health choice and the importance of safeguards against the fallibility of the patient's own individual judgement. Rather than simply a rejection of an adolescent's right to choose, an endorsement of parental involvement might be seen as a conservative approach to complex decisions perceived in terms that require caution and added protection.

By contrast, concrete-operational subjects were strongly in favor of the liberalization of the consent process for teenagers. Only a small proportion endorsed the present legislative requirement for parental consent up to the age of 18 years, and the average ages at which they deemed that all patients apart from the anorexia sufferer should make treatment choices without parental involvement was approximately 15. Possibly their more liberal recommendations with regard to consent criteria reflected lower levels of awareness of adverse outcomes of young people's autonomous health choices against which parental consent might serve as a protective safeguard. This possibility warrants exploration in future research, as does the question of how one's own experiences with parents, peers, and health professionals can affect judgments about patients' competency to consent.

Another unexpected finding was the endorsement of consent ages older than the present legal boundary of 18 years by a considerable proportion of students, especially in response to the dilemmas involving depression. Again this may reflect a cautious strategy in the context of complex health problems since parental consent was always presented in our dilemmas as additional input to be considered along with the views of the young patient. A feature of each dilemma was the explicit mention that a range of treatment options existed, each with specific benefits and risks. Possibly subjects used delaying of the consent age as a way of ensuring that multiple viewpoints would be considered, in the same way that married adults might be advised to consult with their spouse before proceeding with a controversial medical treatment.

The fact that different age boundaries for patients' consent emerged for different types of health problems in our study is relevant to legislation and legislative reform on behalf of minors' consent. As was noted earlier in this chapter, many US states have lowered the statutory age boundary of 18 years to make a specific exception for contraceptive treatment. A lower age for medical than psychotherapeutic treatment has also been a feature of law reforms that have been introduced in jurisdictions such as South Australia, which in 1985 legislated to enable 16-year-olds to consent specifically to the former but not the latter. Conversely, the Mental Health Act of 1974 in Queensland enabled teenagers aged 16 to 18 years to be admitted as voluntary patients to psychiatric facilities without parental consent, though the minimum legal age for medical care is 18 (Queensland Law Reform Commission, 1995). While the "piecemeal" nature of statutes prescribing different minimum consent ages for different health conditions is subject to criticism (Scott, 1992), such an approach is somewhat consistent with the collective opinions of the young people who took part in the present study.

According to the "Gillick" provision that presently governs consent by minors in Australia, Britain, and other Common Law jurisdictions (Devereux, 1991), legal minors of any age can dispense with the parental guardian's consent when a court is satisfied that they possess a full understanding of the nature and consequences of the treatment proposed. In relation to Gillick, both cognitive groups in our study endorsed the patient's understanding of the treatment options as the most important criterion in addition to age for consenting independently of parents. But Gillick competency as a sole criterion would not have satisfied the majority of young people who responded to our dilemmas, as students endorsed multiple prerequisite criteria over and above age, an average of four for the contraception dilemma and three for each of the others. This response pattern appears to reflect concerns similar to those expressed by developmental psychologists (e.g., Scherer and Repucci, 1988; Scott, 1992; Steinberg and Cauffman, 1996) that socioemotional maturity factors need to be considered along with cognitive maturity and chronological age when deciding whether to authorize a young person to select or reject treatment without parental knowledge, advice, or consent.

Practical recommendations

Our study highlights three issues that warrant consideration in legal and moral debates over the criteria for medical consent by minors whose competency to make informed treatment choices is at stake.

First, though chronological age is normally deemed to be the legal requirement for the competency to consent to treatment, chronological age cannot be regarded as synonymous with cognitive development and cannot be well regarded as a sole criterion in appraising the competency to consent. On the measures of Piagetian reasoning levels that we used, only about half the sample of young people aged 16 to 25 years had developed to the stage of formal-operational reasoning. These results are consistent with those of studies conducted in Australia (Connell et al., 1975), Britain (Peel, 1967), and the United States (Neimark, 1975) in showing that formal-operational reasoning does not emerge universally during adolescence, even in the context of high levels of education. In fact, in our study, there was no significance age difference between those who had obtained formal operational reasoning and those who had not; 57 percent of the legally incompetent minors who were under the age of 18 when they took part in our study were nevertheless found to be reasoning at Piaget's most advanced stage of formal-operational thought as compared with 55 percent of those aged 18 to 25 years.

The second issue concerns the relation of cognitive development to perceptions about decision-making competencies. "Libertarian" law reformers (Scott, 1992) have argued on the basis of evidence of this kind for a lowering of the minimal ages for minors' consent to treatment. Yet this was not the stance taken by the majority of formal-operational thinkers in our sample (including the 17 year olds who were themselves disenfranchised from independent medical choice by present statutes in their home state) who recommended the age of 18 or older as the minimum requirement for independent consent to cosmetic surgery and treatment for psychiatric disorders. They advocated not only advanced chronological age boundaries for consent without parental endorsement but also a range of additional protective safeguards including (but not limited to) the cognitive criteria for competency according to the Gillick test. The relatively conservative position taken by those with advanced cognitive development may reflect a growing awareness among adolescents and young adults of the inherent limitations of scientific knowledge, even in domains of medicine and health where rapid strides in the advancement of understanding and therapeutic technology have been made. In this sense, cognitive development rather than chronological age can be seen as a more cautious basis on which to appraise adolescents' competency to consent to treatment.

The third issue follows from this proposal. If even those minors who are more advanced on measures of cognitive development than many who have attained the age of majority advocate that consent for treatment should not be allowed independently of the family, it is important to consider the conditions under which the views of parents and children coincide. As adolescents mature, they naturally seek independence from parents and many conflicts are over matters they deem to be personal and prudential rather than within the moral regulative force of the adult. Formal-operational adolescents may see that even such health dilemmas can have an effect on the welfare of others. Building on the importance of conversational understanding in early cognitive development (Donaldson, 1978; Siegal, 1997, 1999), a central role here may be seen for authoritative parenting that involves reasoning, explanations, and appeals to the child's sense of others' interests and feelings (Baumrind, 1971, 1991). Adolescents who perceive their parents to employ authoritative parenting methods are liable to agree with statements such as "My mother/father has always encouraged verbal give-and-take whenever I felt that family rules and restrictions were unreasonable" (Smetana, 1995). In such instances, the frequency and intensity of conflict between parents and children is minimized. Perceptions of authoritative parenting can extend to decision-making about medical and psychotherapeutic treatment. To invoke the Gillick test and request courts to intervene by overturning the usual processes of family autonomy would be unnecessary. If both parties agree, there is no need to ask for intervention in such cases.

Therefore with respect to the competency to consent to treatment, these results suggest a practical need to involve parents, young patients, and their medical and therapeutic helpers in a "team" approach to health decision-making and to preserving the autonomy of the family. Wide-ranging dialogues both within the family, and in the arenas of health education and health care, are likely to stimulate the development of adolescents' reasoning skills. By articulating their viewpoints, desires, and anxieties in explicit discussion, teenagers may gain the cognitive skills for weighing up risks and benefits that will serve them well when it comes to making independent medical and therapeutic decisions. At the same time, conversations about health with a range of professional and lay adults are likely to broaden and deepen adolescents' levels of understanding both of specific treatment options and of the important contribution of patients themselves to the therapeutic process. Thus the same practical goals that many therapists seek to serve by granting young patients the right to make treatment choices without parental involvement may sometimes also be served by actively engaging parents and their children together in constructive dialogues leading to a collective therapeutic decision.

Concluding comments

Moving from practice back to theory, these observations about the importance of conversations with parents and therapists in boosting children's and adolescents' health knowledge and decision-making has relevance to the broad question of how cognition develops in the health domain and its significance for development in adolescence. There is evidence already to suggest that family conversation in general may contribute to the growth of formal operational reasoning skills in adolescence (Connell et al., 1975; Peterson et al., 1986), though no known published study has looked explicitly at parent–adolescent dialogues about medical or therapeutic choices. By extrapolation, however, it seems conceivable that conversations within the family about the explicit health choices that young people may have occasion to make (for example, dilemmas like those we presented in our hypothetical scenarios, or those facing "Kate," "Helen," and "Valerie" in an earlier section of this chapter) might contribute in a special way to adolescents' cognitive development.

When a therapist consults a teenager in the unfamiliar atmosphere of a hospital or other health care environment, new strategies for expressing opinions and preferences may be called for than when conversing at home with family members or at school with peers. At the same time, by actively discussing their treatment choices with their parents or with health professionals, adolescents may learn to articulate their concerns and desires in a more explicit way than would be possible simply through private thought. Reasoning skills may be facilitated by the need to convince parents of a "Gillick-style" understanding. The three-way conversations that are entailed when therapists consult young patients and their parents together with a view to obtaining consent from the patient and parent jointly might serve a similar developmental function in boosting decision-making skills. Such interactions that involve the exchange of factual information may help parents to communicate more effectively with their children about treatment decisions.

In this sense, communication both at home and in specialized health settings may exert a formative role as long as cognitions about health and treatment themselves remain on a developmental trajectory. We suggest that parents who engage their children in conversations about treatment choices may stimulate children's thinking about health and capacities to perform risk-benefit analyses in the health context. Consequently, rather than granting complete treatment autonomy to adolescents either prematurely or too late to be of optimal benefit, a conversational approach can assist parents to tailor the making of health choices to their children's cognitive skills that will ultimately ensure mature, autonomous medical and psychotherapeutic decision-making.

REFERENCES

Alderson, P. (1993). In the genes or in the stars? Children's competence to consent. *Bioethics News*, 12, 24–32.
Baumrind, D. (1971). Current patterns of parental authority. *Developmental Psychology Monographs*, no. 4 (1, part 2).
  (1991). Effective parenting during the early adolescent transition. In P. A. Cowan and E. M. Hetherington (eds.), *Advances in family research*, vol. II (pp. 111–165). Hillsdale, NJ: Erlbaum.
British Columbia Supreme Court (1993). *Ney v. Attorney General of Canada 102*

DLR (4th) 136 at s.16

Cashmore, J., and Bussey, K. (1996). Judicial perceptions of child witness competence. *Law and Human Behavior*, 20, 313–335.

Connell, W. F., Stroobant, R. E., Sinclair, K. E., Connell, R. W., and Rogers, K. (1975). *12 to 20: Studies of city youth*. Sydney: Hicks Smith.

Devereux, J. (1991). The capacity of a child in Australia to consent to medical treatment. *Oxford Journal of Legal Studies*, 11, 283–302.

Donaldson, M. (1978). *Children's minds*. London: Croom Helm.

Eekelaar, J. (1984). *Family law and social policy*, 2nd edn. London: Weidenfeld and Nicolson.

Elkind, D. (1985). Egocentrism redux. *Developmental Review*, 5, 218–236.

Inhelder, B., and Piaget, J. (1958). *The growth of logical thinking from childhood to adolescence*. New York: Basic Books.

Lewis, C., Lewis, M., and Ifekwunigue, M. (1978). Informed consent by children and participation in an influenza vaccine trial. *American Journal of Public Health*, 68, 1,079–1,082.

Limber, S. P., and Flekkoy, M. G. (1995). The U.N. convention on the rights of the child: Its relevance for social scientists. *Society for Research in Child Development Social Policy Report*, 9, 1–15.

Luetke-Stahlman, B. (1995). On deciding to implant. *American Annals of the Deaf*, 140, 5–6.

Marschark, M. (1996). Consensus on cochlear implants? *Journal of Deaf Studies and Deaf Education*, 1, 213–215.

Melton, G. B., and Stanley, B. (1996). Research involving special populations. In B. Stanley and J. E. Sieber (eds.), *Research ethics: A psychological approach* (pp. 223–254). Lincoln, NB: University of Nebraska Press.

Melton, G. B., Koocher, G. P., and Saks, M. J. (1983). *Children's competence to consent*. New York: Plenum.

Moores, D. (1995). Cochlear implants and hearing aids. *American Annals of the Deaf*, 140, 245–246.

Mulvey, E., and Peeples, F. (1996). Are disturbed and normal adolescents equally competent to make decisions about mental health treatments? *Law and Human Behavior*, 20, 273–287.

Neimark, E. (1975). Intellectual development during adolescence. *Review of Child Development Research*, 4, 541–594.

Newcombe, P. A., and Siegal, M. (1997). Explicitly questioning the nature of suggestibility in preschoolers' memory and retention. *Journal of experimental Child Psychology*, 67, 185–203.

Peel, E. A. (1967). *The pupil's thinking*. London: Oldbourne.

Peterson, C. C. (1991). What is a lie? In K. Rotenberg (ed.), *Children's interpersonal trust* (pp. 5–19). New York: Springer-Verlag.

Peterson, C. C., Peterson, J. L., and Skevington, S. (1986). Heated argument and adolescent development. *Journal of Social and Personal Relationships*, 3, 229–240.

Piaget, J. (1932). *The moral judgment of the child*. London: Routledge and Kegan Paul.

  (1970). Piaget's theory. In P. H. Mussen (ed.), *Carmichael's manual of child psychology* (pp. 703–732). New York: Wiley.

(1972). Intellectual evolution from adolescence to adulthood. *Human Development*, 15, 1–12.

Queensland Law Reform Commission (1995). *Consent to medical treatment of young people*. Brisbane: Queensland Law Reform Commission (legal citation: QLRC W.P. 44).

Scherer, D., and Repucci, N. (1988). Adolescents' capacities to provide voluntary informed consent. *Law and Human Behavior*, 12, 123–141.

Scott, E. (1992). Judgment and reasoning in adolescent decision making. *Villanova Law Review*, 37, 1,607–1,669.

Scott, E., Repucci, N., and Woolard, J. (1995). Evaluating adolescent decision making in a legal context. *Law and Human Behavior*, 19, 221–244.

Shields, J. M., and Johnson, A. (1992). Collusion between law and ethics: Consent for treatment with adolescents. *Journal of the American Academy of Psychiatry and Law*, 20, 309–323.

Siegal, M. (1997). *Knowing children: Experiments in conversation and cognition*, 2nd edn. Hove, UK: Psychology Press.

(1999). Language and thought: The fundamental significance of conversational awareness for cognitive development. *Developmental Science*, 2, 1–34.

Siegal, M., and Peterson, C. C. (1996). Breaking the mold: A fresh look at questions about children's understanding of lies and mistakes. *Developmental Psychology*, 32, 322–334.

Siegal, M., Newcombe, P., and Peterson, C. (1998). Secrets, lies and suggestibility: A conversational perspective on memory and cognition in young children. In R. Vasta (ed.), *Annals of child development*, Vol. XIII (pp. 165–206). London: Jessica Kingsley.

Smetana, J. G. (1995). Parenting styles and conceptions of parental authority during adolescents. *Child Development*, 66, 299–316.

Spencer, J. R., and Flin, R. (1990). *The evidence of children: The law and the psychology*. London: Blackstone.

Steinberg, L. (1990). Autonomy, conflict and harmony in the family relationship. In S. Feldman and G. Elliott (eds.) *At the threshold: The developing adolescent* (pp. 255–276). Cambridge, MA: Harvard University Press.

Steinberg, L., and Cauffman, E. (1996). Maturity of judgment in adolescence: Psychosocial factors in adolescent decision-making. *Law and Human Behavior*, 20, 249–273.

Wald, M., Carlsmith, M., Leiderman, P. H., and Smith, C. (1983). Intervention to protest abused and neglected children. In M. Perlmutter (ed.), *Cognitive aspects on children's social and behavioral development: Minnesota symposia on child psychology*, Vol. XVIII (pp. 207–231). Hillsdale, NJ: Erlbaum.

Weithorn, L. (1985). Children's capacities for participation in treatment decision making. In D. Schetky and E. Benedek (eds.), *Emerging issues in child psychiatry and the law* (pp. 22–36). New York: Brunner Mazel.

Weithorn, L., and Campbell, S. (1982). The competency of children and adolescents to make informed treatment choices. *Child Development*, 53, 1,589–1,598.

Appendix: Hypothetical dilemma vignettes

SUSAN[1]

Susan has become increasingly listless and unhappy for several months, showing little interest in her work, her studies, her friends, or her family. Her appetite is poor and she complains that she sometimes feels that her life is not worth living. Her doctor diagnoses that Susan is suffering from depression. The doctor says that there are three treatment options available to her: (1) she could have drug therapy; (2) she could go into hospital and have intensive in-patient psychiatric treatment without the use of drugs; or (3) she could do nothing and hope that her condition will cure itself over time. Each treatment option has certain advantages and disadvantages and the risks associated with each one are also different, as the doctor explains.

SANDRA

Sandra has been sexually active for several months, protecting herself against pregnancy by insisting that her partners use a condom. She consults a doctor because she wants information on other birth control options. The doctor says there are three options available to her: (1) she could begin taking the contraceptive pill; (2) she could have an intrauterine device (IUD) inserted so, with the use of spermicidal cream, she would be protected from pregnancy without the use of drugs or condoms; or (3) she could do nothing and continue to insist that her partners use condoms, which would help to protect against venereal disease, but the failure rate of condoms as a contraceptive protection is not insignificant. Each treatment option has other advantages and disadvantages and the risks associated with each one are also different, and the doctor outlines each of these briefly.

SOPHIE

Sophie has a birthmark at the base of her neck about which she feels very self-conscious. The mark is about the size of an olive and is dark brown. It is completely harmless with no risk of becoming cancerous if untreated. Sophie consults a doctor because she wants information on cosmetic surgery to have the mark removed. The doctor says there are two options available to her: (1) she could have cosmetic surgery to remove the mark but there would be a small risk of scar tissue forming in such a way that would be much more obvious and unsightly than the mark itself; or (2) she could do nothing and accept the mark, or hide it with makeup.

SHARON

Sharon is extremely diet conscious and has been losing weight steadily over the past several months although she was already quite thin. Lately she has been feeling very ill and lethargic with persistent nausea, headaches, and dizziness. She has difficulty concentrating on her studies and spends most of her time alone. She consults a doctor who diagnoses her condition as anorexia nervosa, an eating disorder precipitated by extreme dieting which can prove life-threatening. The doctor says there are three treatment options available to Sharon: (1) she could go into hospital for an intensive program of dietary intervention with psychotherapy; (2) she could have weekly counselling on an out-patient basis along with tablets to help her gain weight; or (3) she could do nothing except try to eat a better diet and the problem could improve by itself. The doctor explains that the last option entails some risk, as anorexia nervosa is fatal in 10–20 percent of untreated patients and only 30 percent recover spontaneously without the help of psychotherapy.

NOTE

1 These dilemmas are presented here in the order in which they appeared in the questionnaire booklet, and describe medical problems involving depression, contraception, cosmetic surgery, and anorexia nervosa respectively. However, proper names rather than diagnostic categories were used as headings so as to focus attention on the individual and facilitate the respondents' identification with each dilemma.

Author index

Abu-Saad, H. H., 140, 141, 143, 146
Achenbach, T. M., 144, 174–176
Achterberg, C., 175
Ackerson, J. D., 149
Adams, J., 146
Addicoat, L.
Ahrens, H. 187, 195
Alderson, P., 260
Alfred-Liro, C., 40
Allen, D. A., 151
Al-Matar, M., 146
Alpert, B., 149
Altshuler, J. L., 249
Aman, C., 236
American Psychiatric Association, 193
Amgott-Kwan, T., 238
Amsel, E., 15, 76
Anand, K. J. S., 140, 141
Andersen, A., 193, 198
Andersen, R., 184
Anderson, C. T. M., 149
Anderson, J. E., 151
Andresen, G., 169
Angyal, A., 174
Anthony, S., 71
Appadurai, A., 191
Arandine, C. R., 141
Armstrong, F. D., 148, 151
Armstrong, S. L., 112
Arts, S., 140, 141, 143
Ashley, L. C., 151
Astington, J., 75
Atkins, A., 149
Atran, S., 29, 46, 124
Au, T. K., 13, 33, 41, 45, 105, 109, 110,
  113, 209–218, 221, 231, 265
Augustoni-Ziskind, M., 12, 190, 191
Austin, L. J., 199

Bachanas, P. J., 150
Backscheider, A. G., 135, 211, 213
Baillargeon, R., 14

Baker, B., 148
Baker, L., 193, 194
Bandura, A., 147
Banos, J.-E., 140
Banoub-Baddour, S., 146
Barajas, C., 140
Bar-Tal, D., 237, 236
Bartlett, J. A., 209
Bartsch, K., 28, 39
Batteman-Faunce, J. M., 248
Baumrind, D., 275
Beales, J. G., 138
Beales, S., 184
Beard, C. M., 193
Bearison, D. J., 239
Beck, M., 171
Beglin, S. J., 193
Belk, A., 13, 105, 113
Belter, R. W., 143
Bennett-Branson, S. M., 147
Berde, C. B., 144
Berman, D., 73, 91
Bernstein, I., 168
Berry, C. C., 141
Berstein, B. A., 146
Beyer, J. E., 141, 144, 151
Bibace, R., 5, 103, 113, 114, 132, 138
Bieri, D., 142, 143
Billman, J., 173
Birch, L., 162, 166, 168–173, 177
Birch, R. A., 236
Bishop, G. D., 111, 124
Bjorkhem, G., 149
Blinder, B. J., 194
Blotcky, A. D., 149
Blount, R. L., 149, 150
Blount, S. D., 150
Boat, B., 236
Booth, D., 179, 184
Booth, J. C., 141
Bornstein, G. K., 236
Boskind-Lodahl, M., 195

Subject index